Darius Milhaud

Modality & Structure in Music of the 1920s

Darius Milhaud

❦

Modality & Structure in Music of the 1920s

DEBORAH MAWER

© Deborah Mawer 1997

All rights reserved. No part of this publication may be reproduced, stored in a retrieval system, or transmitted in any form or by any means, electronic, mechanical, photocopying, recording, or otherwise without the prior permission of the publisher.

Published by
SCOLAR PRESS
Ashgate Publishing Ltd.
Gower House
Croft Road
Aldershot
Hants. GU11 3HR
England

Ashgate Publishing Company
Old Post Road
Brookfield
Vermont 05036-9704
USA

British Library Cataloguing in Publication Data

Mawer, Deborah
   Darius Milhaud : modality & structure in music of the 1920s
   1. Milhaud, Darius, 1892–1974 – Criticism and interpretation
   I. Title.
   780.9'2

Library of Congress Cataloging in Publication Data

Mawer, Deborah
   Darius Milhaud : modality & structure in music of the 1920s / Deborah Mawer.
   Revision of the author's thesis (Ph. D.) – University of London, 1991.
   Includes bibliographical references and index.
   ISBN 1-85928-249-0 (acid-free paper)
   1. Milhaud, Darius. 1892–1974 – Criticism and interpretation.
   I. Title.
MT92.M55M39 1997
780'.92—dc21   97-3007   CIP MN

ISBN 1 85928 249 0

Typesetting by Ronald Woodley, Lancaster University.
Music origination by John Dunn, Comus Music Printing and Publishing, Tixall, Stafford, and Paul McFadden, Lancaster University.
Printed and bound in Great Britain by Biddles Ltd, Guildford and King's Lynn.

For Ron and Michael

CONTENTS

❦

Preface   ix

Acknowledgements   xiii

Introduction   xvii

1. MILHAUD'S MUSIC IN CONTEXT   1

    Milhaud & his Music in Historical Context   1
    The Constituent Elements of Milhaud's Music   9
    The Place of the Early Chamber Music   14
    Selection of Music for Case Studies   16

2. IN PURSUIT OF AN ANALYTICAL APPROACH   18

    'Polytonalité et atonalité' (1923)   19
    Critiques of Milhaud's Article and Analyses of his Music   26
    General Analytical Theory Relevant to Milhaud's Music   33
    Selection of Analytical Approach   44

3. EARLY EXPLORATION: CHROMATICISM   57

    CASE STUDY 1. Chromaticism and Polarity in the 'Funèbre' from the String Quartet No. 4, Op. 46 (1918)   73
        Preliminaries 73   Analysis 74   Conclusion 83
    CASE STUDY 2. Chromaticism and Canonic Devices in 'La Lieuse', from *Machines agricoles*, Op. 56 (1919)   85
        Preliminaries 85   Analysis 87   Conclusion 94
    CASE STUDY 3. Dissonant Mechanisms in the Chamber Symphony No. 5, Op. 75 (1922)   95
        Preliminaries 95   Analysis: I. Rude 97   II. Lent 105
        III. Violent 107   Conclusion 112

4. BRAZILIAN AND JAZZ-INSPIRED MUSIC: BLUES SCALE   113

    CASE STUDY 4. Seventh Complexes in 'Ipanema', from *Saudades do Brazil*, Op. 67 (1920): A Comparative Analysis with that of Keith W. Daniel   134
        Preliminaries 134   Analysis 135   Conclusion 143

Contents

    Case Study 5. Blues and Other Modal Formations in
    La Création du monde: Suite de concert, Op. 81*b* (1926)   145
        Preliminaries 145   Analysis: I. Prélude 150   II. Fugue 155
        III. Romance 161   IV. Scherzo 164   V. Final 167
        Conclusion 174

5. Neoclassicism: Refined Modality   177
    Case Study 6. Modality and Tension Theory in 'La femme
    que j'aime', from *Quatre poèmes de Catulle*, Op. 80 (1923)   198
        Preliminaries 198   Analysis 198   Conclusion 205
    Case Study 7. *Sonatine pour clarinette et piano*, Op. 100 (1927):
    Rethinking Modality and Sonata Principles   206
        Preliminaries 206   Analysis: I. Très rude 207   II. Lent 215
        III. Très rude 219   Conclusion 226
    Case Study 8. *L'Abandon d'Ariane*, Op. 98 (1927) as the
    Culmination of Milhaud's Neoclassicism in the 1920s   228
        Preliminaries 228   Analysis: Scene I. Modérément animé 231
        Scene II. Modéré 235   Scene III. Moins animé 239
        Scene IV. Très modéré 243   Scene V. Très lent 243
        Conclusion 250

6. Conclusion: Milhaud's 'Total Entity'   252
    Modal and Structural Perspectives 252
    Summary and Critique of Analytical Approach 256
    Stylistic and Aesthetic Perspectives 266
    Final Remarks on Milhaud 276
    Scope for Future Research 278

Appendix: Analytical Examples (Case Studies 1–8)   281

Bibliography   388

Index of Names and Works   401

PREFACE

THIS BOOK offers the first major analytical study of a significant portion of Milhaud's music, as a revised and updated version of a doctoral thesis (1991: see below), translated into book form. Its primary aim is to offer an interpretation of pitch-structure in Milhaud's music of the 1920s. Thus, this study serves to complement the largely biographical or descriptive studies of Milhaud published to date, and, on a larger scale, to represent Milhaud alongside recent scholarship on other French composers of broadly similar stature, including Poulenc (Wilfrid Mellers) and Satie (Robert Orledge).[1] The text is concerned primarily with eight analytical case studies on music belonging to that fruitful decade beyond the First World War, centring on the jazz-inspired masterpiece *La Création du monde*. In this sense, the book belongs within what is still a fairly short, but hopefully growing, tradition of analytical texts on twentieth-century French music, including, notably, Richard Parks's work on Debussy.[2]

Doubtless, in the minds of some, the days for engaging in detailed analyses of individual works are over, or at least numbered, and this may be all well and good for areas of study that enjoy a strong and varied history of analytical research, but for studies in this area, where there has been little serious analytical probing, there is still a need to create a foundation upon which to build. It is detailed analytical investigation which Milhaud's music merits but has not in the past received—partly, as observed by Robert Orledge, because of the 'prevailing quest for unknown pieces by great composers at the expense of great pieces by unknown composers'.[3] Of course Milhaud, much more so than Koechlin, has also been a victim of his own prolificacy and apparent lack of self-criticism, so that much sifting is needed to make sense of a vast, uneven compositional output; this notwithstanding, there are 'great

---

[1] W. Mellers, *Francis Poulenc* (Oxford, 1993); R. Orledge, *Satie the Composer* (Cambridge, 1990) and (with translations by R. Nichols) *Satie Remembered* (London, 1995).

[2] Most significantly, *The Music of Claude Debussy* (New Haven, 1989).

[3] R. Orledge, Preface to *Charles Koechlin (1867–1950): His Life and Works* (Chur and New York, 1989), xiii.

pieces' and others which, though not great, are arguably as or more interesting. Whatever the inherent difficulties, the timing of this analytical enquiry seems now appropriate, both as its own post-centenary assessment and celebration, and in view of the fact that other supporting materials have recently appeared: a new, if somewhat free, English translation of Milhaud's full autobiography, *My Happy Life*, and Roger Nichols's *Conversations with Madeleine Milhaud*.[4]

Where its main analytical identity is concerned, this book tests out a broad range of approaches to Milhaud's music, focusing on applications of extended voice-leading and set theory, including pc set genera. Although modally conceived, this music still presents many challenges to traditional perspectives. And beyond its strictly analytical remit, this book acknowledges the need to contextualize the various case studies, both musically and historically. It also engages at some level with notions of intertextuality, in as much as there are collective technical and stylistic elements or 'texts' which develop across a range of works (for example, a prevalent jazz text—admittedly more varied than, say, Stravinsky's ragtime text); and, conversely, multiple texts (or parts of texts) which may be embraced in a single work: thus individual works are considered as 'relational events',[5] rather than in a false isolation. In support, connection has been sought with the findings of more culturally and aesthetically orientated writings, including those of Glenn Watkins, David Meltzer, Stephen Walsh and Joseph Straus.[6]

---

[4] D. Milhaud, *My Happy Life*, trans. D. Evans, G. Hall and C. Palmer, with an introductory essay by Christopher Palmer (London, 1995): the appearance of this new English translation also constitutes, sadly, a fitting tribute to Christopher Palmer for his work in this domain; R. Nichols, *Conversations with Madeleine Milhaud* (London, 1996). Both texts are favourably reviewed by Robert Orledge in 'Notes from a Happy Life', *Times Literary Supplement*, 13 September 1996, 10–11. Nichols's book usefully supplements historical understanding, in an accessible anecdotal form, although it appeared too late for much wider inclusion in this present study. One should also acknowledge the appearance of Barbara L. Kelly's doctoral dissertation, 'Milhaud and the French Musical Tradition with Reference to his Works 1912–31' (Ph.D dissertation, University of Liverpool, 1994), and her subsequent article, 'Milhaud's *Alissa* Manuscripts', *Journal of the Royal Musical Association*, 121 (1996), 229–45.

[5] Joseph Straus, quoting Harold Bloom in discussing his theory of influence in *Remaking the Past: Musical Modernism and the Tonal Tradition* (Cambridge, Mass., and London, 1990), 12.

[6] G. Watkins, *Pyramids at the Louvre: Music, Culture, and Collage from Stravinsky to the Postmodernist* (Cambridge, Mass., 1994); D. Meltzer, *Reading Jazz* (San Francisco, 1993); S. Walsh, *The Music of Stravinsky* (Oxford, 1988); Straus, *Remaking the Past*.

Preface

Regarding the revision and updating involved in the production of this study, it is probably useful to highlight one or two matters. In recognition both of the emphasis on modality as a structural determinant, and of the wide-ranging repertory involved (albeit with the main focus on chamber music), the original title of the thesis, 'The Early Chamber Music of Darius Milhaud: Style and Structure' (Ph.D dissertation, University of London, 1991, under my former name of Roberts), has been modified accordingly. In focusing on 'Modality and Structure', the intention here is simply to signal the areas of greatest emphasis; 'style' should still be seen to figure implicitly, since structure cannot in any case be viewed in isolation from matters of governing aesthetic and stylistic presentation. Hence, the designations used in individual chapter titles ('Early Exploration', 'Brazilian and Jazz-inspired Music', and 'Neoclassicism') have both structural and stylistic ramifications. (Having said this, one could argue that an emphasis on structural techniques is also quite appropriate for a body of music where technique can sometimes outstrip inspiration.) The inclusion of 'Modality' in the title serves to point up the significance of modal references in individual chapters: 'Chromaticism', 'Blues Scale' and 'Refined Modality'. The final part of the title, 'Music of the 1920s', acknowledges the inclusion of some works whose forces lie beyond generally accepted definitions of chamber music: 'Ipanema' (Case Study 4) is for solo piano, whereas, at the other end of the spectrum, *L'Abandon d'Ariane*, though nominally regarded as chamber opera, involves a total of some twenty-five singers and instrumentalists. This new title also acknowledges the broader scope and application of the book beyond the specific bounds of the case studies.

Whilst there have been additions and modifications during revision, most notably in the case studies (and accompanying examples), as a result of the inclusion of pc set genera and engagement with recent literature across the period 1991–96, there have also been omissions, primarily for reasons of space. Some examples in the Appendix have been condensed, or occasionally omitted when they serve largely to substantiate further a point that has already been illustrated: nevertheless, there are still over one hundred supporting examples, supplemented by many tables. Most of the original appendices have been incorporated within the main text, though some other material, such as the original Chapter 7 and the discography, has been omitted. (It is pleasing to observe that CD recordings of Milhaud's music are increasing in number quite rapidly, so that any information supplied here would soon be out of date. The selected lists of recordings held at the BBC and the Phonothèque of the Bibliothèque Nationale in Paris may still be consulted, if desired, in Appendix 3 of the original dissertation.)

Where readership is concerned, this book aims to be accessible both to music analysts/theorists and musicologists; in terms of level, it seeks to be relevant to established academic scholars and students alike.[7] Whilst this may not be a book for reading from cover to cover, exploration of individual case studies is quite feasible—probably best in conjunction with the relevant introductory outline of Chapter 3, 4 or 5, and the conclusions of Chapter 6. Beyond the United Kingdom, and Milhaud's native France, it is hoped that this book may be of interest to readers in the United States where Milhaud himself exerted a strong influence beyond 1940 as a composer and teacher, and where analytical/theoretical interests, not least in set theory, have such a solid foundation. Beyond its specific focus on Milhaud, this book seeks to hold broader appeal for anyone concerned with analytical approaches to post-tonal musics, in particular those of Stravinsky, Ravel, Satie, and 'Les Six' (especially Poulenc) in the context of the 1920s.

Lancaster, April 1997

[7] For the student reader, especially, it may be useful to note that a software Analytical Listening Guide has been prepared by the present author on 'Darius Milhaud: *La Création du monde*' (Lancaster University, 1996); this aims to offer an approachable introduction to this work through on-screen study and listening in 'real time', in conjunction with a commercial CD recording.

ACKNOWLEDGEMENTS

THIS BOOK has had a long gestation, from the initial research begun in the mid-1980s, through its doctoral stage in 1991, to its final form here: consequently the acknowledgements, too, are extensive and varied.

Thanks are due firstly to Arnold Whittall, as the supervisor of the original dissertation, for his constructive criticism and guidance, and also to Jonathan Dunsby who acted initially as one of the examiners, but who offered additional advice in a broader capacity, and was the first to suggest the possible merits of engaging with Forte's system of pc set genera, and the necessity of checking pc set data on computer. In respect of the latter (and for his more general advice and support), I am grateful to Anthony Pople whose neat *SetBrowser* utility did indeed eradicate a couple of arithmetical blips!

Where the early stages of research and writing were concerned, I am appreciative of the response from individuals and institutions in Paris, including correspondence with Madeleine Milhaud and François Lesure (then Conservateur en chef de la Musique at the Bibliothèque Nationale), generous assistance offered by staff at the Phonothèque of the Bibliothèque Nationale, and information provided by the Music Department of the Université de Paris-Sorbonne and the Conservatoire Nationale de la Musique. In the United States, I would like to acknowledge the assistance of Eva Konrad Kreshka of the Milhaud Collection at Mills College, Oakland, California. Information on the availability of elusive scores, articles, and books, was supplied by several publishers, including Universal Edition, Schott & Co. Ltd., and United Music Publishers, as well as by the British Library and University of London Library.

In the preparation of this text for publication, Rachel Lynch of Scolar Press has been most supportive and accommodating; the Music Library of Yale University has supplied the copy of Milhaud's self-portrait sketch which is reproduced with the library's permission as part of the jacket design; Thames and Hudson have kindly given permission to reproduce parts of the English translation of Blaise Cendrars's scenario for *La Création du monde*; Paul McFadden (Lancaster

University) has set the musical examples in the main text, whilst those in the Appendix which support the case studies have been set by John Dunn (Comus Music Printing and Publishing). Reproduction of the numerous musical excerpts is by kind permission of United Music Publishers (agents for Editions Durand, Editions Max Eschig, Editions Heugel et Cie, and Editions Salabert), and by permission of Universal Edition A.G. Wien, with specific details given below.

Financial assistance to offset production costs has been provided through a generous grant from the journal *Music Analysis*, supplemented by funding from Lancaster University.

Finally, I want to express my special thanks to my partner, Ronald Woodley, not only for bearing with me through the trials and tribulations of this project, but for his direct contribution to the production of the finished book, and his fine eye for visual detail.

So this collective body of assistance and advice is very much appreciated, but of course the responsibility for what follows remains mine alone.

I am grateful to the following publishers for permission to use the musical quotations reprinted in this book:

Musical excerpts contained within figures in the main text: *Machines agricoles* © 1926 Universal Edition, copyright renewed 1954 by Darius Milhaud. Reproduced by permission of Universal Edition A.G. Wien; String Quartet No. 3 © 1956 Editions Durand S.A. Reproduced by kind permission of Editions Durand S.A./UMP Ltd.; String Quartet No. 4 © 1922 Editions Salabert. Reproduced by kind permission of Editions Salabert/UMP Ltd.; *Sonate*, Op. 47 (pour flûte, hautbois, clarinette et piano) © 1923 Editions Durand S.A. Reproduced by kind permission of Editions Durand S.A./UMP Ltd.; *Caramel mou* © 1921 Editions Max Eschig. Reproduced by kind permission of Editions Max Eschig/UMP Ltd.; Chamber Symphony No. 6 (pour soprano, contralto, ténor, basse, hautbois et violoncelle) © 1929 Universal Edition, copyright renewed 1956 by Darius Milhaud. Reproduced by permission of Universal Edition A.G. Wien; 'Corcovado' and 'Laranjeiras', from *Saudades do Brazil* (Suite de danses pour piano) © 1922 Editions Max Eschig. Reproduced by kind permission of Editions Max Eschig/UMP Ltd.; Chamber

Acknowledgements

Symphony No. 3 (*Sérénade*) © 1922 Universal Edition, renewed 1950. Reproduced by permission of Universal Edition A.G. Wien; String Quartet No. 6 © 1925 Universal Edition, renewed 1953. Reproduced by permission of Universal Edition A.G. Wien.

Musical excerpts contained within analytical examples in the Appendix: Case Study 1: String Quartet No. 4, 'Funèbre' © 1922 Editions Salabert. Reproduced by kind permission of Editions Salabert/UMP Ltd.; Case Study 2: 'La Lieuse' from *Machines agricoles* © 1926 Universal Edition, copyright renewed 1954 by Darius Milhaud. Reproduced by permission of Universal Edition A.G. Wien; Case Study 3: Chamber Symphony No. 5 (*Dixtuor d'instruments à vent*) © 1922 Universal Edition, renewed 1950. Reproduced by permission of Universal Edition A.G. Wien; Case Study 4: 'Ipanema' from *Saudades do Brazil* (Suite de danses pour piano) © 1922 Editions Max Eschig. Reproduced by kind permission of Editions Max Eschig/UMP Ltd.; Case Study 5: *La Création du monde* (*Suite de concert*) © 1926 Editions Max Eschig. Reproduced by kind permission of Editions Max Eschig/UMP Ltd.; Case Study 6: 'La femme que j'aime' from *Quatre poèmes de Catulle* © 1926 Editions Heugel et Cie. Reproduced by kind permission of Editions Heugel et Cie./UMP Ltd.; Case Study 7: *Sonatine pour clarinette et piano* © 1929 Editions Durand S.A. Reproduced by kind permission of Editions Durand S.A./UMP Ltd.; Case Study 8: *L'Abandon d'Ariane* © 1928 Universal Edition, renewed 1956; new German version © 1953; English version © 1963. Reproduced by permission of Universal Edition A.G. Wien.

INTRODUCTION

THE AIM of this book is to offer an interpretation of Milhaud's early-period music,[1] with primary reference to modality and structure. The abundant output of these years (especially the chamber music composed between 1917 and 1927) is regarded as one manifestation of the neoclassicism predominant in the 1920s.

Chapters 1 and 2 may be regarded informally as constituting the first part of the book, concerned with establishing a background. Chapter 1 places Milhaud's music and attitudes in historical context, making stylistic comparison with Stravinsky, Hindemith, Milhaud's compatriots, and other jazz-inspired composers, and then leads to more detailed discussion of the elements of (or tendencies in) Milhaud's music, these being the subjects of Chapters 3–5. The special place of the chamber music in Milhaud's output is emphasized, with the early period seen as dating approximately from the First Chamber Symphony (1917) to the Clarinet Sonatina (1927). Finally, criteria are established for the selection of eight works for analysis.

Chapter 2 seeks analytical approaches to the chosen repertory, commencing with discussion of Milhaud's short article-treatise 'Polytonalité et atonalité' (1923).[2] Subsequently some attempt is made, within circumscribed contexts, to develop and apply Milhaud's own ideas to his music, although essentially Milhaud's music is viewed as operating, at any one time, within a single composite modality. Thus compositional perspectives are contrasted with more recent analytical perspectives and interpretative strategies, as applied largely to the music of Stravinsky—and in transferring and adapting ideas from Stravinsky studies, it is hoped that approaches to Milhaud's music may in turn inform and feed back into further research on Stravinsky, amongst others. The priority lies in finding ways to interpret pitch-

---

[1] The interpretation of Milhaud's early-period music as constituting that composed before 1930 is supported by Jeremy Drake, in *The Operas of Darius Milhaud* (New York and London, 1989), 318.

[2] D. Milhaud, 'Polytonalité et atonalité', *La Revue musicale*, 4 (February 1923), 29–44.

structure in Milhaud's music, since this seems to predominate over metre and rhythm: 'For Milhaud, the metre serves primarily to give the melody the required rhythmic fluidity.'[3]

Although valuable biographical work on Milhaud has been undertaken by Paul Collaer,[4] analytical thinking has tended to be conventional: Collaer, for one, is more concerned with stylistic and historical issues than with questions of polytonality. And despite Keith Daniel's early application of set theory to some of Milhaud's works,[5] Drake's discussion of modality in the operas,[6] and a number of American dissertations, no one has previously tested the modal concept analytically by applying a mixture of a broadly Salzerian voice-leading, motivic analysis and set theory (including genera) to a representative selection of Milhaud's music. Chapter 2 advocates this mixture, also embracing ideas of Pieter van den Toorn, Joseph Straus, Leonard B. Meyer and Paul Hindemith/David Neumeyer, dependent on context. In view of the paucity of analytical work on Milhaud's music, some experimentation seemed justifiable and desirable, so that alternative readings are sometimes offered. Finally, one should stress the need for open-mindedness and flexibility: the intrinsically French qualities which give Milhaud's music its 'life' cannot be comprehended purely from a structural standpoint. Above all, free melody is paramount.

Chapters 3, 4 and 5 may be viewed informally as constituting a second part, specifically on the music, whose concern is to portray the forging of a style and development of structural techniques. (The reasoning behind the choice of subject-matter for these complementary chapters is detailed in Chapter 1, 'The Constituent Elements of Milhaud's Music'.) Each of these three chapters commences with an introductory outline, explaining the background and nature of a certain element, or tendency, and its typical structural techniques. Breadth of coverage has been gained by studying as much music as possible within the limits imposed by such a sizeable repertory: most chamber works with opus numbers between 40 and 100, together with some coverage of ballet and opera, since the early period is flanked by

[3] Drake, *The Operas of Darius Milhaud*, 195.
[4] P. Collaer, *Darius Milhaud* (Paris and Geneva, 1982); trans. and ed. J. Hohfeld Galante (San Francisco and London, 1988): this English translation henceforth differentiated from the French edition as Collaer/Galante, *Darius Milhaud.*
[5] K.W. Daniel, 'A Preliminary Investigation of Pitch-class Set Analysis in the Atonal and Polytonal works of Milhaud and Poulenc', *In Theory Only*, 6 (1982), 22–48.
[6] Drake, *The Operas of Darius Milhaud*, 'Modality', 201–7; 'Polymodality', 221–30.

masterpieces in these genres: *L'Homme et son désir* (1918) and *Christophe Colomb* (1928) respectively. Depth of coverage is the preserve of eight varied case studies, two or three of which are placed in each chapter.

Chapter 3 begins by discussing Milhaud's training at the Paris Conservatoire; beyond derivative student pieces, there is stylistic diversity, although this is still essentially late-Romantic. Music composed between about 1918 and 1922 develops chromaticism, in association with octatonicism and polarity, in a way that borders occasionally on atonality. These are amongst Milhaud's most radical and extraordinary works which mark a pivotal point in his career where one senses that neoclassicism was not the only option open to him.

Chapter 4 examines Milhaud's interest in Brazilian music and jazz, noting his visits to the United States to experience, assimilate, and express the jazz style within his own aesthetic; it also identifies typical structural techniques that focus on a blues scale. There is a stronger sense of pitch centre here than in the highly chromatic, exploratory pieces. Brazilian-inspired pieces, such as *Saudades do Brazil* (Case Study 4), lead to jazz-inspired ones, culminating in Milhaud's best-known work, *La Création du monde* (Case Study 5). This jazz-ballet, and subsequent *Suite de concert*, also owes much to a developing neoclassicism, and is, ultimately, a synthesis of the two styles. Equally, Milhaud's interest in Brazilian music and jazz is part of a wider, eclectic approach which also embraces Provençal and Jewish folksong, whilst the 'blues scale' is part of a broader modal approach, as is made clear in the following chapter.

Chapter 5 views the most important notion in Milhaud's music of the 1920s: neoclassicism and its use of a flexible, refined modality. Such neoclassicism firstly coexists with, and then supersedes, the overtly jazz-inspired element. Structural processes centre on modality and exhibit some common ground with those described in Chapters 3 and 4, although third relations, the 'triad motive', ostinato, 'pillar chords', ternary and fugal structures are both more prominent and finely nuanced than before. Many modes are employed in a free fashion,[7] especially Lydian, Mixolydian, Dorian and a 'new' mode (Altered Mixolydian). Case studies include the *Sonatine pour clarinette et piano*, Op. 100, and the second of three 'Opéras-minute'.

---

[7] The free use of modality demonstrates Drake's concept of 'inflectional polyvalency': ibid., 206.

The elements, or complementary traits, in Milhaud's music are brought together in the concluding Chapter 6 on Milhaud's 'Total Entity', as a product of the dictum that 'the whole is greater than the sum of its parts'. The subsequent 'Final Remarks on Milhaud' confirm him as a neoclassical modal lyricist who always maintained that he composed polytonally, comparable to a point with Stravinsky and Hindemith, and in keeping with the musical aesthetic of the 1920s. A final, short section indicating 'Scope for Future Research' highlights areas for further analytical research both within and beyond Milhaud's music.

Milhaud's Writings and their English Translations

Throughout the book, there is much translated material from Collaer's biography, *Darius Milhaud* and from Milhaud's own books and articles. Quotations from Collaer's biography are usually taken from the revised version, translated and edited by Jane Hohfeld Galante, with the assistance of Madeleine Milhaud (see above); occasionally, my own translation is given in preference, indicated as such where appropriate. Milhaud produced at least twenty pieces of writing on music and musicians, in the form of articles, essays and books: a full listing of those consulted for this study is given in the Bibliography. Several of these pay tribute to fellow composers, writers and choreographers, including Honegger, Gédalge, Diaghilev, Satie, Bartók, Claudel and Stravinsky; others include conversations, correspondence and Milhaud's views on the music of his own time.[8]

The two versions of Milhaud's autobiography provide witty, anecdotal accounts of his musical life, with some technical details, and are used frequently as a source of stylistic comment. The first French edition of *Notes sans Musique* (1949) was followed shortly afterwards by an English translation, *Notes without Music* (1952).[9] Twenty-five years later, Milhaud completed his autobiography which was retitled *Ma vie heureuse* (1974); a reprint of this revised version subsequently appeared in Paris in 1987,[10] and the corresponding full English translation was published in London two years ago as *My Happy Life* (1995). This latest

---

[8] The collected critical writings are available in French, edited by Jeremy Drake, as *Notes sur la musique: Essais et chroniques* (Paris, 1982).

[9] D. Milhaud, *Notes sans musique* (Paris, 1949); id., *Notes without Music*, trans. D. Evans, ed. R. H. Myers (London, 1952).

[10] D. Milhaud, *Ma vie heureuse* (Paris, 1987).

Introduction   xxi

English edition is, essentially, an expanded version of *Notes without Music*, with translations pertaining to Milhaud's early years largely unchanged. Although it constitutes a readable account of Milhaud's whole life, I have favoured working primarily from the French edition of 1987, usually in the interests of a more strictly literal translation. Consequently, throughout this book, where the source is given as *Ma vie heureuse* the translation is my own.

Of greatest technical interest are the essays entitled *Études*,[11] the articles 'Polytonalité et atonalité',[12] and 'The Evolution of Modern Music in Paris and Vienna',[13] and writings on Brazilian music and jazz.[14] Again, translations are my own unless otherwise stated. Quotations from 'Polytonalité et atonalité' (in Chapter 2) are given in English translation, with the original French in footnotes; this policy was adopted for analytical clarity and consistency since the other analytical sources were in English. In the introductory outlines of Chapters 3, 4 and 5, however, which use a variety of French sources, it was more appropriate to quote in the original language, with English translations in footnotes. Occasionally, a phrase is left untranslated, because it conveys so much more in its original form.

Analytical Notation

Much of the analytical material in this book is in graphic form. The voice-leading notation (including abbreviations) is a combination of that used by Schenker in *Der freie Satz* (*Free Composition*),[15] and by Salzer in *Structural Hearing*.[16] Terminology (including abbreviations) relating to the set-theoretic analysis is from Forte's *The Structure of*

---

[11] D. Milhaud, *Études* (Paris, 1927).

[12] For full reference, see n. 2 above.

[13] D. Milhaud, 'The Evolution of Modern Music in Paris and Vienna', *North American Review*, 217 (April 1923), 544–54; also *Franco-American Musical Society Bulletin*, 1 (September 1923), 8–16.

[14] D. Milhaud, 'Brésil', *La Revue musicale*, 1 (November 1920), 'Chroniques et Notes', 60–1; 'L'Évolution du jazz-band et la musique des nègres d'Amérique du nord', in *Études*, 51–9.

[15] H. Schenker, *Der freie Satz* (*Free Composition*), trans. and ed. E. Oster (New York, 1979). A. Forte and S. Gilbert also offer a standardized version of Schenkerian notation in their *Introduction to Schenkerian Analysis* (New York, 1982).

[16] F. Salzer, *Structural Hearing: Tonal Coherence in Music*, rev. ed., 2 vols. in 1 (New York and London, 1982), ii, xiv.

Atonal Music,[17] and from his later article on pc set genera. Traditional note-values indicate relative positions within a vestigial structural hierarchy, rather than rhythmic durations (though there is of course no strict middleground in the accepted Schenkerian sense). Essentially, four values are used: open-headed note with stem (beamed or unbeamed), filled-in note with stem, filled-in note with stem and tail, filled-in note without stem. Beamed pitches are of the highest structural order, whilst the smallest note-values represent foreground ornamentation. Modes of structural import are also denoted by open notes, and small-scale surface figuration by filled-in notes. Structural connections between pitches are indicated by solid slurs, or horizontal arrows, whilst broken slurs represent 'association' or actual prolongation, occasionally dissonant,[18] as well as transfer of register. (Context should clarify any potential ambiguity here). A note in brackets signifies the expectation of a voice-leading implication. Blues notes (especially thirds and sevenths) are indicated by an oblique line between the competing pitches. Roman numerals, and/or figured bass, indicate chordal identity, together with pc sets and generic designations, where appropriate. Occasionally, most often in a jazz-influenced context, it was more appropriate that the figuring which supplements Roman numeral designations should be taken from the chordal root (rather than literal bass note, in the case of first and, particularly, second chordal inversions): this more flexible figuring is indicated by the presence of inverted commas, e.g. 'V^{11}'. In the Romance of *La Création du monde*, for instance, such a practice also makes for better connection with the jazz chordal symbols given in parentheses in the middle of the stave.

Octave designation complies with the system whereby middle C is c^1, one octave below is c, two octaves below is C, and three octaves below is C_I; when octave position is not specified, the note-name is given in upper-case lettering. In order both to establish Milhaud's patterns of practice with regard to 'major' and 'minor' modes (including the extent of deviation from standard major and minor scales), and to facilitate a compact form of reference (especially in the Appendix of analytical examples), upper-case lettering also denotes the pitch-

---

[17] A. Forte, *The Structure of Atonal Music* (New Haven and London, 1973; repr. 1979).

[18] See J. Straus, 'The Problem of Prolongation in Post-tonal Music', *Journal of Music Theory*, 31 (1987), 1–21.

centre of a major mode (or triad, seventh construct, etc.), whilst lower-case lettering denotes a minor mode.[19] The importance of internal consistency outweighed considerations of the niceties of prose in reversed designations: for example, the salient features of a 'shorthand' expression used on a graphic example: d [minor-third mode]: Aeolian [specific identity/inflection] are maintained in the prose reversal of 'Aeolian on d'. In the latter expression, even if the use of lower-case lettering seems initially curious, the designation of 'd' still has a useful summarizing function, and is justifiable since 'd' is not in any case a finite pitch designation, but an indication of the starting-point of a sequence of pitches. Similarly, the designation of a 'triad of/on d' implies the other pitches of that construction. The consistent employment of this policy across the study has revealed a notably even-handed overall distribution of major and minor 'derivatives'. As before, context should clarify any potential ambiguity of pitch notation.

Figures in the text include short analyses, score extracts and tables which are labelled sequentially through Chapters 2–5 (Figure 2.1, 2.2, etc.). Each case study begins with a formal outline, which includes the total bars for each section and (despite its obvious limitations) does offer general guidelines for comparison since Milhaud's music is almost always regular in its metre. More extensive graphs, numbered sequentially by chapter as Examples (Example 3.1, 3.2, etc.), are given in the Appendix. Musical examples in both the main text and the Appendix are notated at sounding pitch, unless otherwise indicated.

---

[19] 'Major' mode denotes any mode with a major third interval from its final to third scalic degree: i.e. Ionian, Lydian and Mixolydian; 'minor' mode denotes any mode with a minor third interval from its final to third degree: i.e. Dorian, Phrygian, Aeolian, or Locrian.

CHAPTER ONE

Milhaud's Music in Context

IN PROCEEDING from the general to the particular, this chapter offers an initial discussion of Milhaud's music and attitude in relation to his contemporaries, which leads to a consideration of constituent elements of his music (with emphasis on stylistic and aesthetic concerns), and concludes by placing the works selected for analysis in the context of his larger musical output.

Milhaud & his Music in Historical Context

Darius Milhaud (1892–1974) belonged within a musical and artistic culture which was centred on Paris, though for compositional inspiration he often returned to his family home near Aix-en-Provence. Like most composers of his generation, he could not escape the influence of Debussy and Ravel in his works before 1918; in 1920, however, he became one of 'Les Six'—rather by accident than design, though he had already been a member of its forerunner grouping, 'Les Nouveaux Jeunes'. Henri Collet's journalistic epithet helped to gain initial notoriety for the young composers concerned, but suggested a common artistic purpose which was at best tenuous. Milhaud came to resent the fact that by association with Les Six he appeared merely as an exploiter of frivolous novelty. More detailed comparisons with members of Les Six will be drawn later; suffice it to say here that Milhaud was inspired and influenced by the group's mentor and 'mascot', Erik Satie (1866–1925).

Of great significance to Milhaud, especially before 1930, were his friendships with writers: Paul Claudel (1868–1955),[1] Léo Latil (1890–1915), Francis Jammes (1843–1916) and André Gide (1869–1951), as well as Blaise Cendrars (1887–1961) and the cubist painter Fernand Léger (1881–1955). Madeleine Milhaud's view is that Paul Claudel did indeed

---

[1] Paul Louis Charles-Marie Claudel was a poet, playwright and diplomat, whose plays included *L'Otage* (1911), *L'Annonce faite à Marie* (1912), with incidental music later provided by Milhaud, and *Le Soulier de satin* (1919–24). An important theme of his work was that of man's resistance, and final surrender, to the love of God. The extensive correspondence between the two men is collected in *Correspondance Paul Claudel–Darius Milhaud, 1912–1953*, in *Cahiers Paul Claudel*, ed. J. Petit (Paris, 1961).

constitute the single, most important influence upon her husband, and that, musically, Milhaud was more affected by composers from the eighteenth and nineteenth centuries than by any contemporary.[2] Milhaud was, however, a composer of his time, sharing the neoclassical outlook predominant in the Paris of the 1920s, together with something of the *Gebrauchsmusik* philosophy of Hindemith.

Milhaud was ten years younger than his most important musical ally, a man for whom he held great admiration, Igor Stravinsky (1882–1971). Both were active in Paris during the 1920s and in their ideologies were concerned to move away from the German hegemony epitomized by Wagner: Milhaud's antipathy to Wagner ('À bas Wagner!') is expressed forcefully in his autobiography.[3] This was perhaps one reason for Milhaud and Stravinsky favouring modality over tonality, although in Milhaud's case this was mainly the result of his 'double heritage' of Jewish liturgical music and Provençal folksong.[4] In their neoclassicism, both sought economy of means, though Milhaud worked in miniature more readily than Stravinsky.[5] Both composers made prominent use of third relations, an idea explored, in relation to Stravinsky, by Joseph Straus;[6] carefully balanced polarity is also important in their music, especially at the tritone within octatonic contexts.[7] Stravinsky's modal language is generally more blended and integrated than that of Milhaud, whose primary concern to characterize different contrapuntal strands leads to more disparate results.

Both Milhaud and Stravinsky assimilated aspects of jazz within their music, and discovered the close relationship between the textures and rhythmic momentum of baroque music and jazz. Milhaud's contribution is perhaps more authentic than Stravinsky's, though one could compare Milhaud's *Trois rag-caprices for Piano* (1922), later orchestrated,

---

[2] M. Milhaud, undated letter to the present writer [Paris, c. October 1986]: 'Influence: Claudel. Influence musicale: <Berlioz deleted> Je devrais citer cent qu'il admirait: Gounod, Verdi, Mozart, Bach, Berlioz. Voilà!'

[3] Milhaud, *Ma vie heureuse*, 97.

[4] Drake, *The Operas of Darius Milhaud*, 202.

[5] Cf. Drake, ibid., 220: 'The situation is comparable with that of the pretonal, modal music of the Renaissance polyphonists and like them Milhaud is incapable of large-scale harmonic organization.' Although Drake's generalization is useful up to a point, both Josquin and Milhaud might justifiably take exception to the accusation of incapability.

[6] J. Straus, 'Stravinsky's Tonal Axis', *Journal of Music Theory*, 26 (1982), 261–90.

[7] See especially P. van den Toorn, *The Music of Igor Stravinsky* (New Haven, 1983).

with Stravinsky's *Piano-Rag-Music* (1919). There is, however, no equivalent in Stravinsky's output to Milhaud's ballet *La Création du monde* (1923), despite the range of ragtime and other popular allusions in *L'Histoire du soldat* (1918) and *Ragtime for Eleven Instruments* (1919). Whilst Stravinsky concentrated on the more old-fashioned ragtime, studied from scores and recordings, Milhaud endeavoured to understand and assimilate early jazz, with its blues-inspired vocal inflections, at first hand. His interest in popular music had first been awakened by the period that he spent in Brazil, working for Claudel in 1917–18, which was followed by visits to the United States in search of authentic negro music.

Like Stravinsky, Milhaud also wrote for the Parisian ballets: Stravinsky was commissioned by Serge Diaghilev for the Ballets Russes, and Milhaud by Rolf de Maré for the Ballets Suédois. The astounding rhythmic polyphony of Milhaud's *L'Homme et son désir* (1918) was accorded a very similar reception to the riot which accompanied the première of *Le Sacre du printemps* (1913).

Milhaud and Stravinsky were both interested in composing for woodwind in the early 1920s. Milhaud's Fifth Chamber Symphony, subtitled *Dixtuor d'instruments à vent* (1922), was written a year before Stravinsky's Octet, and two years after the *Symphonies of Wind Instruments*. Although Stravinsky's Octet is a more integrated and successful work than Milhaud's Chamber Symphony, the latter work does show Milhaud prepared to experiment radically.

In the later 1920s, both composers were inspired to revitalise Greek tragedy:[8] Milhaud's interest was first manifested in his *L'Orestie* trilogy (1917–22), followed by the fine chamber opera *Les Malheurs d'Orphée* (1925), and the trilogy of 'Opéras-minute' (1927). In fact, the final scene of the second Opéra-minute, *L'Abandon d'Ariane*, has a distinctly Stravinskian character, as will be discussed in Case Study 8. The year 1927 also saw the composition of Stravinsky's *Oedipus Rex*, followed by *Apollon Musagète* (1928).

In the 1920s, both Stravinsky and Milhaud reached their peaks of achievement in chamber music and Greek tragic (chamber) opera, and both maintained their neoclassicism through the 1930s and 1940s, after emigrating to the United States. Both composers wrote about music

---

[8] See R. Zinar, 'Greek Tragedy in the Theatre Pieces of Stravinsky and Milhaud' (Ph.D diss., New York University, 1968).

and left autobiographies: Stravinsky's *Poetics of Music*,[9] albeit 'ghosted', may be compared with Milhaud's *Études* (and, in fact, Milhaud wrote the Preface to Stravinsky's *Poetics*); similarly, the various volumes of the Stravinsky–Craft conversations[10] may be compared with Milhaud's interviews with Claude Rostand.[11] Milhaud's intense admiration for Stravinsky, first acknowledged in his discussion of *Mavra* (1922)[12], was sustained throughout his long life; and indeed both composers died within the space of a couple of years: Milhaud's final tribute to Stravinsky was a miniature for string quartet, entitled *In Memoriam I.S.*[13]

The most obvious connection between Milhaud and his German contemporary Paul Hindemith (1895–1963), lies in *Gebrauchsmusik*, although this developed more in the 1930s than the 1920s. Both were concerned that music should not be esoteric but accessible, and that the composer had a duty to further education through music. Earlier in the 1920s, however, both composers also shared a debt to Bach, through Milhaud's Six Chamber Symphonies (1917–23) and Hindemith's *Kammermusik* series (1922–27). Although both must have been aware of Schoenberg's *Kammersymphonie* (No. 1), Op. 9 (1906), the initial inspiration seems to have come from Bach's Brandenburg Concertos. In particular, one may compare Milhaud's *Dixtuor d'instruments à vent* and Hindemith's *Kleine Kammermusik* for wind quintet, each composed in 1922. In addition to music for chamber ensemble, both composers were interested in the solo sonata: Hindemith's preoccupation with string sonatas is evident in the early to mid-1920s, whilst Milhaud's interest was most apparent before 1920 and after 1940. Their friendship had begun in 1927, while composing miniature operas for the concerts of contemporary music at Baden-Baden, organized by Hindemith. Milhaud produced the first of his trilogy, *L'Enlèvement d'Europe*, and Hindemith his *Hin und zurück*. Two years later, Milhaud wrote his Viola Concerto No. 1, dedicated to Hindemith and first performed by him in December 1929 at the Concertgebouw in Amsterdam, conducted by Pierre Monteux.

[9] I. Stravinsky, *Poetics of Music* (New York, 1947).
[10] Reference to Milhaud appears, for example, in R. Craft, *Stravinsky: The Chronicle of a Friendship 1948–1971* (New York, 1972).
[11] D. Milhaud, *Entretiens avec Claude Rostand* (Paris, 1952).
[12] Milhaud, *Ma vie heureuse*, 110–11.
[13] Published in 'Canons and Epitaphs', Set 2, *Tempo*, 98 (1972) [no pagination]; he also wrote a separate tribute: 'Stravinsky: A Composer's Memorial', *Perspectives of New Music*, 10 (1971), 9–10.

Both composers were concerned to revive baroque contrapuntal techniques[14] within their neoclassicism: Milhaud, especially, was fascinated by fugue, composing at least eight examples in music of the 1920s. The most striking similarity in their musical language concerns third relations and ambiguity, identified as 'indefinite third relation' by David Neumeyer in analyses of Hindemith's music,[15] which develop ideas from *The Craft of Musical Composition*.[16] Such ambiguity abounds in Milhaud's music too, often concerning 'rival' modalities a third apart. Other areas of common ground include structural 'pillar' chords within a predominantly contrapuntal texture (an idea articulated by Hindemith), the importance of 'fundamental bass' and a 'tension theory' based on relative dissonance.[17] The potentially bizarre confrontation of strong dissonance and pure consonance is also found in both Milhaud and Hindemith: often it is the final chord of a movement which reverts to an apparently naive consonance.

Like Milhaud, Hindemith also wrote about his music, primarily in his treatise *The Craft of Musical Composition*. Indeed, in the very title of this book lies a final similarity of purpose between these composers: the idea of composition as a matter of craftsmanship, rather in the eighteenth-century manner, in response to demand and occasion.

Milhaud's style may seem to be the antithesis of that of Schoenberg (1874–1951), yet there was contact between the composers. Milhaud strongly admired Schoenberg although he was never tempted to pursue serialism himself. In fact, one interesting observation which connects Milhaud, Schoenberg and Hindemith is that, despite their differences, the year 1923 represented for each a stylistic landmark. This was the date of Milhaud's crucial article on polytonality and atonality; of

[14] See Milhaud, 'Polytonalité et atonalité', 30. Some of his initial inspiration for 'polytonality' comes directly from Bach's canons and fugues; compare with Hindemith, 'Atonality and Polytonality', *The Craft of Musical Composition*, Book 1, trans. A. Mendel (Mainz and London, 1942), Chapter 4, 152–6.

[15] D. Neumeyer, *The Music of Paul Hindemith* (New Haven, 1986). Analyses of particular interest include those of the *Ludus Tonalis*, the Third Piano Sonata (1936), the Sonata for solo viola, Op. 11 No. 5, and the Sonata for solo cello, Op. 25 No. 3 (1922); for the indefinite third relation, see ibid., 54–5.

[16] Neumeyer's main sources are Hindemith, *The Craft of Musical Composition*, Book 1, and, especially, Book 3 (posth. publ., 1970; Engl. trans. forthcoming), together with *Traditional Harmony*, Book 2 (New York, 1948).

[17] Neumeyer, *Paul Hindemith*: pillar chords, 52, 76; fundamental bass, 59; harmonic fluctuation, 31, 34, 60–1; Hindemith, *The Craft of Musical Composition*, Book 1: fundamental bass, 121–5; fluctuation, 115–21.

Schoenberg's full commitment to the consequences of his earlier serial explorations; and of Hindemith's discovery of a 'New Objectivity'.[18] Milhaud certainly showed his respect for Schoenberg in the dedication of his Fifth Quartet (1920), which, together with the *Cinq études* of the same year, is one of his most radical and uncompromising 'polytonal' experiments, rigorously pursued. Perhaps Schoenberg recognized the courage and conviction needed in such experimentation (so much a hallmark of his own writing), even if he did not identify with Milhaud's polytonal perspective. Indeed, Schoenberg commented to Zemlinsky in a letter of 1922 that 'Milhaud strikes me as the most important representative of the contemporary movement in all Latin countries: Polytonality. Whether I like him is not to the point. But I consider him most talented.'[19]

Schoenberg's *Kammersymphonie* has already been suggested as a possible influence on Milhaud's Chamber Symphonies, but was Milhaud familiar with Schoenberg's Second Quartet, Op. 10, with soprano (1907–8), when he wrote his own sombre Third Quartet for the same unusual combination in 1916? In the second of three letters to the present author, Madeleine Milhaud declares adamantly that Milhaud did not know Schoenberg's Quartet at that time (though surely he knew *of* it); in the third letter, she explains that the first direct contact between the two composers was in Vienna, in 1922, when they met to discuss the success of the French première of *Pierrot lunaire*, Op. 21, directed by Milhaud.[20]

An important difference of approach between the two concerns thematic development, which in Milhaud's music tends to be limited, although he does employ varied repetition, sequence and inversion; Milhaud is, however, in the words of one of his students, Charles Jones, 'allergic to variation form, and this is where his break with the dodecaphonists is most apparent'.[21]

Although there are few stylistic connections, there was some contact between Milhaud and Alban Berg (1885–1935): the quality and uni-

---

18 Neumeyer, *Paul Hindemith*, 117.

19 A. Schoenberg, *Letters*, ed. E. Stein (New York, 1965), 80.

20 M. Milhaud, letter from Geneva, dated 13 July 1986: 'Non! Milhaud ne connaissait pas le Quat[uor] de Schönberg quand il a décidé de composer son 3ème.'; undated letter [Paris, *c*. October 1986]: 'Milhaud a rencontré Schönberg à Vienne en 1922—il venait de diriger P. Lunaire à Paris. . . .'

21 C. Jones, 'Darius Milhaud', *Dictionary of Twentieth-Century Music*, ed. J. Vinton (London, 1974), 487–8.

versality of Milhaud's writing in his Chamber Symphonies (Nos. 1–5) was attested to by Berg, who wrote to Milhaud on 27 April 1923, in order to acknowledge receipt of the new scores:

> My very dear M. Milhaud:
>
> I thank you sincerely for your five symphonies. After a quick glance, I was delighted with them and eager to study them further. My first impression is that I find your work extremely 'sympathique' as well as fresh and original. And, thanks to you, I believe I have come to appreciate polytonality. Furthermore, even though these pieces were composed between 1917 and 1922 and at places as far distant as Rio de Janeiro and Vienna, they possess such unity that I am convinced of the high quality of this composition.
>
> I am sincerely delighted, and I thank you.[22]

Much of Milhaud's style is shaped by his French-Provençal temperament, especially his belief in the priority of free, unfettered melody and his disdainful rejection of restrictive systems. Of his compatriots, Milhaud identified most readily with Erik Satie, appreciating his subtle wit and eccentricity: both advocated delicacy and economy of musical treatment, with occasional biting dissonance, and shared a sophisticated elegance so typical of French neoclassicism. Milhaud's respect for Satie is evident from tributes in *Notes sur Erik Satie* and *Ma vie heureuse*, and from his orchestration of Satie's *Jack in the Box*.[23]

In connection with Les Six, Milhaud was of course in touch with the group's self-appointed impresario, Jean Cocteau (1889–1963). Despite some ideological differences, and Milhaud's resentment at the over-inflation of *Le Bœuf* (for which Cocteau was largely responsible), there is a small volume of collected correspondence which has been published relatively recently.[24] Cocteau also provided the scenario for Milhaud's ballet *Le Train bleu*, Op. 84 (1924), and the libretto for his chamber opera *Le Pauvre matelot*, Op. 92 (1926). Within Les Six, the main comparisons of consequence are with Francis Poulenc (1899–1963) and Arthur Honegger (1892–1955), and, in fact, although Honegger was an exact contemporary, he and Milhaud still had relatively little in com-

---

[22] Quoted in Collaer/Galante, *Darius Milhaud*, 209 (dated 23 April in error).

[23] Milhaud, *Ma vie heureuse*, Chapter 23: 'The Death of Erik Satie'; id., *Notes sur Erik Satie* (Paris, 1943). Milhaud also made a piano reduction of *Cinq grimaces*, and, according to Collaer, four-hand arrangements of *Entr'acte* and [one of?] the *Gymnopédies*, and, for violin and piano, a Suite from *Trois morceaux en forme de poire*.

[24] P. Caizergues and J. Mas, eds., *Correspondance Jean Cocteau–Darius Milhaud* (Montpellier, 1992).

mon. Honegger was notably more Germanic in his approach, so that the two composers were closest ideologically in their early years, before Milhaud's rejection of a Germanically-inspired late Romanticism. Such early works include Milhaud's Second and Third Quartets, with their intense and melancholic Romanticism which still bears Wagnerian influence. Certainly, the string quartet was a medium important to both Milhaud and Honegger, as were large-scale staged works, illustrated for example by *Christophe Colomb* (1928) and *Le Roi David* (1923). The only other common ground lies in a fascination for portraying machinery in music, and in this respect Milhaud's *Machines agricoles* (1919) and Honegger's *Pacific 231* (1923) were just two works of a larger cult in the 1920s, to be discussed at greater length in Chapter 3.

There is more common purpose between Milhaud and Poulenc in their sharing of a tonal-modal approach, although Poulenc was never drawn to exhaustive exploration of polytonality, nor was his style so consistently directed towards neoclassicism as that of Milhaud. Rather, Poulenc was more partial to the frivolity and melodrama of Cocteau's ideas. Nonetheless, Milhaud's respect and affection for his younger compatriot is shown by the dedication of his Sixth Quartet, Op. 79 (1922). Interestingly, exploratory use of set theory has been employed by Keith Daniel in analysis of the early music of both composers;[25] essentially, though, this research serves only to confirm that their fundamental structures are usually directed not by sets, but by an elusively free modality.

Milhaud's Violin Sonatas Nos. 1 and 2, and his Quartet No. 1, were much influenced by French musicians of the previous generation: César Franck (1822–90), Gabriel Fauré (1845–1924), and, of course, Claude Debussy (1862–1918). There is also stylistic correspondence between Milhaud's Fourth Quartet (1918) and the Quartet in F (1903/1910) of Maurice Ravel (1875–1937); and Ravel in turn was clearly aware of the attributes of Milhaud's music when he declared in a lecture, given in Houston, Texas, in April 1928, that 'In the works of Darius Milhaud, probably the most important of our younger French composers, one is frequently impressed by the breadth of the composer's conceptions.'[26] Additionally, Milhaud strongly admired the

---

[25] Daniel, 'A Preliminary Investigation'.
[26] M. Ravel, 'Contemporary Music', in *A Ravel Reader*, ed. A. Orenstein (New York, 1990), 42–3.

little recognized composer Charles Koechlin (1867–1950),[27] who seemed to inspire him in his initial polytonal explorations.

The remaining comparisons involve composers, born or resident in the United States, who exploited jazz, as well as aspects of the Jewish musical heritage. Together with Kurt Weill (1890–1950), George Gershwin (1898–1937), and Aaron Copland (1900–90), Milhaud should be credited with being amongst the first to incorporate elements of true jazz into 'high-art' music. Milhaud's *La Création du monde* appeared just a year before Gershwin's *Rhapsody in Blue* (1924), and there are certain correspondences between the two works (see Case Study 5 below). In assimilating the cabaret atmosphere of the Berliner Band, there is also similarity between the finales of Milhaud's Fifth Chamber Symphony (1922) and Weill's Second Symphony (1933)—both featuring reiterated dotted rhythms and melodic focus on clarinet. Then, early in the 1940s, following Milhaud's emigration to the United States, both he and Copland composed concertos for the great jazz clarinettist Benny Goodman. In addition to their fascination with jazz, all four composers shared a deeply rooted Jewish faith, and one wonders whether they felt an affinity between melancholic Jewish song and the emotionally charged vocal blues, or a sense of identification with another race which had suffered persecution. Whatever the reasons behind this linkage, Milhaud's music is quite strongly influenced by this Judaic context, most obviously in his solo songs and large choral works, but also in his opera *Esther de Carpentras* (1925).

Finally, one may suggest a parallel with the approach of an American (non-Jewish) composer, the great individualist Charles Ives (1874–1954). Both Milhaud and Ives sought to distinguish areas of sound using 'polytonality' and spatial representation, illustrated by Milhaud's Percussion Concerto, Op. 109 (1929–30), with directions for specific stage layout; his Quartets Nos. 14 and 15, Op. 291 (1948–49), which may be played separately or together as an octet; and Ives's early 'philosophical' piece, *The Unanswered Question* (1906).

The Constituent Elements of Milhaud's Music

Before discussing its constituent elements, it may be useful to offer an initial summative statement as to the basic nature and effect of Mil-

---

[27] Koechlin's neglect has been at least partly remedied by the appearance of Orledge, *Charles Koechlin*.

haud's music in which lyrical melodies are predominant. Several melodies tend to be superimposed in loosely imitative counterpoint, with their own modal identities: the overall effect tends to be that a single pitch centre emerges, dictated by the choice of bass-line, and often reinforced by chromatic encirclement (for example, F♯,G; A♭,G: reinforcing G). Varying degrees of tension may exist within the modality, created by chromaticism, or by tritonal polarities characteristic of octatonicism; bimodality may also constitute a localized source of conflict. Texture is most often light and polyphonic, with doubling between the bass and uppermost voice. Repetitive and sequential patterns are important (especially as ostinati). Metre tends to be regular, with several rhythmic patterns in operation simultaneously; there is also a fondness of a 'pastoral' 6/8 metre with lilting rhythms and occasional syncopation. Milhaud often enjoys working in miniature, with ternary structures predominant. The vast amount of music generated by these means spans three compositional periods, the dates for which are largely in accordance with those suggested by Drake:[28] the early period (approximately 1911–30), the middle period (1930–early 1950s), and the late period, revitalising some early ideas (early 1950s–1973).

The idea of discussing Milhaud's early period music in terms of its predominant stylistic/aesthetic 'elements' developed from reading *Ma vie heureuse* and Collaer's biography of the composer. The term 'élément' is employed frequently in French writing on music, including those texts of Milhaud and Collaer, so that it seemed appropriate to use it here; should the term seem awkward in English, one could substitute 'tendency', though this would lose the associated imagery of fundamental 'chemical' units. Although the full exploration of these elements is reserved for Chapters 3, 4 and 5, the governing concept may usefully be introduced here. The starting-point is an important statement made by Collaer, and, despite any reservations one may have on the analytical validity of some of his comments, he has undoubtedly captured the essence of Milhaud's approach here:

> ... from his adolescent years to the end of his life, he conceived his artistic creation as a total entity, the various elements of which could be drawn forth at any moment for whatever purpose.[29]

This is an apposite appreciation of Milhaud's art, from a man who

---

[28] Drake, *The Operas of Darius Milhaud*, 2, 318, 362.
[29] Collaer/Galante, *Darius Milhaud*, 208.

knew the composer well, so that this quotation is returned to as a point of departure for the final Chapter 6. 'Elements' is interpreted broadly by Collaer to embrace issues of style and 'various technical resources', although he notes no 'systematic development of technique'; rather, Milhaud 'chose those elements that suited a particular expressive imperative'.[30] Collaer suggests essentially that Milhaud's music is based on a 'free and universal concept of the world of sonority'. And the corresponding use of 'elements' in the present book also applies broadly to stylistic (and aesthetic) concerns, in association with the structural techniques needed to express such notions.

Across Milhaud's early works up to 1922, there is a strong sense of exploration which is supported by the early chapters of *Ma vie heureuse*: 'Léo et Armand'; 'Paris 1909–12'; 'Le syndicat'; 'La saison 1913–14'; and 'La guerre'. The most telling passage regarding exploration is contained at the end of Chapter 3 of the autobiography:

> Le soir, avant de m'endormir, je fermais les yeux; alors j'imaginais, j'entendais une musique d'une extraordinaire liberté qu'il m'eût été impossible de transcrire. Comment l'exprimer? C'était pour moi un grand mystère dans lequel je me complaisais, comme en un refuge où mon langage musical s'élaborait dans les couches les plus profondes de mon inconscient.[31]

That this music was impossible for Milhaud to write down stresses the idea of Milhaud as apprentice, and the need for further experience. He imagines his musical language developing in the furthest reaches of his subconscious mind; perhaps most interesting is his question 'How could I express it?' which may be interpreted as referring both to verbal and musical means. The question is used to head Chapter 3 of the present book, with the answer gradually focusing through Chapters 3, 4 and 5, so that from this quotation, and that of Collaer above, developed the image of an early 'melting-pot' out of which the main elements emerged. The most noteworthy inflection of 'Early Exploration' occurs in the form of the experimental machinist aesthetic.

---

[30] Ibid.
[31] Milhaud, *Ma vie heureuse*, 25: 'In the evening, before falling asleep, I used to close my eyes; thus I used to imagine, used to hear, music of an extraordinary freedom which it would have been impossible for me to write down. How could I express it? To me it was a great mystery in which I took much pleasure, as if in a sanctuary where my musical language was working itself out in the furthest reaches of my subconscious.'

Still within the formative years, there are so many references to Milhaud's interest in Brazilian popular music and jazz, in *Ma vie heureuse*, *Études*, and individual articles, that the associated music demanded its own chapter here. The Brazilian/jazz-inspired element is detailed in four chapters of *Ma vie heureuse*: 'Le Brésil'; 'Rencontre avec le jazz'; 'États-Unis, 1922'; and 'Ballets'. It was particularly for its rhythmic potential that Milhaud was attracted to Brazilian musical culture: 'Les rythmes de cette musique populaire m'intriguaient et me fascinaient',[32] though his subsequent interest in jazz delved deeper: 'il me fallait auparavant pénétrer plus profondément les arcanes de cette nouvelle forme musicale dont la technique m'angoissait encore.'[33] This latter quotation is appropriate in that it invokes a distinction between musical form and technique: further justification for investigating the jazz-inspired element in its own chapter. Just as there was one particularly apt quotation from the composer for the exploratory element in his music, embodying a question, so too does one emerge for Chapter 4: 'Les voici à la tête d'éléments sonores et rythmiques absolument nouveaux et bien à eux, mais comment les utiliser?'[34] It is worth noting that Milhaud refers specifically to 'sonorous and rhythmic *elements*', so supporting the use of this term here.

The neoclassical element is the most important one to emerge from the early exploration. Again, the separate chapter on neoclassicism here is justified not least because of the attention given to the concept in three chapters of *Ma vie heureuse*: 'Paris'; 'Orphée de Camargue'; and 'De l'opéra-minute au grand opéra'. One particular quotation stands out in elucidating the neoclassical element:

> En réaction contre l'impressionnisme des post-debussystes, les musiciens voulaient un art robuste, plus clair et plus précis, tout en demeurant humain et sensible. . . . Après tous les brouillards impressionnistes, cet art simple, clair, renouant la tradition de Scarlatti et de Mozart ne serait-il pas la prochaine phase de notre musique?[35]

---

[32] Ibid., 67: 'The rhythms of this popular music intrigued and fascinated me.'

[33] Ibid., 100: 'I had first to penetrate more deeply the mysteries of this new musical form whose technique still troubled me.'

[34] Milhaud, *Études*, 54: 'So here we have to the fore sonorous and rhythmic elements [which are] completely new and apt, but *how* should I use them?' It is worth remarking that a chapter of J.E. Berendt, *The Jazz Book* (New York, 1953) is devoted to 'The Elements of Jazz' (175–89).

[35] Milhaud, *Ma vie heureuse*, 81–2: 'In reaction against the impressionism of the

The key phrases are 'more clear and more precise', and 'renewing the tradition of Scarlatti and Mozart' (indicating awareness of baroque and classical principles); and one may also highlight this final question, used here to head Chapter 5, as to whether the renewal of tradition projected by Milhaud will represent the future of French music.

So, supported by Milhaud's own writings, one may perceive his early music loosely in terms of three stylistic/aesthetic elements (or possibly 'texts', as discussed in Chapter 6), the second and third emerging out of the first. These broad domains encompass 'Early Exploration' (including experimentation with a machinist aesthetic), 'Brazilian and Jazz-inspired Music', and 'Neoclassicism'. Such tendencies, represented here by Chapters 3, 4 and 5, are not mutually exclusive—to make them so would be to impose a rigid system such as Milhaud abhorred, and which simply would not suit his music. One must be sensitive to dangers of over-simplification or distortion: there are works such as the Third Quartet (1916) which include incipient blues gestures, even before Milhaud's stay in Brazil. In the words of Drake, the 'influence of jazz on Milhaud's music should not be laboured precisely because the priorities are not easy to establish';[36] nevertheless, one must have some comprehension of the parts in order to appreciate the complex, sometimes contradictory, allusions and tensions which constitute the whole.

Various criteria are used in viewing works (or parts of works) in association with early exploration, jazz or neoclassicism, and such criteria support the listings in Figures 3.1, 4.1 and 5.1 below; clearly, some works may satisfy the criteria for more than one element. Criteria include chronology (the earliest works tend to be exploratory, those of the early 1920s may be jazz-influenced, mature works of the later 1920s are essentially neoclassical); Milhaud's own views (those works discussed in 'Rencontre avec le jazz' are so regarded here); views of other writers (Drake, for example, discusses *L'Abandon d'Ariane* in his essay on the neoclassical operas); choice of title and/or instrumentation (such as *Saudades do Brazil*, and the jazz-band instrumentation of *Caramel mou*); possible literary significance (for example, use of Classi-

---

post-Debussy composers, musicians wanted a robust art, more clear and more precise, whilst remaining human and sensitive. . . . After all the impressionist mists, wouldn't this simple, clear art, renewing the tradition of Scarlatti and Mozart, be the next phase of our music?'

[36] Drake, *The Operas of Darius Milhaud*, 189.

cal Greek or Roman legendary themes in neoclassical works); and emphasis of main technical features, suggesting chromaticism, blues scale, or more refined modality (and defined structure).

In support of this approach to grouping works, and tracing a larger-scaled agenda, association has been made with the findings of texts that are more culturally and aesthetically directed: Glenn Watkins's impressive, interdisciplinary book *Pyramids at the Louvre* (1994), David Meltzer's *Reading Jazz* (1993), parts of Stephen Walsh's *The Music of Stravinksy* (1988), and Joseph Straus's analytical/aesthetic hybrid, *Remaking the Past* (1990). Consequently, this study explores, albeit in a subsidiary capacity, possible applications of a contemporary machinist aesthetic; notions of distance as 'space' and cultural difference in respect of Milhaud's 'borrowings' from popular musics (particularly jazz); and distance as 'time' in his revisiting of baroque/classical practices. Such complementary notions contextualize the case studies, which, in turn, substantiate the notions. Regarding the inter-relationship of these ideas in Milhaud's music, it is largely a semantic argument as to whether, for instance, the Brazilian/jazz element exerts an influence on neoclassicism,[37] or whether a subtle 'eclectic balance' exists between these and other elements (including those pertaining to Jewish and French folksong), albeit with neoclassicism as the core component. This returns us to our original quotation from Collaer, and the idea of various elements in Milhaud's music coming to the fore and receding, infiltrating and complicating the 'total entity', as dictated by particular contexts (and explored further in Chapter 6).

The Place of the Early Chamber Music

Although this book explores a diversity of genre in Milhaud's music of the 1920s, including reference to opera, ballet, and song, coherence is provided by its main focus on chamber music. Chamber music is significant throughout Milhaud's long career, extending over the three periods from the Violin Sonata No. 1, Op. 3 (1911) to the Clarinet Sonatina, Op. 100 (1927); Quartet No. 8, Op. 121 (1932) to Quartet No. 18, Op. 308 (1950–51); and String Quintet No. 1, Op. 312 (1951) to the Wind Quintet, Op. 443 (1973). The string quartets, especially, can be seen as a backbone which supports the total output, spanning almost forty years (1912–50).

---

[37] Ibid., 186ff.

The mature early chamber music (between 1917 and 1927) is distinctive in forming an important, self-contained repertory: the year 1917–18, generally accepted as that of Milhaud's overall compositional maturity, marks the appearance of his first chamber music in Brazil, whilst 1927 represents a clearly defined finishing date, since he wrote no more chamber music for five years. This repertory, which is well represented in the analytical case studies, comprises seven quartets, six chamber symphonies, two early violin sonatas, two wind sonatinas, and music for mixed chamber ensemble with voice; it is supplemented by chamber operas and arrangements of ballets, including *Cinémafantaisie: Le Bœuf sur le toit*, and *Suite de concert: La Création du monde*. In terms of the relationship with larger-scaled works, the early period music is appropriately framed by the polyrhythmic/-metric ballet *L'Homme et son désir* (1918), relevant in discussion of the Brazilian/jazz element, and by the innovative grand opera-oratorio, *Christophe Colomb* (1928). The demands of such operatic projects constituted the main reason for Milhaud's break in chamber music composition between 1927 and 1932, noteworthy for a composer who had written several chamber works each year for the previous fifteen years, culminating in five works in 1927 alone.

In exploring a range of genres in the 1920s, with an analytical focus on the chamber music (itself diverse), the aim is to prove the conviction that the main stylistic and technical traits may be traced across a variety of significant contexts. Another reason which supports this choice is that the early chamber music contains some of Milhaud's finest works: as with other composers before him, Milhaud's innermost sentiments are often reserved for expression in an intimate medium, especially that of the string quartet. (Such early repertory does not suffer from the problems of technique outstripping inspiration which can compromise some of Milhaud's music beyond 1930, and which may also involve much repetition of already well-tested formulae.) Although it might have been easier to select simply the six chamber symphonies, or, as has been attempted before, part of the quartet, or sonata, cycles,[38] this seemed both less original and less representative of the varied imagination of this musician in his younger years.

---

38 P.W. Cherry, 'The String Quartets of Darius Milhaud' (Ph.D diss., University of Colorado, 1980); P.J. McCarthy, 'The Sonatas of Darius Milhaud' (Ph.D diss., The Catholic University of America, 1972).

Selection of Music for Case Studies

After much preliminary study, eight works have been selected as representing a balanced diversity of genre, with the main emphasis on chamber music. It was practicable to contend with this number since the case studies are selective in their brief, the primary concerns being with issues of modality and structure. A brief rationale for the inclusion of each work is given below, with further detail provided in Case Studies 1–8.

The 'Funèbre' from the Fourth Quartet (1918) has been selected because it was essential that the genre of the string quartet be represented; as one of Milhaud's first mature works, composed in Brazil, this work provides a useful starting-point for analytical discussion. It also seems appropriate to highlight one of two somewhat bizarre 'catalogue works': hence the inclusion of *Machines agricoles* (1919), as an example of Milhaud's unconventional approach within the category of mixed chamber ensemble with voice. Although the work was analysed in its entirety, for reasons of space only the third song has finally been included here. Again, it seems important to represent Milhaud's Chamber Symphonies, and although Nos. 4–6 all repay study, Chamber Symphony No. 5 (1922) has been singled out for its experimental nature.

Saudades do Brazil (1920) for solo piano is chosen as one of the best illustrations of the inspiration offered by Brazilian dance music: 'Ipanema' was selected as it facilitates comparison with an analysis of Keith Daniel. *La Création du monde* (1923/26) functions as perhaps the focal-point of the study: it is amongst Milhaud's most successful and popular pieces, and is the largest structure to be analysed. It is an especially attractive choice since there are two versions to compare (thus allowing some contact here with the significant genre of ballet), and since it represents the ultimate in Milhaud's jazz-inspired composition.

It seemed desirable to include an example of Milhaud's songwriting, whilst wishing to avoid reference to the self-contained repertory for voice and piano, which merits separate, extended treatment: the most appropriate choice of work for discussion, therefore, was the *Quatre poèmes de Catulle* (1923), for voice and violin. Although the whole set has been analysed, space has permitted the inclusion of just one song. The Clarinet Sonatina (1927) is selected because it seems necessary to represent sonata-type composition; and in order to gauge its typicality the Flute Sonatina (1922) and the early Violin Sonatas were also studied. As the last chamber music composed before 1930, the Sonatina also offers a suitable point of demarcation. Finally, in order to maintain a balance of genre, it was imperative to represent the significant domain of (chamber) opera. The trilogy of 'Opéras-minute' provides an attractive focus, and realistic in the present context if one concentrates on only one part: hence the selection of the central piece, *L'Abandon d'Ariane* (1927), which also allows direct comparison with the work of Jeremy Drake.

CHAPTER TWO

In Pursuit of an Analytical Approach

❦

IN SEEKING an analytical approach to the chosen repertory, this chapter points up *en passant* differences between analytical and compositional practice: how one might 'hear', or 'read', as opposed to how one 'writes' (Nattiez's 'aesthesic' versus 'poietic'[1]). Essentially, the starting-point for discussion concerns 'polytonality', a term typically used in connection with Milhaud's music—not least by the composer; although 'polytonality' is espoused, however, as a valid compositional approach of the 1920s, it is less helpful from a perceptual or analytical stance. There are reasons to dispute both parts of the term: most importantly, the concept and nature of modality seems a more productive way of approaching Milhaud's music which is broadly modal rather than narrowly tonal: as Drake suggests, 'it is only with qualifications that we may term Milhaud a tonal composer, for the true basis of his music is not tonality, but modality.'[2] Equally, the prefix 'poly' is of dubious perceptual and theoretical value: the concept of the simultaneous existence of several different tonal or modal lines seems invalid since one tends to perceive a resultant accumulation of all pitch material heard at any particular moment, strongly influenced by the bass progression. Still, such composite modality may yet thrive on a measure of ambiguity; and, more rarely, there may yet be a complementary meeting of two modes (most commonly a 'black/white' confrontation)—a complementation with its own inherent dynamism that in turn creates a new kind of unity. Thus localized bimodality may receive some credibility as an expression of balanced polarity, and is a possibility supported by Richard Taruskin amongst others,[3] though of course, even in extended Schenkerian terms, both 'polytonality' and 'bimodality' remain impossibilities.

---

[1] J.-J. Nattiez, *Music as Discourse: Toward a Semiology of Music* (Princeton, NJ, 1990).
[2] Drake, *The Operas of Darius Milhaud*, 201.
[3] R. Taruskin, '*Chez Pétrouchka*: Harmony and Tonality *chez* Stravinsky', *Nineteenth-Century Music*, 10 (1987), 265–86; Taruskin makes explicit comment regarding the classic example from *Petrushka* on p. 278. See discussion below.

Having marked out the initial ground, the pursuit of an appropriate analytical approach to the music of a composer who denounced rigid theoretical systems had nonetheless best begin by examining closely the most important contributions made to the subject by the composer. Only then does it seem wise to assess analytical techniques applied to his music and to contemporary music in similar styles, and thus to determine the most suitable approach for this study.

'Polytonalité et atonalité' (1923)

Milhaud's article on 'polytonality' and atonality warrants serious consideration and critical scrutiny, even if 'polytonality' is regarded today as a rather dubious theoretical concept. Whatever one's theoretical stance, Milhaud did compose by superimposing melodic strata of conflicting tonalities so that his polytonality is a result of contrapuntal encounter. Milhaud commences by defining polytonality and atonality, and asserts that, 'far from destroying basic musical principles', they make new harmonic and contrapuntal resources available to the composer. In his opinion, the polytonal principle was first stated with the occurrence of 'canons' other than at the interval of an octave.[4]

Milhaud argues that if two canonic (more strictly, fugal) lines are read separately, 'they may imply a parallel harmonization in two keys', and that the resulting 'single-key effect' ('le sentiment unitonal')[5] perceived by the listener 'lies in the limits imposed by the laws of two-part counterpoint and harmony'. He perceives a 'tonal independence of counterpoint', with tonalities superimposed, even in Bach's music. The simultaneous unfolding of several tonalities would be highly contentious, and in Schenkerian terms inconceivable, yet Milhaud's suggestion of a 'single-key effect' is plausible. He then mentions the theoretical problems that arise when 'fixed foreign notes' within a chord do not resolve, and again he is forced to accept tonal superimposition since he is not convinced by regarding such pitches as appoggiaturas without resolution. Working to this premise, his ensuing approach is unarguably methodical as he tabulates all combinations of two triads (and, by extension, presumably their full tonalities), embracing inversions and major/minor modes. Fig. 2.1 uses set theory to distinguish the identities of the 'single' chordal sonorities

---

[4] Milhaud, 'Polytonalité et atonalité', 30.
[5] Ibid. Compare Stravinsky's 'complexe sonore' (sound-complex): I. Stravinsky, *Poetics of Music*, trans. A. Knodel and I. Dahl (Cambridge, Ma, 1947), 12, 33, 36.

that he obtains, though this reduces them to atonal collections and reveals their inversional equivalence:

Figure 2.1   Milhaud's Chordal Types and Set Equivalents

Chordal type (Milhaud):	I	II	III	IV	V	VI
Triad/Tonality 1:	D♭	D	E♭	E	F	F♯
Triad/Tonality 2:	C	C	C	C	C	C
Set designation:	6-Z19	6-33	5-32	5-21	5-27	6-30

	VI	VII	VIII	IX	X	XI
	F♯	G	A♭	A	B♭	B
	C	C	C	C	C	C
(Reversed sequence:)	6-30	5-27	5-21	5-32	6-33	6-Z19

Although Milhaud considers two simultaneous keys, he expresses each combination as a single entity, with the '*Petrushka* chord' at the end of the second tableau of Stravinsky's ballet viewed as 'chord VI' of his scheme. The superimposition of D and F♯ major triads in bars 65–8 of Debussy's 'Ondine' from the second book of *Préludes* produces chord IV, whilst bars 1–6 of the first of Bartók's *Fourteen Bagatelles*, Op. 6 (1908) uses chord VII, with minor/minor modal combination, as in inflection 'B' of Fig. 2.2.

Figure 2.2   Milhaud's Minor/Major Combinational Types

Type:	A	B	C	D
Triad/Tonality 1:	major	minor	minor	major
Triad/Tonality 2:	major	minor	major	minor

Milhaud offers alternative interpretations of a passage from Ravel's Sonata for Violin and Cello (bars 14–17 after rehearsal Figure 6), firstly as a progression of eleventh chords, and secondly as a bitonal succession of constructs referable to chord XI, with modal inflection 'D'.[6] Later in the work (bars 5–12 after rehearsal Figure 12), he identifies modal 'mixture' in the cello part based on F: 'tantôt majeur, tantôt mineur'.[7] 'Mélange', or mixture, is an important concept for later chapters of this book, especially Chapter 4.

---

[6] Milhaud, 'Polytonalité et atonalité', 34.
[7] Ibid., 35.

Milhaud makes the case for bitonality more plausible by distinguishing between different harmonic contexts, and by cautioning against illusory types of bitonality. He considers that the apparent existence of independent tonalities may be illusory because one tonality functions merely as a pedal point.[8] Repeated chords or melodic figures (often developed into ostinati in his own works) are so regarded, with his 'monotonal' illustration taken from Satie's *Parade* ('Acrobates': rehearsal Figures 44–5). A second illusory type involves the momentary introduction of 'foreign notes' over a pedal, where the effect is also that of an 'échappée', yet still not bitonality, demonstrated by bars 10–11 of the first of Poulenc's *Mouvements perpetuels*. And though his specific arguments here are not wholly convincing, Milhaud does thus suggest different types, and possibly levels, of bitonality.

This 'travail théorique' is applied to 'chords taken from three keys', so where there were eleven different combinations for two keys, there are 55 for three keys, and eight 'modal' possibilities. Again, Milhaud considers chordal inversions, though whether these would be so perceived by the listener is another matter. He observes that a nine-pitch chord, of triads C, D♭, and D majors, contains those of seven other keys: F, f, f♯, a, A, d♭ and d. He comments on the richness and possibilities so produced, though these observations surely reduce the case for perceiving the original three tonalities independently. Presumably he would argue that these chordal abstractions have the potential for extension, and thus prolongation. Milhaud seems to suggest that this method could serve as a basis for the analytical study of different musical styles.

As the ultimate extreme, Milhaud imagines the superimposition of triads on all twelve chromatic pitches, claiming that the simplest arrangement would be by successive intervals of a fourth or fifth. Quartal and quintal harmony certainly suggests an area of common ground with Bartók and Hindemith,[9] and some valuable comments are made at this point about twelve-note chords:

> Here all the keys are found united and it is as if there were none of them: Polytonality encroaches on the domain of Atonality, because a melody constructed on the notes of this chord (the twelve notes

---

[8] Ibid.
[9] Such chords are common in Milhaud's early music, from 1917 to 1922.

of the scale) will be able to utilize absolutely any note and thus will escape from tonal feeling.[10]

This suggests that it could be appropriate to identify a sound by a single term of reference, possibly by the adaptation of set theory, when the music 'escape[s] from tonal feeling'. Milhaud is most enthusiastic about the expressive possibilities afforded by this 'limitless domain' of polytonality:

> The expressive scale thus finds itself considerably extended, and within the simpler domain of dynamics, the use of polytonality adds more subtlety and sweetness to pianissimos, and more stridency and sonorous force to fortissimos.[11]

The phrase 'force sonore' may again yield some common ground with Stravinsky's 'complexe sonore', and certainly connects with Hindemith's chordal 'tension theory'.[12] Milhaud continues by identifying two types of true polytonality: firstly harmonic (by chordal superimposition), and secondly contrapuntal (by melodic superimposition).[13] This second type accords well with his compositional practice, especially in chamber music, and to do justice to his music any theory must acknowledge that the first priority is melody, whether single- or multi-layered. Milhaud sees the polytonal, layered approach as particularly suited to the medium of the string quartet and other small ensembles. Quoting from his Third Chamber Symphony, he regards the six instruments as proceeding in five keys, at least from a compositional perspective;[14] there are, however, three bars where even the composer does not assign a tonality, but resorts to parentheses.

Usually, Milhaud finds that 'in envisaging the harmonic entity produced by this polytonal counterpoint of diatonic melodies, one obtains vertically aggregations of pitches which cannot be analysed and whose

---

[10] Ibid., 38: 'Ici tous les tons se trouvent réunis et c'est comme s'il n'y en avait aucun: la Polytonalité empiète sur le domaine de l'Atonalité, car une mélodie construite sur les notes de cet accord (les douze notes de la gamme) pourra employer n'importe quelle note et de ce fait échappera au sentiment tonal.'

[11] Ibid.: 'L'échelle expressive se trouve ainsi considérablement étendue, et dans le domaine plus simple de la nuance, l'emploi de la polytonalité ajoute aux pianissimi plus de subtilité et de douceur et aux fortissimi plus d'âpreté et de force sonore.'

[12] On tension theory see 'harmonic fluctuation' in Neumeyer, *The Music of Paul Hindemith*, 31, 34, 60–1, 115–21.

[13] Milhaud, 'Polytonalité et atonalité', 39.

[14] For a comparative interpretation of this passage, see Fig. 5.8 in Chapter 5 below.

harmonic outcome is atonal.'[15] It is unfortunate that he would not conceive of any vertical means of analysis: with due respect to his views on the supremacy of the contrapuntal perspective, any comprehensive analysis must also embrace the harmonic perspective since this is likely to aid understanding of motivic patterning, procedure and coherence.

Whether or not one agrees with the theoretical existence of polytonality, Milhaud's assertion that combined scale systems, with their vast scope, can produce music of clear individual identity is indisputable. Concluding the first part of his article, he gives a possible *raison d'être* for this present analytical study: 'It would be interesting to study all the forms that polytonality assumes in works of the principal contemporary composers'.[16] And this is probably the nearest that he comes to suggesting a relationship between theory and practice.

Milhaud then mentions the wholetone scale system, centred on the augmented fifth chord, which he sees as excluded from diatonic tonality and polytonality because of its lack of semitones and perfect fifths, yet equally excluded from atonality since the latter is derived from chromaticism. He dismisses the resource as very limited because all is based harmonically on one chord and melodically on six pitches,[17] seeming to overlook the fact that there are two distinct wholetone collections a semitone apart, and that there may be a role for chromatic, 'foreign' pitches within a given collection.

The second part of Milhaud's article begins with the statement that 'Atonal music is, as its name suggests, that which escapes from tonal feeling as much by the character of its melodic lines as by harmonic aggregations which result from superimposition.'[18] For the possible origins of atonality, Milhaud returns to a dubious premise propounded earlier, that 'If polytonal music is essentially of diatonic origin . . . atonal music will find its sources in chromaticism.' The fallaciousness, or at least over-simplification, of this reasoning need not, however, detract

---

15 Milhaud, 'Polytonalité et atonalité', 40: 'en envisageant l'ensemble harmonique de ces contrepoints polytonaux de mélodies diatoniques, on obtient verticalement des agrégations de notes inanalysables et dont le résultat harmonique est atonal.'

16 Ibid.: 'Il serait intéressant d'étudier toutes les formes que prend la polytonalité chez les principaux musiciens contemporains'.

17 Ibid.

18 Ibid., 41.: 'La musique atonale est, comme son nom l'indique, celle qui échappe au sentiment tonal tant par le caractère de ses lignes mélodiques que par les agrégations harmoniques qui résultent de leur superimposition.'

from the many useful ideas elsewhere. Milhaud discusses the dominant seventh chord as a possible starting point for chromaticism,[19] viewing this construct as a 'movement in progression' towards a second chord; in turn, that second chord becomes the dominant of another (i.e. circle of fifths), until one arrives at 'a progression of dominant sevenths, the point of departure of chromaticism and first step towards atonality'.

Milhaud searches for common ground between atonality and polytonality, arguing that occasionally the encounter of atonal lines, 'constructed on the twelve pitches of the chromatic scale', produces a type of tonality, when viewed vertically. The 'tonality' may be monotonal or polytonal, not in the sense of superimposed keys, but as 'the result of a contrapuntal movement bringing a superimposition of foreign notes to the seventh chord through added thirds (ninths, elevenths, thirteenths etc.)'.[20] He also mentions minor, major, and augmented triads, produced by the same means; such chords, though, will be isolated and will not be justified contextually in terms of tonal function.[21] Thus, he establishes another type of 'polytonality', using literary images which liken musical structure to architecture ('construite' and 'l'édifice harmonique') in a manner typical of Hindemith.

Milhaud's first example is from Honegger's *Horace victorieux*, where an atonal double bass solo is heard against chords of added thirds (sevenths through to thirteenths), while his second example is from the first of Schoenberg's Three Pieces for Piano, Op. 11. In bars 3–4, Milhaud identifies a chromatically descending upper line, 'harmonized by two perfect minor triads (d and c♯) and two augmented fifth chords (G,B,E♭ and G♭,B♭,D), sustained by an inner pedal on F, and resting on a bass whose melodic line is atonal'.[22] He asserts that the last six bars cannot be analysed since they do not subscribe to any imaginable diatonic combination, and certainly he is correct that tonal analysis would

---

[19] Ibid. One may compare Milhaud's view of the role of the dominant seventh with that of an analyst such as van den Toorn, who considers the chord in detail in a neoclassical context: 'The (0,4,7,10) "Dominant-Seventh" Complexes', in *The Music of Igor Stravinsky*, 323.

[20] Milhaud, 'Polytonalité et atonalité', 41: 'le résultat d'un mouvement contrapuntique amenant une superposition de notes étrangères à l'accord de septième par tierces juxtaposées (neuvièmes, onzièmes, treizièmes, etc.)'.

[21] Milhaud is therefore well aware of non-functional tonality—an important concept in the analysis of his own music.

[22] Milhaud, 'Polytonalité et atonalité', 42–3.

be meaningless. This stance contrasts with that of Hindemith, who attempted unconvincingly to impose a tonal framework on one of Schoenberg's later works.[23] In Milhaud's opinion, the success of atonality depends on 'enlarging its means of expression', possibly by inclusion of quarter-tones, as in Szymanowski's *Mythes*, or Aloïs Hába's String Quartet. Clearly he is aware of contemporary techniques and compositions.

In conclusion, Milhaud declares that polytonality and atonality are not 'arbitrary systems', though it is not clear whether he is condemning systematic procedures *per se*, or only the alleged 'arbitrariness'. He advocates the implementation of complementary technical studies in order to appreciate connections between polytonality and atonality, believing that despite their opposed origins these domains occasionally unite, or at least overlap.[24] Milhaud stresses his melodic priority, and invoking the concept of 'essential melody' argues that

> That which will determine the polytonal or atonal character of a work will be not so much the compositional procedure but the essential melody which will be its source, and which comes from the 'heart' of the composer. It is this absolute, organic, necessity of the initial melody that will prevent these procedures from congealing into an otherwise still-born system.[25]

This concept of a 'still-born' system is further evidence of Milhaud's distrust of excessive strictness, and undoubtedly any workable system must allow flexibility. Thus he concludes: 'The whole life of a work will depend entirely on the melodic invention of its composer, and polytonality and atonality will act merely to provide a greater field, richer means of composition, a more complex expressive scale for his sensibility, imagination and fantasy.'[26] Melody is the source of Milhaud's in-

---

[23] See his analysis of Schoenberg's *Klavierstück*, Op. 33*a*, in Hindemith, *The Craft of Musical Composition*, Book 1, 217–18.

[24] Milhaud, 'Polytonalité et atonalité', 44.

[25] Ibid.: 'Ce qui déterminera le caractère polytonal ou atonal d'une œuvre, ce sera bien moins le procédé d'écriture que la mélodie essentielle qui en sera la source, et qui vient du "cœur" du musicien. C'est cette nécessité absolue, organique, de la mélodie initiale qui empêchera ces procédés de se figer en un système autrement mort-né.'

[26] Ibid., continuation: 'Toute la vie d'une œuvre ne dépendra que de l'invention mélodique de son auteur, et la polytonalité et l'atonalité ne feront que fournir un champ plus vaste, des moyens d'écriture plus riches, une échelle expressive plus complexe, à sa sensibilité, à son imagination et à sa fantaisie.'

spiration and polytonality and atonality are simply the means to a more varied and subtle melodic goal.

Critiques of Milhaud's Article and Analyses of his Music

The work of six writers who reviewed Milhaud's article and/or analysed his music will now be briefly assessed. The earliest review is by Boris de Schloezer, published two years after Milhaud's article,[27] who identifies the essence of Milhaud's style as 'le sens de l'ordre', 'le goût des formes élégantes', countered by 'son extrême exubérance', and regards him essentially as a classical figure. He points out two distinct melodic types in Milhaud's music: short, fragmentary motives, sometimes mere 'dessins rythmiques', and fully shaped, traditional melodies. Clarifying polytonal types, he suggests that rival tonalities might be either 'absorbed' or 'affirmed' by cadence, and that 'la polytonalité réelle' exists only where there is polyphony. In conclusion, he stresses association with Stravinsky: 'Milhaud is, after Stravinsky, the richest, most powerful musical character of our time.'[28]

Proceeding chronologically, 1954 saw the publication of Humphrey Searle's *Twentieth Century Counterpoint*, with its own, related exposition of 'Milhaud and Polytonality',[29] which, though somewhat conventional from an analytical stance, still contains some useful thoughts. His starting-point, as that of Milhaud himself, is that the origins of bitonality might lie in the successive tonal tensions of fugal writing which were then expressed simultaneously; similarly, he is compelled to cite that now infamous passage from Stravinsky's *Petrushka*. Beyond this point, Searle is rightly dubious about the ability to perceive polytonality:

> This is because the ear will always try to relate the *sum total* of the sounds it hears to a definite tonal basis; it is only really possible to listen to and distinguish between two separate tonalities at once.[30]

Arguably, his 'rider', too, is debatable, though this possibility will be considered further towards the end of Chapter 2. Searle then offers some examples from the Chamber Symphonies, *Les Euménides*, and *Christophe Colomb*, which are alluded to in Chapter 3 below. He concludes, appropriately enough, that 'polytonality is chiefly useful to the

---

[27] B. de Schloezer, 'Darius Milhaud', *La Revue musicale*, 6 (March 1925), 251–76.
[28] Ibid., 274: 'Milhaud est, après Stravinsky, la nature musicale la plus riche, la plus puissante de notre époque.'
[29] H. Searle, *Twentieth Century Counterpoint* (London, 1954), 32–43.
[30] Ibid., 34.

composer in helping him to create an elaborate and complex texture; but it is in itself too rigid a concept'.[31]

The second specific critique of 'Polytonalité et atonalité', by Paul Collaer,[32] stresses Milhaud's debt to Koechlin, and asserts that Milhaud's idea of contrapuntal superimposition is hardly more than a matter of submitting to distinctions of consonance and dissonance. This search for patterns of consonance and dissonance, and their polarized relationship, is a valid approach to Milhaud's music, and connects again with Hindemith's 'tension theory'. Like de Schloezer, Collaer classifies contrapuntal contexts, distinguishing between general polyphonic expression, and a more specific 'jeu polyphonique', which leads (as with Searle) to discussion of Milhaud's affinity for fugue in *Les Euménides*, *La Création du monde*, and *Christophe Colomb*.

Collaer's weakness is that he generalizes and regards fastidiousness in discussion of Milhaud's music as undesirable, when it is such fastidiousness that this music deserves but has rarely received. More positive contributions are made on Milhaud's approach to polytonality and word-setting, with Collaer suggesting that it is the demands of putting across contrapuntal complexes which lie behind Milhaud's habitual use of simple, regulated rhythms (excepting his Latin-American and jazz-inspired works). Choice of instrumentation affects the approach to polytonality, with Milhaud's piano textures, for example, seldom exceeding a 'bitonal' expression. His dramatic approach to word-setting is concerned not with the isolated value of each word, but with the overall sense: 'a personal, lyrical declamation, based upon the [collective] values of duration and accentuation of the syllables'.[33] This is a typically French approach which will be considered in analyses of *Machines agricoles* and *Quatre poèmes de Catulle*. Collaer emphasizes that Milhaud's music is primarily melodic, and that harmony results from the interaction of contrapuntal lines, supported by occasional structural chords (similar to Hindemith's 'pillar' chords). Finally, Collaer comments on Milhaud's remaining distant from predetermined schemes or systems, and cautions against inflexible analysis.

---

[31] Ibid., 43.
[32] Collaer/Galante, *Darius Milhaud*, 'The Language', 39–52.
[33] Collaer, *Darius Milhaud*, 263.

The third review is by Jeremy Drake, contained in *The Operas of Darius Milhaud*.[34] Drake consistently endorses modality, so that when discussing Milhaud's article he opts for polymodality, defined as

> the use of two or more modes simultaneously, though Milhaud always used the term polytonality, and it must be understood that the term polymodality may apply as much to combinations of the same mode at different pitches.[35]

Drake notes from *Ma vie heureuse* that Milhaud's article is the result of his research into polytonality some nine years earlier (1914–15).[36] In response to Milhaud's consideration of the ultimate polytonal superimposition of twelve chromatic pitches, Drake believes that, although the concept is valid, the example of superimposed fourths and fifths is not because 'it is the disposition of a composite chord into bands of common chords that is essential for the effectiveness of polytonality.'[37]

With reference to Milhaud's comments about vertical aggregations having an atonal effect and being unanalysable, Drake argues that this is only theoretically and not practically the case, because 'the horizontal momentum is stronger than the vertical weight: the melodies are heard and not the harmony.'[38] This stance seems unconvincing since the listener has both a melodic and an overall harmonic perception of Milhaud's music, strongly influenced by the bass-line. More positively, Drake mentions characteristics of Milhaud's chamber music prior to the period of polytonal research, including Quartets Nos. 1 and 2 (1912, 1914–15), suggesting that this music is polychordal rather than polytonal. In viewing the chamber music as stylistically revealing and relevant to the discussion of opera, he provides further support for chamber music as a logical focus of this book, and for association between chamber music and opera in Milhaud's music.

Although Drake's book has necessarily been mentioned earlier, this is the appropriate place for the main review of an important source of stylistic (and some technical) ideas. Although Drake uses descriptive, not graphic, analysis, his book includes much historical detail and represents valuable research on a subject still short of scholarly assessment. The most applicable part is that on 'The neo-classical operas II:

---

34 Drake, *The Operas of Darius Milhaud*, 221–4.
35 Ibid., 221.
36 Milhaud, *Ma vie heureuse*, 59.
37 Drake, *The Operas of Darius Milhaud*, 223.
38 Ibid.

Essay in stylistic analysis',[39] which has enabled the comparative view of *L'Abandon d'Ariane* in Case Study 8. Of primary importance are observations on pitch-structure and modality, but Drake rightly begins by exploring the rhythmic parameter, and asserting that the flavour of Brazilian music affects, however slightly, most works between 1917 and 1973. The complex rhythms inspired by Brazilian music often produce 'polymetricality' (i.e. two or more metres operating simultaneously), but not 'polyrhythm'. This is certainly true, although Milhaud rarely employs conflicting time signatures; rather he opposes different lengths of ostinato. Drake also stresses the modal aspect of Milhaud's music, commenting on

> an almost total absence of major and minor keys and key relationships, of tonal formal organization, of harmonic functionality, or the cycle of fifths, of modulation, even of a perfect cadence. The minimal exceptions to be found are of only local relevance and by no means decisive.[40]

This is not to say, however, that there is no place for cadential gesture, and Drake certainly acknowledges cadence in modality whilst stressing its different function: 'Milhaud's cadences do not resolve tonal or harmonic tensions, or articulate tonal movement.'[41] He does state, though, that 'Modulation is quite alien to Milhaud', and that 'there is no possibility of being able to prepare for the new mode, as there is in tonality of preparing for a new key'.[42] This is perhaps arguable since, although Milhaud does not use traditional schemes of key relation, one may nonetheless identify modulatory passages, with motivic, and more rarely chordal, pivotal constructions;[43] it is also still possible to use 'dominant preparation' (or emphasis on a new supertonic) to pave the way for a new modality. Although in certain instances, 'modulation' may simply be a matter of a change in emphasis of modal final, there is still some scope for the concept since there can be transition from a mode on one final to the same mode on a transposed final, or between different modes on different (or the same) finals. Further discussion on this is resumed in Chapters 5 and 6 below.

[39] Ibid., 186–241.
[40] Ibid., 201.
[41] Ibid., 214.
[42] Ibid., 205.
[43] See Chapter 6, *Modal and Structural Perspectives*, below.

An important concept used by Drake is 'inflectional polyvalency', which is viewed as 'the possibility of substituting one inflection (be it ♯, ♭, or ♮) for another',[44] whilst preserving the 'diatonic skeleton'. (Such inflectional polyvalency most commonly affects the third scalic degree.) He also uses interesting, if controversial, definitions of modal consonance and dissonance:

> Any interval between two counterpointed notes is consonant if both notes belong to the same mode; if they belong to different modes they are dissonant, though polytonal counterpoint tends to create its own polytonal norm of consonance.[45]

It is contestable that there can be no dissonance within a mode because there may be just the same intervallic combinations of seconds, fourths and sevenths as between two different modes; it is also unclear what role chromaticism might play in dissonant conflict. A better interpretation might be to envisage two distinct dissonant types: 'internal' (i.e. within the diatonic ingredients of a single mode, in 'white-note' or transposed form) and 'external' (i.e. beyond a single 'diatonic' mode, including chromatic and bimodal contexts).

Drake explains that many typical tonal features are absent from Milhaud's (often quite static) modal harmony: the equivalent of the 'tonic' chord is used less emphatically, often disguised by added notes which function as appoggiaturas; chord V rarely functions as the 'dominant' and loses much of its cadential function. This is compensated for by increased use of chords other than I and V, for instance the substitution of chord II for V in passages of 'vamping'. One may add that often the final sonority of a piece is a fusion of chords I and II. Interestingly, Drake makes special note of a surface chordal formation, (F♯,G,A♯,B), observed independently by the present author in several works of the 1920s as set 4-7. He finds little 'polymodality' in the neoclassical operas, concluding that this contrapuntal technique is best suited to chamber music; arguably genuine bimodality (never mind polymodality) is rare even in the chamber repertory. Although Drake focuses on 'polymodality', he refers occasionally to 'bimodal chords',[46] and acknowledges the opposition of 'black' notes in the bass and 'white' in the

---

[44] Ibid., 228.
[45] Ibid., 210; see also 212.
[46] Ibid., 230.

treble, i.e. chromatic complementation:[47] this proves to be a common technique, as shown in Case Studies 7 and 8 below.

Drake observes that a melody is often accompanied by dissonant harmony (i.e. that of a different mode), thus illustrating 'polymodality' (more accurately 'bimodality') and that there can be 'shifting of the two halves of a chordal or chordal and melodic entity harmonically out of phase with one another',[48] also relevant in Case Study 7. 'Polymodality' is seen as a developing aspect of Milhaud's style: 'integration of polymodality into a general harmonic style is a typical feature of Milhaud's middle period.'[49] Drake also remarks that Milhaud's fondness for fugue (discussed in Chapters 3 and 6 below) is curious since fugue is rooted in tonality, so that he interprets its usage as a result of textural considerations. He considers phrase as contributing to neoclassical melodic style and formal construction, identifying 'perfect and self-contained', and 'imperfect' phrases which may be 'complemented . . . diminished, augmented, varied and generally manipulated to construct much larger forms'.[50]

Apart from American doctoral dissertations by Cherry, McCarthy, Morrill, Bobbitt and Baskerville (see Bibliography), there are noteworthy analyses of Milhaud's early music by Ruth Zinar and Keith Daniel.[51] Zinar discusses 'polytonality' in *Les Euménides* (1917–22), the third of the early *L'Orestie* trilogy, viewing pages 23–4 of the full score as four tonal streams or strands then reduced to one, in parallel with the text, as reproduced in Fig. 2.3.

Figure 2.3   Milhaud, *Les Euménides*, pp. 23–4: Zinar's polytonal schema

Chords:	B	B♭	A	G♯	G	F	
	D♭	D	E♭	E	F	G	F♯
	G	F	G	G	G	F	
	F	G	F	F	F	G	
Bass:	D♭	D	E♭	E	F	F	F♯
No. of keys:	4	4	4	4	2	2	1
Text:		'All the streams . . . . then one pure.'					

---

[47] Ibid., 228.
[48] Ibid., 216.
[49] Ibid., 230.
[50] Ibid., 231.
[51] Zinar, 'Greek Tragedy in Theatre Pieces of Stravinsky and Milhaud'; Daniel, 'A Preliminary Investigation'.

The finale consists of twelve sections which Zinar considers to form a polytonal progression: the first section begins with four keys (D♭,E,G,B♭) expanding to six (D♭,G,A,B,F,E♭) in the sixth and seventh sections; they in turn are gradually reduced to two keys on B and C♯ for the climax. Zinar's perspective is interesting as a starting point, but says little about actual sound: her approach to polytonality is logical if uninspired and conventional. Nonetheless, she notes patterns of consonance and dissonance, and regards 'tritonal relationships in bitonality' as associated dramatically with disturbed emotion and revenge: an example cited is in *Agamemnon* (p. 33 of the score), with Dorian modes on a and e♭ (perhaps the earliest acknowledgement of modality in Milhaud's music).

Daniel adopts the diametrically opposed, set-theoretic approach for analyses of *L'Homme et son désir* and *Saudades do Brazil*:[52] this article is perhaps the only published application of pure set theory to Milhaud's music, seeking to move beyond 'the sometimes naive interpretation of superimposed tonalities'.[53] The problems, however, as Daniel admits, are many. Although set theory enables one to approach the vertical perspective, the horizontal by its diatonic nature is largely ignored; any resemblance to music of the Second Viennese School is superficial, and Milhaud's music seems rather simplistic and naive in comparison; set theory usually elucidates only at surface level where structure may already be evident; variety in Milhaud's music is achieved by means not apparent through set theory: sequential repetition, partial transposition, subtle alteration and reversal of ostinati patterns; finally, many disparate sets are produced, most of which must then be discounted. There are also some weaknesses in Daniel's working: criteria behind his 'creative segmentation' are not adequately explained; the 'atonal' label is used loosely: 'Milhaud worked frequently and freely in an atonal idiom',[54] though Daniel later concedes there is little 'genuine atonality'; he claims his choice of works to be representative of Milhaud's output, though he considers only the Brazilian/jazz-inspired repertory, thus excluding the most appropriate experimental material of the Fourth Quartet, *Machines agricoles*, and Fifth Chamber Symphony.

Despite these difficulties, there are some strengths which lie in observing processes of stratification: 'successive layering' of ostinati; the

---

[52] Daniel, 'A Preliminary Investigation', 22–48.
[53] Ibid., 47.
[54] Ibid., 23.

most successful analyses are from *Saudades do Brazil*: 'Botafogo', 'Copacabana' and 'Ipanema'. Some prominent sets from *Saudades* recur elsewhere, especially 'diatonic' ones, such as 4-23 which Daniel lightheartedly refers to as the 'I got rhythm' tetrachord! Like Zinar, Daniel is sensitive to the 'simultaneous tonal and/or modal gestures' that structure Milhaud's music, most strikingly in the decade 1915-25. Although the implementation of set theory is limited in analysis of polytonally conceived music, it still has a role as a supplementary technique.

General Analytical Theory Relevant to Milhaud's Music

The remaining literature surveyed in pursuit of an approach to Milhaud's music is concerned with analyses of works by Stravinsky and Hindemith. Arthur Berger's pioneering article seeks a working theory for music that is 'centric', but not tonally functional,[55] suggesting referential collections and orderings of pitches, 'simultaneities' instead of chords, and pitch 'priority' of the 'first', or 'second order'. Modality is embraced although historical association is avoided by designations such as 'E-scale on A'. Berger also mentions hybrid minor formations, and the properties of the octatonic collection which prove so successful in interpreting the second tableau of *Petrushka*. Like Milhaud, Stravinsky stated that he 'conceived the music in two keys'.[56] Berger considers the 'filtering-out' of pitch content not referable to the octatonic collection, supported by reference to timbre and acoustics, and examines interaction between diatonic and octatonic scales; in analysing works of Stravinsky (and Milhaud) he declares that the difficulty is that

> Confronted with broadly tonal issues such as these, the critical question is, again, where to draw the line between an intervallic, incipiently serial, 'non-tonal' interpretation of this music and the tonal bias that obviously governed its conception.[57]

Some thirty years on, the dilemma persists!

The octatonic discussion (concerning set 8-28) is continued by van den Toorn:[58] particularly apposite are his analyses of the Three Pieces for String Quartet (1914), *L'Histoire du soldat* (1918), *Les Noces* (1917),

---

[55] A. Berger, 'Problems of Pitch Organization in Stravinsky', *Perspectives of New Music*, 2 (1963), 11–42.
[56] I. Stravinsky and R. Craft, *Expositions and Developments* (New York, 1962), 156.
[57] Berger, 'Problems of Pitch Organization in Stravinsky', 41.
[58] Van den Toorn, *The Music of Igor Stravinsky*.

Symphonies of Wind Instruments (1920), and the Octet (1923), as well as chapters on the 'Neo-classical Initiative', '(034/347/367) "Minor-Major Third" Emphasis' and 'The Dominant-Tonic Relation'. Criticisms have been voiced about van den Toorn's book: that it should more accurately have been entitled 'The Octatonic Stravinsky';[59] that most analyses are on a small scale; and that van den Toorn is concerned primarily with unordered collections. Such criticisms, however, are not my main concern here, which is simply to ascertain which aspects may assist in the analysis of Milhaud's early music: octatonicism seems most prevalent in Milhaud's output between about 1917 and 1922.

Van den Toorn compares diatonic progression and octatonic oscillation, and identifies an octatonic Model A (0,1,3,4,6,7,9,10) for Stravinsky's neoclassical music,[60] which is partitioned at (0,3,6,9), with tetrachordal subcomplexes, minor/major triads, dominant sevenths and minor ninths. Commonly, he observes interaction between the diatonic C-scale and the Model A, Collection II of the octatonic scale, and views the pc groupings of (0,1,3,4/3,4,6,7) and (0,3,4/3,4,7/3,6,7), denoting 'minor-major third' emphasis, as entities in their own right.[61] An illustration from the third movement of the *Symphony of Psalms* (1930) shows interaction between Model A, Collection III and the A-scale:[62] common groupings include minor-major thirds, dominant sevenths, and the figuration (C,E♭,E♮/E♭,E♮,G). Since pitches 3 and 4 are both present, and pitch 3 is not simply a chromatic tendency tone, this represents a genuine 'merger'. Van den Toorn is convinced that it is only through 'an interacting partitioning of the octatonic collection (Model A), that we can begin to account for peculiarity in the exhibition of these Baroque and/or Classical conventions, inflections, and gestures'.[63]

Many contexts described by van den Toorn exhibit ambiguity between centres a third apart (0,3 relationship), in a way which is typical of Milhaud. At one point, he refers to a '"background" (0,3) partitioning of Collection II in terms of (D,B)',[64] suggesting that the

---

[59] J. Straus, 'The Octatonic Stravinsky' [review of van den Toorn, *The Music of Igor Stravinsky*], *Journal of Music Theory*, 26 (1983), 129–34.

[60] Van den Toorn, *The Music of Igor Stravinsky*, 50–1.

[61] Ibid.: see 'Pitch Relations' in the 'Neoclassical Initiative', and the opening section of '(034/347/367) "Minor-Major Third" Emphasis', 261–70, 272–5.

[62] Ibid., 295–8.

[63] Ibid., 297.

[64] Ibid., 302.

conflicting triads may achieve fusion: thus he comes close to admitting localized bitonality, albeit of a static nature, and lacking traditional harmonic process. Van den Toorn uses the term 'superimposition' (as does Milhaud) and argues that

> Superimposition will seem conspicuous—or apt as an explanatory notion—to the extent that 'a certain opposition' or 'polarity' is defined in a context which, octatonically, projects this 'opposition' or 'polarity' among the fragments being superimposed.[65]

The octatonic perspective is less convincing in explaining dominant-tonic relations (however limited the traditional, tonal functions in Milhaud's music, cadential gestures are preserved): since the leading note is not present in Model A, one has to regard this as another octatonic-diatonic interaction. The strength of applying van den Toorn's approach lies in its consistency and motivic outlook, although more attention must be directed towards the linear perspective and ordered motivic collections.

Taruskin's work usefully supplements that of van den Toorn,[66] emphasizing the need to account for pitches not present in a given octatonic collection, and arguing for a distinction between embellishment and directed motion. He considers wholetone interaction with the octatonic collection, and partitioning of the French Sixth chord into two incomplete dominant sevenths, a tritone apart. On occasions, he even accepts a polytonal perspective: 'despite the octatonic interpretation of its genesis, there may be some validity after all in regarding the *Petrushka* chord as a polytonalism.'[67] Taruskin also observes 'white-key/black-key opposition': an idea transferable to Milhaud's early music (and used by Drake).

An important article by Forte[68] concludes with three guidelines that should be borne in mind in the analysis of Milhaud's music:

> an effective reading of the large-scale horizontal dimension should relate in specific ways to the motivic structure of the music.
>
> ... where specific non-tonal referential collections are in operation, as in the Stravinsky and Scriabin examples, the reading should discover precisely how these are expressed in the music, without

---

[65] Ibid., 62.
[66] Taruskin, '*Chez Pétrouchka*', 265–86.
[67] Ibid., 278.
[68] A. Forte, 'New Approaches to the Linear Analysis of Music', *Journal of the American Musicological Society*, 41 (1988), 315–48.

violating such important considerations as phrase groupings, rhythmically determined units, registral and timbral associations, and so on.

... the reading of linear structures should take into account onset and closure within the individual linear configuration as well as the relation between linear configurations in combination—'coincidences', as they might be termed.[69]

In comparing analyses of *Le Sacre*, he cautions over forcing relations between small and large-scale features, and in evaluating Mitchell's analysis of Wagner's Prelude to *Tristan und Isolde*, Forte stresses that one need not insist on a simplistic overall tonality where certain chords are viewed uncomfortably as substitute dominants. He also warns against an 'overly rigid adherence to a background model', and sees as far more important 'the dynamic correspondence of horizontal and vertical'. He proposes transformation of (tonal) voice-leading analysis into post-tonal linear analysis where hierarchies are controlled by sets. Vertical 'slices' are used to seek further manifestations of the 'Tristan' chord: potentially a useful practice in analysis of Milhaud's music. Forte examines connections between horizontal and vertical configurations, noting when chords are subjected to rotation.

In the first movement of Skryabin's Fourth Sonata, he cautions against 'illusory tonal harmonies', when the vertical sonorities belong to other modes of organization. He discusses forms of the tetrachord 4-23, including the trichords 3-7 and 3-9 which are also important in Milhaud's music. Three structural strata interact between diatonic and octatonic domains, connected by an augmented triad, the 'core' of 4-19—a context paralleled by one in the 'Funèbre' of Milhaud's Fourth Quartet. Forte's study is so important because it puts earlier discussion into perspective; his analyses of Liszt's *Vallée d'Obermann*, *Via Crucis*, ('Station 8' and 'Station 5') and *Trauer-Vorspiel* are also useful as basic graphic models,[70] with potential application in Milhaud's Fourth Quartet, especially for structures founded on 3-10 and 3-12.[71]

---

[69] Ibid., 346–7.
[70] A. Forte, 'Liszt's Experimental Idiom and Music of the Early Twentieth Century', *Nineteenth-Century Music*, 10 (1987), 209–28.
[71] Ibid., 213 (Example 2) and 221 (Example 9).

Finally, Forte's ideas on genera as discussed in his extensive article of 1988[72] seem relevant in a supplementary capacity, both as a means of mediating between (neo)modality and localized atonality (and their associated methodologies of extended voice-leading, modal partitioning, and set theory), and as some means of 'classifying' types of musical language. This is not the place for a detailed digest and critique of Forte's article, but rather, beyond an essential introduction, for a signalling of ideas which may be transferred or adapted to serve Milhaud's music. It is Richard Parks who perhaps best exemplifies this independent exploratory approach to genera (and whose distinctive contribution may yet have greater long-term potential) in his fine study of Debussy.[73]

Forte's twelve genera (including two subgenera) are formed according to clearly defined criteria from one or two 'progenitor' trichords (as a basis for comparison of intervallic content). The emergent genera are then listed together with their 'type', such as Genus 2 'wholetone',[74] and it is this characterizing of the generic sonorities, albeit in 'very informal descriptive terms',[75] that facilitates a bridging between modal and set-theoretic means of reference. Beyond a consideration of the distribution across the genera of trichords through to hexachords, Forte maps four scalic collections (diatonic, wholetone, chromatic, and melodic minor), and some 'traditional tonal harmonies' (3-8 as the Italian Sixth chord), on to the twelve genera. (It is important to acknowledge, therefore, that these genera are not synonymous with scalic collections.) The significance of these mappings is again in emphasizing the broader musical applications (and comparisons) that may be enabled by pc set genera.

Beyond this basis, Forte offers a Difference Quotient (Difquo) in order to provide a quantitative measure, or 'index', of the extent of difference (from .87058 as maximally different, to .01666 as maximally similar) both between genera, and between four collective supragenera. As Forte acknowledges, 'In all cases, the numbers [of the Difquo] should correspond to our intuitive perception of the character of each

---

[72] A. Forte, 'Pitch-Class Set Genera and the Origin of Modern Harmonic Species', *Journal of Music Theory*, 32 (1988), 187–270.

[73] Parks, *The Music of Claude Debussy*.

[74] See Forte, 'Pitch-Class Set Genera', 201, Table 10; a full listing of the pc set contents of the genera is given in Forte's Appendix, 264–6.

[75] Ibid., 200.

genus as reflected by the informal type assigned to it.'[76] This concept has particular application for Milhaud's music.

Forte then explores more complex relations between genera and Kh subcomplexes, together with rather cursory explanation of a Status Quotient (Squo), whereby 'For each genus in the matrix a real number serves as an index of its relative strength.'[77] Essentially, the equation involves the number of different set representatives of a particular genus (x), in relation to the total number of sets that constitute that genus (y), and the total number of different sets identified within a particular passage of music (z): Squo of any genus = $((x/y)/z)$. 'Rules for the Interpretation of Generic Relations' are followed by various applications, focusing on Debussy's 'La Terrace des audiences du clair de lune' from Book II of the *Préludes*.

Christopher Hasty's article of four years earlier usefully advises on criteria behind set-theoretic segmentation,[78] mentioning matters of psychology and perception, and the important relationship between phrase formation and whole structure. Choice of segmentation is influenced by discontinuities of melody, duration, rhythm, register, timbre, dynamic and tempo. There are types and degrees of closure, which may produce a simple form: 'statement–departure–return' (as in much of Milhaud's music); equally, there may be ambiguity or suspension of closure, threatening coherence, or a subsequent integration of previously non-cohering elements. A special type of closure is achieved by use of original and retrograde formal shapes. Hasty is not averse to overlapping segmentation where purposeful,[79] and with reference to Webern's first Bagatelle he reveals interlocking sets of 4-7,[80] which may serve as a model for passages in Milhaud's early music where this set is also prominent. Hasty discusses how later phrases are interpreted in the light of earlier ones, and, conversely, how an ambiguous earlier phrase may later be clarified. If additions to a structural formation 'threaten its integrity' at a localized level, then 'a shift must be made to a higher structural level.' Finally, Hasty adds that 'closure could be viewed at any stage as a realization of the possible and thus a renunciation of the future.'

---

[76] Ibid., 222.
[77] Ibid., 232.
[78] C. Hasty, 'Phrase formation in Post-tonal Music', *Journal of Music Theory*, 28 (1984), 167–90.
[79] Ibid., 182, Example 6.
[80] Ibid., 185, Example 8.

Straus's research on 'Stravinsky's Tonal Axis' explores 'poles of attraction',[81] and, though he may be criticized for over-simplification, his notion of opposing axes (often concerned with third relations) is relevant to Milhaud's style. He considers levels of tonal polarity: firstly, between two or three competing axes (for example, (E♭–G–B♭; G–B♭–D) in the third movement of *Dumbarton Oaks*) and secondly, within a single axis (such as (G–B♭; B♭–D♭) in *Oedipus Rex*). He observes primary and secondary axes, and believes that it is from this 'competition' that tension results: the 'shaping role' of axial polarity may parallel that of traditional tonic–dominant polarity. His ideas of superimposing triads on C and E♭ as a primary axis (C–E♭/E♮–G–B♭), in the third movement of the *Symphony of Psalms*, could assist in explaining Milhaud's fondness for blues third and seventh chords. Connections between third relations and an octatonic background are implicit here in Straus's overall view of three third-related triads, focused on C,E,G: (A,C♯,E; C,E,G; E♭,G,B♭), i.e. (A,B♭,C♮,C♯,E♭,E♮,(F♯,)G).[82] Such axial harmonies are connected by 'pattern-completion' as a prolongational aspect of voice-leading (albeit rather dubious). Straus claims (rather as Meyer) that repetition causes a 'normative unit', so that the statement of all but one element causes expectation and a sense of directed motion towards the missing element. He concludes that axes and patterning are closely related, both as theoretical constructs and compositional techniques.

Straus's 'The Problem of Prolongation in Post-tonal Music' of some five years later usefully summarizes the arguments for a more defensible pitch 'association', as opposed to 'prolongation', in post-tonal music (especially in respect of a 'middleground'), as well as questioning the validity of Travis's 'dissonant prolongation'.[83] He rightly raises the difficulties (even impossibilities) involved in interpretation of 'voice-leading' motions in some post-tonal contexts. Although Straus considers 'association', theoretically, as having a role within 'large-scale motivic statement',[84] he does not offer a detailed exposition of how such an idea might work in practice. Finally, and more positively, he draws attention to a mimicking of more traditional prolongational spans

---

[81] Straus, 'Stravinsky's Tonal Axis', 261–90, on 262.
[82] Ibid., 279.
[83] Straus, 'The Problem of Prolongation in Post-Tonal Music'; see especially 8–10 for questions of 'dissonant prolongation'.
[84] Ibid., 13.

(by which one should not of course be misled):[85] of a 'surface suggestive of tonality', in a manner which clearly paves the way for *Remaking the Past*, and which is also highly pertinent to this present study. It is worth adding that such ideas are also represented in the 1990s by James Baker's summary of 'Post-tonal Voice-leading' in Jonathan Dunsby's *Early Twentieth-Century Music*, which concludes significantly that 'The innate strength of tonal relations is such that they may undergo extreme modification and obfuscation without losing completely their cohesive force. It is possible that conventional tonality in the strictest sense underlies a far greater amount of twentieth-century music than we have realized.'[86]

Two articles by Arnold Whittall examine issues of dissonance and polarity:[87] the first on *Le Sacre* is concerned with discrepancies between theory and practice (an idea relevant to Milhaud's music). Whittall considers that an approach concentrating on 'the role of conflict' might usefully complement existing analyses of *Le Sacre*. He notes tensions between a 'particular modality' and a 'focused total chromaticism' which may lead to a dissonant norm.[88] Two types of 'focused dissonance' are identified: a single reiterated dissonance and one which embodies 'a degree of motion and transformation within itself': both 'lack the capacity for substantial "prolongation"'.[89] Applicable to Milhaud's music is the view that 'trappings' of tonality (triads, fifth relations, consonance and dissonance) are employed for dramatic effect. Whittall describes an 'E♭/C opposition' in the 'Danse de la Terre' of *Le Sacre*, and identifies the tension as resulting from the 'superimposition of the unrelated'.[90] (The parallels with Milhaud's

---

[85] Ibid., 15.

[86] See J.M. Baker, 'Post-tonal Voice-leading', in *Early Twentieth-Century Music*, ed. J. Dunsby, Models of Musical Analysis (Oxford, 1993), 40. Baker's notable contribution to this topic also includes his essay on 'Schenkerian Analysis and Post-Tonal Music' in *Aspects of Schenkerian Theory*, ed. D.W. Beach (New Haven and London, 1983), 156–86; his fine book on *The Music of Alexander Scriabin* (New Haven and London, 1986); and his article on 'Voice-leading in Post-Tonal Music: Suggestions for Extending Schenker's Theory', *Music Analysis*, 9 (1990), 177–200.

[87] A. Whittall, 'Music Analysis as Human Science? *Le Sacre du printemps* in Theory and Practice', *Music Analysis*, 1 (1982), 33–53; 'The Theorist's Sense of History: Concepts of Contemporaneity in Composition and Analysis', *Journal of the Royal Musical Association*, 112 (1986–87), 1–20.

[88] Whittall, 'Music Analysis as Human Science?', 42.

[89] Ibid., 44.

[90] Ibid., 47–8.

music are strong, as for instance in parts of the first movement of the Clarinet Sonatina, Op. 100). Whittall advocates studying the function of dissonances and regarding elements on their own terms, not as substitutes for something else. He views dissonance as a positive 'structural focus', rather than as a neutral 'polychord' construct.[91]

His second article pursues polarity further, perceiving a balance between 'confrontation' and 'complementation'.[92] Confrontation may exist not only between pitches, but also between old and new, which, in the neoclassical music of Stravinsky (and Milhaud), may 'converge, precariously but consistently', and thus form a certain 'symbiosis'.[93] If there is no such fusion, the juxtaposition, or superimposition, may result in a collage effect. Polarities exist also between the 'extended tonality' and 'integrated atonality' of Maxwell Davies's music (or between Milhaud's 'polytonalité et atonalité').[94] A further 'dramatic' confrontation is that of solo versus instrumental group.[95] Thus, elucidating contrasts, and how they contribute to structure, can be at least as important as seeking a bland, simplistic unity.

One further piece of research on the music of Stravinsky (and other post-tonal composers) may be selected for discussion here: Michael Russ's doctoral study of 1985.[96] In Stravinsky's *Two Poems of Balmont*, Russ stresses balance and complementation between harmonic units rather than functional (hierarchic) relations, and observes recurrent fixed pitches, but not prolongation. He seeks 'interpenetration' between scalic types and attempts to define ambiguities and the degree of divergence: 'Stravinsky's music is very much the sum of its outwardly contradictory, often divergent, and almost always ambiguous parts.'[97] The same is true of Milhaud's music.

In voice-leading, Russ urges distinction between structural elements and the diminution which prolongs that structure, and questions whether Straus's dissonant yet stable axes can be prolonged

---

[91] Ibid., 51. This focus on the role of dissonance is continued in Whittall's accessible contribution to Dunsby, *Early Twentieth-Century Music*, entitled 'Tonality and the Emancipated Dissonance: Schoenberg and Stravinsky' (1–19).

[92] Whittall, 'The Theorist's Sense of History', 2.

[93] Ibid., 6.

[94] Ibid., 17.

[95] Ibid., 20. See also Dunsby's discussion of heterophony in 'Considerations of Texture', *Music & Letters*, 70 (1989), 46–57.

[96] M. Russ, 'Four Studies in the Analysis of Post-tonal Music' (Ph.D diss., University of Ulster, 1985).

[97] Ibid., 92.

at background level if they are not evident on the surface, and whether 'pattern-completion has the power to prolong tones'.[98] He mentions also Travis's directed motion and dissonant prolongation, believing that, in voice-leading analysis, dissonance must be subservient to consonance. After identifying problematic pitches which are neither structural nor the result of diminution, he presents an alternative approach 'based on contextually defined associations',[99] requiring 'convergence' (or Cone's 'unification') 'of elements'.[100] Again, one must assess the extent of both divergence and association between individual pitches and collections, whilst probing the nature of ambiguities: structure thus involves a subtle balance between constant and changing elements.

In Webern's Bagatelle, Op. 9 No. 1, Russ questions the overall functional control of the bass, suggesting that the music may maintain or challenge this concept; he investigates patterning and motivic association, concluding that the piece has 'such a compressed structure that the concept of prolongation is perhaps unnecessary. Events are stated, not extended.'[101] He considers that 'virtually all aspects of [post-tonal] structure are defined contextually, rather than pre-compositionally',[102] and that 'Pc set analysis pursued on its own will never lead to a theory of early twentieth-century harmonic relations.'[103] There should be 'more systematic and wide-ranging enquiry' into pitch-symmetry (and axes), used sometimes to extend tonal hierarchy and sometimes to negate it.[104] Russ relates the decline of the *Ursatz* in early twentieth-century music to the reduced importance of prolongation of 'hierarchic tonal schemes', and thinks that 'large-scale projections of motivic and symmetrical patterns may compensate for the decreasing reliance on prolongation'.[105] Finally, in considering the 'prime motivator' in Webern's first Bagatelle, he stresses a need to move away from the

[98] Ibid., 165.
[99] Ibid., 167.
[100] Ibid., 169.
[101] Ibid., 219. This may also be true of Milhaud's very different miniature structures.
[102] Ibid., 220.
[103] Ibid., 221.
[104] Ibid., 222–3.
[105] Ibid., 224.

'present obsessive concern with the surface and look for deeper structures'.[106]

Apart from ideas applied largely to Stravinsky's music, there are those from David Neumeyer's study of Hindemith's theory and practice,[107] which does still advocate a hierarchical (though not reductive) voice-leading approach, adapted from Hindemith's *The Craft of Musical Composition*. Useful features include equating pitches 1 and 11, and assigning importance to the central pitch 6, as well as invoking 'pillar harmonies' and 'fundamental bass' (to determine the harmonic resultant of 'polytonality'). A parallel exists between Hindemith's 'indefinite third relation' and the (0,3) relation in octatonic theory, whilst Milhaud's use of third relations is one of his most striking and consistent features. Hindemith's qualification of dissonant tensions produced by different intervallic combinations ('harmonic fluctuation') may also be applicable to Milhaud's music. In analysis of Hindemith's early chamber music, Neumeyer suggests a parallel between voice-leading and set-theoretic approaches, in that Stages I and II of his voice-leading analysis equate roughly with the set-complex and nexus sets, though there is no equivalent of a Schenkerian middleground. Neumeyer's view is that

> The relation of melodic configurations (specifically, motivic design and development) to pc-set structures must be considered, even though Forte disassociates pc-set structures from any necessary connection to melodic or thematic process. Pc sets underlie melodic configurations, which include motives. They are not equivalent or identical, nor dependent. But since I have taken a step from these latent structures in favoring tonal process, I must accept a closer connection between motive and 'significant set' whenever possible.[108]

Any adaptation of these ideas must acknowledge two significant differences between Milhaud and Hindemith: firstly, Hindemith's compositional processes derive from harmony, whereas Milhaud's derive from melody; secondly, Hindemith is bound to a tonal interpretation of his and other music, whereas Milhaud admits atonality.

---

106   Ibid., 219.
107   Neumeyer, *The Music of Paul Hindemith*.
108   Ibid., 125.

Finally, in relation particularly to melodic analysis, the work of Leonard B. Meyer should be considered.[109] His views represent a shift away from the *Gestalt* concept of 'expectation', to one of 'implication' and 'realization'. Implications depend on preceding events and stylistic content, and each parameter may have its own contradictory implication, so that there is only ever 'part-realization'. Unrealized implications are seen as potential, and may be equated with a lack of closure of that implication. The approach is attractive in that the music generates its own contextual procedures, but can be for the same reason vague and open-ended. Ideas of 'pattern consistency' may be helpful in blues or jazz-influenced works, as observed by Charles Keil back in 1969: 'Blues pattern consistency or style has never been given the intensive treatment it warrants.'[110] Keil, citing Meyer, advocates 'thorough dissection of a few outstanding contemporary blues selections', investigating 'probability relationships, the expectations and goals, the harmonic habits, the melodic norms, and ranges of permissible deviation, and the techniques for building and releasing tension'.[111]

Selection of Analytical Approach

Milhaud is firstly a modal melodist, so that the primary analytical concern will be melodic (heeding Forte's guidelines on the implementation of linear analysis), with harmonic interpretation as secondary—the ideal in Forte's parlance being to seek the 'dynamic correspondence' between the two. Even if Milhaud composed his music contrapuntally, the lines are also heard together as simultaneities: a motivic approach seems most likely to succeed. Since Milhaud's music is almost always centric at 'background' level, though more conflicting and complex at surface level, a combination of post-Schenkerian voice-leading analysis (broadly Salzerian) and set theory (following guidelines of Forte and Hasty) will usually be employed, noting that the correspondence between motives and significant sets

---

[109] L.B. Meyer, *Explaining Music: Essays and Explorations* (Berkeley, 1973): see especially Part 2 'Explorations: Implication in Tonal Melody'. The principles are also outlined in I. Bent (with W. Drabkin), *Analysis*, The New Grove Handbooks in Music (London, 1987), 69–70, and are further developed in E. Narmour, *The Analysis and Cognition of Basic Melodic Structures: The Implication-Realization Model* (Chicago, 1991).

[110] C. Keil, *Urban Blues* (Chicago, 1969), Appendix B: 'Talking about Music', 203–16, on 207.

[111] Ibid., 208.

which Neumeyer found in Hindemith's music may also be detected in that of Milhaud.

In terms of set-theoretic refinement, the main principles of Forte's pc set genera will be employed as part of an attempt to mediate between modal and atonal means of reference. The notion of genera seems generally more accessible and suitable for Milhaud's music than, say, that of Kh relations (loosely equivalent in offering some larger-scale coherence). The primary purpose will be to establish patterns of, and partiality for, particular genera across a broad spectrum of Milhaud's music, and whilst endorsing and maintaining Forte's generic types, more standardized abbreviations (such as 'chrom.' and 'diat.', for 'chroma' and 'dia', respectively) will be adopted.

Generally, the emphasis is on what Forte would term 'raw counts', though these often happen to be supported by the Squo index:[112] this parallels to some extent the greater emphasis on basic tenets of set theory (set identity, properties, 'sonority', and small-scale relations) rather than on Kh subcomplexes. ('Raw counts' is perhaps misleading since it suggests a greater crudity than is the case; such counts are still employed with discretion—with concern for the presence and role of progenitors and characterizing (singleton) sets, and in relation to understanding gained by other means.) There are several reasons for this: firstly, because of the detailed examination of many short excerpts, not necessarily contiguous, the usefulness of any Squo calculation may be compromised by figures so small as to be almost without meaning; secondly (and only in small part as a consequence of the first reason), the 'Rule of Singleton Extension' frequently obviates the need for the 'Squo'; thirdly, and most importantly, the Squo index can be counter-intuitive, or rather lacking in sufficient sophistication, in that it does not take into account the prominence or frequency of particular sets (and their associated sonorities) within the musical surface. It also assumes the desirability of resolving generic conflict or ambiguity in contexts which may thrive on such qualities. Consequently, injudicious use of the quotient may actually skew one's perception of the true presence of certain generic materials. Having said this, the case studies will invoke the Squo indicator in order to evaluate its usefulness and applicability.[113] Conversely, the 'Difquo' measure-

---

[112] See again Forte, 'Pitch-Class Set Genera', 232.
[113] Squo indices will be presented correct to three decimal places, with the third figure rounded up appropriately. 'Reduced' generic matrices in the case

ment seems to offer considerable potential in substantiating ideas of contrast and polarity in the pitch structure of Milhaud's music, and may enable a more sophisticated successor to the problematic notion of polytonality.

Motivic interpretation will, where appropriate, embrace 'Implication-Realization', and will examine both decorative and directed motion. Third relations, at different levels, will be approached from the perspectives of van den Toorn, Straus (embracing axes), and Hindemith. Polarity, prominent in varying forms in Milhaud's music, will be approached along lines suggested by Whittall and Russ: the 'role of conflict', and nature of 'focused dissonance' (and consonance) will be pursued. (Hindemith's tension theory, or 'harmonic fluctuation', and Milhaud's expressive 'force sonore' may also be relevant here.) Localized bimodality will be viewed as a type of polarity, together with stylistic oppositions of old and new. It is perhaps in the blues/jazz domain that the most original analytical contribution can be made: ragtime and blues are distinct influences on Milhaud's music in the 1920s, so that one could investigate, along Keil's lines, the extent to which Milhaud's music might parody the structures of jazz.[114]

The approach adopted accepts broadly the work of Collaer/Galante and Drake in establishing the essence of Milhaud's style, and the need to heed Milhaud's own views and permit flexibility. Often a variety of possible interpretations will be offered before one is selected as being the most informative and appropriate in a certain context. Although the study focuses on pitch relations, it will still respect the onset and closure of phrases, metric/rhythmic patterns, register and timbral associations.

In acknowledging the approach to modality as of particular significance, traditional terminology (such as Lydian mode on G) is preferred to that of 'E scale on G' since this method is instantly clear,

studies will still show any sets associated with more than one genus so that Squo results may be verified.

114 The following are useful sources here: D. Baskerville, 'Jazz Influence on Art Music to Mid-Century' (Ph.D diss., University of California at Los Angeles, 1965); C. Colin, ed., *Encyclopaedia of Improvisation* (New York, 1972); F. Tirro, 'Jazz', in *Dictionary of Twentieth Century Music*, ed. J. Vinton (London, 1974), 367–76; M. Harrison, 'Jazz', in *The New Grove Dictionary of Music and Musicians*, 9, 561–79; G. Schuller, 'Rags, the Classics, and Jazz', in *Ragtime: its History, Composers and Music*, ed. J.E. Hasse (London, 1985), 79–89; *The New Grove Dictionary of Jazz*, ed. B. Kernfeld, 2 vols. (London, 1988). See also Chapter 4 below.

and since preservation of a historical perspective seems appropriate. Most common are the Mixolydian (G-scale), Lydian (F-scale) and Dorian (d-scale). In determining the modal final of these and other formations, Hindemith's concept of 'fundamental bass' may have a role to play. The partitioning of modal models, as an initial referential framework, seems especially important, with octatonic partitioning maintaining van den Toorn's Models A and B, and other modal formations approached along similar lines, and detailed below.

The simplest formations are perhaps the pentatonic collections, as shown in Fig. 2.4. The purpose of acknowledging five related types (with shared final on C), all referable as set 5-35, is to ascertain which arrangement of pitches Milhaud favours in relation to the modal final, when this is not ambiguous. The essential melodic feature is the (0,2,5) 3-7 construct which can cause ambiguity between 'tonic' and 'subdominant': collection 2, for instance, could be centred on C, or possibly F. The (0,2,5) construct explains the frequency of movement from fifth to sixth degrees and thence to the tonic, omitting the leading note, especially in its most common form as collection 1. It may be through the properties of this construct that Milhaud was drawn to the pentatonic collection (with its negro associations) and thence to jazz.

The critical (0,2,5/0,3,5) construct here may be expanded to (0,2,5,7), set 4-23 and (0,3,5,8), set 4-26, with 4-26 providing a modicum of common ground between pentatonic and octatonic collections (since two such 4-26 constructs separated by a semitone produce the octatonic Model A: (0,1,3,4,6,7,9,10)). The most notable harmonic feature of the pentatonic mode is that full triads only occur on two pitches separated by a minor third—those for collection 1, for instance, occurring on C and A. Moreover, the unordered pitch contents of C^6 (C,E,G,A) and a^7 (A,C,E,G) are identical: hence ambiguity at the third, or in Hindemith's parlance 'indefinite third relation'. This collection seems of most relevance to Milhaud's early music up to about 1920.

Conversely, chromaticism also seems an important component of Milhaud's early exploratory music, so that the Chromatic Matrix (Fig. 2.5), involving a wholetone collection on C across the diagonal (bottom left to top right), is another useful derivation from the work of van den Toorn. This matrix proves most useful in the finale of the Fifth Chamber Symphony (Case Study 3) where the relevant portion is

Figure 2.4 Pentatonic Model (five related collections (0,2,4,7,9): final on C)

Collection	Pitches	
1	C D E G A	(ascent from C: 3 + 2)
2	C D F G A	(ascent from C: 2 + 3)
3	G B♭ C D F	(ascent/descent: axial about C)
4	E♭ F G B♭ C	(descent from C: 2 + 3)
5	E♭ F A♭ B♭ C	(descent from C: 3 + 2)

Pitch occurrences across the collections

Occurrences	Pitches
	G A♭ A♮ B♭ C D E♭ E♮ F
5	C
4	G F
3	B♭ D
2	A♮ E♭
1	A♭ E♮

Collection 1 (symmetrical partitioning):
no fourth or seventh degrees

```
         C    D    E    G    A    C    D    E
        (0,   2,   4,   7,   9)
                      (9,   7,   4,   2,   0)
   1.   (0,   2,   4,   7)  (7,   4,   2,   0)
                  (0,   3,   5,   8)
```
= tetrachords: 4-23 (0,2,4,7); 4-26 (0,3,5,8)

```
   2.               (0,   2,   5)
                         (0,   2,   5)  (0,   2,   [5])
         ([5]  2,   0)  (5,   2,   0)
                              (5,   2,   0)
```
= trichords: 3-7 (0,2,5)

Chords/dyads
Pitches:	C(0)	D(2)	E(4)	G(7)	A(9)
(0,3)(0,7)		D A	E G	G D	
(0,3,7)					A C E
(0,4,7)	C E G				
(0,4,7,9)	C E G A				
(0,3,7,10)					A C E G
	I	II	III	V	VI

Figure 2.5   Chromatic Matrix

0/	12	11	10	9	8	7	6	5	4	3	2	1	0/	12
12	C	C♯	D	E♭	E	F	F♯	G	A♭	A	B♭	B	C	0
11	B	C	C♯	D	E♭	E	F	F♯	G	A♭	A	B♭	B	1
10	B♭	B	C	C♯	D	E♭	E	F	F♯	G	A♭	A	B♭	2
9	A	B♭	B	C	C♯	D	E♭	E	F	F♯	G	A♭	A	3
8	A♭	A	B♭	B	C	C♯	D	E♭	E	F	F♯	G	A♭	4
7	G	A♭	A	B♭	B	C	C♯	D	E♭	E	F	F♯	G	5
6	F♯	G	A♭	A	B♭	B	C	C♯	D	E♭	E	F	F♯	6
5	F	F♯	G	A♭	A	B♭	B	C	C♯	D	E♭	E	F	7
4	E	F	F♯	G	A♭	A	B♭	B	C	C♯	D	E♭	E	8
3	E♭	E	F	F♯	G	A♭	A	B♭	B	C	C♯	D	E♭	9
2	D	E♭	E	F	F♯	G	A♭	A	B♭	B	C	C♯	D	10
1	C♯	D	E♭	E	F	F♯	G	A♭	A	B♭	B	C	C♯	11
0	C	C♯	D	E♭	E	F	F♯	G	A♭	A	B♭	B	C	12
12/	0	1	2	3	4	5	6	7	8	9	10	11	12	/0

Symmetrical partitioning

1.   C   F♯   C
     (0   6   12/0)

   = tritonal partitioning: 2 × 6 semitones

2.   C   E♭   F♯   A   C
     (0   3   6   9   12/0)

   = 4-28: 4 × 3 semitones

3.   C   E   A♭/G♯   C
     (0   4   8   12/0)

   = 3-12: 3 × 4 semitones

4.   (C, C♯, D, E♭) (E, F, F♯, G) (A♭, A, B♭, B)
     (0   4   8)

   = semitonal 'chords' at 0,4,8

5.   C   D   E   F♯   A♭   B♭   C
     (0   2   4   6   8   10   12)
            (1   3   5   7   9   11)
            C♯   E♭   F   G   A   B

   = wholetone collections: C/C♯: 6 × 2 semitones

the segment marked off at the bottom of Fig. 2.5 (and where partitionings 3 and 4 may also be perceived).

One may also apply modal partitioning to the blues collection, which has considerable application for Milhaud's music. The blues scale is a pitch collection which admits minor and major third, (i.e. interval classes 3 and 4), and minor and major seventh (interval classes 10 and 11).[115] In Milhaud's parlance, the scale embodies 'mélange', or modal mixture and this is often 'le sentiment unitonal' resulting from the encounter of two lines composed in Ionian modes a minor third apart, such as C and E♭ (with blues sixth as well as third and seventh), discussed above. (One could even regard the blues scale on C as a composite of three Ionian modes a fifth apart, as in the cycle of fifths: B♭, F and C.) The special properties of the scale are examined in Fig. 2.6, with pitches F♯ and A♭ in parentheses as further blues-type pitches not present in the given collection, yet commonly invoked and supportive of the third of a chord. In listing chordal types, there seemed little point in extending beyond seventh chords, though those of the added sixth could be treated in the same way. One might also consider association between the blues collection and Straus's tonal axes (relevant in Case Study 4): Straus's example of (C–E♮/E♭–G–B♭) in the third movement of Stravinsky's *Symphony of Psalms*[116] shows how blues third and minor seventh might come about through two competing tonal axes, a minor third apart. Beyond its basic pitch requirements, blues style demands a flexible melodic 'bending' between major and minor allusions, illustrated in Chapter 4.

One may consider interaction between blues and octatonic collections, as van den Toorn did between diatonic and octatonic collections. Interaction between the blues scale and Model A yields two trichordal subsets: 3-2 (0,1,3), whereas that between the blues scale and Model B yields two overlapping tetrachords: 4-10 (0,2,3,5), shown in Fig. 2.7. Interaction between the blues and Model B is more significant since it preserves blues third, dominant and flattened seventh. Additionally, one could list the chords produced by such interaction, if this seemed useful.

Other important scalic formations (the use of which may be elucidated by modal models) are the Lydian, Dorian and Aeolian modes, as well as a 'new' mode explored by Milhaud: (G,A,B,C,D,E♭,F,G). This mode, almost always on G, is effectively c melodic minor in ascent, with its final on the fifth degree, as some variant of a plagal form. It

---

[115] See A. Hodeir, 'The Essence of Melody: The Blues Scale', *Jazz: its Evolution and Essence*, trans. D. Noakes (London, 1958), 154–6; and W. Sargeant, *Jazz: Hot and Hybrid*, rev. ed. (London, 1959), 160.

[116] Straus, 'Stravinsky's Tonal Axis', 279.

Figure 2.6 Blues scalic model (symmetrical scale: nine pitches)

Blues scale:	(C)	D	E♭	E	F	G	A	B♭	B	C	(D)
Pitch classes:		0	1	2	3	5	7	8	9	10	
Semitones:	2	1	1	1	2	2	1	1	1	2	

Partitioning of blues scale

	C	D	E♭	E	F	G	A	B♭	B	C	D
1.	0					7				0	
		0				5				0	

= partitioning at 4th/5th

2.		0	1	2	3	5	3	2	1	0	
		0	1		3	5	3		1	0	
		0		2	3	5	3	2		0	

= penta/tetrachords: 5-2, 4-11 & 4-10

3.	4	(2)	1	0				0	1	(2)	4
			0	1	(2)	4	(2)	1	0		

= tetra/trichords: 4-2 & 3-3 (0,1,(2),4)

4.		3	1	0	0	1	3	1	0	0	1	3
		C	D	E♭	E	F	G	A	B♭	B	C	D

= further trichords: 3-2 (0,1,3)

Chords from blues scale

Pitches:	C(0)	D(2)	E♭/E♮(3/4)	F(5)
(0,3,6)			E G B♭	
(0,3,7)	C E♭ G	D F A	E G B	F (A♭) C
(0,4,7)	C E G	D (F♯) A	E♭ G B♭	F A C
(0,3,4,7)	C E♭/E♮ G			
(0,3,6,10)			E G B♭ D	
(0,3,7,10)	C E♭/E♮ G B♭	D F A C	E G B D	F A C E♭
(0,4,7,11)			E♭ G B♭ D	
	I	II	III	IV

Pitches:	G(7)	A(9)	B♭/B♮(10/11)
(0,3,6)		A C E♭	B D F
(0,3,7)	G B♭ D	A C E	
(0,4,7)	G B D		B♭ D F
(0,3,4,7)	G B♭/B♮ D		
(0,3,6,10)		A C E♭ G	B D F A
(0,3,7,10)	G B♭/B♮ D F	A C E G	
(0,4,7,11)			B♭ D F A
	V	VI	VII

Figure 2.7 Interaction of blues and octatonic scales

Blues scale:	C	B	B♭	A	G	F	E	E♭	D	C
Pitch classes:	0	1	2	3	5	7	8	9	10	
Model A:	0	1		3	4	6	7		9	10
Interaction:	0	1		3			7		9	10
Model B:	0		2	3	5	6		8	9	11
Interaction:	0		2	3	5			8	9	

might, though, be regarded more plausibly, and simply, as a Mixolydian mode with flattened sixth (and occasional mixture at this scalic degree): hence the title 'Altered Mixolydian' which will be used hereafter. This collection is symmetrical about C/D, with two 4-11 (0,1,3,5) tetrachords, shown in Fig. 2.8; its lower tetrachord: (G,A,B,C), (2-2-1) is identical to that of the Ionian, whilst its upper tetrachord (D,E♭,F,G), (2-2-1) accords with the Aeolian. The complete mode may be constructed from two adjacent seventh chords: I^7 and VII^7; G^7 and F^7 (Fig. 2.8), which may provide an element of interaction with the blues collection. The Altered Mixolydian may also be partitioned at (0,4,8): G,B,E♭, set 3-12, with prominent triads a third apart on E♭ and G which may, in turn, be encapsulated within a seventh chord: (E♭,G,B,D), 4-19, in the manner of Straus's tonal axes.

Figure 2.8 Altered Mixolydian Model (symmetrical partitioning: seven-note scale on G)

```
              G     A     B     C     D     E♭    F     G
             (0     2     4     5     7     8     10)
                   (10    8     7     5     4     2     0)

    1.        G                 C     D                 G
             (0/5              5/0) (0/5              5/0)
             (0                      7)
                               (7                     0)

        = partitioning at 4th/5th

    2.        G           B           E♭          G
             (0           4           8           0)

        = 3-12 framework: (0,4,8)
```

(continued)

(Figure 2.8 continued)

3. (5   3   1   0)   (0   1   3   5)
       (0   2   3   5)
              (0   2   3   5)
       (0   3   5   8)

= tetrachords: 4-11 (0,1,3,5); 4-10 (0,2,3,5); 4-26 (0,3,5,8)

4. (5   1   0)   (0   1   5)
       (5   2   0)
       (0   2   5)

= further trichords: 3-4 (0,1,5); 3-7 (0,2,5)

Chords from Altered Mixolydian mode

Pitches:	G(0)	A(2)	B(4)	C(5)
(0,3,6)		A C E♭	B D F	
(0,3,7)				C E♭ G
(0,4,7)	G B D			
(0,4,7,8)	G B D E♭			
(0,4,7,10)	G B D F			

Pitches:	D(7)	E♭(8)	F(10)
(0,3,7)	D F A		
(0,4,7)			F A C
(0,4,8)		E♭ G B	
(0,3,7,10)	D F A C		
(0,4,7,10)			F A C E♭
(0,4,8,11)		E♭ G B D	

Seventh chords on G and F produce the complete mode:

```
       G     B     D     F
(F)    A     C     E♭
```

Interaction between Altered Mixolydian and Octatonic modes

Altered Mixolydian
7-34 (0,1,3,4,6,8,10)   G   A   B   C   D   E♭   F   G

Octatonic
8-28 (0,1,3,4,6,7,9,10)   G♯ A   B   C   D   E♭   F F♯

Scalic interaction   A   B   C   D   E♭   F

Similarly, triads on d and F may be heard compositely as d^{m7} (D,F,A,C) 4-26, and thus set 4-26 also represents potential interaction between Altered Mixolydian and pentatonic collections. Additionally, the main portion of the scale, omitting the 'tonic', is identical with the octatonic Model A: i.e. (0,1,3,4,6,7,9) on G♯: (A,B,C,D,E♭,F), also shown in Fig. 2.8.

There are some instances of what may yet best be interpreted as localized bimodality, embodying a precarious balance of opposing forces (relevant to the Fourth Quartet and *Machines agricoles*). Under what conditions, though, if any, could two modes cadence simultaneously, preserving their separate identities and involving the Schenkerian impossibility of more than one *Ursatz*? Similarly, can the listener ever perceive two separate entities simultaneously, as a 'stereo' effect? And is this analytically relevant? Although Searle claims early in his essay that 'it is only really possible to listen to and distinguish between two separate tonalities at once',[117] by the conclusion he too is slightly more equivocal: 'Bitonality is the only form of this procedure which can really represent a see-saw between two different keys, and even this becomes wearisome after a short time.'[118] Still, in order to test out how far it is useful to travel back in the direction from which Milhaud was coming, a list of factors which might aid the perception of localized bimodality is suggested (Fig. 2.9), together with a possible means of bimodal classification (Fig. 2.10). Such apparatus is offered in a spirit of somewhat speculative open-mindedness!

There are connections between the interval separating the finals of two modalities and the likely bimodal type. Considering combined Ionian modes (rather as the triads in Milhaud's article), the finals of which may be viewed as inversionally equivalent dyad sets, one can suggest that composite collections resulting from combinations of C/C♯, C/B (2-1); and C/F♯, C/G♭ (2-6), might be the most likely to result in a totally chromatic/atonal Class 4. Combined modes on C/D, C/B♭ (2-2); C/F, C/G (2-5), with the greatest number of intersecting pitches could favour the 'absorption' Class 1: those on C/F might yield a single Ionian mode with blues seventh: (C,D,E,F,G,A,B♭/B♮,C), whilst those on C/G could yield a Lydian tendency mode: (C,D,E,F/F♯,G,A,B,C). Combined modes on C/E♭, C/A (2-3); and C/E, C/A♭ (2-4), might have most potential for Class 3, though a fusion of C/E♭ could still produce a

---

[117] Searle, *Twentieth Century Counterpoint*, 34.
[118] Ibid., 43.

Figure 2.9 Factors which might aid the Perception of Localized Bimodality

1. Differentiated modal types, such as chromatic and pentatonic collections (in the Fourth Quartet, II), with simple melodic characterization.
2. Motivic mirroring (fourth and fifth songs of *Machines agricoles*).
3. Emphatic (possibly staggered) 'cadential' gestures.
4. Distinctive pedal points which might be elaborated into ostinati, operating over a sufficient time-span.
5. Choice of interval between modalities to avoid many intersecting pitches: Ionian modes on C/F♯ (white/black opposition) would seem more distinctive than those on C/F♮, or C/G.
6. Contrasting (and simple) rhythmic identities.
7. Balance (and clarity) of texture, instrumental forces (as in the Fourth Quartet), dynamic levels, and proportions.
8. Contrasting timbre (small, mixed chamber ensemble of *Machines agricoles*) to highlight separate identities.
9. Clear-cut, small-scaled structures (small ternary forms).
10. Differentiated registral spacings, and spatial layout: stage positions.

Figure 2.10 Suggested Types of Localized Bimodality

CLASS 1 ('absorption': de Schloezer; 'illusory' type: Milhaud)
(a) One main modality, and a subsidiary one (which is 'absorbed' almost immediately), are heard in terms of the stronger, now modified, collection: Ionian modes on C and B♭ might produce a compound C/c^7, with blues third. This class could occur in piano writing where there is less opportunity for timbral differentiation.

(b) A more extreme version of (a), with 'absorption' of both rival modalities then transformed into a new entity. Such a phenomenon might ensue from combining modalities with many common pitches, any one of which could be strongly sustained: Ionian modes on C and D: (C/c♯,D,E,f/f♯,G,A,B,C) could yield a Lydian/blues-type mode on G: (G,A,B,C/c♯,D,E,f/f♯,G) if G were sufficiently emphasized, especially in the bass.

(continued)

(Figure 2.10 continued)

> CLASS 2 (surface-level bimodality)
> One modality predominates whilst the other is subsidiary, though the latter still has a localized identity, and is not 'absorbed' during a phrase (though it would not be cadentially 'affirmed'). Instrumental and textural distinctions, motivic mirroring, and use of conflicting modalities such as C and C♯ might assist perception of this class, which might best be described as an 'unequal partnership'.
>
> CLASS 3 (bimodality)
> (a) Oscillation/ambiguity: the listener may be unsure which one of two modes is in operation, even though they are employed consistently across a section of a work. The phenomenon could occur frequently in ostinati passages.
>
> (b) Bimodality as a rare, precarious balance, or polarity, between two similar modalities, often with modal finals a third apart; or between differentiated modal collections (such as chromatic and pentatonic). The effect could be aided by any of the factors listed in Fig. 2.9, and might be endorsed by generic complementation (slow movement of the Fourth Quartet). Such bimodality would seldom remain audible as distinct, polarized strands for extended periods, but 'affirmation' of each modality through quasi-cadential gesture might be attempted. This parity of equal and opposing collections might be put over most successfully in string quartet format, with balanced pairings (as in the opening movement of the Fourth Quartet).
>
> CLASS 4 (atonality)
> As Milhaud commented in 'Polytonalité et atonalité', combining tonalities (or modalities), particularly in fully chromatic fashion, may result in atonality, at least at surface level.

single blues-type collection: (C,D,E♭/E♮,F,G,A♭/A♮,B♭/B♮,C), in the manner of Straus's example from the *Symphony of Psalms*, discussed above. Thus one can appreciate 'le sentiment unitonal' of which Milhaud spoke in his article of 1923.

CHAPTER THREE

Early Exploration: Chromaticism

❧

> Le soir, avant de m'endormir, je fermais les yeux; alors j'imaginais, j'entendais une musique d'une extraordinaire liberté qu'il m'eût été impossible de transcrire. Comment l'exprimer? C'était pour moi un grand mystère dans lequel je me complaisais, comme en un refuge où mon langage musical s'élaborait dans les couches les plus profondes de mon inconscient.[1]

THIS chapter is concerned with the early stylistic 'melting-pot' up to about 1922, and, although the makings of the Brazilian/jazz-inspired and neoclassical elements are evident in this exploratory phase, discussion of those elements is reserved for Chapters 4 and 5. Even within Milhaud's music before 1922 there is a distinction between works composed as 'apprentice', while a student at the Paris Conservatoire, and works between 1918 and 1922, which show a conscious striving for personal identity (especially those which may be related to a machine aesthetic). The apprentice works are late Romantic in style, influenced by late nineteenth- and early twentieth-century French masters, especially Fauré and Debussy, whereas the slightly later pieces, three of which are discussed below in detailed case studies, are much more experimental.

The apprentice works, exemplifying in Straus's words 'influence as immaturity',[2] were indeed widely influenced by Milhaud's teachers at the Conservatoire, his contemporaries, writer-friends, and external events, especially World War I. Milhaud entered the Conservatoire in 1909, aged 17, studying violin and composition, and after two years there he wrote his Violin Sonata No. 1 and 600 pages of an opera! He attempted to interest his harmony tutor Xavier Leroux (1863–1919) in the compositions, who, knowing that Milhaud had little taste for traditional harmony, had agreed reluctantly. Having heard a section of the Violin Sonata, Leroux exclaimed: 'You're trying to acquire a

---

[1] Milhaud, *Ma vie heureuse*, 25; for translation and discussion, see Chapter 1 above.

[2] Straus, *Remaking the Past*, 9. For further discussion, see Chapters 4 and 5 below.

conventional language when you already have one of your own. Leave the class. Withdraw!'[3] After this, Milhaud was taught by André Gédalge (1856–1926), Professor of Fugue and Counterpoint, whom Milhaud regarded as a more usefully critical teacher. His reaction to Milhaud's Sonata was: 'Why have you got the note D♯ seventeen times on the first page? You don't know how to construct a melody!'[4] Gédalge strongly influenced Milhaud's early music, and indeed Milhaud never wavered from the belief in melodic priority. Soon after their first meeting, Milhaud gave up violin lessons and devoted himself entirely to composition. He also attended the orchestration classes of Paul Dukas (1865–1935), and courses taught by Vincent d'Indy (1851–1931) and Charles-Marie Widor (1845–1937).

Milhaud acknowledges the great influence of Debussy's *Pelléas et Mélisande* and Musorgsky's *Boris Godunov* on his early works,[5] and it is no coincidence that his early style may be deemed late Romantic or Impressionist. In particular, Milhaud shares the use of parallel chord-streams with his early 'mentor', Debussy. Concerning Ravel's music, however, Milhaud felt regret at not finding the 'same depth of feeling' as he did in Debussy.[6] After the Violin Sonata No. 1, Milhaud's next work for similar forces, the Sonata for Piano and Two Violins (1914), won him the Lepaulle Prize for Composition, and was the first (chamber) work that he did not later repudiate. Yet all these compositions, including the Violin Sonata No. 2 (1917) are immature, compared with the achievements of the mid 1920s.

Although Milhaud's apprentice works owed much to French musical tradition, his early style was more affected in its serious, Romantic expression by the work of several writers.[7] Jammes provided Milhaud with the libretto for his earliest opera, *La Brébis égarée*, Op. 4 (1910–14), and with the inspiration for his first, unpublished composition, *Poèmes de Francis Jammes*, Op. 1 (1910–12) and the further set, Op. 6 (1912–13). It is, however, the influence of Léo Latil, killed in action in 1915, which proves the most striking in Milhaud's early music. His texts produced in Milhaud's music a seriousness and intensity without later parallel,

[3] Ibid., 32.
[4] Ibid.
[5] Ibid., 28.
[6] Ibid., 28–9. There are still, however, echoes of Ravel's Quartet (1903/1910) in the first movement of Milhaud's Fourth Quartet: see the introductory outline of Chapter 4 below.
[7] See also the contextual part of Chapter 1 above.

Early Exploration: Chromaticism 59

and characterized by an unashamed Romanticism, with a certain naivety.

Milhaud's memorial to Latil was the Third Quartet, Op. 32 (1916), with added soprano as in Schoenberg's Second Quartet. Apart from the funereal associations ('Qu'est-ce que c'est que ce désir de mort, et de quel mort s'agit-il?'),[8] this association with death is also heard in the slow movements of the Second Quartet, Op. 16 (1914–15), the Fourth Quartet, the finale ('Douloureux') of the Sonata for Flute, Oboe, Clarinet and Piano, Op. 47 (1918), and scenes from *Les Malheurs d'Orphée* (1924) such as Scene XIV: 'Chœur des funérailles'. This is the dark side of the sunny, Mediterranean lyricist. These movements share an intimacy and unexpected depth of expression, which Milhaud evidently felt was inappropriate elsewhere. Admittedly, there are wistful, subdued sections in *La Création du monde*, but never the sense of solitude and despair heard in the Third Quartet, which, though mixed in quality and too protracted for its material, still rewards listening and study. This is the gravity and introspective solemnity of Milhaud, before he became known as one of 'Les Six', and which may also, as suggested by Matthew-Walker, be bound up with Milhaud's Jewish identity: 'it is this intense melodic expression which is the manifestation of this aspect of his Jewish consciousness.'[9] In addition to providing the subject and text for the Third Quartet, regarded as 'an astonishing work for a French composer for 1916,'[10] Latil provided that for Milhaud's unpublished *Trois poèmes de Léo Latil*, Op. 2 (1910–16) ('Prière à mon poète', 'Clair de Lune', and 'Il pleut doucement'), and *Quatre poèmes de Léo Latil*, Op. 20 (1914).

Milhaud's musical outlook gradually developed, as he sought to explore more radically. As quoted at the head of this chapter: 'mon langage musical s'élaborait dans les couches les plus profondes de mon inconscient'. An important part of the search for stylistic identity was fulfilled by rigorous polytonal experiment, partly influenced by Charles Koechlin.[11] The second opera of Milhaud's *L'Orestie* trilogy, *Les Choéphores*, Op. 24 (1915–16), dedicated to Koechlin, should be mentioned in this connection; of this work the composer said:

[8] 'What is this longing for death, and what kind of death does it mean?', a quotation from Latil's diary, used as the text.
[9] R. Matthew-Walker, 'Milhaud's Jewish Consciousness', *Music and Musicians*, (November, 1984), 14. For more on this topic, see the opening of Chapter 4 below.
[10] Ibid.
[11] See Orledge, *Koechlin*.

> For each strophe and antistrophe, indeed, I established in most cases a definite line of harmonic research, applying to sequences of chords the technique used for variations. The essential part of the music, however, remained the general melodic line. Even when I studied chords, I only used them to sustain a diatonic melody, remembering Gédalge's advice: 'Just write eight bars that can be sung without accompaniment'.[12]

Similar experimental techniques were used in the third part of the trilogy, *Les Euménides*, Op. 41 (1917–22). More extreme were those used in two works of 1920: the Fifth String Quartet, dedicated to Schoenberg, and *Cinq études* for Piano and Orchestra, Op. 63, which is noteworthy for the composer's own acknowledgement of its symmetrical *cancrizans* construction:

> The fourth étude, both violent and dramatic in its content, is constructed crab-wise, i.e. the piece is divided into two, the second being an exact replica of the first, but reversed. From the mid-point it runs backwards to the beginning.[13]

Although this large-scale *cancrizans* phenomenon is much less prevalent in the mid-1920s, it does resurface in the grand operatic context of *Christophe Colomb*, Op. 102 (1928), in association with a six-part canon.[14] Additionally, 'Étude' clearly has particular associations for Milhaud, since the finale of the Fourth Chamber Symphony, Op. 74 (1921), which bears this same title, also illustrates a rigorous 'polytonal' procedure, involving 'strict canon in ten parts on two subjects', as observed by Humphrey Searle in his chapter on 'Milhaud and Polytonality'.[15] Interestingly, the actual tonalities, ordered from bass to treble, create a large-scale quintal/quartal construct (F,C,G,D,A; A,D,G,C,F): another early stylistic hall-mark.

Parallels have been drawn between Milhaud's attraction to polytonality and that of Cézanne, the dedicatee of the First String Quartet, to Impressionism. Christopher Palmer considers that Milhaud sought greater linear distinction through polytonality, whereas Cézanne sought this through the light and shadow of Impressionism.[16] The analogy is obviously not exact, but certainly there is an Impressionist quality to Milhaud's apprentice works (e.g. the First

---

[12] Milhaud, *Ma vie heureuse*, 60.
[13] Milhaud, *Ma vie heureuse*, 92.
[14] For an initial description, see Searle, *Twentieth Century Counterpoint*, 40–2.
[15] Ibid., 34–5.
[16] Palmer, 'Milhaud', in *The New Grove Dictionary*, xiii, 307.

Quartet, Op. 5, First Violin Sonata, Op. 3, and First Chamber Symphony, Op. 43) in terms of texture and timbre.

Although the 'polymodal' phenomenon is an integral part of Milhaud's early stylistic identity, it can be attractive to interpret this as something of a musical metaphor: with respect to *Le Bœuf sur le toit*, Nancy Perloff regards 'Polytonality as a musical metaphor for jangling simultaneity', in its various juxtaposed references to 'urban technological life', the Parisian fairground, and Brazilian Carnaval.[17] More generally, Wilfrid Mellers considers that Milhaud 'seems to have cultivated polytonality as a tribute to Nature's polymorphous perversity. In many early works Milhaud "hogs all the keys at once" in a spirit of democratic fair play, breaking down barriers between the artistic and the populist in the process. This lends itself to surrealistic Dadaism'.[18] Other similar metaphors and associations are invoked *en passant* in Case Studies 3 and 4.

In his exploration of extreme 'polytonality', chromaticism and limited pitch 'series', some of Milhaud's early music moves quite surprisingly towards atonality (albeit localized), as for example in passages from the slow movement of the Fourth Quartet (1918), the third song of *Machines agricoles* (1919) and the first movement of the Fifth Chamber Symphony (1922);[19] it is fascinating to speculate where such interest might have led him, had he not opted for a neoclassical approach.

Part of the impetus behind the extreme chromaticism which borders on atonality is bound up with a contemporary interest in what Glenn Watkins terms the 'machine aesthetic'—an idea signalled in Chapter 1, and explored further in Case Studies 2 and 3.[20] The preoccupation with the machine is certainly the most notable feature of Milhaud's 'Early Exploration', and one which balances the concerns in Chapters 4 and 5 with types of 'distance'. 'Distancing techniques' are inherent in the idea of mechanization:[21] the removal of the human variable as 'depersonalization', together with associated notions of

---

17 Perloff, *Art and the Everyday*, 184. For more on *Le Bœuf*, see Chapter 4 below.

18 W. Mellers, 'Polymorphous Celebrations', *Times Literary Supplement*, 30 June–6 July 1989, 717.

19 See below, Case Studies 1–3.

20 For a general discussion of music and machines in this period, see Watkins, *Pyramids at the Louvre*, Chapter 12 'Masks and Machines', 310–38; see also the useful introduction to the broader artistic notion of Futurism given in C. Tisdall and A. Bozzolla, *Futurism* (London, 1977).

21 Ibid., 310.

abstraction and alienation, often achieved musically by means of conflicting, 'fixed' ostinati. Indeed the machine aesthetic offers points of connection with both neoclassicism and modernism, as part of a continuing Parisian fascination with technology and Futurism beyond World War I, which had been sparked initially by the 1889 Exposition and the completion of the Eiffel Tower. Furthermore, in respect of Milhaud's involvement with the aesthetic, the composer's own writings tend to couple consideration of mechanization with (the white (re-)invention of) jazz—for instance his essay 'Les ressources nouvelles de la musique (jazz-band et instruments mécaniques)', published in *L'Esprit nouveau* in 1924; and his chapter on 'L'Évolution du jazz-band et la musique des nègres d'Amérique du nord', in his own *Études* (1927): 'cette musique mécanisée et aussi précise qu'une machine'.[22] As with jazz, and *art nègre*, representation of the machine, too, was inherently paradoxical, or double-edged, with shifting oppositions: freedom and constraint; opportunity and drudgery; inspiration for, yet a stifling of, creativity.

The final, surprising avenue explored in the search for stylistic identity represents an interesting anticipation on Milhaud's part. In 1920, Milhaud wrote an unusual chamber piece for three clarinets and soprano, entitled *Cocktail*, Op. 69.[23] This was a frivolous work, which owed some of its character to Milhaud's increasing interest in jazz, but the striking aspect of the work was its exploration of aleatory or 'chance' elements in the music.[24] This was some forty years before chance music was hailed by the post-war American experimentalists; and indeed Milhaud himself only continued this aleatoric style much later (in his third period beyond 1950), with the *Suite de quatrains* (1962), String Septet (1964) and *Musique pour Ars Nova* (1969).

So the overall impression of Milhaud's early music, with a focus on chamber music, is one of stylistic diversity: elements of late Romanti-

---

[22] Milhaud, *Études*, 56. For further comment see the introductory outline of Chapter 4 below. This French interest in the machinist phenomenon, as part of that late wave of Futurism, parallels and interacts with that of the well documented Bauhaus group in Weimar.

[23] Text by Larsen (from a cocktail recipe!); published in the *Almanac de Cocagne*, though not readily available: see Collaer/Galante, *Darius Milhaud*, 296.

[24] See Nichols, *Conversations with Madeleine Milhaud*, 99: 'Musical phrases of different lengths are repeated ad libitum by the performers. When the singer has finished, the players come to the end of their phrases, holding the last note until everyone has finished.'

Early Exploration: Chromaticism

cism, Impressionism, radical 'polytonal' and chromatic experiment (embracing a machinist aesthetic), and an aleatoric style, co-existing with the emergence of his interest in Brazilian music, jazz and neo-classicism. Some works, such as the Violin Sonatas, are 'hybrids', with one movement suggestive of a late Romantic style, whilst another contains elements of incipient neoclassicism; the majority of early works, however, are connected beneath the stylistic umbrella of late Romanticism.

Having outlined the main stylistic traits in Milhaud's search for identity, it remains to examine the structural techniques and concepts, from an analytical stance. The function of this part of the contextual framework is two-fold: to provide an overview of developing techniques, and to introduce Case Studies 1–3; conversely, the case studies exemplify this exploratory element of Milhaud's composition—particularly regarding total chromaticism, octatonicism, and the high profile of dissonance. More generally, works (or movements) relevant to the process of compositional exploration include those summarized in Fig. 3.1.

Figure 3.1 Early Works (Apprentice/Exploratory)

1911	*Première sonate*, Op. 3 (violin & piano) (I, II, III)
1912	*Premier quatuor*, Op. 5
1914–15	*Deuxième quatuor*, Op. 16
1916	*Troisième quatuor*, Op. 32 (string quartet with soprano) (I, II)
1917	*Deuxième sonate*, Op. 40 (violin & piano) (II)
	[*Première petite symphonie*, Op. 43]*
1918	*Quatrième quatuor*, Op. 46 (II, III)
	Sonate, Op. 47 (flute, oboe, clarinet & piano) (I, IV)
	[*Deuxième petite symphonie*, Op. 49]
1919	*Machines agricoles*, Op. 56 (voice & chamber ensemble) (III)
1920	*Catalogue de fleurs*, Op. 60 (voice & chamber ensemble) (I)
	Cinquième quatuor, Op. 64
1921	[*Troisième petite symphonie*, Op. 71]
	[*Quatrième petite symphonie*, Op. 74]
1922	*Cinquième petite symphonie* (*Dixtuor d'instruments à vent*), Op. 75
	[*Sonatine*, Op. 76 (flute & piano)]

* Square brackets indicate works also relevant in a different connection in Chapters 4 or 5.

Although many works were analysed as part of the original research for this book, it has been impractical to include much of the raw data here—hence this selection of principal features, followed up by Case Studies 1–3. Analysis reveals common techniques underpinning various early works, so that an overview of Milhaud's technical procedures emerges. Structural concepts and techniques are not all discussed in the same detail, as some are of far greater significance and interest than others. Chromaticism is an example of a technique which is prominent, frequently employed and relevant to various compositional phases, and is thus of primary importance; at the other extreme, certain works receive but a brief mention in serving to support a particular feature, as their contribution to this technical discussion. Although the exploratory, or experimental, element is most important between 1918 and 1922, the majority of early works share the priorities of melody, motive and, underlying everything, the concept of modality. Within this technical outline, principles of large-scale form and modality are followed by more detailed consideration of melodic and motivic processes, third relations, chromaticism and semitonal relations, bimodality, octatonicism and the place of dissonance and polarity.

The most common early forms are a free, ill-defined rhapsody, ternary form, rondo, and particularly fugue—often used as a device within a larger form. Milhaud hardly ever uses variation form; his structures tend to lack organic, developmental process of this type. The early forms are invariably over-long and lack clearly directed motion, such as in the two slow movements which comprise the Third Quartet, Op. 32 (1916). There is, however, resourceful variety within a restricted range of forms, especially ternary form, and in this latter respect the Flute Sonatina (1922) alone demonstrates two formal variants. The first movement works to unusual proportions: A [38 bars] B [9] C [30] A' [9], whilst the finale is effectively a modified sonata form, with two clear subjects and balanced proportions: A [19] B [21] A' [22] Coda [21]. On the whole, the most innovative and imaginative procedures operate at surface level, whilst the larger-scale forms created are less original.

Much of this discussion is concerned with the concept of modality, though this is not so clearly expressed in the early works as in later neoclassical compositions. The most commonly found modes are Ionian, Dorian, Aeolian, octatonic and pentatonic (the latter being most prominent in jazz/eclectic contexts), as exemplified in parts of the String Quartet No. 4 (Case Study 1). The years up to 1922 show clear progression in the handling of modality. Milhaud's Violin Sonata,

Early Exploration: Chromaticism

Op. 3 (1911), is very traditional, with an example of the well-tested Beethovenian technique of moving from minor to major tonality: the d♯ minor of the first movement concludes on a D♯ major chord, at the end of a coda marked 'Joyeux, très décidé et très large', and is balanced by a finale marked 'Très rythmé, joyeux', entirely in the major mode on C♯. Five years later, the first movement of the Third Quartet subscribes to the Dorian mode on d, with occasional introduction of the raised seventh, C♯. The overall modal centres of the two movements: (d; c–d) trace a lower neighbour-note progression, emphasizing the flattened seventh on the largest scale. One example of increasing sophistication is in the use of what one might loosely call 'plagal' as well as 'authentic' modal forms, as in the main theme of the finale of the Fifth Chamber Symphony (Case Study 3), where the Aeolian mode is used with 'final' on a, yet with ambitus D–D (i.e. not E–E). Usually a single modal background results from the encounter of 'polytonal' lines, though Milhaud's use of complex combinations of up to six composite tonalities in these early years makes it difficult if not impossible to perceive fundamental lines at background level. The centric nature of a work is rarely in question, but to select an upper-line descent is not often meaningful, with a possible exception in Case Study 2, 'La Lieuse' from *Machines agricoles*.

The Altered Mixolydian mode is most prominent in the exploratory phase before 1922, with the scalic form (G,A,B,C,D,E♭,F,G) almost always on G.[25] Relevant works include the finale of the Fourth Quartet and final song of *Machines agricoles*, as well as certain neoclassical works.[26] The opening and closing bars (1–16; 50–64) of 'La Faneuse' from *Machines agricoles* are nicely elucidated by means of the Altered Mixolydian mode (embodying some mixture at the sixth degree), as shown in Fig. 3.2, which quotes bars 1–4.

Modality may be clarified or extended by pedal-points, an important 'middleground' feature in Milhaud's early music. The finale of the First Violin Sonata (1911) opens with a sustained double pedal in the bass on tonic and fifth degree (C♯/G♯) across bars 1–6, with a similar double pedal occurring across bars 82–8 ('Mouvt. du début') of the first movement of the Third Quartet (see Fig. 3.3). Dominant pedals are also quite common from the Third Quartet onwards, as across bars 106–8 of the first movement, and bars 29–32 of the second movement.

---

[25] This 'new' mode was introduced in Chapter 2 above.
[26] See the introductory outline of Chapter 5 below.

Figure 3.2   *Machines agricoles*: VI, bars 1–4

Ostinato can be a means of prolonging a pitch collection, either consonant or dissonant, subject to reinforcement by neighbour-note progressions and other types of voice-leading. Ostinato undergoes considerable development in the 1920s and will be discussed again in connection with neoclassicism. It can, however, be detected in incipient form, at a localized level, from the first movement of the Sonata, Op. 47 (1918) onwards. Even there, the use of ostinato has developed from the simple repetition of inner parts within the first movement of the Third Quartet. The finale of the Fifth Chamber Symphony marks a further stage of development (Case Study 3).

There is a wide variety of melodic treatment in the early works, with some techniques clearly more successful than others. A criticism of Milhaud's early music is either that limited, repetitive material is overused, or that there are too many disparate ideas, not subject to real development. The Violin Sonata, Op. 3 (1911), whose first theme was severely criticized by Gédalge, illustrates the first melodic limitation. In the opening 'Lent et robuste' in d♯ minor, Milhaud uses too often a simplistic idea in two halves, heavily reliant on the tonic chord. Clearly, he has not yet gauged the critical relationship between the amount of thematic material and the overall scale of a piece. From the late Romantic qualities of this work amongst others, one senses the influence of Fauré's Violin Sonata, Op. 13 (1876), Franck's Sonata in A

(1886) and perhaps d'Indy's Violin Sonata in C, Op. 59 (1903–4). The limitations of this student composition are evident; yet it does use the technique of melodic/motivic 'exchange', a notion similar to invertible counterpoint, which was to become a hallmark of Milhaud's style. There are many sequels, including those in the first movement of the Fifth Chamber Symphony.

The Third Quartet shows a more motivic approach to melodic construction, the second movement focusing on two four-note motives. An ordered wholetone tetrachord 4-21 (B♭,A♭; D,C) in the violins, competes against an ascending 'minor' tetrachord 4-10 (C,D,E♭,F), within a basic modality of Aeolian on c.[27] Ultimately, the opposition is between a second wholetone tetrachord 4-21 (C,D,E,F♯) and the semitonally contracted 4-3 (C♯,D,E,F), ordered as (E,F; C♯,D), between bars 71 and 83. Ideas are subjected to transposition and some inversion, though the melodic motion is not always clearly directed. 'Melodic combination' is part of the essence of Milhaud's compositional technique and is a specific type of counterpoint where two distinct melodies, introduced separately, are later heard together. Usually the device is reserved for recapitulations, such as bar 82 of the opening 'Très lent' of the Third Quartet, where the main theme on violin I, constructed of two third motives, is combined with a subsidiary appoggiatura idea in the inner strings (Fig. 3.3).

Figure 3.3 Third Quartet: I, bars 82–4.

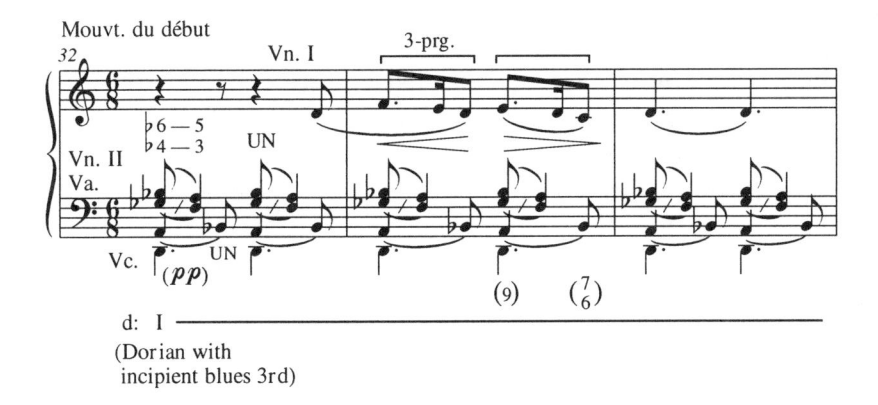

[27] The 4-10 tetrachord is employed later as a 'pillar-chord' (F,G,A♭,B♭) in Scene XII, 'Lamentations d'Orphée', of Milhaud's chamber opera *Les Malheurs d'Orphée* (1924).

Melodic combination and imitation can be employed together, as in the finale of the Fourth Quartet (bars 98–100), where three subjects combine along with the imitation in stretto of the second subject (Fig. 3.4).

Figure 3.4 Fourth Quartet: III, bars 98–100

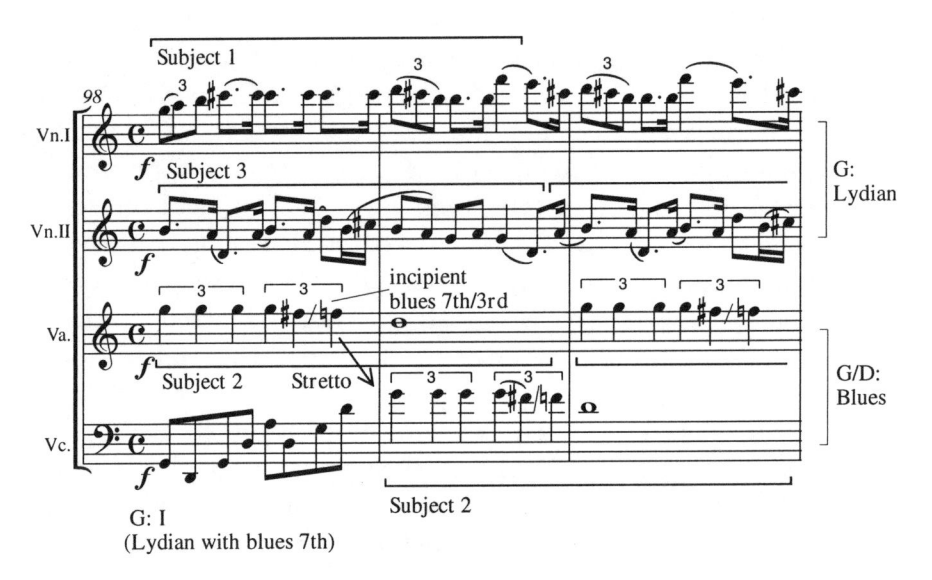

In melodic and contrapuntal domains, and at various structural levels, third relations play a significant role in Milhaud's music throughout the 1920s. They may occur as melodic third progressions, as found in the opening 'Très Lent' of the Third Quartet (Fig. 3.3), the basis of the material being a third motive with dotted rhythm, heard on the tonic (D–F,E,D), and answered imitatively on the dominant. This is extended sequentially, using the Aeolian on d (D–F,E,D; E,D,C–D) and is initially effective, but again is repeated too often either directly or in sequence (Fig. 3.3). Equally, third relations may operate within a vertical perspective, such as between two melodic lines in different modalities a third apart: the opening 'Animé' of the Fourth Chamber Symphony (1921) exhibits third relation between a main modality on C (descant and bass), and a subsidiary treble strand in e♭ minor, first alluded to by Searle.[28] Third relations are increasingly important through Milhaud's early period (up to 1927), and are already evident at background level by

---

[28] Searle, *Twentieth Century Counterpoint*, 36. For more on possible bimodality, see below.

1922, as illustrated by the choice of modal centres for each movement of the Flute Sonatina: G♯–f/c–A♭.

Discussion of Milhaud's apprentice and exploratory works must invoke the term 'chromaticism', with reference to the relationship between non-diatonic pitches and a strong diatonic collection. Chromaticism of various types, including incipient blues third, is prevalent at foreground and middleground levels. Early works use the same gesture excessively, though some simple devices are effective, such as the descending semitonal appoggiaturas at bars 36, 38, 40, and 46–8 of the first movement of the Third Quartet. At foreground level, chromaticism exists in dissonant, contrary motion devices, in two, three, four or six parts.[29] Further details are given in Case Study 3: Fifth Chamber Symphony, 'Rude', and Case Study 1: 'Funèbre' from the Fourth Quartet, which also shows conflict as the result of a process of chromatic complementation, in its opening bars. Dissonance is significant as a main structural component in works before 1922, usually as a result of chromaticism or bimodality.

'Semitonal relations', as a term which may be applicable across a broader musical spectrum than chromaticism, tends to imply one of two states (in reference to motivic activity): firstly, one or more pairs of semitones operating in a diatonic collection; secondly, semitones operating in an atonal collection (as interval-class 1).[30] The first state is illustrated by the ending of the Third Quartet, restricted to two ascending appoggiaturas (E–F; C♯–D), which reaffirm the work's overall centre on d. At bars 75–7, for the first time, the voice employs the same pitches as the haunting line about death is intoned. The reordering of the motive (C♯–D, E–F) offers a new twist, however, suggesting a resolution on to the third degree F. Examples of the second state—semitonal relations within localized atonality—are found in Case Studies 1–3. Vertical semitonal relations, especially those within set 4-7 (F♯,G,A♯,B), constitute important dissonant gestures at foreground level, as shown in Case Study 3. This particular construction permeates

---

[29] The device persists in the second and third 'Opéras-minute', for passages of heightened emotion: bars 43–4 in Scene II of *L'Abandon d'Ariane* (Case Study 8) and bars 154ff. in Scene VI of *La Délivrance de Thésée*, with the text: 'Ô douleur! Ô tristesse!'

[30] I tend to dispute the view taken by Howard Boatwright, in *Chromaticism: Theory and Practice* (Fayetteville, NY, 1994), that chromaticism need have little or no connection with notions of pitch centricity, and still more that it may be employed in any discussion of twelve-note music.

several works, including the second movement of the radical Fifth Quartet (1920), and continues through to 1927, in works which are stylistically neoclassical.[31]

Semitonal relations at middleground/background level are prominent in Milhaud's early output, the first instance occurring as a complex of such relations in the second movement and finale of the First Violin Sonata, Op. 3. The 'Très lent' commences in E major, with emphasis on the dominant B; a move to c minor (via D♭) for the central section is followed at the 'Mouvt. du début' by a semitonally transposed version of the opening, now on E♭ with prominent B♭, whilst the final bars, marked 'Très ralenti', employ enharmonic change of E♭(D♯) to close back on a chord of B major.[32] The ensuing finale then commences on C♯ major, a semitone away from the central section of the slow movement. Similar relations at middleground level may be observed through the semitonal transposition of discrete phrases, as varied repetition—a common device in popular music. In the 'Vif' of the Second Violin Sonata, bars 1–11 in the Aeolian mode on f are transposed up to the Mixolydian on F♯ for the recapitulation (bars 89–99). The practice highlights common ground between early exploratory works and the jazz/Brazilian-influenced repertory, with *Saudades do Brazil* (1920) and *Trois rag-caprices* (1922) sharing the technique.

Background semitonal relations which govern a complete movement are found in the opening movement of the Fifth Chamber Symphony (Case Study 3), with an overall progression of b–b♭–b; the reverse procedure occurs in 'La Lieuse' (Case Study 2) where the main pitch centre on B♭ is articulated by means of part of a central section focused on b. Equally, one might interpret the slow movement of the Fourth Chamber Symphony in this way since it consists of a compositional superimposition of semitonally related modalities on e♭, e♮, and f, as observed by Searle.[33] Semitonal relationships between tonal/modal centres of movements include the A–A♭–G descent of the First Chamber Symphony (1917), the D♮–D♯ (3 of B)–D♮ upper neighbour-note progression of the Third Chamber Symphony (1921), and the b–B♭–C interrupted ascent of the Fifth Chamber Symphony.

---

[31] The list includes the opening 'Très rude' of the Clarinet Sonatina and Scenes v and vi of the first 'Opéra-minute', *L'Enlèvement d'Europe*, bars 109–25, with the impassioned text: 'Ne me retenez pas! Mon honneur outragé!'

[32] It is worth acknowledging the prominence of enharmonic change itself, another procedure more in keeping with late Romantic than neoclassical practice.

[33] Searle, *Twentieth Century Counterpoint*, 36.

Localized 'polymodality' may itself be a source of polarity and thus of conflict, as suggested by the example of the Fourth Chamber Symphony above. Some of the most radical polymodal contexts occur in the early works, as in the attempt to sustain six simultaneous 'tonalities' in *Les Choéphores* (1915–16). Other illustrations are found in *Machines agricoles*, *Catalogue de fleurs*, the Fourth and Fifth Quartets, and the Third Chamber Symphony, discussed later in Chapter 5 with regard to its neoclassical dimension. In Chapter 2, a possible classification for 'localized bimodality' was suggested, with a list of factors likely to aid its perception, and it is appropriate now to illustrate these classes, initially with small-scale examples from *Machines agricoles*. Bars 1–4 of the first song could accord with the most common Class 1*a* 'absorption': two separate modalities combining to form one, on the stronger pitch centre, producing in this case a Mixolydian on C with blues third (C,D,E♭/E♮,F,G,A,B♭,C). Bars 5–8 illustrate Class 2 'bimodality at foreground level', i.e. localized bimodality with one modality predominant and the other subsidiary. Class 3*a*, a more penetrative 'oscillation/ambiguity', often occurs in ostinato passages, as in the ensuing bars 10–14. The ambiguity is between C and A♭ majors, though the case for C is probably stronger, being supported by voice, cello and piccolo. (Another example of this phenomenon was given earlier, with reference to third relations.)

There are rare instances when two pitch centres may be construed as operating at the equivalent of a middleground level, i.e. Class 3*b*. The opening of the Fourth Quartet reveals a carefully balanced polarity between centres on F and A, across bars 1–4 and 8–11, as a special type of third relation, with the effect enhanced by exchange of material and invertible counterpoint. Although the passage could be viewed within a single F-based mode, with C♯ incorporated, or as derived from a 3-12 (F,A,C♯) augmented triadic framework, this would not satisfactorily explain the precarious balance and harmonic tension. Similarly, the fourth and fifth songs of *Machines agricoles* also fulfil the requirements of Class 3*b*, with constructs about A/D and G/E respectively, whilst the other catalogue work, *Catalogue de fleurs*, contains an excellent illustration of divergent and convergent modalities in the fourth song, 'Les Jacinthes', typical of Milhaud's early music in the way that bimodality emerges from a single centre which later reasserts itself. The song is founded on a strong 'tonic' pedal on C, although many incompatible triads, including those on A, B♭, B, C♯, D, G, F, A♭ and G♭, emerge to challenge.

In the exploratory years (1918–22), tritonal relations are frequently and prominently expressed, as an extreme manifestation of polarity—sometimes part of a more elaborately developed octatonic framework. The earliest example of localized tritonal relations shows simplicity and balance: bars 38–9 and 76–7 in the 'Tranquille' of the Sonata for Flute, Oboe, Clarinet and Piano (1918). The e♭^{7} and a^7 chords of bars 38–9 may be viewed collectively as the octatonic collection, Model A: 0,1,3,4,6,7,9,10 (E♭,E♮,G♭,G♮,A,B♭,C,D♭), but ultimately it is the sense of polarity which is important (Fig. 3.5). Tritonal relations persist in the second and third 'Opéras-minute' and the Clarinet Sonatina, and can be traced in the Brazilian/jazz domain, through *L'Homme et son désir*, Op. 48 (1918).[34] More sophisticated octatonicism operates in the 'Funèbre' of the Fourth Quartet (Case Study 1), and in the first movement of the Chamber Symphony No. 4, with its C–F♯ opposition. This step towards atonality is further developed in localized 12-note contexts in the 'Funèbre', and the third song of *Machines agricoles* (Case Study 2), whilst a similar procedure operates in the first movement of the Fifth Chamber Symphony (Case Study 3) where all 12 pitches are introduced across bars 1–3. Even these contexts, however, have their source in chromaticism.

Figure 3.5 Sonata for Flute, Oboe, Clarinet and Piano, Op. 47: I ('Tranquille'), bar 39.

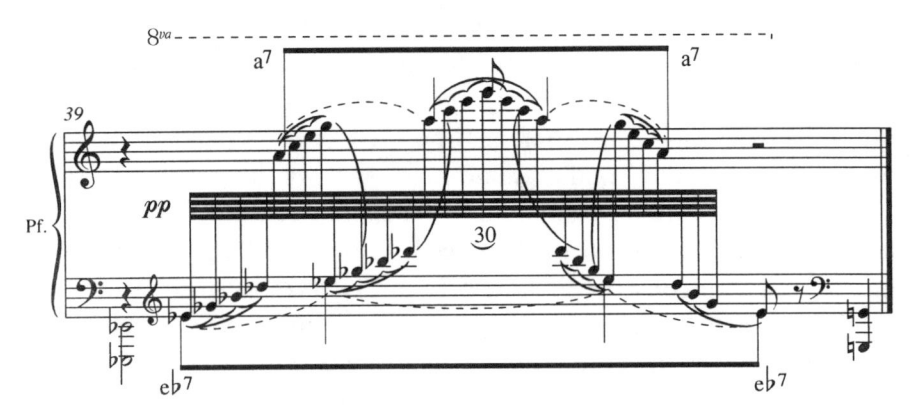

[34] A tension between C and F♯ exists throughout Scene II.

CASE STUDY 1
Chromaticism and Polarity in the 'Funèbre' from the
String Quartet No. 4, Op. 46 (1918)

Preliminaries

Composed in Rio de Janeiro in 1918 and dedicated to Félix Delgrange, Milhaud's Fourth Quartet was regarded by Walter Cobbett (in 1929) as his most popular of the genre—indeed, amongst the most performed of any of his works.[35] The Quartet was first performed to warm acclaim at the Concerts Delgrange, in Paris, on 5 April 1919, by the Quatuor Capelle, and was also well received at a subsequent performance given by the Pro Arte String Quartet, at the SMI Concerts on 6 January, 1921. When reviewing this later performance for *La Revue musicale*, Georges Migot declared that 'C'est une œuvre d'un réel musicien qui doit encore contrôler quelquefois sa facilité.'[36]

The Quartet has three movements: 'Vif', 'Funèbre' and 'Très animé', lasting approximately 9' 45", which Migot viewed as

> un triptyque dont le panneau central est très developpé et les deux ailes latérales très brèves. Ces deux ailes semblent s'inspirer de la construction du mouvement vif de l'école française du xviiie siècle, alors que le mouvement lent procède du lied mendelssohnien.[37]

The association with Mendelssohn is arguable, but the 'central panel' is certainly the weightiest and most interesting of the three movements, and as such is the logical choice for detailed analysis. As Migot suggests, the Fourth Quartet is well proportioned and balanced; material is not over-used, but is succinct and coherent. Despite the fact that Milhaud was only twenty-six at the time of its composition, a consistent style is emerging. The Quartet shows the craftsmanship of a maturing musician, with many of Milhaud's compositional hallmarks already present. Since this is one of his first mature works, it has been chosen as the earliest representative example of his chamber music before 1930. The analytical approach consists of a mixture of voice-

---

[35] Cobbett, *Cyclopedic Survey of Chamber Music*, 2nd ed. (Oxford, 1963), ii, 142.
[36] 'It is a work of a real musician who still needs sometimes to control his facility.' (G. Migot, '4e quatuor à cordes', *La Revue musicale*, 2 (February 1921), 167).
[37] Ibid.: 'a triptych whose central panel is highly developed, whilst the outer wings are very brief. These two wings seem to be inspired by the construction of the *vif* movement [typical] of the eighteenth-century French school, whilst the slow movement proceeds in the manner of a Mendelssohnian lied.'

leading and set theory (used especially to examine processes of chromatic complementation), modal partitioning and octatonic axes, derived, respectively, from van den Toorn and Straus.

Analysis

The form of the 'Funèbre' is a ternary variant: AA'BCA, as outlined in Fig. 3.6. The characteristic surface feature of this elegiac slow movement, which operates within an overall modality on d, is the all-pervasive dotted figure, with its funereal association, first assigned to violin II. Accompanying this is an equally unrelenting 'basso ostinato' in viola and cello. In the words of Paul Collaer:

> Above an ostinato bass consisting of viola and cello lines that are placed at intervals of the minor 7th and 9th, a march-like motive emerges which gives rhythmic cohesiveness to the entire movement. From time to time it is interrupted by a succession of translucent, ethereal chords.[38]

Figure 3.6 Fourth Quartet: II ('Funèbre'): Formal Outline

Ternary Variant: A A' B C A

	Bars		*Total bars*
SECTION A	1–16		16
Dotted theme, motive A	1–7	Violin II	
Ostinato, motive B^I	1ff.	Viola/Cello	
Countertheme, motive B^2	5	Violin I	
Dotted theme, motive A	9–10	Viola	
	11	Cello	
Link	12–13		
'Mouvement'	14		
Dotted theme, motive A	14	Violin II	
	15–16	Violin I	
SECTION A'	17–27		11
(Second 'verse')			
Dotted theme, motive A (as opening)	17–20	Violin II	

(continued)

---

[38] Collaer/Galante, *Darius Milhaud*, 195.

(Fig. 3.6 continued)

	Bars		Total bars
New countertheme (pentatonic idea: derived from B¹)	17–21	Violin I	
Dotted theme, motive A (reinforcement)	21	Violins I/II	
Link (1 + 2; 1 + 2 bars)	22–7		
Dotted theme, motive A	24–25	Cello	
SECTION B 'Au mouvement'	28–44		17
Dotted figure (from motive A; chromatic identity from B)	28–40	Cello (upper strings: chordal)	
Dotted rhythm (from A)	36–9	Infiltrates all parts	
Link: 'Très lent'	41–4		
Fragment of dotted theme (motive A)	43	Violin II	
SECTION C	45–68		24
Link	45–8	Tutti: chordal texture	
Fugato	49–64		
Fugal subject (from chromatic motive B²)	49–56	First stated on Cello	
Climax of movement	65–7		
Chromatic dotted theme (from motives A and B)		Tutti presentation	
Link back to recapitulation 'Très retenu'	67–8		
SECTION A 'Mouvement du début'	69–80		12
Recapitulation (condensed, varied)	69–75		
Integral CODA	76–80	Chordal texture	

As a starting point, Appendix Ex. 3.1 gives a polymodal view of bars 1–3, operating in D major/minor, and e and a 'minors', perhaps offering something close to Milhaud's interpretation (see Ex. 3.1*a* and *b*). The diatonicism of motive A on violin II: 4-10 (A,B,C,D) contrasts with the chromatic lines of viola (motive B^I inverted) and cello (motive B^I): 5-1 sets on (D♯,E,F♮,F♯,G) and (D,E♭,E♮,F♮,F♯) respectively, as the first of several polarities (Ex. 3.1*b*). This exlusivity of material is nicely articulated in terms of Forte's pitch-class set genera,[39] as shown in Ex. 3.1*c*. The 4-10 set of violin II is assigned, by means of Forte's 'Rule of Singleton Extension',[40] to Genus 7, itself regarded as embodying a 'chromatic-diatonic synthesis'.[41] One 'progenitor' of Genus 7 is evident motivically as the subset 3-2,[42] whilst the other, 3-7, is arguably implicit (A,B,D; A,C,D), although its importance only becomes apparent later (bars 17ff.) in more overtly pentatonic contexts. Meanwhile, the chromatic material of viola and cello beneath subscribes in the main to Genus 5 (chromatic), which embraces both its progenitor sets: 3-1 (the triplet figure F,E♭,E♭), and 3-2 (implicit as the modal framework of the bass (D-F,E,D)), together with the 'singleton set' 4-1, and 4-2, 5-1, and 5-2.[43] Some sets have duplicated representation in respect also of Genus 6 (semichromatic),[44] whose progenitor sets 3-3 and 3-2 are also present. If one chooses, however, to invoke Forte's Status quotient (Squo) to establish the genus with primary role, Genus 5 is firmly endorsed, as evidenced by the reduced matrix in Fig. 3.7.[45] Although the Squo rating is affected by the small size of Genus 5 in comparison with Genus 6 (leading to its greater proportional representation), Genus 5 does in any case seem the most suitable choice in reflecting the collective, total chromaticism of lower strings. Additionally, Genera 5 and 6 may be viewed compositely as Supragenus II, and thus one can consider a generic complementation between this Supragenus and Genus 7.[46]

---

[39] Forte, 'Pitch-Class Set Genera'; see also the initial discussion of this article in Chapter 2 above.

[40] Forte, 'Pitch-Class Set Genera', 234, Rule 4: 'The Rule of Singleton Extension causes pitch-class sets which are attached to only one genus ("singletons") to engage that genus in its entirety'.

[41] See 'Genus 7' in Forte, 'Pitch-Class Set Genera', Appendix, 265, and designation of the characteristic 'chroma-dia', ibid., 201.

[42] The 'progenitor(s)' may be seen as the 'source-set(s)' from which any genus may be deemed to emanate. For further discussion, see Forte, 'Pitch-Class Set Genera', 190–2.

[43] See 'Genus 5' in Forte, 'Pitch-Class Set Genera', Appendix, 265.

[44] See 'Genus 6', ibid.

[45] The actual calculations, as given in Fig. 3.7, were arrived at as follows: Squo (G5) = ((6/8)/29) = .259; Squo (G6) = ((5/8)/45) = .139; and Squo (G7) = ((3/8)/45) = .083.

[46] Having said this, given some level of chromatic common ground between these materials, the genera involved are not in fact as different as they might be.

Figure 3.7 Fourth Quartet: II ('Funèbre'), bars 1–3
Matrix to show Sets in relation to Genera

Potential Genera:	G5	G6	G7
Sets			
3-1	o		
3-2	o	o	o
3-3		o	
4-1*	o		
4-2	o	o	
4-10*			o
5-1	o	o	
5-2	o	o	o
Counts:	6	5	3
	G5	G6	G7
	[SG II]		

Counts	Squo Indices in descending order with Genera
6	.259: G5 (chromatic)
5	.139: G6 (semichromatic)
3	.083: G7 (chromatic-diatonic)

* denotes a 'singleton' set

Alternatively, embracing these elements within a single term of reference, one might also view the viola/cello ostinato and the dotted theme of violin II as making use of complementary segments of a Dorian-type mode on d, as shown in Ex. 3.1*d*.[47] The material of viola and cello is carefully organized, the two parts being related by a mixture of inversion and transposition (Ex. 3.1*e*); between bars 1 and 3, sets 4-1 and 3-3 sets are exchanged and then transposed from D to E♭ and vice versa (Ex. 3.1*f*). The overall modal perspective is focused on the common pitch D, with the chromatic pitches (D♯/E♭) inessential, and the conflict which exists between the pitch patterns of viola and cello is appropriately mirrored by the rhythmic conflict of duplet versus triplet.

This is borne out by Forte's Table 23 'Genera Comparison: Difference Quotients' ('Pitch-Class Set Genera', 221), which gives a reading of .31459 for the extent of difference in the opposition of Genera 7/6, and one only slightly higher at .46759 for the opposition of Genera 7/5. This is within the context of a 'maximally different' (or genuinely complementary) reading of .87058.

[47] A similar scalic division is employed later in *La Création du monde*: see Case Study 5 below.

The introduction of violin I at bar 5 (with motive B²) bridges the upper and lower segments of the mode on d, as shown in Ex. 3.2*a*. With the second violin's fragment here, the dotted figure (of motive A) has now been combined with the chromatic character (of motive B)—the first suggestion of a potent fusion which will lead ultimately to the climax of the movement. Thus there is a new generic homogeneity between the violins, with exclusive invocation of the chromatic Genus 5. As with cello and viola, the two upper voices are connected by inversion, starting in this case with interval class 11, and creating a chromatic, contrary-motion device common in Milhaud's early music (Ex. 3.1*b*). With the entry of violin I, the modalities of the four separate lines, D/d, e, f, a, tend to support the main centre of d, by outlining its triad (Ex. 3.2*a*). Continuing the idea of complementary segments, observed in bars 1–3, the pitch contents of violins I and II between bars 1 and 7 are exactly complementary: violin I, 4-1 (F,G♭,G♮,A♭); violin II, 8-1 (A,B♭,B♮,C,D♭,D♮,E♭,F♭), as illustrated in Ex. 3.2*c*. This represents the ultimate polarity of pitch and arises through extensive chromaticism.

Bar 9 is the subject of Ex. 3.3, commencing once more with the type of polymodal perspective which Milhaud would be likely to have endorsed (Ex. 3.3*a*). The recurrent principle of inversion between the violins is highlighted in Ex. 3.3*b*, the process also commencing at interval class 11. The final Ex. 3.3*c* charts the continuing set-theoretic perspective with Genus 5 maintaining its profile in embracing sets 3-1, 4-1 and 4-2. Rogue elements appear in the form of the 4-24 set (of Genus 2 or 4?), and, more importantly, set 4-7, a member exclusively of Genus 8. Although the reference here is very much *en passant*, this set has quite an illustrious career across Milhaud's music of the 1920s.[48]

The chordal transitional passage between bars 12 and 16 (shown in Ex. 3.4*a* and *b*) acquires an octatonic flavour. Set 5-32 is featured four times in bar 12 (and again at bar 23), with a horizontal 4-28 (0,3,6,9) framework evident across the four transposed chords, and the whole subscribing clearly to the diminished Genus 3 (of Supragenus I). Ex. 3.5 focuses in more closely on the octatonic pitch patterning of bar 12. Four pitches (B,A♭,F,D) and their semitonal transpositions (C,A,F♯,D♯) form the octatonic collection Model A: 0,1,3,4,6,7,8,10 (B,C,D♮,D♯,F♮,F♯,A♭,A♮) also used in *Machines agricoles* (Case Study 2).

---

[48] See especially Case Studies 3 and 7.

Early Exploration: Chromaticism

A more traditional harmonic interpretation would acknowledge triadic combination at the minor third interval: (A♭/B), (F/A♭), (D/F), (B/D).

Moving back briefly to the larger-scale Ex. 3.4, there is a significant discontinuity at the 'Mouvement' of bar 14, with the appearance of the 5-35 pentatonic set, arranged in perfect fourth intervals, with set 3-9 on lower strings (indicative of the diatonic Genus 11).[49] The invocation of Genus 11 is sandwiched between brief references to Genus 7 (implied by 4-10 (and 5-25)) in a resurfacing of violin II's opening argument, but is consolidated in bars 15–16 by occurrences of the singleton set 4-23, and the other progenitor, set 3-7. The localized discontinuity of diatonic/pentatonic language, however, provides an aspect of large-scale unity, since pentatonicism is both a continuing form of reference from the opening 'Vif' (to be resumed in the finale), and since its reintroduction at bar 14 heralds a more sustained projection by violin I at bar 17.

The 'Funèbre' has a verse-type structure, in the manner of a strophic song, so that a varied repeat of Section A occurs at bar 17 (Ex. 3.6*a*), with violin I developing further the pentatonic argument, in contradiction to the chromatic lines beneath—another instance of diatonic/chromatic polarity (and generic opposition), albeit mediated by isolated, staggered diatonic cells in viola and cello. Ex. 3.6*b* explores this further use of the pentatonic mode in more detail, identifying a main Collection 5 on b: (B,D,E,G,A,B), but one with inherent ambiguity of modal final and sense of 'modulation' to other pentatonic shapes (Collections 4, 3 and 2). ('Chords' here refers simply to aggregates of melodic pitches drawn from the violin line.) The modal partitioning after van den Toorn seeks to capture this fluidity, whilst the generic identity of this material is essentially a continuation of the diatonic Genus 11 (of bars 14–16), with a small-scale inflection as Genus 12 (signalled by the singleton set 4-26), creating a composite Supragenus IV.

In this 'verse', the compass of the second violin line is extended: the previous span between A and F♮ is modified to A and F♯, focusing on the C–F♯ tritone (bars 18 and 20: see again Ex. 3.6*a*). The framework of the violin II pitches across bars 17–20 is a diminished triad: set 3-10 (A,C,F♯), and is part of a continuing octatonic structure (as the

---

[49] The strength of the discontinuity is underlined by the Difference Quotient (Difquo) between Genera 3 and 11, measuring .81409 (much closer here to the 'maximally different' [complementary] .87058 than was the case in bars 1–3).

'progenitor' of Genus 3), confirmed by its association with the viola/cello pitches (E♭,G♭) in bars 19–20: the collection is still Model A, as used around bar 12: (B,C,D,E♭,F♮,F♯,A♭,A♮). Additionally, the lower string material invokes Genus 5 (and 6), as in the opening, thus producing something of a generic complex.

Bars 21–7, which link into the formal Section B (at bar 28), are examined in Ex. 3.7*a* and *b*. The octatonic perspective continues, involving a symmetrical structure composed of three axes, which provide a 3-10/4-28 diminshed framework: Axis 1 (B,D,F,A♭), Axis 2 (C,E♭,F♯,A) and Axis 3 (B♭,C♯,E,G). Open-headed and filled-in pitches (with beams) are used to differentiate between any two axes in operation at one time. Intervallic symmetry occurs with the (0,6)(0,3), (0,3)(0,6) patterning of Axes 2 and 3 (Ex. 3.7*b*, across bars 21–3), together with a symmetry of actual axes (and intervallic patterning) from the end of bar 22 through to bar 27: Axis 3 (Axis 1 embedded in the inner lines)—Axis 2 (centre of symmetry, at the essentially repeated bars 23/24)—Axis 3 (Axis 1 embedded). All sets examined in Ex. 3.7*b* produce another occurrence of Genus 3, though one should acknowledge the wider generic menu, as suggested in Ex. 3.7*a*, with further instances of the chromatic Genus 5 (especially cello), together with Genus 7 (inner strings), and the much less frequently invoked wholetone Genus 2.

From this point on the main structural arguments of the movement are all in play, so that it makes sense simply to summarize the remaining activity, and draw attention to occasional new ideas, or new combinations of pre-existing ones.

In Section B (bars 28–44), it is the cello that assumes the independent pentatonic identity (as had violin I at bar 17), whilst maintaining the dotted figure, with the upper three voices in rhythmic unison, and diatonic chordal homogeneity. The cello line subscribes initially to a Pentatonic Collection 1 on F♯ (F♯,G♯,A♯,C♯,D♯: bars 28–30), then re-centring on the D♯ (bars 33–6), whilst upper voices favour a largely white-note modality, with a Lydian/whole-tone melodic leaning. The following 4-21 tetrachords are invoked here: (F,G,A,B), (B♭,C,D,E), (D,E,F♯,G♯), with two augmented triads implicit within: (B♭,D,F♯) and (C,E,G♯). This is an effective illustration of increasing rhythmic and harmonic tension, reaching the first peak of the movement, heightened by careful use of register, at bars 37–40. Significantly, across these bars, the cello resumes once more its chromatic 4-1 identity. Thus these bars offer a development of the initial diatonic/chromatic opposition observed in the opening bars of the 'Funèbre'.

The 3-12, augmented triad hinted at above assumes a new significance in bars 41–4, marked 'Très lent'. Through similar treatment to that given to the 3-10/4-28 construct in bar 12, two semitonally opposed augmented triads, (D,F♯,B♭) and (E♭,G,B), a composite 6-20, provide an architectural framework for bars 41–2, now rooted back on the main pitch centre of D. The vertical occurrences are of 6-32, as against 5-32 at bar 12. This augmented construct on D is maintained across two repeated phrases of two bars' duration, bars 45–8, which link into Section C. And although one also perceives hints of an incipient blues third F♮/F♯ here, the main chordal set is 5-21 (F♯,C♯,B♭,D,A), together with subsets 4-19 and 3-12, all Kh-related to 6-20, and, furthermore, all members of the augmented Genus 4.[50]

Section C (bars 45–68) is distinctive in avoiding polarities of pitch or instrumental grouping. This main climactic part of the movement is strongly integrative and chromatic. Across bars 49–52, a chromatic fugal subject on D (from motive B²), first stated by the cello, and illustrated in Ex. 3.8*a* and *b*, seems to be a precursor to the fugue theme of *La Création du monde*. The two are connected by the common centre on D, the preoccupation with chromaticism—especially concerning the blues third F♮/F♯ (G♭)—and the choice of cello/bass for the first statement, with successive entries at increasingly higher pitches. Violin II provides the fugal answer a fourth higher on G, at bar 53, whilst the accompanying countersubject from bar 53 to 57 is an entirely chromatic affair, enlivened by occasional octave displacement (see again Ex. 3.8). Of greater significance is that, from its initial establishment of D (through a process of chromaticized voice-leading), the large-scale

---

[50] See Forte, 'Pitch-Class Set Genera', Appendix, 264. As with 3-10 in relation to the earlier presentation of Genus 3, the 3-12 'progenitor' of Genus 4 has a high profile in this passage. It is worth adding that juxtaposition of the predominant Genus 5 and the localized Genus 4 yields the highest Difquo (.87058), as the ultimate generic complementation, though one should acknowledge that the genera operate at rather different structural levels, and across varying time-spans. Paradoxically, although on the large scale the chromatic Genus 5 predominates over other generic concerns, on the small scale chromatic diminution is subservient to constructs such as the augmented triad. See comments on Section C below, including n. 51.

framework of cello pitches across bars 49, 53, and 57 emphasizes once more the 3-12, augmented triad (D,B♭,F♯).[51]

After a moment of repose on the F♯ pedal, across bars 57–8, as the viola assumes the subject on C, the cello again outlines the augmented triad, now in ascent. The framework is filled in by further chromatic passing notes grouped in fours—hence the recurrent set 4-1, now in quaver diminution. The remaining answer is provided at bar 61 by violin I, a further fourth higher, on F. Horizontally, all lines tally with the 4-1 set. At bar 61, the cello has a reiterated B♭, again part of the augmented triad axis, with the chromatic ascending line of bars 61–4 continuing to feature 4-1 groupings, the initial pitches of which outline a second augmented triad axis (E,A♭,C).

The real climax of the movement occurs across bars 65–7, with bar 65 characterized by the augmented triad first heard in the preceding four bars (E,A♭,C), with the addition of E♭ in violin I producing set 4-19 (and reinvoking Genus 4). Drama is heightened by the sudden rhythmic unison of all four voices on the chromaticized dotted figure (motives A and B combined), at a *fortissimo* dynamic, and with use of octave displacement from the fugal countersubject. These bars leading into the recapitulation are unified by the continued prolongation of 3-12 (E,A♭,C) as a horizontal framework, still filled in by the 4-1 chromatic sets. Set 4-19 remains the source of vertical reference, with occurrences at bar 65 (E,A♭,C,E♭), bar 66 [beat 3] (G♯,C,E,G), and bar 67 [beat 3] (C,E,G♯,B). In bar 68, the cello descends through the 3-12 triad: B♭–F♯–D, with the re-sounding of this D pitch having been carefully reserved for the start of the recapitulation.

The recapitulation is a much condensed version of Section A, typical of Milhaud's procedure in other early works. Bars 69–72 approximate to bars 2–5, with a reinvocation of the chromatic/diatonic polarities. The pentatonic pitch content of violin I, at bar 75, alludes to the second 'verse' which began at bar 17, followed across bars 76–80 by a brief coda which explores a harmonic area whose reference set might

---

[51] Thus, in simple generic terms, we have a continuation of complementary opposites in respect of the chromatic Genus 5 melded with the augmented Genus 4. Clearly though, such an observation also demands qualification, since, again, the genera are effectively operating at different levels. Furthermore, where small-scale replication is concerned (across bars 53–6), the decoration of an augmented triad framework by chromatic infill (or, conversely, the partitioning of a chromatic scale, within 4/4 metre, as 3 groups of 4 pitches which thus trace an augmented triad) is hardly remarkable.

be 5-21 (C♯,D,F♮,F♯,A), i.e. chord 'I⁷', with incipient blues third. (Set 5-21 was heard earlier at bars 45 and 47, within the distinct augmented framework of Genus 4, and its reappearance in this blues-type setting suggests its acting as a pivotal element, now relating to a possible Genus 9.) The emphasis is still on a simultaneous, harmonic clashing of major/minor third, as opposed to the more subtle, jazz-like 'bending' of the third degree. Nonetheless, the critical 'blues' chord 4-17 (D,F♮,F♯,A), the singleton tetrachord of Genus 9, emerges in its own right at bars 76–7, and forms the final sonority of the 'Funèbre', whilst the cello's pitches in the coda (D,F♯,A♯,C♯) bear some affinity with those at the start of Section B (bars 28–30).

By means of this cross-referencing, the movement is successfully unified, although even in these final bars, the chromatic/diatonic argument (with its articulation of generic oppositions) that occasioned the movement is not totally resolved. Paul Collaer expresses well this sense of denied repose:

> The tension is finally held by an appealing call on the cello, which drives the harmony towards a resolution that is desperately sought after, but which is not granted.[52]

Conclusion

The Fourth Quartet exhibits a wide range of scalic structures (and pitch-class set genera), including Ionian, Lydian, pentatonic, incipient blues and localized octatonic modes (of Model A). The pentatonic mode is used to achieve structural unity, by connecting the central 'panel' with the outer 'wings'. The characterizing intervals of the pentatonic mode include the major second and minor third, and, significantly, the pitch centres of the movements comprise these intervals (F,D/d,G) (0,2,5), i.e. set 3-7. An awareness of octatonicism provides a continuing structural framework where more conventional terms of reference fail: the Model A collection first appears in bar 12 and returns in bars 17–27, but is implicit across a larger time-span. In addition to the diminished triad framework 3-10, extended to 4-28 (i.e. Genus 3), and often an indication of octatonic activity, the 'Funèbre' utilizes an augmented triad framework 3-12 (i.e. 'progenitor' of Genus 4). In association with its 'elaborated' form of 4-19, 3-12 offers an important source of reference across bars 41–69 (including the climactic

---

[52] Collaer, *Darius Milhaud*, 312 (my translation).

point at bars 65–7), and is also relevant in the opening 'Vif', concerned with (F,A,C♮,C♯), and in the final 'Très animé', concerned with (G,B,D,E♭). In fact, collectively, the octatonic tetrachord (B,D,F,A♭) and the augmented triad (D,F♯,B♭) both serve to preserve the centre of the 'Funèbre' on D, though with inherent conflict between F♮/F♯ and B♮/B♭, as part of a complex process of complementation and polarization.

In the realm of rhythm too, ideas taken to their extreme in the 'Funèbre' (such as dotted-note patterns) are also discernible elsewhere. The opening 'Vif' features a simple, lilting crotchet–quaver pattern, leaving scope for the rigorous characterization in the 'Funèbre' as dotted semiquaver–demisemiquaver, and the fourfold augmentation of dotted crotchet–quaver. The latter pattern continues in the finale, which also features diminution at halved duration: dotted quaver–semiquaver.

The attention paid to details of pitch and rhythm contributes to the success of this central movement, and indeed to that of the whole Quartet. The 'Funèbre' illustrates well the varied features of the late Romantic/exploratory phase, founded on chromaticism, with a definite interest in exploiting polarity.

Employment of pitch-class set genera has enabled more detailed distinctions in the perception of a chromatic/diatonic opposition (or a bimodal complementation), and has also offered a measure of the extent of difference. Essentially, it has suggested a pitting of the chromatic Genus 5 (and 6) against the more diatonic Genera 7/11, together with high profiles for the strongly differentiated diminished Genus 3 and augmented Genus 4.[53] This movement also suggests that the seeds of Milhaud's developing interest in jazz were already sown. Thus analysis of the 'Funèbre' provides an appropriate starting-point to an investigative study of Milhaud's music in the 1920s.

✧

---

[53] The perception of Genera 3 and 4 as balanced opposing forces across the 'Funèbre' is supported by their high Difference Quotient of .85454 (the third from highest differential rating of a pair of genera out of a total of 43 readings): see Forte, 'Pitch-Class Set Genera', 223, Table 24.

CASE STUDY 2
Chromaticism and Canonic Devices in 'La Lieuse', from *Machines agricoles*, Op. 56 (1919)

Preliminaries

Machines agricoles was composed in Aix-en-Provence in 1919, and was first performed at the 'Concerts Section d'Or',[54] in Paris on 11 March 1920, with the soprano Madame Vié and ensemble (piccolo, clarinet, bassoon, violin, viola, cello and double bass) conducted by Félix Delgrange.[55] One wonders whether this set of six so-called 'pastorales' for voice and seven instruments, lasting about twelve minutes, is a witty *divertissement* in the same spirit as Walton's *Façade* (1923), or an entirely serious celebration of harvest, as Milhaud would have us believe. Whatever the answer, *Machines agricoles* is one of Milhaud's most unusual, experimental works, both stylistically and technically. Milhaud explains the background to the piece and its companion, *Catalogue de fleurs* (1920), in a chapter entitled 'Musique d'ameublement et pour catalogue' in *Ma vie heureuse*.[56] The inspiration for *Machines agricoles* stemmed from visiting an exhibition of agricultural machinery:

> I had been so impressed by the beauty of these great multi-coloured metal insects, magnificent modern brothers to the plough and scythe, that I thought of celebrating them in music.[57]

---

[54] In these circumstances it is always tempting to compare significant events in the music with the ratios of the Golden Section ($\approx$ 0.618/0.382). In fact the most significant finding does relate to 'La Lieuse' (34 bars' duration), whose Section B commences at bar 13 (0.382 ratio = 12.988). Frustratingly, the start of the second part of Section B (bar 20) is just one bar out from the closest whole-bar approximation to 0.618 (i.e. bar 21); equally, divisions across the six songs are very close to those of Golden Section, though also falling a bar short: Songs I and II contain 86 bars of a total 228 (0.382 ratio = 87.096), whilst Songs I–IV contain 140 bars (0.618 ratio = 140.904). (This is supported by a balancing of tempi and character of Songs I and VI, and II and V.) Other lesser observations are that song I (51 bars' duration) has its first intensifying *tutti* beyond the second half of bar 19 (0.382 ratio = 19.482); song IV (24 bars' duration) has its only *tutti* crescendo at bar 15 (0.618 ratio = 14.832); song V (20 bars' duration) has its first articulatory peak at bar 8 (0.382 ratio = 7.640), marked instrumentally by the conclusion of the first continuous string passage.

[55] Details from Catalogue compiled by Madeleine Milhaud, in Collaer/Galante, *Darius Milhaud*, 295.

[56] Milhaud, *Ma vie heureuse*, Chapter 16, 103–5 ('Musique d'ameublement et pour catalogue' [Furnishing and Catalogue Music]).

[57] Ibid., 104.

Milhaud goes on to say that he composed a small suite 'in the style of my little symphonies', with the original ordering of songs quoted in *Ma vie heureuse* differing slightly from that in the published score: II, III, IV, I, V and VI.[58]

Two writers offer usefully contrasted views of *Machines agricoles*: Martin Cooper suggests that the work has a 'strong pastoral vein, combined with the objective impersonal style of a shop catalogue, which it was fashionable to exalt at the expense of the hermetic poetry of the symbolists'.[59] He asserts that Milhaud is deliberately embracing the symbols of modern life, in a defiant, aggressive manner.[60] And although Cooper is quite right to stress the 'machinist', modernist aesthetic of this work (to some extent paralleling contemporary concerns of Futurism), he rather underplays the role that wit and sophisticated humour have to play within this scheme. Malcolm Hayes takes a more light-hearted view: 'Some settings from a catalogue of agricultural machinery, suggesting some wonderful uncharted regions of music theatre—members of the Nash Ensemble driving an assortment of reapers, mowers and drain-diggers around the stage of the Queen Elizabeth Hall'.[61]

Although Milhaud may have taken exception to Hayes's attitude, the reviewer is certainly justified in bringing to our attention this implied aspect of music-theatre within Milhaud's work. Milhaud himself complained that none of the critics writing at the time of the first performance understood what had inspired him to create the work. He parallels his intention in *Machines agricoles* with Honegger's desire to glorify the locomotive in *Pacific 231* and Fernand Léger's exaltation of machinery in the sphere of painting.[62] Contemporary critics cited Milhaud's work as evidence of his tendency to 'leg-pulling' and eccentricity, to which Milhaud retorted that he could not see why it should be imagined 'that any artist would spend his time working, with all the

---

58 Ibid.
59 M. Cooper, *French Music, from the Death of Berlioz to the Death of Fauré* (London, 1951), 190. Cooper is among the first to suggest that *Machines agricoles* marks the start of a fashion in the 1920s, followed by such works as Antheil's *Airplane Sonata* and Poulenc's *La Voix humaine*.
60 Ibid.
61 M. Hayes, *The Listener*, 6 February 1986, 41, reviewing a South Bank performance.
62 Milhaud, *Ma vie heureuse*, 105.

agonising passion that goes into the process of creation, with the sole purpose of making fools of a few of them'.[63]

Clearly, it is simplistic to subscribe to either extremity of view, yet Milhaud's apparent denial of the innate humour of the work is curious. Irony abounds, from the first incongruous juxtaposition of the ideas of machinery and pastorale—almost Dadaist in its bringing together of the mundane and the poetic. The music itself is outrageously 'mechanistic' in its employment of 'devices' that are deliberately predictable, sometimes even trite, such as the contrived exchanges of material between instruments in the first and last songs. Similarly, the rather pompous tone of the text, too, seems to invite a light-hearted and theatrical approach, with dramatic declamation: 'it is the truly economical drainage'![64] Surely there has to be significance also in the dedication of these six songs to the other members of that publically acknowledged clique of 'les Six', together with their impressario Jean Cocteau (the dedicatee of the first song, 'La Moissoneuse Espigadora'). The third song of the set, 'La Lieuse' (The Binder), dedicated to Francis Poulenc, has been selected as perhaps the most interesting: it will be approached by means of a mixture of post-Schenkerian voice-leading and set theory (particularly in order to investigate processes of chromatic complementation), together with some consideration of octatonic issues.

Analysis

Since the text is an integral part of the work, it is appropriate to consider this first. In fact, this setting of a section from a salesman's catalogue sometimes contradicts the natural stresses and importance of particular words, producing an intentionally artificial and 'synthetic' effect. The voice is used as another instrument of the ensemble with the text almost incidental, so that the result is similar to that in Walton's *Façade* where it is the sound and rhythm of the words, rather than their meaning, which matters most. In terms of balance, the singer has to work hard to be heard against the seven instruments, which include piccolo in its upper register. The text, divided into two parts, is as follows:

---

63 Ibid.
64 Quoted from the fifth song, 'La Fouilleuse-Draineuse' (The Digger-Drainer).

> Le bâti principal est entièrement en acier, cornières et tubes carrés; ce genre de tube a été employé parce qu'il offre plus de résistance à la torsion. Les chaînes sont extraordinairement fortes et durables et chaque d'elle est essayée à l'usine sous une traction considérable. Les rabatteurs ont un vaste champ de développement. Ils peuvent être relevés pour la coupe des récoltes hautes ou abaissés quand le blé est versé ou tourbillonné. Les diviseurs peuvent se plier. Ce qui est une commodité quand il s'agit de transporter ou de remiser la lieuse.
>
> Grâce à son tendeur, la durée de la toile de la platforme est prolongée. Les leviers sont convenablement placés, le levier d'inclinaison et le levier des rabatteurs sont sur l'avant entre les jambes du conducteur, le levier du lieur est à droite sous la main. Le levier du tablier est à droite du siège. La lieuse peut être élevée ou baissée au moyen de dispositif placé à cet effet à la roue motrice et à la roue à grain.[65]

In 'La Lieuse', the harmonic language of chromaticism and polarity previously encountered in the 'Funèbre' of the Fourth Quartet is developed further. This short ternary structure of regular 4/4 metre, marked 'rythmique', contains some passages of surprising harmonic angularity. On the large scale, two sections centred on B♭ are separated by a predominantly fugal, central section ('Moins vif'), loosely based upon the semitonal, upper auxiliary of B♮. A formal outline is given in Fig. 3.8.

Before discussing pitch structure in detail, it is helpful to consider texture, since modal diversity in this piece owes much to the textural diversity of superimposed, yet far from wholly unintegrated, contrapuntal strands which are at times suggestive of mechanical devices. At the extremities of pitch, the piccolo usually doubles the

---

[65] 'The main chassis is entirely of steel, with corner-irons and square tubing; this type of tubing has been used because it offers greater resistance to torsion. The chains are extraordinarily strong and durable, and each of them is factory-tested under considerable traction. The beaters have vast scope for development. They can be raised up for cutting tall crops or lowered when the corn is flattened or wind-swept. The dividers can be folded up, which is convenient when it comes to transporting, or putting the Binder away.

Thanks to its tightener, the wear of the platform canvas is extended. The levers are conveniently situated: the lever for tilting and the lever for the beaters are in front between the legs of the driver; the binder lever is on the right under the hand. The deck lever is to the right of the seat. The Binder may be raised or lowered by means of devices positioned for this purpose at the driving wheel and at the grain wheel.' (My translation)

Figure 3.8   'La Lieuse' from *Machines agricoles*, Op. 56: Formal Outline

TERNARY FORM

	Bars	Total Bars
SECTION A	1–12	12
Incipient blues mode on B♭		
Sub-divisions of phrase	1–5; 6–9	
Arrival on B♮	10–12	
SECTION B	13–26	14
'Moins Vif'		
Modality centred on B♮		
First canonic subject	13–15; 16–19	
Second canonic subject (heightened chromaticism)	20–6	
SECTION A'	27–34	8
Condensed return to incipient blues mode on B♭		
Integral CODA	32–4	

bassoon at four octaves' distance: a crazy set of gears, or cogs, running in parallel. This practice occurs during both the opening and closing bars, where the upper voice seems to be the more important of the two. Placed between them, the clarinet has a largely independent and ornamental part, creating a delicate filigree. The voice occupies both the middle of the pitch range and of the score layout, and is again largely independent (and incongruously 'pastoral'), though occasionally supported by the violin doubling an octave higher. In the string group, violin and viola are often paired, opening with a mechanical device of superimposed fifths (D,A,E), set 3-9. Cello and double bass have their own independent identities: the double bass is especially striking, focused upon B♭ yet with a prominent F♯.[66] The intervals are decidedly angular, mainly major sevenths and ninths, and the overall texture of the opening is dense, with considerable rhythmic repetition and conflicting patterns, typical of Milhaud's chamber music composed before 1920.

Nonetheless, much of the pitch activity in 'La Lieuse' can still be perceived in terms of post-Schenkerian voice-leading analysis, as demonstrated by Exx. 3.9, 3.10 and 3.11. Some sense of pitch priority is

[66] This initial attention to detail at foreground level, emphasizing (B♭–F♯), and suggesting a possible octatonicism, supports the later middleground reference pitches suggested in n. 71 below.

usually preserved, whether within chromatic, pentatonic, octatonic or other modal contexts. Certain traditional formulae are encountered: neighbour-note, third and fifth progressions, and occasional cadence, albeit unorthodox. A sense of hierarchy remains, so that even though the voice-leading analysis is not strictly reductional, there is still a distinction between the harmonic background and a more immediate foreground. It is possible to suggest an overall melodic descent from 3̂ (d3), although this clearly involves modal 'mixture', and the progression can never hold the significance of the *Urlinie*, or 'fundamental line', within a Schenkerian context. It may be, however, that the concept of a referential pitch collection, such as the ostinato (A,B♭,F♯,G), set 4-3, actually proves more helpful in attempting to characterize the movement.

Modally, the most important collection in Section A (and A') is an incipient blues scale on B♭, involving much chromaticism: (B♭,C,D♭/D♮,E♭,F♮,F♯/G,A♭/A♮,B♭). 'Incipient' is used to stress that the mixture at the third degree is relatively undeveloped, compared with its culmination in *La Création du monde*. Nevertheless, 'La Lieuse' uses the blues mode more authentically than any other song in *Machines agricoles*. In more localized contexts, one may consider possible octatonic collections, to be explored further below, while there are other bars which subscribe to the Aeolian on b♭, both with and without blues third (bars 33-4, and 7, respectively).

The opening of 'La Lieuse' is detailed in Ex. 3.9*a*, *b* and *c*. The first interpretation (Ex. 3.9*a*) establishes B♭ as the indisputable pitch centre, within a Class 1*a* harmonic context.[67] The incorporation of set theory in Ex. 3.9*c* produces clear patterning, with the 6-33 set of bar 3 seemingly the most appropriate reference set (its pitches (B♭,C,D,E,G,A) usually arranged so that perfect fifths predominate), encompassing 5-29, 4-23 and 4-26 within a Kh relationship. Unfortunately, one of the most important 'subsets' is, however, excluded from 6-33 because of its F♯ pitch: the bass ostinato set 4-3, (F♯,G,A,B♭). At the end of the song, the final bars 32-4 balance the opening, and are almost identical to bars 1-3, so that the conclusion also makes use of 6-33, and the problem of its non-compatibility with 4-3 persists. The non-compatibility of this language is underlined by pitch-class set

---

[67] Class 1*a* suggests that one centre predominates (i.e. B♭), but that other modalities, such as D 'major', have been absorbed within it. For further detail, and rationale, see Chapter 2, 'Suggested Types of Localized Bimodality', above.

genera, since all sets identified in Ex. 3.9c are members of the diatonic Genera 11 and 12 (Supragenus IV), with the greater emphasis on Genus 11 (as endorsed by the Squo measurement), the exception being the 4-3 ostinato which is a singleton set referable only to Genus 6.[68] Ex. 3.9c offers a 'reduced representation', focused primarily on Genus 11, so that other genera are invoked only in respect of sets which would otherwise be unrepresented, i.e. the singleton sets 4-26 and 4-3. From an outline of referential pitches, it seems that this opening passage might be elucidated by an octatonic interpretation.

Pursuing such octatonic possibilities, with reference again to Ex. 3.9a and b, the Model A collection (on B♭) generally proves more useful than Model B (on B♭), since it preserves the critical D♭/D♮ oscillation. In broad terms, bars 1–3 may be seen collectively to exhibit a type of octatonic complementation between Model A in the treble, and Model B in the bass. One could qualify this by saying that Model A (B♭,B♮,D♭/D♮,E,F,G,A♭,B♭) (0,1,3,4,6,7,9,10), is most applicable in its lower segment: (B♭–F); and that Model B (B♭,C,D♭,E♭,E♮,F♯,G,A,B♭) (0,2,3,5,6,8,9,11) is most relevant in its upper scalic segment: (F♯–B♭), i.e. the basso ostinato, set 4-3. In other words, the octatonic interpretation respects the same division as did the generic one; unfortunately, though, neither discrete octatonic collection (or even an unorthodox hybrid) is able to account convincingly for the prominence of third progressions, especially (B♭,C,D) and (D,E,F♯).

Beyond octatonicism, one might argue a case, particularly in bar 1, for a 'new' mode with a wholetone perspective: (B♭,C,D,E,F♯ [G,A],B♭). By bar 2, this is modified to a Lydian mode on B♭ with blues third and fourth: (B♭,C,D♭/D♮,E♭/E♮,F,G,A,B♭) and, by bar 3, to one with blues third and fifth: (B♭,C,D♭/D♮,E,F♮/F♯,G,A,B♭). Thus modal flexibility is demonstrated within the first three bars. On the large scale, the all-embracing blues-type mode (B♭,C,D♭/D♮,E♭/E♮,F/F♯,G,A♭/A♮,B♭) probably provides the best source of reference, in combination with set 6-33.

The first part of Section B comprises bars 13–19, the opening of which lies within a Phrygian-type mode on b♮, with incipient blues third: (B,C,D/E♭,E,F♯,G,A,B: see Ex. 3.10a). This move to a centre on b♮ represents perhaps the ultimate polarity in relation to Sections A

---

[68] The Squo calculations on a basis of seven sets: (3-7), 3-9, 4-3, 4-23, 4-26, 5-29 and 6-33, are as follows: Squo(G11) = ((5/7)/29) = .246; Squo(G12) = ((4/7)/45) = .127; and Squo(G6) = ((1/7)/45) = .032.

and A'. The identity of the mode, however, is soon compromised in bars 17–19, when it is challenged by that of the 'third relation' Mixolydian on G, suggesting a bimodal Class 1*a*; alternatively, in acknowledging the high profile of chromaticism, in the quasi-'note-row', one could move towards a non-tonal Class 4. The eight pitches of the mechanized (and fixed) Canonic Subject 1 are presented by the violin across bars 13–14 and 16–17: (B,F♯,G; C,A,E♭/D♯,D♮; E♭), set 8-26,[69] with a superficially Schoenbergian angularity (Ex. 3.10*a* and *b*). The few pitch repetitions tend to provide symmetry: e.g. 1,2,3,[2,1]. At one bar's distance, a second entry of the subject occurs on viola, as a slightly stricter presentation of these pitches, followed two bars later by the final violin entry. Against these lines, the voice offers a free melodic countersubject,[70] supporting the overall modality on b♮(/G), and consisting initially of an elaborated scalic descent. Three of the four pitches of the complementary 4-26 are presented by the clarinet 'free part' across the same bars: (F,A♭,B♭), set 3-7. These pitches are highlighted by registral placement, with B♭ representing the peak of the clarinet line (after which a short descent leads back to a sustained middle D♮ (d¹) at bar 16). The clarinet's 3-7 set, in bar 15, is also supported in the same bar by the voice on (E,D,B), whilst the remaining twelfth pitch C♯ is reserved as a 'leading-note' for d minor (bar 23: double bass). Thus the music moves both towards and away from tonal allusion; the texture is already imitative, though not as rigorously applied as across bars 20–6.

The second part of Section B (bars 20–6), has a somewhat bizarre pitch structure, with no clear overall centre.[71] What is far more evident is the striking linear opposition of chromaticism and 'white-note' diatonicism (Ex. 3.11*a*), with these bars involving a textural crescendo of intensifying activity prior to the reprise at bar 27. The main material is again presented in canon, as a distinctly clockwork device, accompany-

---

[69] By virtue of its complement equivalence with the singleton set 4-26 (incidentally also of relevance in the opening bars), set 8-26 is also, somewhat ironically, referable to the diatonic Genus 12.

[70] It is a moot point whether the voice accompanies, or is being accompanied. Indeed it is one of the ironies of this piece (as in the Fifth Chamber Symphony) that the apparent accompaniment (the mechanistic instrumentation) is often more engaging than the supposed vocal solo.

[71] In terms of the actual subject which predominates, a possible progression of centres across these bars is: B♭–d–F♯–d–(B♭), thus outlining the augmented triad—a favoured construct in Milhaud's early music, as used in the Fourth Quartet.

Early Exploration: Chromaticism 93

ing a free, diatonic vocal line (which, conversely, acts as a type of countersubject), with instrumental points of imitation always entering on E♭ at one bar's distance, shown in Ex. 3.11*a* and *b*. All instruments, including the clarinet, are now locked into this dissonant mechanism. This second chromatic 'note-row', stated initially by double bass, makes reference back to Section A, in that pitches 4 to 7 are the reversed pairs of the opening basso ostinato (A,B♭,F♯,G), set 4-3. The frequency with which major sevenths and ninths occur in the Canonic Subject 2 is reminiscent of passages in the 'Funèbre' of the Fourth Quartet of the previous year. As with Canonic Subject 1, eight pitches are presented, though now without any internal repetition: (1,2,3; 4,5,6,7; 8) (E♭,D,E♮; B♭,A,G,F♯; F♮), producing set 8-4 (exclusively of the atonal Genus 8). The pattern of pitch-groupings 3 + 4 + 1 is also identical with that of the earlier bars, whilst six of the pitches of set 8-4 are in common with those of 8-26, i.e. (E♭,D,E♮,A,G,F♯), thus indicating a measure of common ground beyond the generic distinction. Beyond the 8-4 set, the remaining four pitches (C♮,C♯,B,G♯: set 4-4) do occur soon after, though they are scattered within the more tonally orientated bars 21–2, with the use of C♯ still restricted until its reiteration in bar 23, as the leading-note of d minor.[72] Ex. 3.12 examines the 'prime form' and intervallic patterning of the Canonic Subject 2: reduced within an octave, the ordering of pitches within small cells favours an alternation of interval-classes 1 and 2 (in this respect exhibiting some similarity, albeit superficial, with octatonic scalic construction). In the complex tutti bar 26, immediately preceding Section A', the double bass places the now familiar C♯ on the first beat, followed by a horizontalized A^7, chord V of d minor, which then functions as a 'leading-note' to B♭.

The ensuing, condensed recapitulation (bars 27–34) contains no new material, but serves to emphasize the most salient features of 'La Lieuse': an underlying modality, including an increasingly important, if still incipient, blues scale, and localized octatonic activity, all of which is at times obfuscated by an intrusively high level of chromaticism.

---

[72] In addition to the C♯ functioning within d minor, it is of course also an enharmonic D♭ in terms of the B♭-based recapitulation (and possible melodic descents from a prolonged 3̂).

Conclusion

The employment, albeit limited, of pc set genera in this work has probably proved less useful than in the Fourth Quartet, although it has served to underline the presence of non-compatible materials, with the initial diatonic Genera 11/12 rubbing up against the 'semichromatic' Genus 6 of the 4-3 basso ostinato. This incongruence was maintained through Section B, with the first canonic subject, 8-26, still indicative of a continuing Genus 12, whilst one's perception of the second canonic subject as representing the most remote area of the piece was, up to a point, confirmed by set 8-4 being referable to the atonal Genus 8.[73] In qualification of these findings, one should add that there is a danger that use of the generic perspective may overplay the non-compatibility of materials in Section B since, conversely, this interpretation rather underplays the indisputable chromaticism already present in the first canonic subject (and thus a significant area of common ground with the second subject).

Machines agricoles, as a whole, makes use of a more varied technical vocabulary than either Milhaud's jazz-inspired, or his more clearly neoclassical, works. This repertory embraces the idiosyncratic, chromatic 'serialism' of the central section of 'La Lieuse', the emergence of an Altered Mixolydian mode (with flattened sixth) in the sixth (final) song, and a continuing interest in pentatonicism and complementary processes. In terms of the consequences of extreme chromatic activity, *Machines agricoles* is perhaps indicative of what Milhaud could and might have gone on to explore, had not the lure of neoclassicism—already evident in this work—proved too attractive to resist!

◈

---

[73] As the complement of 4-4, set 8-4 is referable to Genus 8 by virtue of the 'Rule of Singleton Extension': see Forte, 'Pitch-Class Set Genera', 234. Although, Genus 8 is nominally 'atonal', it is part of Supragenus III, which in respect of Milhaud's music is loosely styled as the 'Blues Supragenus': indeed 4-4 is one of two critical 'blues tetrachords'.

Early Exploration: Chromaticism

CASE STUDY 3
Dissonant Mechanisms in the Chamber Symphony No. 5, Op. 75
(1922)

Preliminaries

Milhaud's fifth *Petite symphonie* or *Dixtuor d'instruments à vent*, Op. 75 is a highly concise work of only five minutes' duration, consisting of three movements, 'Rude', 'Lent' and 'Violent'.[74] It is scored for piccolo, flute, oboe, cor anglais, clarinet (B♭), bass clarinet, two bassoons and two horns. The work was composed in Vienna and Warsaw during February 1922,[75] with the first performance in May 1923, given by the 'Société instrumentale à vent', in Paris. Publication was immediately taken up by Universal Edition, who publish the series of six chamber symphonies.

The Fifth Chamber Symphony is best understood in the context of the whole series, even though in some respects it stands alone; although the main discussion of the series is reserved for Chapter 5, it is useful to offer a brief summary here. Milhaud had composed the First Chamber Symphony in Rio de Janeiro in 1917, before working on the Fourth Quartet. Some four years later, he had completed the Fourth Chamber Symphony, or *Dixtuor d'instruments à cordes*, which is the closest companion piece for the Fifth, and is only slightly more substantial, at six minutes' duration; it is scored for four violins and two each of violas, cellos and basses. The Sixth and last of the series was composed in New York in 1923, for vocal quartet with oboe and bassoon, and shows increased emphasis on blues-scale procedures, especially in the finale.[76]

The question may be asked why the Fifth Chamber Symphony is being considered in a chapter concerned with 'exploration'. The reasoning here is that, although the general notion of a set of chamber symphonies owes much to a neoclassical aesthetic, the language of the Fifth Chamber Symphony is often idiosyncratic, or experimental. Al-

---

[74] An earlier version of this Case Study was presented at the Lancaster Music Analysis Conference (LancMAC, 1994).

[75] Milhaud was in Vienna with the Polish singer Marya Freund (the dedicatee of the Fifth Chamber Symphony), to meet Schoenberg, following the success of the French première of *Pierrot lunaire*, which Milhaud had directed.

[76] Further details on the background to the Six Chamber Symphonies, together with Milhaud's own views, are given in the introductory outline of Chapter 5 below.

though certain features are typical of neoclassical practice,[77] the language is less consistent: the first and last movements are in keeping with the more dissonant, chromatic syntax of the 'Funèbre' from the Fourth Quartet, or 'La Lieuse' from *Machines agricoles*, whereas the central movement makes more use of blues-scale procedures.[78]

Paul Collaer discusses Milhaud's style and methods in the Fifth Chamber Symphony, and regards this work as perhaps the finest of the set, commenting:

> Le premier mouvement, rude, entrechoque les instruments par des mouvements contraires, houleux. La partie lent est une chose frissonnante, d'une sensibilité inquiète et étrange. Sur de longs trilles s'appuie, comme une respiration oppressée, l'harmonie voilée des bois. La clarinette-basse déroule ses volutes étayées par les bassons et les cors en sourdine. . . . Le joyeux final retentit de violents piétinements et traduit un sentiment affirmatif, solide, volontaire.[79]

It is difficult to agree that the Fifth Chamber Symphony is necessarily the finest of the set: such an accolade is better reserved for the Sixth, or Fourth. The Fifth is an interesting, if flawed, work. Nevertheless, it illustrates well Milhaud's early experimentation, showing him, as did *Machines agricoles*, at a stylistic cross-roads, where other more atonal destinations might have been open to him had not the enticing qualities of 'le nouveau classicisme' proved too strong.

Although the Fifth Chamber Symphony is underpinned by a developing neoclassical aesthetic, and is imbued with his innate lyricism, analysis reveals an array of rigorously employed chromatic devices, involving both complementation and symmetry. Such devices operate in extended modalities (sometimes ill-defined, yet at other times themselves polarized as precarious bimodal constructions), as well as in more dissonant pc set referential contexts.

Additionally, textural and timbral effects operate across a broad spectrum, from opposition to synthesis between distinct instrumental

---

[77] See ibid.

[78] Blues-scale procedures are investigated in the introductory outline, and Case Studies 4 and 5, of Chapter 4 below.

[79] Collaer, *Darius Milhaud*, 335: 'The rugged first movement jostles the instruments together, by opposing, turbulent movements. The slow part is a trembling thing, with a troubled and strange sensitivity. The veiled woodwind harmony, like constricted breathing, leans on long-held trills. The bass clarinet unwinds its twisting line, supported by bassoons and muted horns. . . . The elated finale resounds with fierce outbursts and conveys an affirmative, solid and determined feeling.' (My translation)

Early Exploration: Chromaticism

groups. Complementation fuels the 'dialectic' (though not in a strict Hegelian sense) between solo and accompaniment, or in Birtwistle's preferred terms 'cantus' and 'continuum',[80] which helps to generate the form of the piece. Furthermore, pitch and texture are intricately linked by complementation, since chromatic complementation and symmetry are usually focused on the 'ripieno' (and, as in 'La Lieuse', ironically often more engaging than the supposed solo), whilst the 'concertino' is more freely and diatonically conceived. Thus one encounters in Milhaud the 'chromatic-non-chromatic dialectic' which Wallace Berry identified in Bartók's Third Quartet,[81]—in fact, Milhaud himself articulated similar ideas, which will be discussed and applied a little later.[82]

The analytical approach adopted is flexible, reflecting the varied nature of the music: a mixture of voice-leading and set theory (to investigate processes of chromatic complementation), together with octatonic axes (after Straus and van den Toorn) and, in the finale, Meyer's contextually determined 'implication-realization'.[83] The emphasis on polarity and balancing seeks to avoid an artificial overstating of unity, and presents dissonance, disjunct ideas and discontinuity as powerful, positive forces.

Analysis

I. Rude

The indication 'Rude' suggests that the movement should have a rusticity and rugged harshness of sonority in performance. Such a direction is in keeping with the dissonant nature of the harmony, though this is still within the bounds of a sophisticated and highly stylized music. In fact, the terms with which Milhaud heads the three movements: 'Rude', 'Lent' and 'Violent' are similar to the sequence employed later in the Clarinet Sonatina (1927): 'Très rude', 'Lent' and a

---

[80] These are the (perhaps more equally balanced) terms which Birtwistle uses in discussion of his own *Secret Theatre* (1984): 'Notes made by Harrison Birtwistle prior to composing *Secret Theatre*': extract reproduced in the programme notes for the first performance by the London Sinfonietta on 18 October 1984.

[81] W. Berry, 'Symmetrical Interval Sets and Derivative Pitch Materials in Bartók's Third Quartet', *Perspectives of New Music*, 18 (1979–80), 287–379, on 359.

[82] Milhaud, 'The Evolution of Modern Music in Paris and Vienna'.

[83] See Meyer, *Explaining Music*, esp. Part 2, Chapters 6 and 7.

final 'Très rude'.[84] As an analytical starting point, a formal outline of the opening movement is given in Fig. 3.9.

As with much of Milhaud's composition up to 1922, the language is highly chromatic, but, despite the contradictions, the opening 'Rude' does operate within an ill-defined modality on b, which tends to favour the minor third over the major, and which also invokes C♮ as a Phrygian inflection. It is dangerous, however, to classify the type of tonal/modal language too narrowly, because Milhaud is obviously exploring and broadening his terms of reference, in a way which at times results in atonality. Even if the music was conceived 'polytonally', in horizontal strands, the overall effect—at least on the small-scale—can be atonal.

Figure 3.9 Fifth Chamber Symphony: I ('Rude'): Formal Outline

TERNARY FORM

	Bars	Total Bars
SECTION A	1–9	9
Chromatic modality on b		
Reference set 4-7: (F♯,G,A♯,B)		
Introduction of all 12 pitches	1–3	
Octatonic axis: (G,E,C♯,B♭)	7	
(use of B♭ as substitute dominant; also the centre for movement II)		
SECTION B	10–20	11
Second statement of 4-7 material	10–14	
Chromatic, symmetrical patterns	15–16	
	19–20	
Substitute dominant: B♭	17–20	
SECTION A'	21–9	9
Contracted statement of 4-7	21–2	
Continuing principle of semitonal opposition		
Integral CODA	23–9	
Repeated cadential formulae		
Sets 4-7 and 4-1: modified octatonic collection		
Conclusion on blues chord: (F♯,D♯,B,D♮)		

---

[84] Milhaud's fondness for this carefully judged uncouthness of sonority is also evident through his use of the term much later, in the Quartet No. 17 (1950).

Early Exploration: Chromaticism

As in the nature of experimentation, the results are not always successful: pitch relations are sometimes poorly defined and there are probably too many diffuse ideas stated without development, using too many different pitches.

Setting aside the criticisms, dissonance clearly has a high profile, with harmony ranging between mild and strong dissonance. This may occur within contrapuntal and harmonic gestures, often by means of semitonal/tritonal tensions, and at both foreground and background levels. Dissonance may be linked with large-scale ostinati, or other smaller-scale patternings.

A new departure in Milhaud's early treatment of dissonance is his use of vertical semitonal relations, which can constitute important gestures at foreground/middleground levels, as with the referential set 4-7 (F♯,G,A♯,B) (the upper tetrachord of a harmonic minor scale), which forms the basis of the first elaborate complementary (and implicitly symmetrical) device. The 4-7 pitch collection is strongly associated with aggressive, violent sentiment here and elsewhere, often appearing as a defiant, accented gesture.[85]

Ex. 3.13 considers the opening of the piece (Ex. 3.13*a*: music; and Ex. 3.13*b*: a derived theoretical schema). As in the 'Funèbre' of the Fourth Quartet and 'La Lieuse' from *Machines agricoles*, particular 12-note principles (as a form of chromatic complementation) also apply in the *Dixtuor*. All twelve pitches are introduced across the opening three bars, as indicated by the circling of pitches in Ex. 3.13*a*, and their corresponding positions in the theoretical abstraction of Ex. 3.13*b*. The structure commences with set 4-7 (F♯,G; A♯,B), of the so-called 'atonal' Genus 8, as two semitonally opposed pairs of pitches, and is first extended upwards by the fifth pitch: C. Pitches 6 and 7 extend the two emerging chromatic fragments down by a further semitone: (F♮,F♯,G) 3-1 and (A♮,A♯,B,C) 4-1. The procedure of balancing chromatic pitches on either side of a theoretical axis of symmetry about G♯/A continues, and finally produces two pitch-exclusive hexachords: E♭–G♯ and A–D, articulated about the tritone (referable to the chromatic Genus 5). Set 4-7 is restated in bars 10 and 12, after which, in

---

[85] In addition to providing a strong source of reference in this opening 'Rude', the feature also permeates later, more overtly neoclassical works, as mentioned above in the introductory outline.

bars 13–15, set 7-1 (C–G♭) emerges, in the main, complementary to 4-7.[86]

The 4-7 referential set is expanded twice during the final section of the movement (Ex. 3.14*a* and *b*). At bar 21, the addition of C♯/D on piccolo and flute produces set 6-Z19 (still maintaining the 'atonal' Genus 8: Supragenus III), or two principal triadizations from the major third dyads of the original set, i.e. F♯,A♯,C♯ and G,B,D. Two bars later, the incorporation of a final pairing, D♯/E, produces 8-17 (referable to the 'atonal-tonal' Genus 9, also of Supragenus III), as a fusion of 4-7 and the chromatic 4-1, which acts as a referential superset.[87] The 8-17 material can also be viewed as a modified octatonic-type collection of two instrumentally opposed and pitch-exclusive 4-3 sets: A♯/B, C♯/D, against D♯/E, F♯/G; or indeed as a symmetrical modal process of adding two further minor thirds below the original dyads, and thereby producing two seventh constructs: d♯^{7} and e^7.

This brings us to Milhaud's own possible perspective on this passage, through the vehicle of the composer's article 'Polytonalité et atonalité' (1923). Although viewing his resultant sonorities as pitch-class sets does nicely highlight theory in practice where set 6-Z19, specifically, is concerned,[88] presumably Milhaud would have regarded bars 23–9 (Ex. 3.14) as a superimposition of four overlapping triads, on d♯,e,F♯ and G, expressed in an equal minor/major 'mélange', as a doubled-up version of his 'inflection D'.[89] Polytonal theory also relates to practice in the discrete use of the 'black' and 'white' components of set 8-17, with piccolo and clarinet at bar 23 presenting the white-note construct in contrary motion (thus with a horizontal plane of symmetry), and pitted against the black-note version (flute and bass clarinet). Although Milhaud does not articulate this explicitly in 'Polytonalité et atonalité', he does cite the end of the second tableau of

---

[86] Again there is a tritonal/octatonic aspect, with (C–G♭(F♯)): the same pitches are in fact used in this way in the finale.

[87] This combination of 4-7 and 4-1 was in fact anticipated, though not consolidated, in an isolated occurrence, on oboe, cor anglais and bassoons, at bar 14 of Section B. Although set 8-17 is referable to Genus 9, as the complement of the singleton set 4-17, its significant subsets are other singleton tetrachords whose allegiance lies elsewhere. For further consideration of this point, see the conclusions on pc set genera in Chapter 6 below.

[88] 6-Z19 results from the superimposition of two major triads a semitone apart, as illustrated and discussed in Fig. 2.1, Chapter 2 above, derived from Milhaud's article ('Polytonalité et atonalité', 32).

[89] Milhaud, 'Polytonalité et atonalité', 33. See also Chapter 2, Fig. 2.2.

Petrushka, with its C/F♯ superimposition, as an illustration of his 'Chord VI', and later quotes a black/white opposition in Satie's *Parade*.[90]

Referring again to Ex. 3.14, and the theoretical schema of Ex. 3.15, one should acknowledge the high musical profile, within the 8-17 material, of its complementary 4-17: this 'blues set' is presented as harmonic pastiche in a second inversion chordal format which embraces the final bass note, and uppermost pitch: (F♯,D♯,B,D♮). Additionally, with specific reference to Ex. 3.15*a* and *b*, the pitches not represented by the 8-17 collection would constitute an occurrence of 4-17 once more at the tritone: (F,G♯/A,C),[91] and, across bars 26–9, the main pitches of the first horn (C,E,G,B♭), set 4-27, beg the resolution to these 'missing' pitches, though this is not forthcoming. The attractive incongruence of the horn's melodic fragment based in the Mixolydian on C creates a further Phrygian relation to B, whilst the final sonority of the horns produces another tritonal relationship: E–B♭. The emphasis on the flattened seventh B♭, as the uppermost pitch of a seventh construct, also bears testimony to Milhaud's increasing preoccupation with blues procedures, just a year before embarking on his most thorough exploration of this inflectional phenomenon in *La Création du monde*.

To digress briefly, it may be worth considering a contemporary 'cult' which seems to have a bearing on the Fifth Chamber Symphony. There is, as mentioned earlier, a great fascination with, and respect for, mechanisms in Milhaud's music of the 1920s: the most obvious illustration is of course the subject-matter and treatment of *Machines agricoles* (Case Study 2). Some two years earlier Stravinsky had composed his Study for Pianola (1917), and one is reminded here of Cocteau's tag applied to the new French music of Auric, amongst others: 'musique à l'emporte-pièce', literally 'punched-out [production-line] music'.[92] Other contemporary manifestations of the 'machinist' phenomenon include Antheil's *Airplane Sonata* and *Ballet mécanique* (1925), in which he collaborated with Léger, as well as Hindemith's unpublished *Musik*

---

[90] See again Chapter 2, Fig. 2.1 and discussion (from Milhaud, 'Polytonalité et atonalité', 32–3, 35).

[91] It is worth noting that G♯/A marked the centre of symmetry in bars 1–3, with F and C the first pitches added beyond the 4-7 set.

[92] In *Le Coq et l'arlequin*, according to Collaer/Galante, *Darius Milhaud*, 20, though not in the version printed in *Œuvres complètes de Jean Cocteau*, 11 vols. (Paris, 1946–51), ix (*Le Rappel à l'ordre*), 13–69. See also Milhaud, *Ma vie heureuse*, 83: 'il réclamait une musique dite française, à l'emporte-pièce.'

für mecanische Instrumente (1926), and Mossolov's *The Iron Foundry* (1927). As alluded to earlier in this chapter, in 1924 Milhaud himself published an article in *L'Esprit nouveau* (originally given as a lecture at the Sorbonne earlier that year), on 'Les Ressources nouvelles de la musique (jazz-band et instruments mécaniques)', whilst an earlier issue of that same journal, in 1921, had seen Le Corbusier's article, 'Le Purisme', on 'mechanical selection', as a successor to 'natural selection'.[93] Even Ravel declared that 'My own *Bolero* owed its inception to a factory. Some day I should like to play it with a vast industrial works in the background.'[94]

One can also make association with the world of film, a genre to which Milhaud contributed several scores, including that for the experimental *La P'tite Lilie*, Op. 107 (1929). Two years earlier, Fritz Lang's dramatic *Metropolis* had first been screened, whilst the satirical stance on the new factory-governed life was perhaps epitomized by Charlie Chaplin's *Modern Times* (1936).[95]

In this opening movement of the Fifth Chamber Symphony, the various chromatic and rhythmic devices of the 'ripieno' may be regarded as musical mechanisms. Casting an eye back over Ex. 3.13*a*, one is struck by the—surely deliberate—mechanical employment of the device associated with the 4-7 set. Rhythmically, the overall effect is of repeated semiquaver punctuation; yet within this, the alternating patterns and emphases of oboe/cor anglais against bassoons perhaps give a brief whirring semblance of the piston engines that came to fascinate Honegger. The short time-spans and abrupt phrasing mimic the stop-start of an on-off switch, whilst the grating semitonal dissonances hint at the cacophony of machinery. The very circularity of

---

[93] D. Milhaud, 'Les Ressources nouvelles de la musique (jazz-band et instruments mécaniques), *L'Esprit nouveau*, 25 (1924); A. Ozenfant and C.-E. Jeanneret [Le Corbusier], 'Le Purisme', *L'Esprit nouveau* (1921), repr. in R.L. Herbert, ed., *Modern Artists on Art: Ten Unabridged Essays* (Englewood Cliffs, NJ, 1964), 58–73. For further information, see also N.J. Troy, *Modernism and the Decorative Arts in France: Art Nouveau to Le Corbusier* (New Haven, 1991), esp. 216ff.

[94] M. Ravel, 'Finding Tunes in Factories', *New Britain*, 9 August 1933, 367: reprinted in A. Orenstein, ed., *A Ravel Reader* (New York, 1990), 399.

[95] For further information, see E.A. Kaplan, *Fritz Lang: A Guide to References and Resources* (Boston, 1981), and J. McCabe, *Charlie Chaplin* (London, 1973), esp. 181–8. Milhaud, an aficionado of Chaplin's early comedies (screened in Paris from about 1917), had originally intended *Le Bœuf sur le toit* (or *Cinéma-fantaisie*) to accompany one of Chaplin's silent films.

motion and little varied repetitions are also in keeping with the metaphor.

Developing this notion within a neoclassical aesthetic, one might view *Fortspinnung* ('sewing-machine music') as a possible eighteenth-century equivalent of the machine aesthetic, as a means of leading to the versatile dialectic involved in re-thinking 'ripieno' and 'concertino' (often in association with bimodality). Comparing Ex. 3.13*a* and Ex. 3.16*a*, which cover the same opening bars, the 4-7 'ripieno' mechanism (pitches 1-4) is presented antiphonally against the 'concertino' of flute and clarinet (pitches 6-12), and is mediated by bass clarinet, with something of a dual function in its trilled pitch 5 of C♮. Ripieno material (usually highly chromatic) is indicated by shaded blocks, concertino material (generally more diatonic and melodic) by open blocks, and the more ambiguous connective material (often employing trills, or a modicum of chromaticism) by single hatching.

Frequently Milhaud's concertino lines 'dissolve' into chromaticism before being absorbed into the ripieno, at which point a new soloist, duo or trio, moves into the spotlight. Chromatic infiltration thus acts as a metaphor for mechanization. This is demonstrated for the first time by the hint of chromatic activity in flute and clarinet, in bar 3, which heralds an immediate repeat of the 4-7 mechanism in bar 4, and a cue for the subsequent horn solo entry in bar 5. Milhaud himself was sensitive to this chromatic-diatonic dialectic (a type of bimodal complementation): indeed, in his other main article of 1923, 'The Evolution of Modern Music in Paris and Vienna', he suggested that 'Diatonicism and chromaticism are the two poles of musical expression'.[96] And so, perceiving his music, at least partially, as an expression of this polarity seems especially apt.

By the end of the first movement (Ex. 3.16*b*), the ripieno-concertino dialectic is somewhat different. Flute and piccolo, originally members of the concertino, have been absorbed to form the expanded semitonal mechanism at bar 21; only the first horn, with its incipient blues motif, manages to maintain diatonic independence. Mechanization is in danger of taking over, but for the time being the momentum is rhythmically reduced and the tension diffused: the clockwork machinery winds down from semiquavers, through quavers, triplet crotchets and standard crotchets, to a final semibreve.

[96] Quoted in S. Messing, *Neoclassicism in Music, from the Genesis of the Concept through the Schoenberg/Stravinsky Polemic* (Ann Arbor, 1988), 124.

Focusing finally on the central section of the movement, Exx. 3.17 and 3.18 present two illustrations of a more overt set symmetry (bars 15–16, 19–20). Intricate mechanisms in four, and then six parts emerge as a product of total chromaticism in conjunction with contrary motion and voice-exchange,[97] and serve to anticipate the expansion of the 4-7 mechanism in the recapitulation. Regarding possible association with film techniques, the magnified attention to detail here creates the effect of a cinematic 'close-up'. The four-part progression (Ex. 3.17*a* and *b*) extends from extreme dissonance (semitonally opposed) to relative consonance ('tonally' opposed), and back again. This observation is well supported by the resultant pitch-class set genera: 4-1 (× 2: chromatic G5), 4-10 (chromatic-diatonic G7), 4-23 (diatonic G11), and back again. It should, though, be acknowledged that the nature of the dissonance in, for instance, the 4-1 set, is affected by registral placing: Milhaud favours wide, angular spacing of sevenths and ninths, only occasionally requiring the harshest close-position spacing.

In Ex. 3.18*a* and *b*, the six-part device consists of four main convergent lines (horns and bassoons), plus two divergent clarinet lines. The structure commences with the B♭/D♭ dyad, which has been sustained by the bassoons since the end of bar 16, and leads to a centre of pitch-class symmetry (set 6-30) as the bass reaches C♯/E, with G/B♭ above. The total sets of the ripieno produce the formula: 3-2; 5-2 (inc. 4-10: Genus 7); 6-Z10 (inc. 4-17: Genus 9); 6-30 (inc. 4-28: diminished Genus 3), and back again. The pattern is completed at the arrival of the bass on E/G. Thus an axial construct, set 4-28, on B♭, C♯, E and G, does seem to function as a substitute dominant (a 'polar' opposite) to the outer sections on B♮.

As regards the theory behind Milhaud's practice of total chromaticism, in 'Polytonalité et atonalité' he does of course imagine, as the ultimate extreme, the superimposition of twelve chromatic keys (triads), and the consequent 'escape from tonal feeling'.[98] And despite the blurring of the edges, in failing to distinguish fully between keys and triads, the main thrust of Milhaud's theoretical argument is applicable to this passage of his music. Milhaud talks also of a 'force

---

[97] Although there was a similar two-part structure in the 'Funèbre' of the Fourth Quartet, both the four-part and six-part versions represent a new departure, with increased complexity. The device does occur, albeit less frequently, in the later 1920s: see n. 29 above.

[98] Milhaud, 'Polytonalité et atonalité', 38.

sonore', a 'power of sonority', which can result from polymodal tensions;[99] and, with reference again to Ex. 3.18, the dynamic surge and increasingly frequent and prominent embellishments which herald the return at bar 21 are supported by the increased (i.e. six-part) chromatic 'force sonore'. And, although audibility of pitch priority is lost in the amorphous chromaticism of these bars, it is still fascinating that the 4-28 construct of Section B is the pitch-exclusive complement of 4-17 (B,D♮/D♯,F♯: Section A'), taken compositely with its tritonal mirror of (F,G♯/A,C), as shown in Ex. 3.19. Thus the theoretical relations between the material of Sections A/A' and B involve a complex of interlocking, complementary constructs of 4/8-17 (Genus 9: Supragenus III) and 4/8-28 (Genus 3: Supragenus I).

II. Lent

A formal summary of the 'Lent' is given in Fig. 3.10. Ex. 3.20*a* quotes the opening of the movement, based on the semitonal lower neighbour-note of B♭, with its theoretical abstraction and voice-leading interpretation in Ex. 3.20*b* and *c*. A composite complementation is presented, with a textural/instrumental opposition, and the rigorous semitonal pitch-symmetry of a new ripieno mechanism which produces subtle timbral distinctions of the chromatic set 5-1 (B♭,C♭,C♮,D♭/D♮), of the recurrent Genus 5. The mechanized pattern involves reorderings of a 4-1 cell, in constant relation to a B♭ pedal: (C♭: 1, C♮: 2, D♭: 3, D♮: 4); (2 1 3 4); (3 2 4 1); (4 3 2 1), after which the scheme is reversed (Ex. 3.20*b*).

The abstraction of the second flute line (Ex. 3.20*b*) reveals further blues 'mélange' at the third, within this modality on B♭. The seventh degree (A/A♭) receives similar treatment at the beginning and end of the bass clarinet solo, with the motivic set 4-4 (B♭,A♮/A♭,F), of the 'atonal' Genus 8, recurring in transposed form both in the finale (bar 9), and, perhaps most distinctively, in the Middle Section of the Fugue from *La Création du monde*. Milhaud's increasing fascination with blues melodic inflection, contemporary with the Fifth and Sixth Chamber Symphonies, is a subject much discussed both in his autobiography and in *Études* (1927).[100]

---

[99] Ibid.
[100] See the introductory outline of Chapter 4 below.

Figure 3.10 Fifth Chamber Symphony: II ('Lent'): Formal Outline

TERNARY FORM

	Bars	Total Bars
SECTION A	1–15	15
Chromatic ripieno mechanism on B♭	1–7	
Opening statement of first theme: bass clarinet, with blues set 4-4[101] (Concertino/ripieno division)	3–7	
Move to G♭ modality	11	
Second theme: oboe	11–15	
Second theme: bassoon	14-16	
SECTION B (Development)	16–34	19
Thematic combination: flute, clarinet, cor anglais		
Bimodality: E♭/A; A♭/D	20–3	
Second theme: cor anglais	22–7	
Second theme: clarinet	27–32	
Chain of supporting seventh sonorities (4-27)	28ff.	
SECTION A' (Recapitulation)	35–43	9
Material condensed		
First theme: bass clarinet (final appearance)	39	
Final use of 5-1 set on B♭: (B♭,C♭,C♮,D♭/D♮)	43	

Ex. 3.21 illustrates bimodal complementation, as a precarious polarity between pitch centres a tritone apart: firstly A♮ and E♭, then D and A♭. (In terms of a possible film analogy, one could view the superimpositions that comprise this passage as a musical metaphor for the camera's 'double exposure'.) These combinations of two keys would be classified, within a single term of reference, as 'Chord VI', in Milhaud's theory, as expounded in 'Polytonalité et atonalité.[102] In Ex. 3.21, the tritonal relations are further supported by Lydian inflections in each mode, as a modified version of Milhaud's major/major combination,

---

[101] Note that set 8-4, the complement of 4-4, was also an important source of reference in Case Study 2 above.

[102] See Chapter 2 above. Milhaud cites the opening of Albert Roussel's *Fête de printemps* and part of Ravel's Sonata for Violin and Cello as further instances of this phenomenon, to supplement his initial example of *Petrushka* ('Polytonalité et atonalité', 33 and 34).

'inflection A'.[103] Also typical of Milhaud's neoclassical works is a tiny 'triad motive', denoted by α, and almost insolent in its diatonicism![104]

The final recapitulatory section runs from bars 35 to 43, in highly condensed form, with the final chord at bar 43 featuring, for the last time, the all-pervasive reference set for the ripieno: 5-1 (B♭,C♭,C♮, D♭,D♮). Tonally, one perceives a B♭ major/minor ninth chord, with mixture at the third.[105]

III. Violent

The finale, designated 'Violent', requires a fierceness and stridency not dissimilar to that of the first movement, and also continues the concertino/ripieno textural analogies of both preceding movements. A formal outline is given in Fig. 3.11.

This swift double-dotted march, projected tersely by clarinet (within a Mixolydian-type mode on G), and articulated percussively, somehow evokes the sound-world of the Berliner Band, and is strangely prophetic of the finale of Kurt Weill's Second Symphony (1933).

The overall modality of the finale is centred on C, though not without internal tensions, and the main source of pitch reference is that afforded by octatonic-type collections (nominally of Genus 3), especially Model B: (0,2,3,5,6,8,9,11) (C,D,E♭,[F♮,]F♯,G♯,A,[B,]C). There is inherent conflict between the diatonicism of the solo clarinet line (on G) and the strong tritonal relations (C–F♯), expressed by an alternating bass pedal. What is indisputable is that the process of semitonal opposition (with small cells of semitonal pairings), which has operated through the first and second movements, continues in the finale.

The clarinet's Mixolydian mode 'modulates' to the Lydian with a C♯ substitution (G,A,B,C♯) in bar 8, followed in bar 9 by a hint of the blues on A: (D,C♯/C♮,A), set 4-4.[106] The bass tritone (C–F♯) still dominates, with further exploration of this same dyad between bars 14 and 20, by means of a horn ostinato, of varying length, metric positioning and rhythmic presentation. In fact, there are five lengths and types of

---

[103] See Chapter 2 above.
[104] This triad motive is discussed in Chapter 5 below.
[105] This aspect of chromatic conflict is discussed in Chapter 4 below.
[106] This pitch-class set previously appeared in bar 3 of the second movement, on bass clarinet: (B♭,A♮,A♭,F).

Figure 3.11   Fifth Chamber Symphony: III ('Violent'): Formal Outline

TERNARY FORM

	Bars	Total Bars
SECTION A	1–13/14	14
Overall modality on C		
(Lydian inflection: C–F♯)		
Clarinet theme	1–4; 5–9; 10–13	
SECTION B	14/15–24	11
C–F♯: horn ostinato	14–24	
Clarinet theme	15–24	
Pentatonicism	14–16	
Ostinati (ripieno)	17–24	
Possible octatonicism:		
(C,D,E♭,F♮,F♯,G♯,A,B,C)		
SECTION A'	25–38	14
(Recapitulation)		
Overall modality on C		
Main theme: concertino of		
Flutes, Oboe, Clarinet		
Chromatic ostinato: ripieno	25–36	
Integral CODA	36–8	
Final chord: blues-type on C,		
with chromatic appoggiaturas		

ostinato operating between bars 14 and 24, but their centres on C,E,G,(B♭) tend to reinforce the sense of an overall centre on C.

The recapitulation of the main material (bars 25–38) is controlled by a final intriguing mechanism: a chromatic ostinato (in the ripieno, on cor anglais, bass clarinet and bassoons) of gradually increasing length, from one to nine crotchet beats (Exx. 3.22 and 3.23). These are the fixed mechanical elements against which the instruments of the concertino (piccolo, oboe, clarinet, and the first four pitches of the flute) present the main thematic material, transposed up a tone to the 'pseudo-plagal' form of the Aeolian on a (ambitus D–D), as shown in Ex. 3.22*a*. For an understanding of this structure, generated organically, an application of Meyer's contextually determined 'implication-realization' proves a useful ploy. In considering the horizontal process of implication-realization, reference is restricted to the bass line: the chromatic appoggiatura C♯–D on second bassoon (Ex. 3.22*b*). In order for Meyer's 'implication' to operate, there has to be repetition, so that the ear has gained familiarity with a particular piece of musical information;

only then is it possible to anticipate the next step of the pattern and for that step to be 'realized'. After the initial material has been stated on the strong beat, it is repeated and followed by the additon of a new element, E♭, following which the steps back to the initial C♯ are retraced. The ostinato has now doubled in length from one to two crotchets. Having added the extra semitonal step up to E♭, the rest of the growth process of the ostinato is already logically implied. The next repetition (of the 'known' element) implies a further new completion, the pitch E♮, which is then supplied and concluded by a return to the starting point, and so the elements consist of a statement and its reversion, articulated by means of a centre of symmetry. Each repetition is itself punctuated by the horns, with their own symmetrical semitonal gesture on G/A♭.[107]

This is 'implication-realization', to some extent mirrored by Straus's 'pattern-completion', because there is a sense in which the pattern—as we are familiar with it—is incomplete before the logical addition of each 'new' highest pitch. The process continues until the minor sixth above the (C♯–D) is attained: (A–B♭) in bars 35–6, at which point the ostinato has grown to nine beats' duration, once more starting on the strong beat of the bar.

There is also a vertical perspective to this symmetrical device (with a harmonic logic in completing the ostinato at this point), but before discussing this, attention should be drawn to an element which connects subtly between 'horizontal' and 'vertical' planes: if one adopts the filmic metaphor, this involves an object which is viewed from two different camera angles. A hexachordal set, 6-Z38 (C♮/C♯,D/E♭,G/A♭), common to concertino and ripieno, is found horizontally as a five-beat ostinato in the fluid flute line across bars 25–36, and as a vertical punctuation at every repeat of the ripieno pattern (as in bar 25 of Ex. 3.22*a*, and bar 34 of Ex. 3.23*b*). Harmonically, the workings of the device are demonstrated across the final nine-beat version of the ostinato (bars 34–6, Ex. 3.23*a* and *b*). Set 6-Z38(/Z6) is classified as a member of Genera 1/2, and thus, in generic terms, is unrelated to other material, though its chromatic perspective is unquestionable.

Furthering the vertical perspective, all twelve pitches are brought into play, simply and logically, with three occurrences of the chromatic set 4-1 (Genus 5), on C♮,C♯,D,E♭; E♮,F♮,F♯,G; and G♯,A,B♭,B♮, across a

---

[107] Compare with the F/G♭ occurrence on horns, across bars 13–15 of the first movement.

3-12 augmented triadic framework, with C♯–F–A bass pitches (see the chordal constructs numbered 1, 2, and 3 in Ex. 3.23*a* and *b*).[108] When the twelfth pitch is reached at the start of bar 35, there is opportunity for just one final upper neighbour-note embellishment, A–B♭–A, in the bass-line before the steps of the phrase are retraced.[109] In order to halt the process, Milhaud returns to the opening statement (C♯–D), and subjects this to repetition. With this achievement of horizontal and vertical pitch saturation (i.e. total chromaticism), the energy of both mechanism and finale has been spent—almost too quickly .

All that is possible now is the miniature two-bar coda, delivered in condensed 2/4 metre *fortissimo*, and consisting simply of a chromaticized V–I cadence in C. Appropriately enough, the main pitches of the final sonority present once more the 4-17 blues set C,E♭/E♮,G (with D and F♯ functioning as chromatic appoggiaturas to E♭ and G), and thus provide a correspondence in pitch-relations with the end of the first movement.

Additionally, there is a textural correspondence with the opening 'Rude', since the finale also presents a concertino-ripieno dialectic broadly concerned with a progression from diatonic-chromatic opposition to relative synthesis. Whereas at the conclusion of the first movement the first horn maintained melodic (diatonic) independence, in the finale both horns have been subsumed by the chromaticism of the ripieno. Indeed it was part of the horns' role to punctuate the repetitions of the ostinato, and drive the chromatic forces to their ultimate pitch saturation. The irony of bars 37 and 38, however, is that, there being nothing left to say in the chromatic domain, the syntax of all lines, other than those of the horns, is actually diatonic (though construed polytonally, and still creating resultant chromaticism).

Returning finally to the 'machinist' perspective, a further irony presents itself in that the ripieno mechanism fails ultimately because, albeit on a small scale, it has been over-extended. At the end of the finale, unlike that of the first movement, the machinery is not allowed to wind down. Visual imagery and analogy return. Picture 'Charlie as a semi-automaton in a factory, tightening nuts on double bolts on a

---

[108] See beats 1 and 3 of bar 34, and beat 1 of bar 35. C♯ provides a Phrygian tension against C♮, as at a similar point in the first movement.

[109] For the theoretical background, refer back to the marked segment of the Chromatic Matrix in Chapter 2, Fig. 2.5 above.

Early Exploration: Chromaticism

relentless conveyor belt',[110] or the scene in Lang's *Metropolis* where 'tired workers endlessly manipulate the levers that run the machines. One worker, unable to continue, allows his machine to go out of control and there is an explosion.'[111]

Perhaps, though, this is all too serious. Milhaud's own aesthetic in these tiny compressed symphonies accords rather better with that of contemporary cartoonists, whose few deft strokes produce caricatures, where the power of suggested meaning far exceeds the literal content. One could consider instead the early animation cartoons of Disney: what more appropriate analogy, indeed, than his set of small-scaled 'Silly Symphonies' introduced in 1929? After all, the first Mickey Mouse cartoons played on the aspirations of technological endeavour: *Steamboat Willie* of 1928, followed a year later by *Plane Crazy*, which was directly inspired by Lindbergh's solo flight from New York to Paris.[112]

In the journal *Comœdia*, of 20 December 1920, Cocteau described Satie's *Parade* in the following terms: '*Parade* is neither dadaist, nor cubist, nor futurist, nor of any school. *Parade* is *Parade*, that is to say a big play-thing.'[113] Whatever doubts one may have about the consistency of Cocteau's argument, the notion of a 'play-thing' is apt. Perhaps Milhaud's piece is simply a small play-thing: a deliberately crude, even clumsy, toy which is unduly strained by over-winding. The mainspring of the clockwork mechanism is subjected to ever-increasing tension— uncoiled further and further, so that bars 37 and 38 represent irrevocable mechanical failure: self-destruction. Extending the metaphor back to the music, the compositional process itself is taken to breaking-point, as an ironization, or parodying, of self-enclosed 'system'. As Milhaud himself says, it is only the 'absolute, organic necessity of initiating melody that will prevent these procedures from congealing into an otherwise still-born system'.[114] But the melody itself has been subsumed. So, the ending of the Fifth Chamber Symphony is inevitable; as in cartoon images of a defunct cuckoo-clock, the spring snaps.

---

[110] McCabe, *Charlie Chaplin*, 182.
[111] Kaplan, *Fritz Lang*, 48.
[112] R. Pickard, *The Hollywood Studios* (London, 1978), 252–3.
[113] Cited in Perloff, *Art and the Everyday*, 151.
[114] Milhaud, 'Polytonalité et atonalité', 44. See also Chapter 2 above.

Conclusion

The Fifth Chamber Symphony consists of an interrupted ascent from the centre on b♮ (through the 'Lent' on B♭), to the finale on C, a progression also used later in the Clarinet Sonatina (1927). Some similarities between the works have already been noted, concerning the character and markings of the movements; others hardly need amplification, such as the appeal of the clarinet to Milhaud in the 1920s.

The *Dixtuor d'instruments à vent* is a fascinating (albeit flawed) work of the early 1920s, concerned with total chromaticism, octatonic axial constructs, symmetries, complementary complexes of pitch, mode, texture and timbre. As Milhaud himself acknowledged in part of his autobiography where he described his early compositional experiences, 'I used to imagine, used to hear, music of an extraordinary freedom which it would have been impossible for me to write down. How could I express it?'.[115]

So the Fifth Chamber Symphony, particularly, represents a working-out of part of Milhaud's quest, and it is probably for this reason, i.e. the highly experimental, somewhat disparate, nature of the music, that pc set genera are not especially revealing. Nonetheless, the technique has emphasized the dominance of total chromaticism: 4-1, 5-1 (Genus 5), instances of localized octatonicism: 4-28/8-28 (diminished Genus 3), together with a predilection for constructs which inhabit that dangerous but seductive no-man's-land between tonality and atonality: 4-4 and 4-7 (with 6-Z19) of the 'atonal' Genus 8, and 4-17/8-17 (with 6-Z19 again) of the 'atonal-tonal' Genus 9. (These may be viewed collectively within Supragenus III.) Pc set genera also articulated nicely the wide-ranging linguistic palette of the mechanisms, albeit small-scaled, in Section B of the first movement.

Concluding by moving back towards tonality, in anticipation of Chapter 4 on jazz, blues and modality, the slow movement, in particular, demonstrates Milhaud's increasing interest in gestures associated with blues. In fact, he visited the United States in 1922, and soon after embarked on his major jazz-inspired project: *La Création du monde* (1923).

---

[115] See the epigraph to the present chapter, above.

CHAPTER FOUR

Brazilian and Jazz-inspired Music: Blues Scale

❦

Il me vint à l'idée d'utiliser ces rythmes et ces timbres dans une œuvre de musique de chambre, mais il me fallait auparavant pénétrer plus profondément les arcanes de cette nouvelle forme musicale dont la technique m'angoissait encore.[1]

Les voici à la tête d'éléments sonores et rythmiques absolument nouveaux et bien à eux, mais comment les utiliser?[2]

THE topic under investigation here is Milhaud's eclecticism—his interest in Provençal folksong and awareness of his Jewish heritage, and, more particularly, the influence exerted by Brazilian popular music, blues and jazz, together with his increasing desire to respond to these latter stimuli. As detailed in this chapter, Milhaud's travels to Brazil and the United States, from 1917 onwards, were of critical importance, enabling him to experience such styles at first hand, and thus facilitating his assimilation and subsequent reinterpretation, or reworking, of them within his own musical language. Milhaud's experience of travel connects directly with the concept of 'distance as space', both literally in terms of geography, and, by extension and association, in terms of cultural difference; these ideas are balanced in Chapter 5 by a parallel concern with 'distance as time' (and place). There is also connected common ground with Chapter 5 regarding what Joseph Straus calls the theory of 'influence as generosity', in terms here of a distinct ethnological musical tradition acting as 'a source of inspiration, a touchstone of musical value',[3] together with more limited application of 'influence as anxiety', and the consequent struggles of 'misreading'.[4]

[1] Milhaud, *Ma vie heureuse*, 100; partially translated and discussed on p. 12 above.
[2] Milhaud, *Études*, 54; translated and discussed on p. 12 above.
[3] Straus, *Remaking the Past*, 5. 'Influence as generosity' is explored by Straus in more detail as the second of three theories of influence, with reference to T.S. Eliot and Charles Rosen, ibid., 10–11.
[4] Ibid., 5, 12–20. These ideas are considered more fully in Chapter 5 below. On 'reading' and 'misreading', see also Meltzer, *Reading Jazz*, discussed later in the present chapter.

Before any apparent concern with music from other cultures, Milhaud was nevertheless deeply interested in the cultural tradition of his native France, often through literary settings; he was also strongly committed to his Jewish faith, and its associated heritage. The importance of French literature and early settings of poetry by Jammes, Latil, Lunel, Gide and Claudel has already been discussed in Chapters 1 and 3; in respect of the influence of Jewish liturgical and secular melody, one can cite the well-known *Poèmes juifs*, Op. 34 (1916), *Six chants populaires hébraïques*, Op. 86 (1925), *Deux hymnes*, Op. 88 ('Hymne de Sion' and 'Israël est vivant': 1926) and the opera *Esther de Carpentras*, Op. 89 (1925–27). These two interests remain constant throughout his career: indeed Milhaud's receptiveness to various examples of cultural 'otherness' may have been stimulated partly by his own position as a Jew in Provence.[5]

In 1917 Milhaud travelled to Rio de Janeiro as assistant to Paul Claudel, who had been appointed as the French minister there, during his war service. The two artists spent almost two years in Rio, returning to Paris in late autumn 1918. Milhaud was immediately attracted to the native music, which was the subject of his earliest article in *La Revue musicale*, published in 1920.[6] In *Ma vie heureuse* he explains his fascination with the rhythms of Brazilian popular music: 'Il y avait dans la syncope une imperceptible suspension, une respiration nonchalante, un léger arrêt qu'il m'était très difficile de saisir.'[7]

The products of the stay in Rio included the First and Second Chamber Symphonies (1917 and 1918), the Second Violin Sonata (1917), and the Fourth Quartet (1918), discussed in Chapter 3. However, the period also produced more strikingly original works, indebted to the Brazilian heritage and influenced by the Carnival of Rio, such as the fantastic polymetric (and polyrhythmic) ballet *L'Homme et son désir* (1918); this work is described in the score as a 'poème plastique', and is the first of many successful collaborations with Claudel.

The extraordinary textures in *L'Homme et son désir* are created by combinations of solo instruments. The ensembles include vocal quar-

---

[5] 'Je suis un Français de Provence, et de religion israélite' (Milhaud, *Ma vie heureuse*, 9). Thus he enjoyed a rich, dual cultural heritage, but also an awareness of difference and the sense of being, in some contexts, an outsider himself.

[6] Milhaud, 'Brésil'.

[7] Milhaud, *Ma vie heureuse*, 67: 'There was an imperceptible pause in the syncopation, a subtle catch of the breath, a slight halting which I found very difficult to grasp.'

tet; piccolo, flute, clarinet, bass clarinet; oboe, trumpet, harp and double bass; string quartet; and a percussion ensemble 'with drums of all shapes and sizes, cymbals, rattles, a triangle, a whistle, castanets, whips, and a hammer'.[8] Milhaud's purpose here was as follows:

> Je désirais conserver une entière indépendance, aussi bien mélodique, tonale, que rythmique à ces divers groupes. Je mis à exécution mes aspirations et sur ma partition écrite pour certains instruments à quatre temps, pour d'autres à trois, pour d'autres à six-huit, etc., afin de faciliter l'exécution, je marquai une barre de mesure arbitraire tous les quatre temps, en ajoutant des accents afin de conserver le rythme authentique.[9]

Later in 1918 there appeared a percussive sequel to *L'Homme et son désir* in the rather different form of *Deux poèmes tupis*, Op. 52. These remarkable, unpublished songs,[10] entitled 'Caïné' and 'Catiti', were inspired by native Indians of Brazil and Paraguay; the word 'Tupi' refers to both the people and the language of this tribe. Milhaud wrote the songs on Indian texts for four women's voices and hand-clapping (presumably involving his favoured technique of rhythmic ostinati): such was his striking originality of expression in this early period. (One is reminded here of Milhaud's best-known pupil, Steve Reich (b. 1936), who composed his own *Clapping Music*, for two players, in 1972.)

During his time in Rio, Milhaud heard traditional dance-forms, such as the chôros, tango and samba, but may also, where contemporary Brazilian composition is concerned, have heard music by the young Heitor Villa-Lobos (1887–1959) whose *Sexteto místico* appeared in 1917. Milhaud was certainly most inspired by the tango and samba, the former dance being of urban Argentine origin from the turn of the century, appearing in Europe and the United States about 1910, whilst the latter represented an older dance of Portuguese-Brazilian origin. In Brazil, the samba is a traditional form of carnival music and, authentically, is danced by groups of people in a circle. It has also been popularized in the ballroom, in stylized form and at a more moderate tempo.

---

8 Collaer/Galante, *Darius Milhaud*, 65.

9 Milhaud, *Ma vie heureuse*, 72: 'I wanted to preserve absolute independence, tonal and rhythmic, for each of the various groups. I realised my desire and, in order to facilitate the execution of my score, written for some instruments in common time, for others in triple time, and for others in 6/8, I inserted an arbitrary bar-line every four beats, adding accents to preserve the authentic rhythm.'

10 See Collaer/Galante, *Darius Milhaud*, 340: the manuscript is apparently missing.

The tango, as its complement, is performed at a more relaxed pace, and is an important source of inspiration behind *Saudades do Brazil*, discussed here a little later.

The Brazilian theme continues in some of Milhaud's first works composed back on French soil. Jean Cocteau was responsible for the (now rather over-exposed) pantomime staging of *Le Bœuf sur le toit* (1919), inspired by Brazilian dance material and loosely based on a much repeated popular song, 'O boi no telhado'. In *Ma vie heureuse*, Milhaud explains how 'je m'amusai à réunir des airs populaires, des tangos, des maxixes, des sambas et même un fado portugais et à les transcrire avec un thème revenant entre chaque air comme un rondo.'[11] The work exists in orchestral form, but also as a *Cinéma-fantaisie*, Op. 58*b* for violin and piano, and as a *Tango des Fratellini*, Op. 58*c* for solo piano. Although this divertissement met with immediate popular success, it cost Milhaud quite considerably where his longer-term credibility was concerned. The rest of his output seemed to be trivialized by association with *Le Bœuf*, so that he was labelled merely as a comic composer, with a 'music-hall-circus aesthetic'.[12]

Saudades do Brazil, Op. 67 (treated in part in Case Study 4) then appeared in 1920 as perhaps the most obvious tribute to Brazilian culture, apparently based, if only loosely, on the music of the Brazilian composer Ernesto Nazareth.[13] The collection comprises two sets of six tangos, with the formal characteristics of the dance providing an overall unity. Each tango evokes a district of Rio: Group 1 'Sorocaba', 'Botofago', 'Leme', 'Copacabana', 'Ipanema' and 'Gavea'; Group 2: 'Corcovado', 'Tijuca', 'Sumaré', 'Paineras', 'Laranjeiras' and 'Paysandú'. Each has a different character, despite duplication of structural devices: 'there is elegance in 'Sorocaba', tenderness in 'Leme', and brilliance in 'Ipanema'; and 'Gavea' explodes in rhythm and shattering harmonies before settling into amiable nonchalance.'[14] The final 'Paysandú' is, in Collaer's somewhat syrupy language, 'a serene meditation'.[15]

---

[11] Milhaud, *Ma vie heureuse*, 86: 'I enjoyed bringing together popular tunes, tangos, maxixes, sambas, and even a Portuguese fado, and transcribing them with a theme recurring between each tune like a rondo.'

[12] Ibid., 88.

[13] Palmer, Preface to Milhaud, *My Happy Life*, the recent English translation of *Ma vie heureuse*, 16.

[14] Collaer/Gallante, *Darius Milhaud*, 185.

[15] Ibid.

Returning to Paris after the end of World War I, one should explain briefly the cultural context in which Milhaud found himself, and which influenced strongly his creative output in the early 1920s. 'Primitivism', as exemplifying a Western perception of cultural 'otherness', is a most important artistic concept of this period, with clear application to *La Création du monde* and, indeed, already implicit in *L'Homme et son désir*. The concept is, of course, epitomized in its Russian inflection by Stravinsky's monumental *Le Sacre du printemps* (1913), which cast such a daunting shadow across the second decade, though the complex origins of primitivism in early modernist 'high art' stretch back across several decades.

In 1889, at that famous Exposition, the Parisian public was introduced to 'exotique' cultures of the Far East, perhaps most notably to the Javanese gamelan. Orientalism and exoticism emerged as potent forces in late nineteenth- and early twentieth-century Paris, although such notions also spawned more than their fair share of mediocrity in respect of shallow, stereotyped 'constructions' of the East, as perceived by the West.[16] At their most exemplary, the 'oriental' and the 'exotic' were manifested in paintings by Gauguin (whose Tahitian-inspired paintings were clearly also inextricably bound up with 'primitivism' itself), and Rodin (whose watercolours of 'Cambodian dancers' were produced in 1908), in dramatic costume designs by Léon Bakst, and in the music of Debussy, Ravel and Rimsky-Korsakov (whose *Shéhérazade* was produced in Paris in 1910).

In the first decade of the twentieth century, Picasso and Derain, amongst other artists, became fascinated by artefacts brought back from tribal Africa, and exhibited at the Musée Ethnographique. The year 1917 saw the celebrated exhibitions of *art nègre* organized by Paul Guillaume, who was perhaps the 'cheer leader for primitivism'.[17] *Art nègre*, as Negro/African art, became a phrase with almost a cult significance beyond World War I, regarded by some as the essential primitivist source, somehow separated from European/Oriental tradi-

---

[16] Cf. especially E.W. Said, *Orientalism* (London, 1978). For a more detailed musical exposition, see Watkins, *Pyramids at the Louvre*, 'The Orient', 13–60; and E. Brody, *Paris: The Musical Kaleidoscope 1870–1925* (London, 1988), 60–76.

[17] P. Rose, *Jazz Cleopatra* (London, 1989), 45. For further consideration of primitivism, see Watkins, *Pyramids*, esp. Chapter 3 'Out of Africa and the Steppes', 63–83; C. Butler, 'Subjectivity and Primitivism', in *Early Modernism: Literature, Music and Painting in Europe (1900–1916)* (Oxford, 1994), 106–31; and C. Harrison, *Primitivism, Cubism, Abstraction: The Early Twentieth Century* (New Haven, 1993).

tion, and thus representing a possible means of by-passing Bloom's 'anxiety of influence' of the immediate past.[18] Thus there is a temporal aspect to the present chapter, as well as to Chapter 5, except that the concern here is rather with the 'timeless', the idealism of apparent connection back to a 'primordium'.

Musically, a repertory evolved whose inspiration lay in a loose assemblage of American negro styles (especially cake-walks and ragtime), including Debussy's 'Golliwog's Cake-Walk' from the *Children's Corner* Suite (1908), Satie's 'Ragtime du paquebot' from *Parade* (1917), Stravinsky's 'Ragtime' from *L'Histoire du soldat* (1918), *Ragtime for Eleven Instruments* (1919), and *Piano-Rag-Music* (1919). It should perhaps be emphasized that composers in Paris at this time were generally unfamiliar with genuine blues and jazz, as distinct from ragtime (with Ravel's 'Blues' movement from the Violin Sonata, for instance, appearing in final form as late as 1927).

For many, including the poet/novelist Blaise Cendrars (with whom Milhaud collaborated in *La Création du monde*), there was celebration in the discovery of African and Negro culture,[19] as witnessed by the Pan-African Congress of 1921, and by Josephine Baker's success in the *Revue nègre*, presented (as was Milhaud's *La Création*) at the Théâtre des Champs-Élysées, in 1925. The response to *art nègre* was, however, double-edged: artistic fascination, coexisting with a barely concealed racism, evidenced for instance even in the poster design for the *Revue nègre*, which used gross racial caricature.[20] (Not for nothing does Phyllis Rose entitle one chapter of her biography of Baker 'Savage Dance'.) For those fearful of cultural submergence, 'Degeneration was the dark underside of Darwinian thought.'[21] This represents an apt point, perhaps, with which to cue the recent critical work of David Meltzer in his thoughtfully provocative, if idiosyncratic, source-book *Reading Jazz*, which will be referred to again in relation to Milhaud's explorations of jazz. Meltzer sees jazz in terms of 'forms of permissible racism', to the

---

18 For further on this, see again Straus, 'Toward a Theory of Musical Influence', in *Remaking the Past*, 1–20.

19 Chefdor, Cendrars's biographer, talks specifically of this sense of celebration: M. Chefdor, *Blaise Cendrars* (Boston, 1980), 74.

20 See the reproduction in M. Horsham, *'20s and '30s Style* (London, 1994), 76.

21 Rose, *Jazz Cleopatra*, 33. This stance is adopted, for example, in L. Stoddard, *The Rising Tide of Color against White-World Supremacy* (New York, 1921), with an introduction by Madison Grant, whose own *The Passing of a Great Race* appeared in New York in 1916; see also M. Muret, *Le Crépuscule des nations blanches* (Paris, 1925).

extent that without racism there is no jazz: 'jazz as mythology, commodity, cultural display is a white invention and the expression of a postcolonial tradition.'[22]

This, then, is the backdrop against which much of Milhaud's creative activity in the early 1920s should be viewed. The world of jazz held a deep fascination for Milhaud at this time,[23] and he made several visits to the United States, particularly New York, in 1918, 1922, 1923 and 1926 to experience jazz at first hand. This is in marked contrast to contemporaries such as Stravinsky, whose knowledge of rag-time was gained essentially at second hand, mainly through sheet music, although one should add that Milhaud did supplement his understanding with the Black Swan recordings that he brought back from the United States.[24] Milhaud's first encounter with 'cette école de rythme' was, however, provided in Paris in 1918, by the arrival of jazz-bands from New York.[25] His interest in the jazz-band was further aroused, in 1920, by the visit of Billy Arnold's Band to the Hammersmith Palace, in London. Indeed, this latter experience may have been the inspiration for *Caramel mou*, Op. 68, written for a jazz-band of clarinet, trumpet, trombone, piano, percussion and voice (or saxophone), for performance in a show at the Théâtre Michel in May

---

[22] Meltzer, *Reading Jazz*, 5 and 4 respectively. Lynn Haney's *Naked at the Feast: A Biography of Josephine Baker* (London, 1981) also considers the role of jazz, and perceptions of it. Meltzer and Haney both make the point that the term 'jazz' derived from 'jass' as a slang term for sex.

[23] 'Fascination' is the appropriate term here, and one usefully elucidated by Meltzer in the creative jottings of his 'Preamble': 'Most of the texts [on jazz] reflect this fascination, the creating and re-creating of a romantic other; acts Aldon Lynn Nielsen calls "romantic racism". (Implying a dialectic that polarizes between racism of hate and racisim of desire. Also suggestive of the impossibility of Romance; the participatory blindness of either two-way or one-way ardor.)'; and '"Fascination", another key word with roots in magic and magical empowerment.' (*Reading Jazz*, 9).

[24] Perloff cites two specific titles that Milhaud purchased in New York on the Black Swan label: *I wish I could shimmy like my sister Kate*, and *The wicked five blues* (Perloff, *Art and the Everyday: Popular Entertainment and the Circle of Erik Satie* (Oxford, 1991), 96). Milhaud's comments in *Études* suggest that he had also heard early recordings/performances of other specific blues numbers, including *Aunt Hagar's Children's Blues*, and W.C. Handy's *Saint-Louis Blues*. (*Études*, 57). Perloff elaborates on this, remarking that he 'probably [also] had opportunity to hear recordings of *St. Louis Blues* on the Pathé, OKeh, and Columbia labels when he was in New York in 1922' (ibid., 204).

[25] Milhaud, *Études*, 20.

1921. The style of *Caramel mou*, subtitled 'Shimmy',[26] is a curious mixture, reflecting Milhaud's increasing interest in jazz and the witty Parisian scene, and is dedicated to Georges Auric, one of the short-lived 'Groupe des Six'. The text is again that of Jean Cocteau and is an archetypal period-piece of the 1920s. In translation:

> Take a girl,
> Fill her up with ice and gin,
> Shake it all about,
> To turn her into an androgyne,
> And send her back home to Mummy and Daddy.
>
> Hello, hello Miss, don't hang up. . . . Miss, don't . . . don't hang up. . . .
> Ah! Oh! Oh! How sad it is to be King of the Beasts,
> Nobody there.
> Oh, oh, love really sucks. . . .
>
> Take a girl,
> Fill her up with ice and gin,
> Put a drop of angostura on her lips,
> Shake it all about
> To turn her into an androgyne,
> And send her back home to Mummy and Daddy.
>
> I once knew a guy really unlucky in love,
> Who played Chopin nocturnes on the drum.
>
> Hello, hello Miss, don't hang up,
> I was talking to . . .
> Hello, hello, nobody there.
>
> Take a girl,
> Fill her up with ice and gin,
> Don't you find that art is a little . . . ?
> Shake it all about,
> To turn her into an androgyne,
> And send her home to Mummy and Daddy.
>
> You say to your kid, 'Wash your hands',
> You don't say, 'Wash your teeth'.
>
> Soft caramel.

A considerable amount of information about Milhaud's 'love-affair' with, in Meltzer's words, the 'sexual utopia' of jazz can be gleaned from his various writings. In 'Rencontre avec le jazz' within *Ma vie heureuse*,

---

[26] A 'Shimmy' was a lively American ragtime dance involving much girating of the shoulders and hips. Hindemith also composed an example around this time, as one movement of his Suite for Piano (1922).

he makes comparison with Bach, as he stresses the rhythmic parameter of jazz: 'la musique syncopée exigeait la regularité d'un rythme aussi inexorable que celle de Bach, dont il est la base même.'[27] He is intrigued by the improvisatory syncopation and rubato superimposed on this regular rhythmic background. Melody and timbre were also part of the appeal of jazz:

> l'apparition . . . du trombone lyrique frôlant de la coulisse le quart de ton dans le crescendo du son et de la note, ce qui intensifiait le sentiment; et le piano reliait, retenait cet ensemble si divers mais non disparate, à la ponctuation subtile et complexe de batterie, espèce de battement intérieure, de pulsation indispensable à la vie rythmique de la musique.[28]

Milhaud details the instrumental roles of piano, percussion, trombone, trumpet, clarinet, banjo and violin within the jazz ensemble, and is fascinated by the use of glissando, portamento, vibrato, tremolo, oscillation and the variety of timbral expression.[29] In his opinion, blues style merits special attention: 'À cette cataracte sonore a succédé une mise en valeur remarquable des éléments mélodiques: c'est la période des "Blues".'[30] Milhaud continues by alluding to the idea of 'la mélodie depouillée': melody stripped of inessentials.[31] He also seems drawn by the sense of tragedy and desperation inherent in much negro spiritual song, as the expression of a persecuted people (with his empathy resulting in part perhaps from his own Jewish experience). As Milhaud remarks, thus also supporting the relevance of 'primitivism' in respect of his aesthetic outlook, 'Le côté primitif africain est resté profondément ancré chez les noirs des États-Unis et c'est là qu'il faut voir la source de cette puissance rythmique formidable'.[32] Further developing this

---

[27] Milhaud, *Ma vie heureuse*, 101: 'syncopated music required a regularity of rhythm just as inexorable as that of Bach, of which that rhythm is the very basis.'

[28] Ibid., 100: 'the lyrical use of the trombone, gliding with its slide over quartertones in crescendos of volume and pitch, thus intensifying the feeling; and the piano holding together the ensemble, so varied and yet not disparate, subtly punctuated by the complex rhythms of the percussion, a kind of inner beat, the vital pulse of the rhythmic life of the music.'

[29] Milhaud, *Études*, 20-1.

[30] Ibid., 53: 'From this eruption in sound there followed a remarkable development of melodic elements: this was the age of the "blues".'

[31] Ibid.

[32] Ibid., 56: 'The primitive African side has remained deeply rooted in the blacks of the United States and it is there that one must seek the source of this formidable rhythmic force.'

stance in connection with contemporary (mis)conceptions of 'the primitive' as, at some level, necessarily synonymous with 'the ancient', one can note Milhaud's comment concerning 'une Noire dont la voix granuleuse semblait sortir du fond des âges'.[33]

Milhaud rightly considered that in the early 1920s most American musicians had not realized the value of jazz as an art-form. He comments on his own views having been regarded with some astonishment: '"Milhaud admire le jazz", ou bien "Le jazz pèse sur les destinées de la musique en Europe".'[34] As expressed in the opening quotation of this chapter, he became convinced that he wanted to use these timbres and rhythms in a piece of chamber music, although first he needed to research further in order to increase his formal and technical understanding.[35] The answer to the second quotation at the head of this chapter, which questions how this new knowledge might be used, is surely to be found in *La Création du monde*.

With the composition of this piece, Milhaud became one of the first composers to assimilate successfully and imaginatively a variety of jazz techniques within classical art music. Most had, thus far, confined themselves to 'interpretations of dance music', by recreating the rhythms and set formulae of ragtime.[36] Stravinsky had written his ragtime pieces and those with a wider range of popular allusions, e.g. *L'Histoire du soldat*; but Milhaud went further, incorporating and synthesizing elements of the timbre, instrumentation and scalic forms of ragtime, blues and New Orleans styles within his own distinct aesthetic. His main concern was to absorb the emotional spirit of jazz, especially the melancholic, vocal inflections of the blues.

As Milhaud explains at the end of 'Rencontre avec le Jazz', his creative thinking at this time was also supported by avant-garde Parisian shows, such as that put on by Pierre Bertin in May 1921, in which Satie's extraordinary play *Le Piège de Méduse* was performed (together

---

[33] Milhaud, *Ma vie heureuse*, 115: 'a black woman whose grainy voice seemed to emanate from the depths of the ages'.

[34] Milhaud, *Ma vie heureuse*, 114. The quotations are apparently the titles of interviews given with New York journalists, though no exact sources are given. Meltzer confirms this perception: 'Europeans, especially French, British, and German, were first to fully receive jazz as art, as an aesthetic and expressive practice worthy of serious creative and intellectual engagement. America's initial difficulty with the music may have been due to vestigial nineteenth-century republican rigidities, its anti-urbanism, anti-intellectualism...' (Meltzer, *Reading Jazz*, 37).

[35] Milhaud, *Ma vie heureuse*, 100 and 116.

[36] Ibid., 100.

with Milhaud's own *Caramel mou*). Such imaginative ventures, like jazz itself, acted as catalysts for technical experimentation, leading to new means of musical expression:

> Les spectacles de ce genre, de caractère si varié, étaient excellents pour nous, ils nous permettaient d'expérimenter toutes sortes de techniques et de rechercher continuellement de nouvelles formes d'expression.[37]

That the opportunities for 'technical experimentation' which Milhaud so valued here existed in equal measure within his perception of jazz is evidenced, and balanced, by his opening statement in the essay on jazz in *Études*: 'La force du jazz vient de la nouveauté de sa technique dans tous les domaines.'[38] Thus he seeks to experiment with, and develop, the sources of his inspiration. He is not interested in mere pastiche, but in rethinking, reworking and intensifying what he finds, often involving an increase in complexity within both rhythmic and modal domains: hence, as possible examples of 'misreading', the tritonally-related seventh complexes of 'Ipanema' (Case Study 4), and the so-called polyrhythm, criticized by Hodeir, in the Fugue of *La Création du monde* (Case Study 5).

Some years later Milhaud disappointed American reporters by telling them that his interest had waned, the reason being that jazz had become official and won universal recognition.[39] He explains in *Ma vie heureuse* that, by 1926, there were even instructional manuals which analysed and dissected jazz as, in the apt words of Meltzer, 'bagged difference',[40] with the consequence that the popularity and explanation deprived the music of its spontaneous charm. Interestingly, in his corresponding comments in the more contemporary *Études*, he refers somewhat more ambivalently to the (implicitly 'white') music resulting from such instruction as 'cette musique mécanisée et aussi précise qu'une machine',[41] and, whatever the inappropriateness of 'mechanized music' for Milhaud in this context, it is useful to note his acknowledgement of the concept as deployed here in Chapter 3. Furthermore,

---

[37] Ibid., 102: 'Shows of this kind, so varied in character, were excellent for us: they allowed us to experiment with all sorts of techniques and to search continually for new forms of expression.'
[38] Milhaud, *Études*, 51: 'The strength of jazz comes from the novelty of its technique in all parameters.'
[39] Milhaud, *Ma vie heureuse*, 158.
[40] Meltzer, *Reading Jazz*, 40.
[41] Milhaud, *Études*, 56: 'this mechanized music, just as precise as a machine'.

in his detailed descriptions of the teaching of jazz (represented in both sources, but condemned more overtly in his autobiography), Milhaud illustrates well his own familiarity with its structure. That he was aware of all the following criteria, and may have incorporated them into his music, is most valuable from an analytical stance:

> Les différents moyens d'assimiler le jazz y étaient enseignés, ainsi que le genre d'écriture pianistique et d'improvisation; sa liberté dans un cadre rythmique rigoureux, toutes les échappées, les dissonances de passage, les accords brisés, les arpèges, les trilles, les embellissements, les ornements, les variations, les cadences qui peuvent surgir "ad libitum" comme un contrepoint d'une fantaisie extrême.[42]

He adds regretfully that

> Même à Harlem, le charme était rompu pour moi! Les snobs, les Blancs, amateurs d'exotisme, les touristes de la musique nègre avaient pénétré dans ses plus intimes recoins. C'est pour cela que je me retirai.[43]

Evidently Milhaud does not classify himself as a (white) musical tourist! Nonetheless, his stance is one which is well supported by Meltzer, who considers that 'jazz was mythologized, colonialized, demonized, defended, and ultimately neutralized by white Americans and Europeans. This is about the white invention of jazz as subject and object.'[44] From Milhaud's point of view, however, it is unfortunate that he did not maintain his interest long enough to hear the extraordinary genius of Louis Armstrong, who was emerging at this time.[45]

The second, more technical, part of this contextual framework is, as in Chapter 3, two-fold: to survey techniques derived from, or inspired by, Brazilian popular music and jazz, and to introduce Case Studies 4–5 which provide the main analytical illustrations to substantiate the out-

---

[42] Milhaud, *Ma vie heureuse*, 158: 'The various ways of assimilating jazz were taught there [at the Winn School of Popular Music], as well as the style of writing for the piano and improvisation; its freedom within a rigorous rhythmic framework, all the *échappées* and passing dissonances, the broken chords, arpeggios, trills, embellishments, ornaments, the variations and cadences which can arise "ad lib." as in some highly fantastic counterpoint.'

[43] Ibid.: 'Even in Harlem, the charm was broken for me! Snobs, Whites, amateurs of exoticism, tourists of negro music had penetrated even its most intimate nooks. That's why I gave it up.'

[44] Meltzer, *Reading Jazz*, 4.

[45] Armstrong had a significant presence from about 1918, joining King Oliver at Lincoln Gardens in 1922, and culminating in the establishment of 'Louis Armstrong's Hot Five' in 1925.

line. 'Ipanema' from *Saudades do Brazil* (Case Study 4) is inspired by popular Brazilian dance, and is a work mentioned *en passant* in Milhaud's chapter on jazz in his autobiography,[46] whilst *La Création du monde* (Case Study 5) is in some respects the centre-piece of the present book. Works showing the influence of Brazilian popular music and jazz are listed in Fig. 4.1.

Figure 4.1 Brazilian and Jazz-influenced Works

1918	[*Quatrième quatuor*, Op. 46 (III)]*
	[*Sonate*, Op. 47 (flute, oboe, clarinet & piano) (I)]
	L'Homme et son désir, Op. 48 (ballet)
1919	*Cinéma-fantaisie: Le Bœuf sur le toit*, Op. 58*b* (violin & piano)
1920	*Saudades do Brazil*, Op. 67 (piano solo)
	Caramel mou, Op. 68 (voice & chamber ensemble)
1922	[*Cinquième petite symphonie* (*Dixtuor à vent*), Op. 75 (II)]
	[*Sonatine pour flûte et piano*, Op. 76 (I)]
1923	*Trois rag-caprices*, Op. 78 (piano solo)
	Sixième petite symphonie, Op. 79
	[*Quatre poèmes de Catulle*, Op. 80 (voice & violin) (IV)]
	La Création du monde, Op. 81 (ballet: 17 solo instruments)
1926	*La Création du monde: Suite de concert*, Op. 81*b*
	(piano quintet)

* Square brackets indicate works also relevant in a different technical connection in Chapters 3 or 5.

As before, discussion of general principles of large-scale form and modality, including pentatonic, wholetone, Mixolydian and especially blues collections, is followed by more detailed consideration of structural procedures in Milhaud's employment of jazz, e.g. blues third/seventh, seventh chordal axes, harmonic riffs, chromaticism, third relations, rhythmic characteristics and metrical structures.

Ternary structures still predominate in Milhaud's Brazilian and jazz-influenced works, as in the tangos of *Saudades do Brazil* (1920), and the Romance and Finale of *Trois rag-caprices* (1923). Often the B section of an ABA form is third-related to the main modality, as in 'Sorocaba' from *Saudades*, based in B♭, with a central section in g 'minor', or 'Sumaré', based in G, with a central section in E♭. Additionally, there may be bimodality at the interval of a third. Extended ternary forms

[46] Milhaud, *Ma vie heureuse*, 99.

may also derive from the basic model, as in *Caramel mou* (1920), which has the following scheme: A (1–47), B (48–82), A (83–129), B (130–165), A (166–185) and Coda (186–203).

Rondo form has many illustrations in the jazz-influenced repertory: the Scherzo of *La Création* (Case Study 5), 'Gavea', 'Corcovado' and 'Tijuca' from *Saudades* and the 'Sec et Musclé' from *Trois rag-caprices* with the modification: AB/AC/ABA. The *Cinéma-fantaisie: Le Bœuf sur le toit* offers the best example of a loosely structured rondo-fantasy, sometimes simply a medley of ideas. The first part (bars 1–135) in C 'major', employs a large-scale 4-28 progression (C,E♭,F♯,A), as in the Fourth Quartet, and always moves from major to minor mode. Hence it is evident structurally that *Le Bœuf* is still an early work.

Milhaud's jazz-influenced repertory does employ stylized blues forms, such as the modified 12-bar form found in the Romance of *La Création du monde* (Case Study 5). Additionally, prelude and fugue are employed in the ultimate synthesis of jazz and Bachian techniques, again illustrated in Case Study 5 and discussed further in Chapter 6. Milhaud's Brazilian and jazz-influenced works are strongly centric, with less modal ambiguity than in the late Romantic/exploratory works. Pentatonicism seems to be the compositional source of Milhaud's Brazilian/jazz-influenced idiom, appearing mainly as a foreground phenomenon. The end of the first movement of the Fourth Quartet, for instance, composed in Rio de Janeiro, features a prominent submediant degree within what is essentially the Pentatonic Collection 1 on F: (F,G,A,C,D), as shown in Fig. 4.2. Although occasional inclusion of B♭ (and E) in bars 87 and 88 suggests a more expanded scalic form, bars 89–91 reduce to a pure pentatonicism across all parts which highlights pitch D($\hat{6}$), in association with C($\hat{5}$).

In the first and last movements of Milhaud's Fourth Quartet there are perhaps reminiscences of Dvořák's 'American' Quartet in F (brought about by the strong emphasis on the sixth scalic degree, D), as well as of Ravel's String Quartet in F (1903). Both Dvořák and Milhaud also make use of their native folksong idioms, whether Czech within an 'American' context, or French/Provençal. In most pentatonic collections one of the missing scalic degrees is the leading-note, with the minor third between $\hat{6}$ and $\hat{1}$ especially prominent. This phenomenon applies to parts of Milhaud's Fourth Quartet, the end of the Scherzo of *La Création du monde,* and a number of traditional negro spirituals. Thus, Milhaud's jazz and folk-influenced works may have a common

Figure 4.2 Fourth Quartet: I, bars 87–91

source in pentatonicism. Melodic and harmonic processes are inextricably linked, with exclusive use of (0,2,5) cells producing only mild dissonance within the vertical perspective.

The wholetone scale also forms an important localized source of reference, with its inherent tritonal framework. Melodic and harmonic perspectives are well illustrated across bars 186–96 of *Caramel mou*, the (0,2,4,6,8,10) collection operating on B♭ (B♭,C,D,E,F♯,A♭), with introduction of 'foreign' pitches F and G, used chromatically, as shown in Fig. 4.3.

Figure 4.3 *Caramel mou*, bars 186–9: wholetone collection

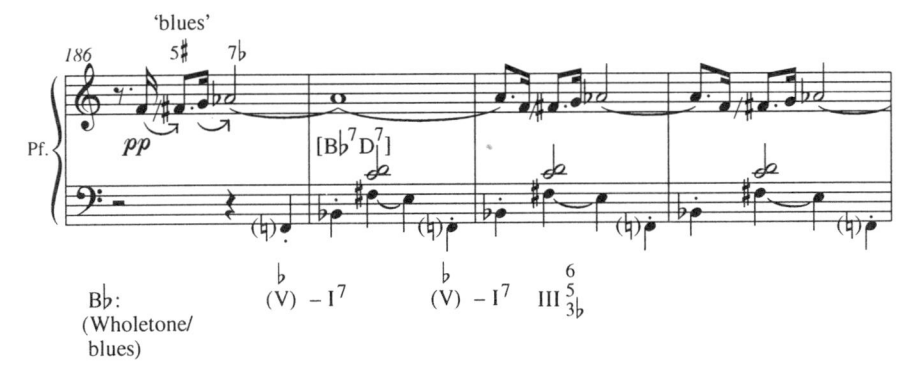

Aeolian and Mixolydian modes may be perceived at background level, such as the sustaining of Mixolydian on E♭ across the central section of 'Laranjeiras' from *Saudades do Brazil* (1920). This concept of background modality is demonstrated in the complete analysis of *La Création du monde* (Case Study 5), as well as in the neoclassical context of Chapter 5. Additionally, some limited bimodal conflict persists, as in 'Gavea' from *Saudades*, which has its first and final sections centred on C, but with A and F♯ conflicting in the central section. The overall progression of *Trois rag-caprices* (1923) also stresses tritonal relations between F♯ and C, with movements centred on F♯–F♮–C.

Undoubtedly, the most important modal collection here is a 'blues scale', whose salient feature, as noted in Chapter 2, is its blues third. The phenomenon of melodic blues third has its source in chromaticism, as mixture predominantly at the third scalic degree. This oscillation between minor and major third, or 'bending', is best suited to vocal technique (i.e. more microtonal) and can only be parodied on instruments with fixed pitches, such as the piano. Instances of the blues third phenomenon in Milhaud's music are numerous: it pervades the majority of his works between 1918 and 1926. The earliest instance (both melodic and harmonic) may occur in the first movement of the Third Quartet (1916), with its G♭/F inflection within an Aeolian modality on d;[47] this is followed by the finales of the Sonata, Op. 47 and the Fourth Quartet (1918): see Fig. 4.4*a* and *b*. The blues third surfaces again in the Flute Sonatina (1922) and the second movement of the Fifth Chamber Symphony (Case Study 3).

In 'strict' jazz only the horizontal expression of blues third is genuine, the vertical expression suggesting 'high art' pastiche, and frequently linked to large-scale third relations emerging from bimodality at the minor third. Centres on C and E♭, as shown in Fig. 4.4 for instance, produce a tonal axis in the manner of Straus's models for Stravinsky's music of the late 1920s/early 1930s: (C–E♭/E♮–G(–B♭/B♮)).[48] The essence of the blues third principle is found in the openings of *Caramel mou*, 'Sorocaba', 'Tijuca' and 'Sumaré' from *Saudades do Brazil*, *Trois rag-caprices*, and the second and third movements of the Sixth Chamber Symphony. This horizontal expression of blues third has a much higher profile in Milhaud's jazz-influenced compositions than in those of his contemporaries. The

---

[47] For illustration, see Chapter 3, Fig. 3.3.
[48] Straus, 'Stravinsky's Tonal Axis', esp. 265.

Figure 4.4*a* Sonata Op. 47: IV, bars 55–6
(also bars 2–3, 19–20, 25–6; 39–40, 44–5; 65ff.)

b Fourth Quartet: III, bars 18–21 (also bars 111–14)

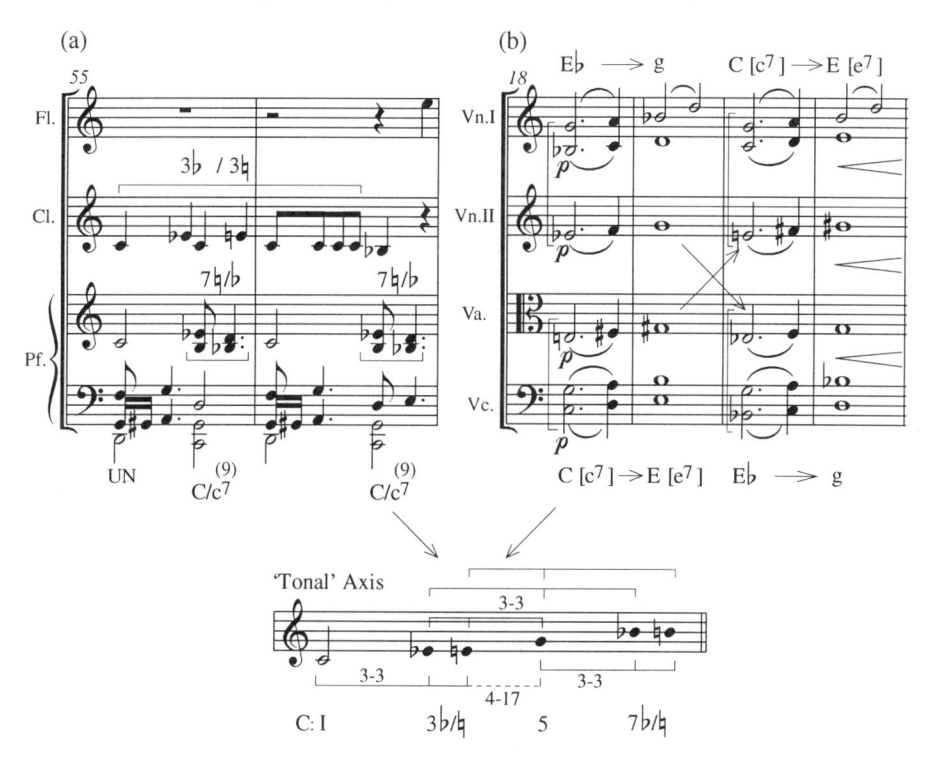

opening of *Caramel mou* (bars 1–6), which prolongs an initial structural 3̂, with 'mixture', and the ending of the Sixth Chamber Symphony (bars 25–7), shown in Fig. 4.5*a* and *b*, are typical, with the ultimate synthesis of vertical and horizontal presentation found in *La Création du monde*.

Large-scale blues third progressions can exist at background level, across a movement or work, such as occurs across *Quatre poèmes* (1923): (G–B♭–B♮–G), or across the *Suite de concert* version of *La Création du monde* (1926): (D–d–F♮–F♯–D). Even after the waning of Milhaud's interest in jazz, vestiges of blues third persist in the Seventh Quartet, *Les Malheurs d'Orphée* (Scene IX: 'Duo d'Eurydice et d'Orphée'), and the 'Opéras-minute'. The feature has become an instinctive part of Milhaud's vocabulary.

In addition to mixture at the third, the trait is encountered commonly at the leading-note, as a result of modal ambiguity between centres a fourth apart, a phenomenon exploited in the Fugue of *La Créa-*

Figure 4.5a *Caramel mou*, bars 1–6

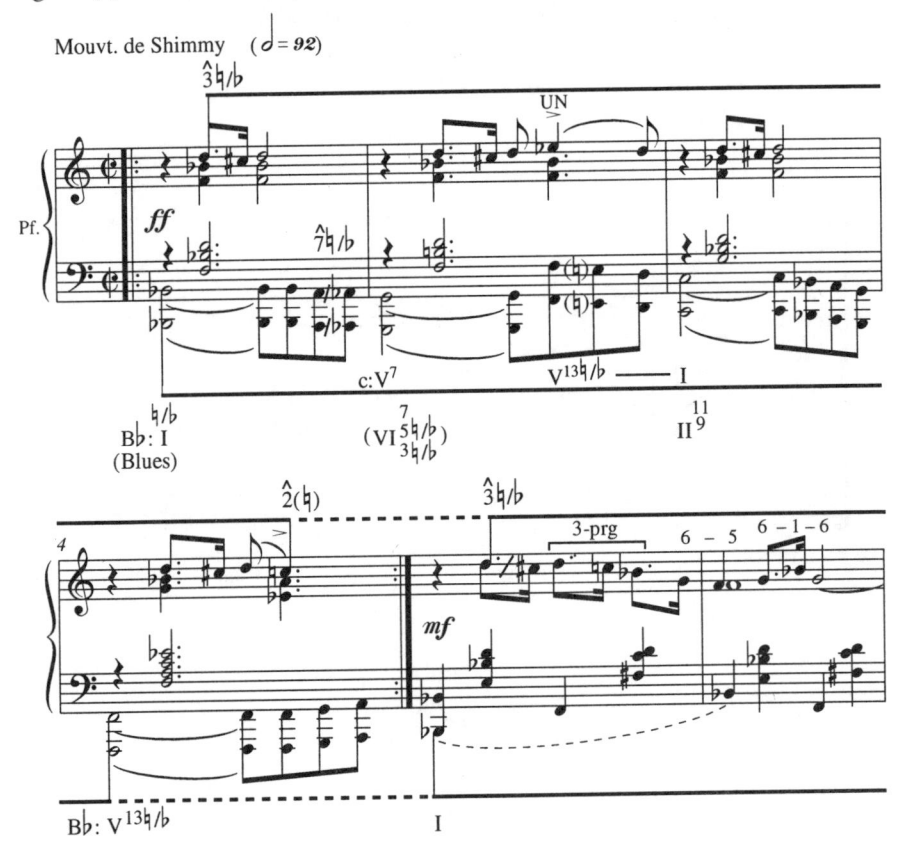

tion (bars 22–6). Other examples include the opening bass line of *Caramel mou* (see again Fig. 4.5a), the ending of the Sixth Chamber Symphony (Fig. 4.5b), and the second movement of the Fifth Chamber Symphony (1922). More rarely, mixture occurs at the submediant, as in the last of the *Quatre poèmes*.

Such specific treatment of blues pitches, involving microtonal intervals in performance, is still within the context of a more general continuing chromaticism, demonstrated in the Fugue of *La Création*, and in much of the passage-work for violin in the *Cinéma-fantaisie: Le Bœuf sur le toit* (1919). Additionally, at middleground level, semitonal relations are still part of the make-up, with similar transposed repeats of whole phrases.[49] The usual practice is to transpose sections up by a semitone, as in *Saudades do Brazil* or *Trois rag-caprices*. Although not restricted to

---

[49] For other examples, see Chapter 3 above.

Figure 4.5b Sixth Chamber Symphony, bars 25–7

the jazz-influenced repertory, there is a continuing partiality for third progressions, especially the small-scale, melodic kind. In the jazz-influenced repertory, progressions on F♯ are employed frequently, as in the openings of *Trois rag-caprices* and the Scherzo from *La Création du monde*.

There are several means of extending modal structures in the jazz-influenced repertory, some shared with the exploratory and neoclassical dimensions. Tonic and dominant pedals abound, as found in 'Sumaré' from *Saudades*. Another means of extending and securing the coherence of modal structure is by using a (dominant) seventh chordal axis, at any structural level. The V^7 and I^7 constructs (vertical or horizontal) are prominent at the conclusions of main sections, particularly at the end of the second movement of a three-movement work. This is an identifiable trait of traditional jazz, as an expression of the flattened seventh of Mixolydian or 'blues' modes. A seventh axis on (C,E,G,B♭), for instance, could be constructed along the lines of Straus for application in the F-based Romance in *La Création* (Case Study 5). The ultimate example may be a large-scale tonic seventh axis across 'Ipanema' from *Saudades do Brazil* (Case Study 4). Other examples of strategically placed dominant seventh chords are found in the second movement of the Flute Sonatina and in the second of the *Trois rag-caprices*, together with a significant tonic major seventh sonority at the end of *La Création*. Vestiges of the dominant axis are detected in the 'Lent' of the Clarinet Sonatina (1927) (Case Study 7).

The harmonic 'riff' is an acknowledged rhythmic/pitch formula for extending blues structures, as a jazz equivalent of ostinato, the effect extending to middleground level. Many similar illustrations are found in *Saudades*: 'Sorocaba', 'Gavea', 'Corcovado', 'Paineras', 'Laranjeiras', 'Paysandú' and 'Ipanema' (Case Study 4). The favoured pattern is tonic–supertonic–tonic, i.e. an upper neighbour-note progression. This substitution of supertonic for dominant in 'passages of vamping for example (especially in connection with Latin-American rhythms)', was first observed in Milhaud's operas by Jeremy Drake.[50] The clichéd gesture usually begins section A of the dance, almost as a mannerism (shown in Fig. 4.6*a* and *b*), after which the pattern changes. Rather more sophisticated patterns operate, as will be seen, in the Final of *La Création* (and, a little later, in the 'Tango' of *L'Abandon d'Ariane*).

Figure 4.6*a* 'Corcovado', bars 1–3

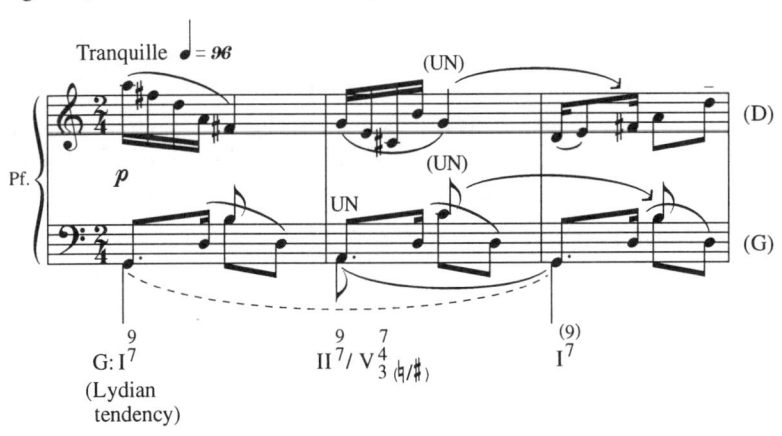

[50] Drake, *Operas of Darius Milhaud*, 213. See also Chapter 2 above.

Discussion of techniques influenced by jazz and Brazilian popular music must include the parameters of metre and rhythm, their processes being closely linked to the exigencies of particular dances. The most frequent metres are 2/4 and 4/4. Metrical changes within a movement are uncommon but can be striking, for instance in the finale

Figure 4.6*b* 'Laranjeiras', bars 1–3

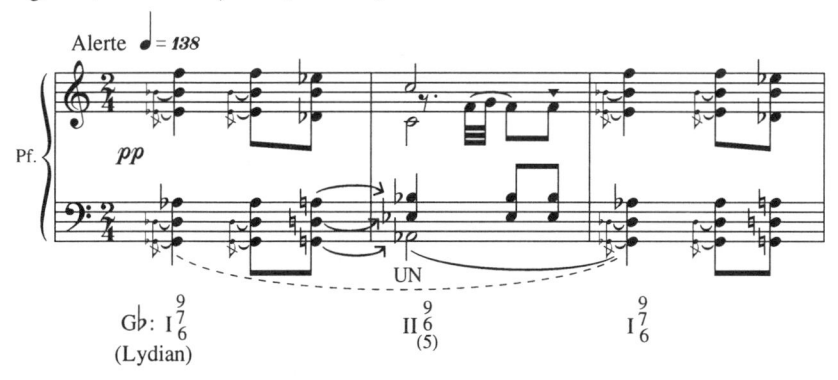

Gb: I$^{9}_{6}$^{7}
(Lydian)   II$^{9}_{6}$ I$^{9}_{6}$^{7}
            (5)

('Précis et nerveux') of *Trois rag-caprices*, where the 4/4 metre alternates firstly with 3/4 bars to form seven-beat groupings, and then with 2/4 bars. A 5/4 bar is introduced at bar 85, as a metric suspension, before the recapitulation at bar 86. There are patterns of anacruses, especially of three quavers in 4/4 metre, e.g. the Fugue of *La Création*, or of the same pattern in double augmentation, e.g. the Romance of the same work. The first (and third) of the *Trois rag-caprices* uses the three quaver motive, followed by the three crotchet version, in the slower section beyond bar 30 (this latter characteristic also being shared by the central Romance). More rarely, the first semiquaver of the bar can be removed, causing a sensation of halting, or tripping (cf. Milhaud's 'léger arrêt' above), as in, for example, 'Corcovado' or 'Tijuca' of *Saudades*.

The characteristic rhythmic identity of the tango is: dotted quaver + semiquaver + two quavers, in 2/4 metre; yet beyond this prerequisite, Milhaud's tangos in *Saudades* exhibit great variety. The samba also uses 2/4 metre, characterized by simple syncopation as semiquaver + quaver + semiquaver. This pattern is used in augmentation in *Le Bœuf*, and indeed in fourfold augmentation (crotchet + minim + crotchet) in the Scherzo of *La Création*. Tied note-values may contribute to the effect: the repeated samba pattern, for instance, sometimes has the semiquaver notes tied across the middle of the bar, as in 'Tijuca', or tied across the bar, as in 'Corcovado'. The first of the *Trois rag-caprices* has a crotchet tied across the barline to a quaver. Although the rumba developed somewhat later, with the 3 + 3 + 2 pattern of dotted crotchet + dotted crotchet + crotchet, in 4/4 metre, the second movement of Milhaud's Sixth Chamber Symphony (written in New York in 1923) nicely anticipates a distorted rumba in 7/4 metre: 'Souple et Vif', divided into 2 + 3 + 2.

Case Study 4
Seventh Complexes in 'Ipanema',
from *Saudades do Brazil*, Op. 67 (1920):
A Comparative Analysis with that of Keith W. Daniel

Preliminaries

Saudades do Brazil was composed in Copenhagen and Aix-en-Provence in 1920, and was first performed on 21 November of that year at the 'Concerts des Six', Galérie Montaigne in Paris, by the pianist Nininha Velloso Guerra. There exists also an orchestrated version, Op. 67*b*, together with various arrangements for violin and piano, and for cello and piano. Dissension between sources persists as to whether the première of Op. 67*b* was the performance at the Théâtre des Champs-Élysées, or that at the Spectacle Loïe Fuller (directed by Vladimir Golschmann), in Paris of 1921.[51] Where the original Op. 67 is concerned, whatever the nature of the connection with the Brazilian composer Ernesto Nazareth, mentioned earlier in this chapter, Milhaud does not help to clarify the situation with his seemingly contradictory remark that *Saudades* is 'une suite de danses pour piano inspirée par des rythmes sud-américains pour laquelle je n'utilisai aucun élément de folklore'.[52]

'Ipanema' is the fifth of the set of dances, and is dedicated to Arthur Rubinstein. It is a typical, ternary-structured tango, selected from *Saudades do Brazil* by Keith W. Daniel as the most suitable for a set-theoretic interpretation in his article, which was discussed in Chapter 2;[53] it is partly for reasons of direct comparison that 'Ipanema' has been chosen here. In addition to evaluating Daniel's analysis, this Case Study also investigates Joseph Straus's notion of seventh axes, and assesses its suitability within this context.

---

[51] The respective sources are Milhaud, *Ma vie heureuse*, 297, and Collaer, *Darius Milhaud*, 269.

[52] Milhaud, *Ma vie heureuse*, 99: 'a suite of dances inspired by South American rhythms in which I made no use of any element of folk music'. Milhaud's meaning here is presumably that he made no direct quotation of pre-existing folk melodic material.

[53] Daniel, 'Preliminary Investigation': see Chapter 2, 'Critiques of Milhaud's Article and Analysis of his Music', above.

Analysis

The central question in the analysis of 'Ipanema' is: how relevant are atonal techniques to modally conceived, centric music, albeit encompassing complex bimodal constructs? The following comparative analysis attempts to answer this question. As before, a formal outline is given before embarking upon more detailed discussion. The small difference of opinion with Daniel over the breakdown into formal sections is indicated in Fig. 4.7 and argued below.

Figure 4.7   'Ipanema', from *Saudades do Brazil*, Op. 67: Formal Outline

STANDARD TERNARY FORM

	Bars	Total Bars
SECTION A	1–33	33
	(Daniel: 1–31)	
Flexible Dorian mode on e♭		
(Lydian inflection), with triads		
of e♭ and F superimposed		
(progression: e♭–E♮–F– G♭ [Section B])		
SECTION B	34–61	28
	(Daniel: 32–61)	
Seventh complexes on G♭ and C		
(possible octatonic framework:		
(E, G, B♭, D♭))		
[For detail, see Fig. 4.8.]		
SECTION A'	62–85	24
Return to Dorian-type mode		
on e♭, with triad on F superimposed		
INTEGRAL CODA	75–85	
Final chord including triad of G♭	85	

Daniel commences with the statement that 'Ipanema provides a more interesting and tightly-organized example of the use of pc sets [than other pieces from *Saudades*].' Sets are used as a 'coordinating element' and 'the set family can be reduced to a more compact complex, with more multiply-represented sets'.[54] He asserts that 'Most importantly, the use of sets transcends the surface structure of the piece.'[55] Daniel concentrates on the central section of the piece, which proves of

---

[54] Daniel, 'A Preliminary Investigation', 32.
[55] Ibid., 33.

greatest interest, and his implementation of set theory is generally convincing. There are nevertheless possible criticisms, such as in respect of his Example 7,[56] which examines bars 32–61, but offers little detail regarding the criteria employed in segmentation, beyond the assertion that this is 'creative segmentation'. A second point of contention concerns his Figure 4,[57] where the segmentation of bars 62–8 is offered without an annotated score, so that there is no way of verifying Daniel's results without re-working the section.

Daniel rightly regards the work as a standard ternary structure, divided A (bars 1–31); B (32–61); A' (62–85). The only point with which one may take issue here is in identifying the start of Section B, which is better argued as from bar 34 onwards. The reason for this lies beyond the brief of a set-theoretic analysis, and in many ways it is regrettable that Daniel restricts himself to this technique alone, because the piece can only properly be appreciated through a more flexible mixture of post-tonal voice-leading analysis and set theory. It seems better to regard the section as beginning at bar 34, firstly because this bar represents one of several strategically placed consonances, within a predominantly dissonant syntax (as shown in Appendix Ex. 4.1*a*). One might even suggest the idea of 'focused consonances', as the converse of Arnold Whittall's term 'focused dissonance', because this indeed is what they are. These rare, pure consonances (discussed in detail below) appear on G♭ at bars 34 and 45; on C at bar 55; on G♭ at bar 68; and on C at bar 74, in a large-scale e♭ modal context. The first four occurrences are relatively evenly spaced, at distances of 10, 9, and 12 bars.

The second reason for favouring bar 34 is that this bar also represents the conclusion of one of several chromatic progressions, in this case (E♭–E♮–F–G♭), operating at different structural levels. By bar 32 the progression which began at bar 29 has reached only as far as F. The third, connected reason in support of bar 34 is that the whole movement constitutes a typical third progression from e♭ (with F in Section A), to G♭ as the final chord of Section A': bar 85 (see the schema in Ex. 4.1*b*). The transition to Section B mirrors this progression on the small scale, based primarily on G♭ (with an important tritonal rival on C). For all these reasons, bars 32–3 are only part of a link into Section B, rather like the isolated octave on C at bar 74, used as a transition to the coda, at bar 75.

[56] Ibid., 35.
[57] Ibid., 33.

There are occasions when Daniel's segmentation overlooks important pitch connections: bar 55, for instance, is the first 'focused consonance' on C, which develops into C^7 at bar 56, i.e. 4-27 (unmarked by Daniel), and thus parallels his observation of 4-27 (G♭^{7}) at bar 57, shown in Ex. 4.2. This polarized juxtaposition is overlooked because the segmentation only operates in crotchet beats, or whole-bar groupings. For similar reasons, the 4-27 (G^7) formation of the bass is overlooked in bar 50. Sometimes the introduction of extra sets would reveal further relations: in bar 56, Daniel identifies one occurrence of 4-16 in the second crotchet of the bar: pitches (D♮,D♯,G,A), but, in fact, the pitches across the centre of the bar (the central, syncopated crotchet unit) are also related in this way: 4-16 (A,B♭,D,E), as indicated in Ex. 4.2.

In order to contribute to the overview of pc set genera in Milhaud's music of the 1920s, generic designations are interpolated within this case study, accepting of course that Forte's research on genera postdates Daniel's analysis. In Ex. 4.2, the importance of the modal perspective to this music is underlined by the prominence of the 'diatonic-tonal' Genus 12, embracing sets 3-11, 4-27 and 6-Z50/Z29; indeed, this passage is founded on sonorities which are almost entirely concerned with triadic/dominant seventh syntax. This, however, is not the whole picture, since rogue elements infiltrate in the form of the wholetone Genus 2, embracing the occurrences of 4-16, 4-21, and mediated perhaps by 4-27 (common to Genera 12/2 and Genus 3). Such infiltration is still of little threat, though, since it involves merely the (almost accidental) vertical aggregates of one transitional bar (with no reference to the progenitor of Genus 2). Whatever one's view on the actual value of the Status quotient (Squo), its use in this context does endorse the given interpretation, with Genus 12 receiving the substantially higher rating (.133), in comparison with that for Genus 2 (.094).

Daniel considers bar 54 of the central section to be of special significance: 'finally, 6-Z50, the complement and Z-related set of 6-Z29, the most important set of the two outer sections of the piece, is derived from the total pc content of measure 54'.[58] In post-tonal terms, however, the bar functions simply as part of a modified cadential I$^6_4$–V (with blues seventh/third), *en route* to the more significant C major consonance at bar 55, referred to above (Ex. 4.2). It seems strange to single out this bar, when it is just a structural and voice-leading sequel to bar

---

58 Ibid.

44, whose motion was directed towards the opposite 'pole' of G♭. In his Figure 5, Daniel illustrates the set complex, with its K and Kh relations, concluding that '4-27 seems to be the logical nexus set, because of its frequent use in the piece, and because it contains 3-11, and is contained in 6-Z25, 6-Z29, 6-30, and 7-31.'[59]

Daniel is certainly justified in assigning significance to the all-pervasive set 4-27, though it may yet be inappropriate to elevate this to a 'nexus set'. After all, the piece still owes much to tonal principles, however modified, so that the frequent appearance of 4-27 as the dominant seventh chord, is hardly remarkable. What is more interesting, and illuminating, is to distinguish between the appearances of 4-27, so that a tightly structured dominant seventh complex emerges (suggestive perhaps of a deliberate 'misreading' in respect of the Latin American dance style of Milhaud's inspiration, mentioned above). Thus, it may be possible to view the dominant seventh as a framework for the Mixolydian mode: an incipient jazz construct. The central Section B of 'Ipanema' features four tritonally-related dominant seventh constructs: two of primary, and two of secondary, importance, as shown in the theoretical schema of Ex. 4.3*a* and *b*. The latter two are D♭^{7} (C♯^{7}) and G^7, whose chords of resolution are the two primarily opposed constructs: G♭^{7} (F♯^{7}) and C^7. The resolution of G♭^{7} is never stated; as for that of C^7, the juxtaposition of F/e♭, and F/G♭ in Section A' (bars 62–3, 66–7, 70–3, 75–83), is justified as the logical 'implication-realization' of C^7 in the central section. The full listing of occurrences (including superimpositions) of the four types of 4-27 in the central section is given in Fig. 4.8.

The dominant seventh construct is involved in the prominent complementary set relations, observed by Daniel: 'the large set 7-31 provides foundational support in measures 40, 42, and 52, while its complement 5-31 appears in measures 38–39 and measure 52',[60] shown in Ex. 4.4*a*. The connection with complementation is that the dominant sevenths in bars 38–9, 48–9 and 52 contribute to set 5-31 (C,E,G,B♭,D♭), whilst the complementary 7-31 features C♯^{7} in bars 40 and 42, and G^7 at bar 52 (Exx. 4.3 and 4.4). The dominant seventh construct also connects with octatonicism, in that the interaction of polarized dominant sevenths: (G♭,B♭,D♭,E[F♭]) and (C,E,G,B♭), illustrated in Ex. 4.4*b*, produces the octatonic set 6-30.

---

[59] Ibid., 34.
[60] Ibid., 33.

Brazilian and Jazz-inspired Music

In terms of the generic perspective, Genus 12 remains the main source of reference, encompassing 5-31/7-31 (together with the triadic constructs 3-11/4-27), and 6-30. It is, however, worth signalling that 5-31 and 6-30 also feature in the make-up of two other contenders: Genus 9, and Genus 3—which also sports 4-27). These elements of common ground are significant in facilitating the generic progression which occurs across the piece.

Figure 4.8 'Ipanema': occurrences of tritonally-related dominant seventh chords and triads: D♭⁷, G♭⁷; G⁷, C⁷

Secondary construct	Primary construct
D♭⁷ (V⁷)	G♭⁷ (I⁷)
Bars	Bars
	34 (triad)
	35–7
44	43–4
	45 (triad)
	58–61
	68 (triad)
G⁷ (V⁷)	C⁷ (I⁷)
Bars	Bars
	47–8
	53–4
55	55 (triad)
	56
D♭(C♯)/G (combined) (V)	G♭/C (combined) (I)
Bars	Bars
	38–9
40	41
42	
	48–9
50	51
52	

Exploring further the role of 4-27, endorsed by Daniel as one of 'several strategically-placed set repetitions', one may suggest that it is used as a means of signalling imminent change. The G♭⁷ construct, at both the beginning (bars 35–7) and the end (57–60) of the central section, 'implies' a change which, in the parlance of Meyer, is then 'realized'.

Similarly, bars 35–7 prepare for the full opposition of 38–9, with the F♭ of G♭⁷ represented enharmonically as E♮, in readiness (as the new third), for the imminent C triad at bar 38; bars 43–4 also feature G♭⁷ in a transitional context. Bars 46 and 56 are loosely equivalent in serving to bridge the two parts of the primary, tritone-related seventh complex G♭/C: bar 46 features a chromatic descent in the bass which links G♭ to C, whilst bar 56, commencing on C, features a chromatic ascent in the treble: D–D♯–(E), with bass G leading chromatically to G♭. Pitches B♭ and E represent the intersection of C⁷ and G♭⁷, used across bars 56–7 (see again Ex. 4.2). In bars 57–61, E continues to act as a pivot (reached by means of the C major triad of bar 55), functioning as the seventh of G♭ and acting as a 'leading-note' to create suspense in advance of the return of the upper pitch on F at Section A' (bar 62).

Some of the most interesting processes can only be fully appreciated as expressions of bimodal polarity, in keeping with sections of *L'Homme et son désir* and contemporary, exploratory works. The centres on G♭ and C are confirmed by their own separate, but simultaneous, cadences maintaining superb balance. This dynamic correspondence between 'polar' opposites is achieved with unfailing logic, almost as a literal musical portrayal of cultural 'otherness'. The G♭ centre of the bass in bars 38–9 and the C centre of the treble, are confirmed by their respective (second-inversion) dominants—D♭⁷ and G⁷—in bar 40 (see again Ex. 4.4). Referring to the C and G♭ triads collectively as part of an octatonic (Model A) complex: 6-30 (C,D♭,E,G♭,G,B♭) is feasible, as described above, but may detract from the remarkable duality. The passage is clearly significant to Milhaud, who has designated it, unusually, 'très strict, sans nuances'. In terms of cadencing, bar 41 features resolution to the 'tonics', followed by the dominants in bar 42. The 'focused consonance' on G♭ at bar 45, approached by means of D♭⁷, is strategically placed before the inverted counterpoint of bars 48–9, where C now occupies the bass and G♭ the treble position. Bar 50 features their dominants (as bar 40), and bars 51–2 their tonics (as bar 41). G♭⁷ of bars 35–7 is balanced by C⁷ at bars 53–4; the 'focused consonance' on G♭ (bar 45) balances that on C (bar 55).

Of the outer sections, Daniel mentions only the main set 6-Z29, which comprises the superimposition of triads of e♭ and F (indeed, suggesting, in combination, a continuing seventh chordal presence: F⁷⁽¹¹⁾, and, by extension, e♭⁷). The effect is collage-like, with e♭ in the bass, and F in the treble (bars 1–2), followed by the reverse arrangement (bars 3–4: Ex. 4.5), in which the dissonance is more acute since the closer spacing highlights the A/B♭ opposition. The idea of the reversal procedure might also suggest the possibility of hearing the full construct in relation to F$^{(13)}$: F,G,A,C,E♭,G♭,B♭,(D♭). On the one hand, the bass motion of E♭–F–E♭ across bars 1–5 is seen to confirm e♭, by means of an upper neighbour-note progression; on the other hand, the upper voice of bars 9–14 reinforces F by means of another upper neighbour-note gesture (F–G♭–F), then followed by a parallel gesture on the 'dominant': D♭–C (upper voice: bars 15–20). In this sense at least there is also dominant-tonic activity in the opening section. Meanwhile, G♭/F triadic opposition is introduced in bars 11–12 and 15–16, as a foretaste of the G♭ centre, so important in the central section and conclusion. The most 'biting' dissonance is reserved for the 'fortissimo' superimposition of E♭^{9} and D, at bars 21, 23 and 25–7. This semitonal opposition is cadentially affirmed in bars 22 and 24, with chord IV^9 (A♭^{9}) of E♭ in the bass, and V^7 (A^7) of D in the treble. Additionally, melodic chromaticism permeates the opening section (as it does the central section), such as the isolated instance of incipient blues third in the bass of bar 30: (G♯/A) within F. This is a clear expression of voice-leading and cannot be understood in set-theoretic terms alone (as in Daniel's Figure 4).

With the hindsight provided by having begun with the central section, the generic aspect of the opening may be seen as first suggesting the basis within Genus 12 (sets 3-11, 6-Z29/6-Z50, later confirmed by the importance of 4-27). Such an interpretation, though, demands the qualification that, on the data of Ex. 4.5 alone, Genus 9 would be as strong a contender, and so should be seen as a 'background' participant.

There are small modifications in the return of Section A at bar 62 (Ex. 4.6). The continuing relevance of melodic chromaticism, as indicative of modal voice-leading principles, is noted in the chromatic ascent in the 'tenor' line at the start of the section (bars 62–8). The F/G♭ opposition (bars 70–4) is 'softened', as the triads are presented successively rather than simultaneously, with the effect of tonic-dominant oscillation. The triad on F (bars 70ff.) is further clarified by the octave on C, at bar 74, as an implied dominant, before the resolution back onto the triad on F at the start of the coda (bar 75).

Nine of the eleven bars of the coda ('Mouvt.': bars 75–85) sustain the 6-Z29 e♭/F opposition, whose tension is not resolved, but simply remains static, whilst the rhythmic fabric disintegrates (Ex. 4.7). The final chord 6-20, supposedly unrelated to previous sets, still does not constitute a resolution, although it does provide the conclusion of the large-scale e♭–G♭ progression, first discussed in relation to Ex. 4.1 (and developed schematically in Ex. 4.8a).

The set-theoretic relationship which is not immediately apparent, but is significant nonetheless, is provided by pc genera. The ending is where the 'atonal-tonal' Genus 9, having been present throughout in a dormant, or embryonic, state, finally asserts itself (embracing sets 3-11 and 6-20, in addition to 6-Z29, and sets 5-31 and 6-30 of Section B). Genera 8/9/10 (Supragenus III) may be seen collectively as the blues complex, and so the progression from the 'diatonic-tonal' Genus 12 to Genus 9 seems appropriate in a piece which is leading the way towards an increased focus on blues constructs. (Blues third is, after all, implicit with A♭/A♮ in relation to F (Section A) and G♭/G♮ (Section B) in relation to an overall E♭.) Invoking Forte's Status quotient (Squo) again, within an abstract schema that summarizes the main set content across 'Ipanema', supports the essential findings here, as shown in Figure 4.9.

Figure 4.9 'Ipanema': Matrix to show summary of Sets in relation to Genera

Potential Genera:	G2	G3	G9	G12
Sets				
3-11			o	o
4-16	o			
4-21	o			
4-27		o		o
5/7-31	o	o	o	o
6-20			o	
6-Z29/Z50	o	o	o	o
6-30	o	o	o	o
Counts:	5	4	5	5
	G2	G3	G9	G12

Counts	Squo Indices in descending order of Genera
5	.152: G9 (atonal-tonal)
5	.139: G12 (diatonic-tonal)
4	.116: G3 (diminished)
5	.098: G2 (wholetone)

The generic interpretation above, with Genus 12 seen as the main protagonist whose position, at the 6-20 chord, is finally usurped by Genus 9 (which has been waiting quietly 'in the wings') is seemingly vindicated by the finer details of the Squo calculations. Genus 12 receives an overall value of .139, which is exceeded by an overall value of .152 for Genus 9; if, however, the final set 6-20 is removed from the calculations, the overall rating of Genus 9 is reduced to .122, which puts it firmly in second place.

Tonally speaking, the final set 6-20 is a first inversion chord of G♭⁷, with 'interference' of pitches D and A: (B♭,G♭,D♭,B♭; D,F♯,A; D♭,F,B♭,D♭). It exhibits similar pairings of semitonal opposition (A/B♭, D♭/D♮, F/G♭) to the earlier 6-30, and in fact embraces the blues set 4-17. Finally, the bass pitch is B♭ (of chord III in first inversion), in relation to a centre on e♭: thus, like many of Milhaud's jazz-inspired works, 'Ipanema' concludes on the fifth scalic degree.

Conclusion

It would be tempting to view the whole piece in relation to one of Joseph Straus's seventh axes: (E♭,G♭,B♭,D♭), as demonstrated in Ex. 4.8*a*, which would explain the close third relations between e♭ and G♭. In this scenario, the piece focuses initially on the lower part of the axis (E♭,G♭,B♭), and then moves to the upper part for Section B (G♭,B♭,D♭); a return to the lower part for Section A' is balanced by a conclusion on the upper portion. One would need, however, to qualify this seventh axis so that it acknowledged the innate conflict between e♭ and F (6-Z29) in the outer sections, and the antagonism of C and G♭ (6-30) in Section B. In fact, from the latter point of view, one might suggest a diminished axis (C,E♭,G♭), so that the movement is focused on e♭ as the main centre, with subsidiaries on G♭ and C, both a minor third from the 'tonic'.

Alternatively, Section B might be viewed schematically as operating in an octatonic collection (at least nominally) on E (Ex. 4.8*b*): this pitch both begins and concludes the section (bars 35–9, 57–61), and links Section B to the outer portions. The whole piece could be seen as an interaction between the seventh axis on E♭ and the octatonic framework on E♮; or the octatonic terms of reference might actually be extended to embrace the whole piece within a Model A collection on E♭: (E♭,E♮,G♭,G♮,A,B♭,C,D♭), with a consequent raising of the status of Genus 3 within the work (Ex. 4.8*b*).

This second stance, however, still rather ignores any role that the pitch F may have in the outer sections of the piece. Consequently, a final idea is to envisage the piece as an expression of a flexible Dorian collection on e♭ (with blues third), as in Ex. 4.8*c*. The scalic form (E♭,F, G♭/G♮,A♭,B♭,C,D♭,E♭) (0,2,3/4,5,7,9,10) would still be useful in explaining the interaction between G♭ and G♮ in Section B and the concept of the seventh axis (E♭,D♭,B♭,G♭,E♭), stressing the modal basis of the work. It would also provide the most plausible explanation for the polarity of G♭ and C in Section B, since these pitches exist symmetrically within this collection, in relation to the 'tonic'. Moreover, it would also recognize the pitch F as of some significance in the outer sections.

Whichever stance one adopts, set theory provides only part of the solution in respect of a work with modal foundation. Although Daniel's implementation of set theory is reasonably convincing as far as it goes, there are nevertheless few significant sets (apart from 4-27) which appear in transposition, and the outer sections of 'Ipanema' do not reward the set-theoretic approach as much as the more complex central section. There is still doubt whether even Section B does 'offer a convincing argument for set consciousness in this piece.'[61] The background is still a centric, modal one, outlining a third progression (Ex. 4.8*a*), and procedures at middleground level are heavily reliant on prolongation through pedal-points, articulated by neighbour-notes and appoggiaturas. One should acknowledge, though, that a study of pc set genera does offer some mediation between set theory and modality, and usefully raises the idea of a possible 'generic' progression from Genus 12 to 9 (or at least a shift of generic emphasis), where other means of reference fall short. Finally, it is indisputable that 'Ipanema' provides one of the best illustrations of 'bimodal' polarity in Milhaud's Brazilian/jazz-derived repertory.

⟡

---

[61] Ibid.

CASE STUDY 5
Blues and Other Modal Formations in
La Création du monde: Suite de concert, Op. 81*b* (1926)

Preliminaries

La Création du monde, that tour de force of jazz-ballet, exists in two versions: the original ballet, Op. 81 (1923) and a *Suite de concert*, Op. 81*b* extracted from the ballet (1926).[62] The original version was first performed on 25 October 1923, by the highly inventive and avant-garde Ballets Suédois[63] directed by Vladimir Golschmann (1893–1972), at the Théâtre des Champs-Elysées in Paris, whilst Op. 81*b* was first performed in 1927, by the Kolisch Quartet, at the annual Festival for Contemporary Music in Baden-Baden. The work is dedicated jointly to Milhaud's biographer and life-long friend, Paul Collaer, and to the conductor, Roger Desormière (1898–1963). Strangely, perhaps, in view of its evocation of African mythology, the first performance with negro dancers did not take place until 1939, when Agnes de Mille choreographed the work as a 'Black Ritual', at the Ballet Theatre in New York.

In his autobiography, Milhaud explained that for the music of *La Création*, 'I set up my orchestra like those of Harlem, with 17 solo musicians'.[64] The instrumentation,[65] however, as he acknowledged in *Études* (1927), was also inspired by a contemporary musical, Maceo Pinkard's *Liza*. From this, Milhaud borrowed the idea of the string quartet, with viola replaced by alto saxophone, and double bass.[66] By contrast, Op. 81*b* requires a more homogeneous ensemble of piano quintet. Essentially, the original score layout of two violins, alto saxophone, cello and double bass is transferred to two violins, viola, cello

---

[62] An introductory Analytical Listening Guide to the original ballet version of *La Création du monde* is available as a software package from Lancaster University, written by the present author: for further details, see the Preface above.

[63] The Ballets Suédois (Swedish Ballet) was an influential and innovative ballet company based in Paris, which, although existing for only five years (1920–25), in that period arguably eclipsed its better known rival, the Ballets Russes (1909–29). Rolf de Maré (1888–1964), of Swedish origin, was the adventurous and imaginative director of this company, which viewed ballet as an integrated 'multi-media' art-form. See B. Häger, *Ballets Suédois* (London, 1990).

[64] Milhaud, *Ma vie heureuse*, 125.

[65] Op. 81: 2 . 1 . 2 . 1 – Sax. – 1 . 2 . 1 . 0 – T. B. – 2 Vln. Vc. Cb. – Pno.

[66] Details from *Études*, 'L'évolution du jazz', 51–9, on 57.

and piano. Both versions last about 15 minutes and consist of five movements: Prélude, Fugue, Romance, Scherzo and Final, although the titles are used only in Op. 81*b*. The basic material is common to both versions, though there are fewer repeats, doublings and expressive markings in Op. 81*b*.

Although the primary concern in this Case Study is with the Concert Suite rather than the ballet, the actual genesis of ideas is essentially the same, and so it seems desirable to discuss briefly the dramatic collaboration behind *La Création* and the musical genesis of the work. The scenario for *La Création*, focusing on African myths of creation, was developed by Blaise Cendrars (1887–1961)[67] from his own *Anthologie nègre* (1921), and the poetic expression of this exotic and fanciful mythology certainly generated part of the initial momentum for the collaborative project:

> Le couple s'est étreint.
> La ronde se calme, freine et ralentit et vient mourir très calme alentour.
> La ronde se disperse par petits groupes. Le couple s'isole dans un baiser qui le porte comme une onde.
> C'est le printemps.[68]

The visual aspect of *La Création* was shaped by the cubist painter and aestheticien Fernand Léger (1881–1955), who produced the sets and costumes,[69] together with Jean Börlin (1893–1930), the leading dancer of the Ballets Suédois, who devised the choreography. Léger, in particular,

---

[67] Cendrars was a prolific poet and novelist of French nationality (though born in Switzerland), whose collected writings extend to some eight volumes. Like Milhaud, he was a very keen traveller, and sought to view his journeys as literary allegories. In the early years of the twentieth century, his name was frequently associated with Guillaume Apollinaire (1880–1918), as well as with Léger. In her biography *Blaise Cendrars*, 74, Chefdor explains that the *Anthologie nègre* evolved from tales collected by a 19th-century missionary, Father H. Trilles. Chefdor also includes a section on 'Cendrars and the Ballets Suédois', ibid., 75ff.

[68] Scene v of Cendrars's scenario, quoted in Collaer, *Darius Milhaud*, 121: 'The couple embraces. | The [dancing] circle quietens, checks itself and slows and starts to die down peacefully all around. | The circle breaks up into little groups. The couple is separated off in an embrace, which carries it along like a wave. | It is springtime.'

[69] Léger was strongly interested both in Futurism, as represented in its second wave by the contemporary journal *L'Esprit nouveau*, and, by association, in the powerful potential inherent within industrial mechanization. His ideas sprang from a concern with geometry, abstraction and space. Although his most famous collaboration is probably that with George Antheil on the *Ballet mécanique*, his finest sets are undoubtedly those for *La Création*.

was fascinated by the innovative possibility of 'mechanical theatre',[70] and introduced radical and dramatic strategies for rethinking the conventional relationship between actors/dancers and their sets. He imagined the shallow stage as a moving image, in effect almost anticipating video art, and wanted the sets and figures to be as one.[71] Characters wore animal costumes and masks, as illusory African sculptures; the gods of creation were huge figures, several metres in height! In accordance with Léger's fantasy, no recognizable human figure was to be seen. The aim was to depict the very processes of creation, with partly formed creatures: insects, birds, animals and man himself, developing before one's eyes. Form from chaos. The choreography of the disguised dancers was then created by Börlin, who had made his name with a stunning solo display in the highly acclaimed *Sculpture nègre* (1920). In sympathy with the aims of Léger, Börlin sought a new approach to dance and movement which would be in keeping with the new technological age.

So, in collaboration with Cendrars, Léger and Börlin, Milhaud aimed to portray the creation as suggested by negro legend and ritual, without the innate violence of Stravinsky's *Le Sacre* of a decade earlier, and yet embracing somewhat similar oppositions of the 'primitive' and the 'modern'.[72] It was in *La Création du monde* that Milhaud considered that he 'at last had the opportunity to use the jazz elements that I had studied so seriously'[73]—especially those of the blues: 'The melodic lines, punctuated by the percussion, overlapped in a breathless counterpoint of broken and twisted rhythms.'[74] The work nevertheless involves a synthesis of seemingly opposed musical discourses of jazz and neoclassical (or neobaroque) features, as will be discussed in Chapter 6.

---

[70] For further detail, see 'The Invented Theater' (1924), in H. Rischbieter, *Art and the State in the Twentieth Century* (Greenwich, Conn., 1968), 97. This interest in mechanization connects of course with that of Milhaud, discussed in Case Studies 2 and 3.

[71] For an illustration of one of Léger's sets from *La Création*, see Häger, *Ballets Suédois*, 192–3.

[72] For more on the 'primitivist' stance behind *La Création du monde*, see the thorough exploration offered by Watkins, *Pyramids*, Chapter 5 'The Creation of the World', 112–33.

[73] Milhaud, *Ma vie heureuse*, 125: '*La Création du monde* m'offrit enfin l'occasion de me servir des éléments de jazz que j'avais si sérieusement étudiés.'

[74] Ibid., 115: 'Les lignes mélodiques scandées par la percussion se chevauchaient en contrepoint dans un halètement de rythmes brisés, tordus.'

Milhaud's inspiration derives in fact from diverse sources: from the jazz that he heard in Harlem in 1922 (and previously at the Hammersmith Palace, in 1920, when Billy Arnold's American Band visited London), from the Black Swan recordings that he brought back from New York, from Parisian night-life—the ambience of the Rue des Lappes and the Boulevard Barbès—and, indirectly, from his Latin American experiences (evident from *Saudades do Brazil* right through to *Scaramouche* (1937)). The necessary musical expertise had been acquired through earlier collaborations, including that with the dramatist Paul Claudel, on *L'Homme et son désir* (1918), itself a celebration of South American primitivism and legend, and another production of the Ballets Suédois, in 1921.

Although the first performance of *La Création du monde* did not meet with the riots that had marked the première of Stravinsky's *Le Sacre* some ten years earlier, the Parisian critical response was still decidedly mixed. Some were shocked by the ballet, particularly by its staging and unconventional use of dancers, whilst others complained that the music especially was not shocking enough! Émile Vuillermoz, for example, commented in uncompromising fashion, in *La Revue musicale* of December 1923, that 'The scenario by Blaise Cendrars and the decor and costumes by Fernand Léger seemed intent on making of this evening an audacious manifestation of the avant-garde. This did not happen, however.'[75]

Meanwhile, the notably conservative ballet critic André Levinson was shocked by the outlandishness of the concept, writing in *Comœdia* of 28 October 1923: 'What an aberration, taking on living dancers to imitate the formulas of exotic sculptors by contorting themselves. No one can ever create a work for dancers by translating the conventions peculiar to the plastic arts by means of saltatory movement. . . . the glamour of Negro sculpture, exalted to the sky by some great modern artists and adopted by the snobs.'[76] It is worth drawing attention here to the derogatory nuances concerning the 'exotic', and the perhaps justifiable scepticism with which the primitivist enterprise was viewed; equally, one should note the unwitting misconceptions, and thinly veiled hints of racism.

---

[75] Quoted in Watkins, *Pyramids*, 126.
[76] Quoted from the English translation by Ruth Sharman in Häger, *Ballets Suédois*, 44.

Whilst Vuillermoz complained that Milhaud's music 'becomes meeker with every passing day, another contemporary critic, Pierre de Lapommeraye declared in *Le Ménestrel* of 2 November 1923 that 'The feeling one gets listening to Darius Milhaud's latest productions is rage. . . . Going back to tom-toms, xylophones, bellowing brass and noise is not progress!'[77] Again, the inaccuracies contained in this account (regarding, for instance, the non-existent tom-toms) suggest a preconceived and prejudiced stance which typically does not trouble itself with the facts.

Milhaud sums up the initial critical response, recounting in his autobiography that 'The critics decreed that my music was not serious and was better suited to dance-halls and to restaurants than to the concert-stage.' He adds though, somewhat wryly, that 'Ten years later, these same critics were discoursing on the philosophy of jazz, and demonstrating learnedly that *La Création* was my finest work.'[78]

Although somewhat standard practice where staged works of the early twentieth century are concerned, it is still curious that Milhaud should have wished to produce a Concert Suite from *La Création du monde* at all. By 1926 his enthusiasm for jazz, on his own admission, was already waning, so why should he have wanted to revise and rearrange his most overtly jazz-inspired composition? The only explanation has to be that he wanted to 'update' the work to fit the dictates of his emerging neoclassical aesthetic. At the risk of over-simplification, the original ballet, Op. 81 may be identified as the 'jazz version' and the Concert Suite, Op. 81*b* as the 'neoclassical version'. In fact, both versions to some extent share the synthesis of jazz/blues procedures and neoclassical modality.

The analytical approach to Op. 81*b* focuses here on the use of the blues scale, employing post-Schenkerian voice-leading and motivic analysis, with modal partitioning (of blues, Aeolian and Dorian modes). Traditional terminology tends to be employed in preference to that of set theory, because the music is so strongly centred and obviously jazz-influenced. Having said this, limited use of set theory is made in the

---

[77] Ibid.
[78] Milhaud, *Ma vie heureuse*, 128: 'Les critiques décrétèrent que ma musique n'est pas sérieuse et convenait plutôt aux dancings et aux restaurants qu'au théâtre. Dix ans plus tard, les même critiques commentaient la philosophie du jazz et démontraient savamment que *La Création* était ma meilleure œuvre.' For further details on the early reception history of *La Création,* see Häger, *Ballets Suédois*, 43–4, and Watkins, *Pyramids*, 126–7.

concluding thematic summary that illustrates modal complementation, in order to contribute to the overview of pc set genera in Milhaud's music of the 1920s. Melodic/thematic process tends to be examined in advance of harmonic process, in keeping with the premise that, in Milhaud's music, harmony emanates from melody (such a melodic priority applies also to the negro music of Milhaud's inspiration). In harmonic analyses, traditional Roman numeral chord symbols are used, together with jazz symbols and an indication of the mode. The main concern is with pitch formation although it is impossible to ignore rhythmic treatment, which is particularly subtle and effective. Stylistic comparison and critique is also included in terms of the relationship of Milhaud's score to basic principles of jazz, taking on board the views of early jazz critics such as André Hodeir and Winthrop Sargeant. This embraces matters such as blues form, harmonic riffs, blues melodic patterning and techniques of embellishment. Comparative comments are also offered where specific differences of treatment between Op. 81 and Op. 81*b* are concerned. In all respects, the Prélude and Fugue are treated in most detail since these movements first state the main thematic material of the work.

Analysis

I. Prélude

This is the introductory portion of the original ballet, serving as a kind of overture, prior to the rise of the curtain. The formal framework of the Prélude is a four-part structure of roughly equal segments, from 24 to 30 bars in length, shown in Figure 4.10. Alternatively, one might view the Prélude as ternary, since the second and third sections are both concerned with the development of the main thematic idea: i.e. Section A (1–30); Central Section (31–82); Section A' (83–106); equally, one could regard Section A as (1–55); Central Section (56–82), Section A' (83–106). A resulting lack of balance would, however, tend to invalidate these two later suggestions. The Prélude (as its more developed counterpart, the Final), is a complex, sectionalized yet rhapsodic, structure.

The main material consists of Theme A and Counterthemes 1 and 2, as marked on the annotated score in Appendix Ex. 4.9*a*. Theme A has a clear motivic construction, with elements labelled 'a', 'b' and 'c', as shown in Ex. 4.9*b* and *c*. (See also the illustrations of Thematic Extension and Transformation: Exx. 4.10–4.11). Label 'a' denotes the opening

Figure 4.10 I. Prélude: Formal Outline

MONOTHEMATIC SONATA-TYPE FORM
2/2 metre (3/2 irregularity at bar 45)

	Bars	Total Bars
SECTION A	1–30	30
Expository portion		
SECTION B	31–55	25
Developmental episode 1		
Climactic point	46–7	
SECTION C	56–82	27
Developmental episode 2		
Climactic point	68–72	
SECTION A'	83–106	24
Recapitulatory portion		

perfect fourth in ascent; 'b' a third progression in descent; and 'c' a kind of inverted mordent used as a cadential figure. There is also a significant larger-scale motive 'α', an extension of 'a' consisting of a perfect fourth plus major second—which in a sense sums up Theme A, itself of great importance in both the Prélude and Final. Whereas Theme A favours predominantly the upper segment of the Aeolian on d: A–D, Counterthemes 1 and 2 (shown in Ex. 4.9) use only the lower segment: D–A and are mainly concerned with the small cadential motive 'c', derived from the end of Theme A itself. Thus the mode on D is partitioned about A. Inherent in the D–A segment is the fifth progression: 'β', consisting of two successive occurrences of the third progression 'b'. Although the Countertheme material might seem unimportant here, it is crucial as the basis for the Fugue, as well as influencing the Romance and Scherzo—especially the tonic–supertonic–mediant ('b'' inv.) part of the phrase. Each half of Countertheme 2 is a combination of retrograde and inversion of Countertheme 1, shown in Ex. 4.9c.

In Section A, 'mélange' at the third scalic degree is immediately evident, though it is simply a non-linear superimposition of major and minor, and so, as discussed by the jazz critic André Hodeir, does not yet justify the term 'blues'.[79] Hodeir believes also that this is in any case

---

[79] For the harmonic perspective on the opening, see again the annotated score, Appendix Ex. 4.9a. Roman numeral chords are used, together with an indication of

too early for harmonic instability, in a piece where tonality is later important.[80] In response to his criticism, one would certainly concede that the blues third of the opening is not authentic, but serves rather as a parody of jazz practice. It can be argued, however, that the basis of the work on D is still clearly established by a tonic pedal which extends across bars 1–30 (see Ex. 4.9a), and that Milhaud's use of ambiguous 'mélange' creates an appropriate sense of expectancy.

A second source of conflict, or polarity, concerns phrasing: whilst Theme A is constructed in three-bar phrases, with supporting bass, Counterthemes 1 and 2 utilize two-bar units. Even when a 12-bar 'blues' form is thought to operate, it is invariably this parody of 4 × 3 bars, as opposed to a traditional blues pattern of 3 × 4 bars. The Aeolian modal nature of Theme A means that, in keeping with modal practice, the raised seventh is reserved for moments of special melodic, or harmonic impact, such as the subtly 'pointed' effect of bar 24 (Thematic Extension: Ex. 4.10c). The next C♯ is employed at bar 31 to mark the start of the first developmental episode, Section B (which features far more harmonic movement than the expository section), on the dominant modality of Aeolian on a.

In Section B (bars 31–55), Theme A is played by the string quartet with added tonal warmth, in contrast to Section A where it was stated by the piano in bare octaves. Both the wistful character of the melodic contour and the accompaniment figure seem reminiscent of the first of Mahler's *Lieder eines fahrenden Gesellen* (also founded on d). Typical harmonic techniques include chromatic encirclement of D, by E♭ and C♯, across bars 35–6, and suggestions of bimodality at the minor third (F♯ 'major' and a 'minor', bars 37–9). Bars 41–6 show a favourite developmental device: multiple sequential transpositions of a second inversion chord (heralded in the original by slithering glissandi and blues notes on trombone), resolving at an initial climactic point across bars 46–7 on to a tonic pedal on D. It is common practice in Milhaud's music of the 1920s for main sections of material to be endowed with harmonic stability, whilst the passages which link them are unstable. A modulatory effect is created across bars 50–5 with fourth-interval patterns: a basic 'quartal' harmony in conjunction with a stepwise progression linking into Section C.

---

figuring, whilst a freer interpretation of likely jazz chordal symbols is given above. Most chords of tonic modality feature added sevenths, ninths or thirteenths.

[80] Hodeir, *Jazz: Its Evolution and Essence*, 255.

A second developmental episode, Section C (bars 56–82), commences on f 'minor',[81] with the major mode conflicting in bar 58 and superseding in bar 59.[82] Both counterthemes are now presented simultaneously at the third statement of Theme A which appears in the middle of the piano texture, embellished by grace-notes. Significantly, across bars 56–64, Countertheme 2 (on lower strings) has acquired the distinctive rhythmic identity of three anacrusic quavers (with syncopation) from which the main subject of the Fugue will be derived. Soon after arriving on a B♭ pedal, a parallel, if smaller, climax occurs (bars 68–73): Countertheme 2 has already been robbed of its recent rhythmic identity and is presented firstly as equal minims, with a process of diminution into crotchets and quavers operating through bars 73–5. This second climax subsides as the piano acquires the quietly surging repetitions of the syncopated quaver figure from Countertheme 2 (bars 77–81). There is some affinity with the later Romance in the use of harmonic constructions on F^7/B♭ (bars 75–80). Milhaud then smooths the join into the recapitulation (rather as he did into the developmental episodes), with a phrase marked 'Cédez' (bars 81–2), similar in effect to a jazz 'break'.[83]

The return of Section A reasserts the tonic, by means of a chromatic progression (E♭–D) across bars 83–6 (pointed at bar 86 in the original by the reintroduction of timpani, absent from the second developmental episode). Theme A (Ex. 4.11, Thematic Extension: Fourth statement) now features the viola, with the initial fourth interval 'a', explored in ascent and descent, then expanded to a sixth 'd' (bars 83–90; 90–5). Again there are hints in Countertheme 2 (bars 87–8), presented in the bass-line of the piano, of the imminent fugal subject with its linear expression of blues third. The interpolation of extra bars between 83 and 106 (for instance, bar 91), contributes to a distinctive, irregular phrasing: 4 + 5 + 3 + 2 + (2 × 5). A second reinforcement of the modality on D occurs at bar 94, with the use of a C♯ lower neighbour-note.

---

[81] The term 'minor' is used since, as only the lower scalic segment: F–C is employed, with no information about sixth and seventh degrees, it is impossible to be more modally specific.

[82] This section of the original featured the *tambourin de Provence*, commonly described as the 'Provençal long-drum'—double-headed, but with a single snare. The most famous usage of the instrument is in Bizet's 'L'Arlésienne' where it is still often thought, mistakenly, that the indication is for a tambourine.

[83] A 'break' in jazz is a brief improvised solo, interpolated between the lines of a verse, or between a verse and a chorus, which serves to dovetail different sections.

The Prélude ends with an integral coda (bars 97–106), just after the bass has come to rest on a definitive pedal on D, which resounds in the bass register of the piano, doubled at the octave. It is struck percussively five times, with the effect rather like that of a tolling bell. Above this, the strings are reduced to the rhythmic anonymity of even crotchets, and the melodic anonymity of mere scalic descents, within the Aeolian collection on d. Appropriately enough, the final occurrence of the raised leading-note is reserved for the final cadence (bars 105–6), with its allusion to Baroque practice.[84] The $^{5}_{4}$–3 dissonance in the piano part resolves onto a pure d 'minor' chord.

In summary, the Aeolian on d is the main modal collection for the Prélude, with others of lesser importance, including the blues collection and small-scale Dorian, Phrygian and pentatonic fragments. Given the dominance of the Aeolian, it might be argued that even the Dorian passages are modified Aeolian (melodic minor) in transposition. Additionally, there are bimodal passages operating at foreground level and 'fused' or combined modes, exhibiting characteristics of more than one standard mode: thus modal interaction is considerable.

In terms of the comparative perspective between Op. 81 and Op. 81*b*, at the start of the Prélude, the piano assumes the original saxophone line (now lacking the indication 'chanté')—a curious substitution, since the piano can only mimic blues notes imperfectly. The cello meanwhile takes the double bass line. String trills are introduced into violin II (bars 1–9) and viola (bars 12–19), possibly as compensation for the lack of large timpani (on D, F♯), and bass drum, which maintains a minim pulse though the original, rather like a heartbeat. The inner strings also provide a double-stopped, syncopated gesture in place of the muted roll on tenor drum (*caisse roulante*, bars 10–11, 20–1). Such substitutions, however, bring new timbral qualities of their own. Further embellishment is introduced with the piano's decorative 'fourth' transpositions (bars 50–5), balanced by textural simplification in the strings at bar 53: again the changes are superficial and the harmony is hardly modified. At bar 59, viola and cello assume the clarinet's material, but the piano accompaniment remains close to the original. Generally, the piano writing tends to be heavier in the chamber version, as octave doublings are introduced for added weight. Accentuation, also, is more frequent and forceful than in the original,

---

[84] The momentum into the cadence is provided by triplet crotchets on viola (bar 104), presented in allusion to the triplets of the piano (bars 91 and 94).

such as at bar 74 where Op. 81 accentuates beats 2 and 4, whilst Op. 81*b* accents every crotchet beat.

In the recapitulation of Op. 81*b* (Ex. 4.11, bar 83), the viola finally assumes the role of the alto saxophone, a logical substitution since in Op. 81 the saxophone was included at the point in the score where one would expect the viola; the pitch ranges and mellow tone qualities of the two instruments are not dissimilar. In Op. 81, bar 96 onwards continues to feature the saxophone, whereas the chamber version effects a change of instrumental colour, with melodic material transferred from viola to violin I. Scalic patterns across bars 97–105 of the original are assigned to a diverse group of horn, saxophone, bassoon and cello, whereas in Op. 81*b* the material is assigned to the homogeneous string quartet. Although the Prélude is not so named in the original, its 106 bars correspond exactly, at the end of which, according to the published full score of the ballet, the curtain rises.

II. Fugue

> The curtain rises slowly on a dark stage. In the middle of the stage we see a confused mass of intertwined bodies: chaos prior to creation. Three giant deities move slowly around the periphery. These are Nzame, Medere, and N'kva, the masters of creation. They hold counsel, circle round the formless mass, and utter magic incantations.[85]

The Fugue, by contrast with the Prélude, has an unambiguous tripartite structure, with the final recapitulatory section reduced from 21 to 15 bars, as illustrated in Fig. 4.11. It is a short movement with no tempo changes and the only metrical irregularity occurring in the final three bars. The main subject of the Fugue, i.e. Subject/Theme B, shows the authentic handling of a blues collection on D, featuring the minor third motive 'b'' particularly in inversion, its extension as a fifth progression 'β', and 'c'' in a mixture of retrograde and inversion (a possible case for Réti's 'interversion'), as shown in Ex. 4.12*a* and *b*. This is a classic illustration of the flexible blues collection of pitches that allows major/minor inflections, and microtonal 'bending', particularly of the third and seventh degrees.[86] The first four pitches of the subject: (D–

---

[85] Cendrars, trans. Sharman, in Häger, *Ballets Suédois*, 190.
[86] See Sargeant, 'The Scalar Structure of Jazz', in *Jazz: Hot and Hybrid*, 147–172. References to Sargeant throughout are to the 1959 edition; the book was further revised and enlarged as *Jazz: A History* in 1964.

E–D–F) were, in the words of Hodeir, 'particularly prized' by jazz-inspired composers.[87] The first part of the subject is concerned with the span (D–A), to which it returns after a short excursion to the upper tetrachord (A–D).

Figure 4.11   II. Fugue: Formal Outline

MONOTHEMATIC TRIPARTITE FORM
Common time metre
(irregularities at bar 56: 6/4, and bar 57: 5/4)

	Bars	Total Bars
EXPOSITION	1–21	21
MIDDLE SECTION	22–43	22
FINAL SECTION (Recapitulation)	43–58	15

The voice-leading interpretation of the fugal subject and counter-subjects (Ex. 4.12*a* and *b*) has heeded basic principles of jazz, as embraced in Stuart's *Encyclopedia*.[88] This includes the premise that 'a neighbour-note [appoggiatura] always precedes the main note, unless the main note is returned to directly after a neighbour-note [i.e. mordent]'.[89] The subject features blues third with its main pitch as F (preceded by F♯) in bars 2–3, then F♯ (preceded by E♯) in bar 4.[90] The flattened seventh is also introduced in bar 4, with a confirmatory (C♯/C♮) progression in bar 5. Hodeir believes that 'the composer got close here to the true significance of the blues scale: its instability'.[91] The rhythmic structure of the subject also contributes to its effectiveness, with consistency and momentum afforded by the three-quaver anacrusic grouping (from Countertheme 2), so typical of jazz. This figure is all-pervasive, with detailed patterns of accentuation: (1 + 3 quavers) across bars 6–11, maintaining the dynamic drive.

Hodeir finds the way in which Milhaud brings the subject around to its subdominant at the conclusion of the phrase (bar 6) especially significant: 'The harmonic climate and evolution of the blues do not

---

[87] Hodeir, *Jazz: Its Evolution and Essence*, 254. As observed by Hodeir, the motive is also used in Gershwin's *Rhapsody in Blue* (1924).

[88] W. Stuart, *Encyclopedia of Improvisation* (New York, 1972).

[89] Ibid., Part 4, 3.

[90] In the blues collection on D, if F precedes F♯, then F♯ is deemed to be the main, structural pitch on the third scalic degree, and vice-versa.

[91] Hodeir, *Jazz: Its Evolution and Essence*, 253.

depend solely on the more or less frequent use of blues notes. They result above all from a perpetual interplay between the tonic and subdominant. Darius Milhaud seems to have understood this perfectly.'[92] This move of a fifth interval across the duration of the subject embodies one of the ironies of this movement, since it is both a typical feature of jazz, and one which operates apparently very naturally in the alien, neobaroque context of fugue (simply as part of the 'cycle of fifths'). In the domain of jazz itself lies a second incongruity in that, although melodic transposition to a new tonic a fourth higher is common,[93] both negro music (according to Sargeant) and Milhaud's fugal subject tend to avoid melodic reference to the fourth scalic degree, because of the former's heavy reliance on the pentatonic collection.[94]

The countersubject, in the flexible blues scale on E, also features motives 'b', 'β' and 'c" (see again Ex. 4.12*b*); and incorporated within both the countersubject and free part is a quotation—surely deliberate—of one of the most famous of blues themes: the *St. Louis Blues* (1914) of W.C. Handy (1873-1958). The free part is also of interest in that it reintroduces the prominent fourth: (A–D), so crucial to Theme A of the Prélude. The second free part (bars 17–21) restates the blues quotation and fourth interval back in the blues collection on D; it also features the minor sixth motive 'd', effectively a distortion of the opening fourth interval, motive 'a'.

The order of fugal entries in the exposition is shown in Fig. 4.12. Harmonically, the pattern is consistent with the formula for a basic jazz 'riff': I, II, V, I (a formula used later in the Final), and, motivically, the progression corresponds with the most important motive of Theme A from the Prélude: 'α'—i.e. perfect 4th and major 2nd intervals.

Figure 4.12   II. Fugue: Pattern of Fugal Entries

Pitch	*Material*	*Bars*
D (I)	Subject: cello	1–6
E (II)	Answer: viola	6–11
A (V)	Subject: violin II	11–16
D (I)	Answer: violin I	16–21

---

92   Ibid., 254.
93   Sargeant, 'The Scalar Structure of Jazz', in *Jazz: Hot and Hybrid*, 147–72 (esp. 160, 163, 167), 203.
94   Ibid., 149, 151, 166.

Most harmonic movement occurs in the Middle Section (bars 22–43), where the chromatic bass-line from bar 27 onwards is especially striking. (This section was cued in the original by the introduction of woodblock, *tambourin* and 'piccolo timpani': very small timpani, notated in the treble clef, and relatively rarely used.) At bar 22, a varied countersubject is presented by the piano (Ex. 4.12*c*) which is preoccupied primarily with the upper tetrachord (A–D), involving motive 'a'' and its compound 'α', both in inversion; and although the varied countersubject material is first heard in the blues collection on D, the possibility of a localized centre on A becomes increasingly feasible across bars 22–6.[95] The main figure is (D,C♯/C♮,A), set 4-4, and the classic ambiguity concerns whether (C♯/C♮) is the blues seventh of D, or the third of A. (A similar context involving set 4-4 exists in the second movement of the Fifth Chamber Symphony, Case Study 3.) Again, one should stress the authenticity of Milhaud's modulatory technique here, whereby a blues note on the third is transformed into one on the seventh degree of a new tonic, relevant both here and in the ensuing Romance. This practice relates back to the concept of 'perpetual interplay' discussed earlier, which, in Hodeir's view, Milhaud develops in order to create a 'complex of blue notes',[96] which exploits tonal ambiguity. The irony is that Milhaud's music explores the blues phenomenon more thoroughly than the music he sought to emulate. His constant fluctuation between lowered and raised seventh degrees 'creates an harmonic relation that Duke Ellington came across on his own several years later and used as one of the bases of his dissonant system'.[97]

There are further instances of 'pastiche' blues treatment, with vertical opposition of F♮/F♯, on violin I and piano across bars 22–6, superimposed against the lower line of the piano which expresses the blues pitches melodically, though still without 'bending'—a practice which is reserved for the final section. In the middle of the texture at bar 22, violin II and viola allude to Countertheme 2 of the Prélude, now presented in the 'major' mode on D. Beneath, the cello produces a conflicting 'walking-bass' ostinato (of five-beats' duration), which spans

---

[95] The 'triad motive' is implicit across bars 23–24 (as a development of motives 'd' and 'a'): a hall-mark of Milhaud's more overtly neoclassical works, discussed below in Chapter 5.
[96] Hodeir, *Jazz: Its Evolution and Essence*, 254.
[97] Ibid., 255.

four bars and operates in a localized Ionian mode on C. Its inclusion prepares for a more persistent source of conflict and disruption in the bass of the piano part across bars 44–56. From bar 35 onwards, material is fragmented, creating a mosaic-like texture, with direct imitation between violins across bars 39–43.

The recapitulatory Final Section synthesizes aspects of the preceding ones, maintaining, with admirable consistency, the contrapuntal intricacy and semblance of improvisation. It commences with the last three quavers of bar 43 (articulated in the original by the reintroduction of cymbals and snare drum at the equivalent of bar 44). The main material, consisting of the varied countersubject (now on cello, with a diminution on the violins) and the scalic 'walking-bass' (on piano), is closer to that used at the start of the Middle Section.[98] At bar 48, however, the original subject reappears emphatically on viola, presented in high tessitura within the 'tonic' blues collection on D. The answer is heard on A (bar 52), played by the cello, also in high tessitura. Polyrhythmic groupings, first apparent in the Middle Section, reach their culmination in the Final Section: six simultaneous patterns stress unexpected beats, particularly the second quaver of the bar: Cendrars's 'confused mass of intertwined bodies'. Additionally, there is conflict between differing lengths of competing ostinati: the treble line of the piano features a six-beat group which is set against a five-beat group in the bass.

Failing to appreciate fully Milhaud's programmatic intentions in portraying Cendrars's 'chaos prior to creation', and his right to an independent artistic aesthetic inspired by jazz, Hodeir criticizes this use of rhythmic accentuation and the conflict of one line against another, declaring that 'The resulting impression of disorder is undoubtedly intentional, even though the composer does not always seem to be completely in control of the forces he unleashed.'[99] Furthermore, he asserts that 'Not one of these rhythms, syncopated or otherwise, has more than an incidental similarity to good jazz of the period.' Hodeir considers this rhythmic treatment inauthentic because the real jazz beat has been compromised by Milhaud's penchant for polyrhythm:

---

[98] The blues pitches of the varied countersubject can now be inflected with subtle portamento on strings, whilst the role of the piano is one of percussive punctuation.

[99] Hodeir, *Jazz: Its Evolution and Essence*, 258.

the composer of *La Création* was set on going jazz rhythms one better. By introducing a certain type of polyrhythm, he destroyed the very bases of jazz rhythm.[100]

In response, Milhaud would presumably have taken much exception to the accusation that he had destroyed the pulse since, in *Ma vie heureuse*, he comments on the 'inner beat' as being one of the main attractions of jazz for him.[101] Equally, of course, there is no reason why he should not be entitled to exaggerate and distort the rhythmic component of jazz as a particular 'misreading' within his own 'revisionary strategies'.[102]

The miniature three-bar coda contains the only metrical expansion, where, as at the close of the Prélude, melody is reduced to scale, and rhythm to an even quaver pulse. The movement ends with an unworldly bimodal superimposition of Dorian on g♯ and Ionian on C (perhaps simply C 'major' with added notes). One could argue that since the flattened fifth is the most pronounced pitch feature of jazz after the blues notes on third and seventh, introduction of the enharmonic g♯, in relation to a tonic D, is hardly surprising. Equally, introduction of the C major tonality could be justified as the dominant of F, the focal pitch of the ensuing Romance. Ultimately, though, the movement ends by moving off at a tangent to the main argument: perhaps this is simply to remind the listener that this movement is still only a parody of jazz.

Where comparison between the two versions of the score is concerned, the Fugue perhaps loses something in the chamber transcription since one original strength lay in the percussive backing of the fugal material, with muted bass drum (in a conflicting triple metre), *tambourin*, snare drum, and very dry, fast and 'nervous' arpeggios on the piano. Additionally the timpanist dovetailed the join between Prélude and Fugue with an appropriate roll to mark the rising of the curtain. Op. 81*b*, by contrast, exhibits a new timbral consistency, with fugal entries appearing on cello, viola, violin II and violin I, as opposed to the disparate entries on double bass, trombone, saxophone and trumpet. Nonetheless, the first subject entry is definitely more novel and dramatic when played by the original double bass, than by the

---

[100] Ibid., 260.
[101] See n. 27 above.
[102] See Straus, 'Toward a Theory of Musical Influence', *Remaking the Past*, 1–20; Meltzer, 'Preamble', in *Reading Jazz*, 4ff.; and Chapter 5 below.

cello. Whilst accentuation and dynamic levels of the original are preserved in the transcription, there are small instrumental changes in Op. 81*b*, where oboe and saxophone were originally prominent. The piano writing (as in the Prélude) tends to be more intricate and complex in Op. 81*b*, a feature which sometimes extends to other aspects of the writing, such as in the miniature coda which utilizes descending upper woodwind scales in Op. 81, but both descending and ascending string patterns in Op. 81*b*. This embellishment has the effect of 'placing' the final sustained chord of Op. 81*b*, whilst the equivalent bars 164–5 of Op. 81 flow onwards to a return of the Prélude, in synthesis with material from the Fugue at bar 179 (creating a large-scale ternary form). Although the repetition of the Prélude is omitted in Op. 81*b*, this is hardly a weakness since the material was in danger of being overstated anyway.

III. Romance

> There is movement in the central mass, a series of convulsions. A tree gradually begins to grow, gets taller and taller, rising up straight, and when one of its seeds falls to the ground, a new tree sprouts.[103]

The Romance comes closest to blues chordal progressions and forms,[104] within an elaborated, overall ternary form, shown in Fig. 4.13.

The main thematic idea of the Romance involves a re-working, and new characterization, of the fugal subject (now combined with the cadential formula from Theme A): hence the labelling as Theme B in Appendix Ex. 4.13*a* and *b*. The introductory bars 1–4 constitute 'α''— encompassing 'a' and 'c'', after which Theme B commences with two further statements of motive 'c', so that a concluding gesture is now re-characterized as an opening idea (bars 4–12). Motive 'a' recurs in the third phrase of the theme, embracing again Milhaud's favoured 'triad motive', followed by 'b' and 'β', and concluded by 'α'', formerly used as an opening gesture, and now framing Theme B (presented here as a piano solo, though originally heard in the plaintive timbre of the oboe).

The harmonic content of bars 1–17 in the Mixolydian on F is considered in Ex. 4.13*a*, with the introductory bars 1–4, which emphasize 'F⁷', functioning as opening and closing gestures both in this movement and

---

[103] Cendrars, trans. Sharman, in Häger, *Ballets Suédois*, 190.
[104] See B. Kernfeld, 'Blues progression', in *The New Grove Dictionary of Jazz*, ed. B. Kernfeld (London, 1988), i, 129–30.

Figure 4.13   III. Romance: Formal Outline

TERNARY FORM (Monothematic)

	Bars	Total Bars
SECTION A	1–4, 4–17, 18–19	4 + 14 + 2
SECTION A'	20–31, 31–4	12 + 4
SECTION B (Developmental portion)	35–42, 43–7, 48–51	13 + 4
Link back to return of opening	52–8	7
SECTION A' Integral CODA	59–83 79–83	25

in the Final. Despite the dominance of Mixolydian modality on F, there is persistent ambiguity (or, more positively, 'polyvalence') in respect of the Dorian on c and Ionian on B♭. Such ambiguity is created by the alternation of F^7/C^9 chords (bars 4–12), in conjunction with a melodic line centred on c (albeit as the upper tetrachord of F), and a significant perfect cadence in B♭ (bars 13–14). The relationship between these centres is itself an implied statement of the germinal motive 'α': B♭–C (major 2nd); B♭–F (perfect 4th). Ultimately, though, the indisputable status of the F^7 chord, and the expanded melodic line of phrase B (bars 12–17), endorses an interpretation of Mixolydian on F. Furthermore, the F^{M7} scale is featured in the 'break' at bars 18–19, with F^7 continuing as the main source of reference in Section A'.

Ex. 4.13a aims to show that this initial structure is also a skilful stylization of a classic three-line blues formula in as much as it shares an AAB phrase construction, within a 12-bar form (plus two-bar extension), and gives prominence to the subdominant relation of B♭ (bar 14). The more wide-ranging third phrase (bars 12–17), with expressive sixth and seventh intervals, does not finish, but simply hangs inconclusively on a G^{13} supertonic of F.

In keeping with the blues formal analogy, a two-bar scalic 'break' leads to a modified repeat of the piano solo material across bars 20–31 (Section A'). The centre on F is asserted melodically through bars 28–31, thus continuing support for the interpretation of the Romance within a Mixolydian modality on F. The close of Section A' (bars 31–4) is marked by the return of the introductory bars, the first two-bar phrase heard on piano, the second transferred to the warmer string tones.

At the start of Section B (bars 35–51), Theme B is transposed up a tone, into the upper tetrachord of a Mixolydian mode on G, and transferred to the warmer timbre of violin I. The piano now assumes an accompanying role with increasingly chromatic scalic diminution, and consequent sense of intensification. (This point in the original score featured the re-introduction of snare drum and *tambourin*, followed by bass drum and wood-block.) In bars 42–7 a figuration from the Fugue using the subsidiary fragment B' would seem strongly influenced by Gershwin's *Rhapsody in Blue*, were it not that Milhaud got there first![105] Ex. 4.13c details this figure, with motive 'b'' as the minor inflection of 'b', and 'c'' comprising a hybrid of retrograde and inversion. The importance of the neoclassical device of sequence cannot be over-emphasized here, with Theme B on violin heard twice on G^7 (bars 35–8, 39–42), then on F^7 (bars 43–4), E♭ (bars 44–7), and directed through b♭ 'minor' ('Cédez'), back to the 'pillar chord' of F^7 (bar 51). So, in addition to the small-scale blues formula, Milhaud cleverly replicates the AAB idea on a larger scale (i.e. A: bars 1–19, A: bars 20–34, B: 35–51). The linking passage across bars 51–8, 'Animez beaucoup', is triggered by the F^7 chord and involves another piano 'break'. Descending scalic sequences move through G and on to $F\sharp^7$ as dominant preparation for the return of Section A, with Milhaud's typical octave doubling using notes one step out of phase.

Section A returns at bar 59, transposed down a semitone from the opening to an overall Mixolydian mode on E, with a melodic centre on b (Dorian). (This return is punctuated in the original score by a pianissimo entry of bass drum, played dryly with a hard stick.) Apparent bimodality and harmonic ambiguity arise again between modalities whose roots are a perfect 4th (B–F♯) and major 2nd (F♯–E) apart, whilst the introduction of sonorities within F♯ (in the piano part) nicely prepares the centre of the ensuing Scherzo. The peak is achieved at bar 72, with the (G♯–F♯) pitches of violin I left 'hanging', as a more dramatic version of the piano's statement at bar 17. This leads to the parallel scalic break at bars 73–4 which explores E 'major', and is followed by a four-bar piano solo that modulates back to the centre on F. Bar 78 sees

---

[105] Gershwin's *Rhapsody in Blue* was composed in 1924, although Nancy Perloff suggests that Milhaud may have experienced Gershwin's music, at the Bar Gaya in Paris, back in 1921 (*Art and the Everyday*, 92–3). This passage (bars 42–7 of the Romance) can be connected with the similar bars 18–24 of the Scherzo.

the only instance of metric expansion in order to allow time for an enharmonic conversion from E♯ to F♮.

The Coda (bars 79–83) returns to the F^7/C^9 alternation of the opening section, with Theme B reduced to ostinato, back on its c-centred melodic pitches. The final cadence, as with other sections of this jazz-derived movement, concludes on an F^{11} chord—still with a hint of dominant function. The recurrent bivalence between E♭ as the third of c 'minor', or the seventh of F (paralleling a similar bivalence in the Fugue), was first noted as intrinsic to the modality of jazz by Hodeir.[106] On the large-scale, however, the Mixolydian mode on F is undoubtedly the appropriate collection for the Romance.

Timbral contrast is undoubtedly reduced in Op. 81*b*, but is replaced by a new intimate quality of chamber music: the piano solos are important in this respect. Orchestral-type markings are usually omitted from Op. 81*b*, such as the 'swell' markings originally contained in bars 16–17. Milhaud is concerned to vary register when using the more limited forces of Op. 81*b*, such as in the pianistic treatment of the Gershwin-like section, at bar 42. Each version has its merits: Op. 81*b* (bars 51–8) features an effective pianistic development of an original flute pattern, whereas Op. 81 (bars 250–7) has the special colouring of flutter-tonguing: 'trémolo en roulant la langue'. Some sections of the chamber version are contracted from the original, yet others are expanded, e.g. the final seven bars of the Romance expanded from the original two bars 347–8. Additionally, some passages, such as bars 59–83, are reordered so as to appear earlier in the chamber version than they did in the original.[107]

IV. Scherzo

> Each creature, with a dancer bursting from its centre, evolves in its individual way, takes a few steps, then gently begins to move in a circle, gradually gathering speed as it revolves around the three initial gods. An opening appears in the circle . . . this is man and woman, suddenly upright. They recognize one another; they come face to face.[108]

---

[106] Hodeir, *Jazz: Its Evolution and Essence*, 254.

[107] Bars 59–83 of the Romance occur originally beyond the main portion of the Scherzo, as bars 329–48 (through-numbered from the start of the ballet).

[108] Cendrars, trans. Sharman, in Häger, *Ballets Suédois*, 190.

In contrast to the lyrical Romance, the F♯-based Scherzo displays a stark neoclassicism; beyond this, the two movements share a strong emphasis on the 'dominant', often as a bass pedal. The Scherzo utilizes a ternary/rondo hybrid form, as detailed in Fig. 4.14.

Figure 4.14   IV. Scherzo: Formal Outline

TERNARY FORM (with elements of rondo)

	Bars	Total Bars
A	1–24	24
SECTION A	1–16	
SECTION B (from Fugue)	17–24	
B	25–54	29
SECTION A'	25–40	
SECTION B'	41–54	
A'	55–67	13
SECTION A''	55–62	
CODA	63–7	

The main Theme C, shown in Appendix Ex. 4.14*a* and *b*, is derived largely from Countertheme 1. Instrumentally, this theme maintains its original main focus on the violins, although it lacks the distinctive additional timbres of flutter-tonguing trumpets and bass drum. Motivically, it consists of three statements of 'c', followed by a fifth progression, motive 'c' inv.', and 'b", and concluded by 'a'. Section A consists of two eight-bar phrases, divided at bar 8 by a loud articulatory chord (with added cymbal clash in Op. 81). Bars 1–12 operate within a modality on F♯, whose Lydian predilection becomes increasingly clear from bar 4 onwards; and it is the strength of Lydian inflection that causes the inevitability of the 'modulation', in neoclassical fashion, to the Ionian on C♯ (bars 13–16)—a move which had already been strongly signalled in the melodic parameter by bar 8. The harmony of bars 1–16 tends to consist of a simple I–V oscillation, with periodic punctuation by a I$^6_4$–V construction over the C♯ pedal (Ex. 4.14*a*). Occasional chordal fusions occur such as the concluding construct of bar 8: essentially an elaborated tonic, 'I^{9}6', yet comprising distinct elements of chords I and II.[109] Typical of jazz are the simple syncopations: crotchet–minim–crotchet; two quavers–minim–crotchet. Texturally, this chordal opening contrasts strongly with the fugal counterpoint which inspires the ensuing Section B.

Sections A and B are neatly dovetailed at bar 16 to effect a change from four- to three-bar phrases, and from chordal to contrapuntal style. The insistent interjections of Section B (bars 17–24) are derived from both the Fugue and the Romance. This syncopated passage again anticipates most strikingly the jazz-derived sequential motives that were to ensure the fame of George Gershwin.

At the fortissimo appearance of Section A' (central episode: bars 25–40), Theme C in the white-note modality on F conflicts with partial pentatonic black-note figures in the bass (C♯,D♯,F♯): this bimodal conflict is encapsulated in the piano part. The introduction of the pitch-centre F, in possible allusion to the Romance, balances the reference in the Romance to the F♯ modality of the Scherzo. As in the Romance, there are occasional 'romanticized' gestures, such as the elaborate, scalic anacrusis into bar 33. A more vivacious rendition of Section B' (bars 41–54) also incorporates elements of Fugue and Romance, such as a three-crotchet ostinato on cello featuring successive fifths: (D♯–G♯–C♯), above which upper strings offer a conflicting three-quaver ostinato. Bars 44–5 demonstrate another scalic 'break', with bar 46 stressing dominant and tonic pedals: 'gardez la pédale'. Upper string register and piano doublings intensify the activity at a fortissimo dynamic, with a more extensive four-bar scalic passage exhibiting tritonal conflict between C and F♯ in the lead back to the recapitulation.[110] Bars 48–54 represent the climactic moment of the movement, marking, in terms of the scenario, the creation of man and woman. (In the original, this climax is held over until the start of the reprise at *fff* some six bars later.)

The final Section A" occurs at bar 55, designated *f* 'très sec'; as in the Romance, material is transposed down a semitone to F (bars 55–8), with an abrupt switch to F♯ for the next four bars. Quadruple trills appear (bars 59–62) as a feature both of Milhaud's neoclassical and jazz-

---

[109] Milhaud's preference for chord II over V, especially in Latin American/jazz-inspired contexts involving vamping, was considered above in the introductory portion of this chapter.

[110] Conflict between C and F♯ is typically found in early pieces, e.g. the Fourth Quartet or Fifth Chamber Symphony, but is less common later.

influenced works. Bars 63–7 form a five-bar coda over an F♯ 'tonic' pedal, above which an attractive, unexpected melodic twist occurs in the form of an elaborated tetrachordal formula (A♯–C♯,D♯,E,A♯–F♯: Ex. 4.14*c*). This formula exhibits characteristic ambiguity between centres of C♯ and F♯ and minimizes reference to the leading-note/fourth scalic degree, i.e. pitch B. The authenticity of this particular figure is supported by Sargeant, who quotes a remarkably similar shape when discussing typical endings of negro melody which 'coincide with the principle of melodic movement peculiar to the blues tetrachordal grouping: A,C,D,E♭(E♮).'[111] The movement ends with a punctuating pizzicato, in keeping with this motivic, scalic and rhythmic movement, not highly melodic by Milhaud's standards.

In the original score, the Scherzo and Romance materials return briefly in synthesis[112] after the main statement of the Scherzo, as was the case with the Prélude and Fugue. Although the basic instrumentation of the two versions corresponds closely: two violins, cello, double bass, as against two violins, viola and cello, the percussive effects on snare drum (requiring the player to place one stick across the rim and head of the drum, and to strike this with the second stick) and bass drum, which support the fugal interpolations, are obviously unavailable in Op. 81*b*. Conversely, the chamber version is striking in its stripping of inessentials: the sparse markings (including those of accentuation), and the succinctness of the coda (bars 63–7 are condensed from an original nine bars); it also features (inevitably) a more demanding piano part than the original version.

V. Final

> And while the couple perform the dance of desire, followed by the mating dance, all the formless beings that remained on the ground stealthily creep up and join in the round dance, leading it at a frenetic dizzy pace.[113]

The Final draws together ideas from the earlier movements, and commences with a stronger assertion of D 'major' than hitherto. The complex and large-scaled ternary form, outlined in Fig. 4.15, is extended at either side by an introduction and coda, with two occurrences of Section B, each leading into an episode that recalls the

---

111 Sargeant, *Jazz: Hot and Hybrid*, 203; see also 167 and 175.
112 See bars 329–48 of Op. 81.
113 Cendrars, trans. Sharman, in Häger, *Ballets Suédois*, 190.

Figure 4.15 V. Final: Formal Outline

EXTENDED TERNARY FORM

	Modal Basis	Bars	Total Bars
INTRODUCTION		1–15	15
(Prélude material)	D: Ionian		
Bass chromaticism:	D♮–D♯–D♮		
SECTION A		16–65	50
(Theme D)	F♯: Mixolydian (Lydian/blues)		
	Subsection *a*	16–31	
	Subsection *b*	32–40; 41–52	
	Subsection *a'*	53–9	
Linking material	Motive: A♯–F♯	60–5	
SECTION B (WITH EPISODES)		66–115	50
SECTION B1			
(Theme E)	F♯: Lydian/blues	66–76	11
EPISODE 1			
(Prélude material)	b: Aeolian/ harmonic minor	77–88	12
Linking material: 3-bar 'riff'	G: Lydian tendency	89–91	3
SECTION B2			
(Theme E)	G: Lydian/blues	92–103	12
Linking material: 3-bar 'riff'	E♭: Lydian tendency	104–6	3
EPISODE 2			
('Prelude' material)	E♭: Ionian	107–9	3
	d: 'minor/major'	110–15	6
SECTION A'		116–65	50
(Theme D)	D: Mixolydian		
(Recapitulatory)	(Lydian/blues)	116–31	
		132–40	
		141–52	
		153–9	
Short transition	Motive: F♯–D	160–5	
CODA		166–90	25
	D: blues collection		
Romance material		166–80	
Cadential linking gesture		181–2	
Fugue material		182–90	

Prélude. A loose symmetry exists in terms of the progression from the introduction forwards through to Section B, and then backwards from the second occurrence of Section B to the Coda; furthermore, the incorporation of material, particularly from the Prélude, also affords a sense of symmetry to the whole work. Techniques for formal extension and development include repetition, sequence, augmentation, diminution and intervallic distortion.[114]

Theme A of the Prélude is heard initially on the viola, now featuring the raised seventh of the broadly Ionian mode (see Ex. 4.15*a* and *b*: Thematic Extension & Transformation: Theme A (fifth statement)); Countertheme 1 returns on the violins, followed by an interpolated fragment of Theme B (Romance). The procedure of bars 1–6 is repeated across bars 7–12 with new instrumentation. The Final contains several possible parodies of blues form, and one could regard these introductory bars as a 12-bar blues structure, with an additional three-bar linking passage, reminiscent of bars 13–15 of the Romance. Nevertheless, the phrase structure is still (4 × 3) bars, with D♮–D♯ bass movement, as opposed to standard blues phrasing and harmony. The harmonic perspective of bars 1–15, similar to that of the opening Prélude, is considered beneath the score of Ex. 4.15*a*.

Section A commences at bar 16 with Theme D: Cendrars's 'dance of desire', derived from Theme A in its use of a prominent fourth and step-wise motion (Ex. 4.16*a* and *c*). Theme D subscribes to the Mixolydian mode on F♯, with strong emphasis on the sixth scalic degree, particularly in its initial 'pentatonic' motive 'α'.[115] This first motive uses the pitches of the upper tetrachord only (albeit with octave displacement to highlight the sixth degree), whereas the second motive 'β' inv.' frequents just the lower scalic segment. Allusions to the other movements are strong: the modal basis on F♯, the Lydian tendency in the accompaniment, and the piano's suggestion of the rhythmic figure crotchet–minim–crotchet, allude to the Scherzo, whilst the accompanying pattern on strings (e.g. bars 16–19) evokes the rhythmic identity and blues notes of the Fugue, and could be construed as a parody of a 'riff': a repeated formulaic device in jazz, similar in effect to

---

[114] These techniques are all demonstrable within the extension of Theme D, part of which is detailed in Appendix Ex. 4.16*c* and *d*.

[115] This emphasis on the sixth scalic degree is also a common feature of the negro music of Milhaud's inspiration, as attested to by Sargeant (*Jazz: Hot and Hybrid*, 155, 163, 164–5, 203) and as evidenced, for example, by the spiritual 'Swing low, sweet chariot'.

an ostinato. This four-bar chordal riff is explored in Ex. 4.16*b*, with the simple harmonic pattern (I–'II⁷'–V¹¹–I⁷) underpinning a strongly directed chromatic descent reused from the Fugue.[116] Milhaud's practices of octave doubling (in the piano part) and instrumental variation on repetition of the riff, produce the characteristic texture. The strings assume a percussive, punctuating role, as if acknowledging the importance of this parameter in Op. 81, at the point where cymbal, *tambourin*, snare and bass drum return.

The material of Theme D, based on F♯, is extensive, and its development may be regarded as consisting of patterns of three distinct types of material: the first derived from Theme A (Ex. 4.16*c* bars 16–24; also 30–5, 53–60); the second derived from Theme B (Ex. 4.16*d* bars 25–30; also 35–42, 44, 48, 49–52); and the third, of lesser status, involving the chromatic descent of the accompanying riff (bars 16–40, 41–51, 53–6, 57–60). Bar 41 marks a more powerful phase within Section A (subsection *b*), supported by transposition of the main material up a tone, this technique being commonly employed in popular music for the same purpose. The end of Section A is indicated by the simplified string 'riff', no longer employing the anacrusic three-quaver figure, but simply unadorned crotchets (bars 57–60). At the slower, linking bars 60–6 ('Cédez'), another textural change is provided by the mimicking of a further jazz 'break' on solo cello (evoking bars 42–5 of the Romance), with a repeated third motive on piano (A♯–F♯), and further chordal punctuation in upper strings: I⁷–'II♯⁹'–V¹³(–I⁶₅) (Ex. 4.17). Harmonic emphasis is still on F♯, in reminiscence of the Scherzo.

Section B (bar 66) features Theme E (Ex. 4.18*a* and *b*), another derivative of Themes A and D, which now enjoys indulgent triplet minims. Again fourth intervals are prominent, together with motive 'd'', the minor 7th in ascent, based in what appears initially to be a Lydian mode on F♯. The first phrase of the theme (bars 66–9) is restricted to the pitches of the lower scalic segment F♯–C♯, albeit with a clear octave displacement of F♯ which in fact signals the activity of the second phrase (bars 69–71). (This displacement technique first came to the fore in Theme D.) The response is an exclusive exploration of the upper tetrachord, directed through the blues seventh E♮/E♯ to the upper 'tonic'. At bar 71, Theme E is restated in its 'minor' inflection,

---

[116] This is the same basic progression as used for the order of fugal entry in the second movement. The simple chordal progression has many counterparts in the popular repertory of jazz standards, for instance in the tune 'Sweet Lorraine'.

transferred now from first to second violin, whilst Countertheme 1 on piano beneath supplies 'mélange' at the third scalic degree (A♮/A♯). Section B contains many subdivisions into 'Cédez' and 'Mouvt'. bars and is itself just a link into the episode which follows. Episode 1 (bars 77–88), alluding to the Prélude in the mediating Aeolian/harmonic minor mode on b, suggests a type of blues structure, albeit highly stylized. The two violins share Theme A, in combination with Countertheme 1 (generally on inner strings), and the violent spasms of the syncopated riff on piano. All the material of the Final is now in play, and the remainder of the movement may be viewed loosely as a structural retrograde of the portion heard so far.

Section B returns (bars 92–103), transposed up a semitone into a Lydian/blues modality on G, with bars 97 and 70 corresponding; texturally, glissandi and triplet/quintuplet groupings are introduced in semblance of improvisation. The transitional bars 104–6 (marked 'Animez') correspond with bars 89–91, based now in a Lydian-type mode on E♭, whilst bars 107–15 (Episode 2) are reminiscent of the E♭–D progression at the start of the recapitulation of the Prélude' (bars 83ff.). Bar 110 ('Mouvt.') marks the restoration of the d minor/major modality with a d^{13} chord. Episode 2 is, however, only a fleeting reminder of the Prélude, almost immediately reduced to the familiar, inert scales of undifferentiated crotchets, with a sense of 'winding down' before the ultimate frenzy.

In the recapitulation, a reworking of Theme D (third statement: bars 116–52) on D, played by violin I, combines with an unrelenting presentation of the varied fugal countersubject on viola, and the four-chord riff. The music thrives on mesmeric repetitions of mosaic-like patterns, so creating its own momentum, and a 'mock' improvisatory effect. This is the period of most intense activity, with constant reinforcement of the 'tonic' modality of D by the bass, midst a myriad of blues inflections above. (In Op. 81, unpitched percussion offer reiterated flourishes on snare drum, cymbal, small timpani, metal- and woodblocks, anchored by the bass drum.) Cendrars's description is most apt here: 'All the formless beings that remained on the ground stealthily creep up and join in the round dance, leading it at a frenetic, dizzy pace.'[117]

The inexorable building of the 'dance of fulfilment' (in the words of Paul Collaer) leads to the most forceful and ecstatically intense *fff* cli-

---

[117] Cendrars, trans. Sharman, in Häger, *Ballets Suédois*, 190.

max of the piece (bar 147), where the viola, still locked into its continual repetition of the varied countersubject, drives now with increased semiquaver diminution. Such intensity, though, cannot be maintained indefinitely; finally, and inevitably, the dynamic power diminishes, cued by the start of the fourth statement of Theme D (bars 153–9). At the end of Section A' (bars 159–64), the melodic third motive (F♯–D) derived from the fugal subject, is most prominent, sounded jointly by violin I and piano. Bars 160–5 link into the Coda (echoing and balancing the previous transitional 'Cédez' across bars 60–5), with D^7 clearly asserted in the bass (bar 160), followed by the remainder of the riff pattern, considerably augmented. Each chord spans a two-bar period, in an effective reduction of momentum, yet still creating an effective sense of expectation through repetition and sequence. Further material from the Fugue includes the three-note chromatic descent which is subjected to much sequential extension, whilst the cadence across bars 165–7 derives from the introduction of the Romance.

> The [dancing] circle quietens, checks itself and slows and starts to die down peacefully all around. The circle breaks up into little groups. The couple is separated off in an embrace, which carries it along like a wave. It is springtime.[118]

Bars 166–90 constitute the Coda of the whole *Suite de concert*— effectively a type of 'Epilogue' which was regarded as a separate final scene in the original ballet. The first portion ('Mouvt.', bars 166–80) employs a cadential figure (on D^7) from the opening of the Romance, using the crotchet augmentation of the three-quaver figure, on viola, that initially characterized material B. Another distant echo of this material is heard on the piano, then imitated by, and set against, the meandering and melancholy chromatic counterpoint of the viola (similar to the piano part across bars 36–41 of the Romance proper). The result is a lyrical interlude (exclusively for viola and piano) in reminiscence of the Romance whose main theme B appears in the work's tonic, in the piano part at bar 176. This portion ends as it began, with the introductory D^7 chord (bar 180).

The second portion of the Coda (bars 182–90: Ex. 4.19) is signalled at bars 181–2 by another expectant cadential gesture, presented by the quartet, outlining the 'A^{11}' chord of an imperfect close (from bar 13 of

---

[118] Ibid. (Scene v of Cendrars's scenario (my translation): for original French, see p. 146 above.)

the Final, and the Romance). Silence and space are as telling as sound: 'The couple is separated off in an embrace, which carries it along like a wave.' There is appropriate intimacy in the final allusions to the fugal interplay, heard in the original blues collection on D, now with initial emphasis on the major third. The three-quaver anacrusis returns and, in a last gesture of dialogue, material is assumed by each string instrument in turn, first descending, then ascending in pitch, whilst the piano resumes its accompanying role with the four-chord riff, first heard at bar 16: D–E^7–A^9–D (still maintaining the Lydian tendency). This incomplete seven-bar phrase is balanced by the final two bars (189–90, as a development of 181–2), which employ the cadential figure from the Romance for the last time. The viola provides the last chromatic gesture, highlighting the blues seventh, and ending with a deliciously subtle dissonance on the leading note (C♯), sustained against the D major chord ($I^{♯7}$). In keeping with the 'real' blues, there is no resolution.

In terms of comparison between Op. 81 and Op. 81*b*, the chamber Final constitutes Scenes IV and V of the original ballet. As before, some material is reordered: the introductory bars 1–15 in Op. 81*b* which refer to the Prélude correspond with bars 525–37 in the final Scene V of Op. 81. Condensation in allusion to the Prélude also occurs in relation to Episode 2: 19 bars of Op. 81 (bars 440–58) are reduced to a mere 9 bars in Op. 81*b* (bars 107–15). With regard to instrumentation, some details of the piano accompaniment are simplified in Op. 81*b* (e.g. around bar 36), whilst the cello part is more wide-ranging, as a means of compensating for the lack of double bass (e.g. bar 41 of Op. 81*b*, compared with bar 374 of Op. 81). As a connected matter, there are certain registral changes, such as that across bars 131–2 of Op. 81*b* where violin I descends a semitone, as opposed to the angular seventh contour on saxophone (bars 474–5 of Op. 81). Obviously, the percussive effects on metal-/wood-blocks and cymbals cannot be reproduced in Op. 81*b*. Generally, the effect in the *Suite de concert* is less dramatic but arguably more controlled. Both versions use 'tutti' forces for the climax achieved at bar 147 (Op. 81*b*) and bar 490 (Op. 81), with notably more accentuation marks in the chamber version than in the original. The harmony tends to correspond closely, although there are often small textural changes as a result of modified arrangement (the 'riffs' offer a typical example). In respect of the ending, bar 182 (Op. 81*b*) and bar 538 (Op. 81) correspond, although the melody which was originally assumed solely by the flutter-tonguing flute is now distributed amongst the quartet. The final cadential bars correspond exactly, with viola and piano of Op. 81*b* assuming the original saxophone line.

Conclusion

La Création du monde makes widespread use of modality, invoking the Aeolian and Dorian modes, and, particularly, a blues collection on D. Consequently, the conclusion too focuses on issues of modality, considering firstly a summary of modal types, following extensive monitoring within each movement (Appendix Ex. 4.20). A major/minor third distinction has been made here in order to consider the deviation from standard major or minor scales: thus modes 1–3, as labelled in this example, are regarded as 'major' third forms, and modes 4–7 as 'minor' third forms. Each mode is divided into upper and lower tetrachords, and patterns of symmetry are established by calculating the semitonal pitch content. Of note in this respect is the Dorian mode (No. 6) which offers a good example of complete tetrachordal symmetry, although it occurs less frequently in *La Création du monde* than does the Aeolian. Equally, the blues collection may be viewed as a direct consequence of modal mixture: a hybrid of Ionian/Aeolian, or Mixolydian/harmonic minor, although it is of course used in a distinctive manner, highlighting interplay between the 'blue' and 'real' note on the third, seventh and sometimes sixth degrees.[119] The creation of modal models from contexts within *La Création*, as shown in Ex. 4.20, seeks to stress the instinctive, flexible nature of Milhaud's modality, with close-knit relations between collections.

The thematic basis of *La Création* is founded on processes of modal complementation, exhibiting a discrete partitioning into upper and lower scalic segments, pivoting about the fifth degree (Ex. 4.21).[120] Some themes are focused on the upper segment (A–D) i.e. material A, and others on its complement, the lower segment (D–A) i.e. material B, each segment featuring strongly the blues notes. Designations of material A and B are used simply because the initial Theme A (Prélude) utilizes the upper tetrachord 4-11 and subset 3-7 (i.e. one singleton set, and one progenitor referable to Genus 7), whilst its Counterthemes refer only to the lower part of the scale: 5-23 (Genera 7/11). (It should be

---

[119] For further discussion, see J.B. Robinson, 'Blue note (i)', in *The New Grove Dictionary of Jazz*, i, 120.

[120] Refer back to the partitioning of the blues scale in Chapter 2 above.

noted that consideration of genera is included here mainly to facilitate comparison across the various case studies.)

Sometimes upper and lower segments are each enclosed within a distinct part of the same theme. The main motive that constitutes the subject of the Fugue subscribes to the lower scalic portion, to which it returns after an excursion to the upper tetrachord in the second phrase. Material B in the Fugue embraces the main motive of both subject and countersubject: set 4-2, with subset 3-3, and, in the countersubject, superset 5-11 (all of Genus 6, though exhibiting some common ground with Genus 5). The varied countersubject (bar 22) inhabits the upper tetrachord (material A), with its main motive denoted as 4-4, including subset 3-3 (i.e. one singleton set, and one progenitor referable to Genus 8). The main material of the Romance is of course ambiguous in its tetrachordal orientation, consisting of sets 4-11, and 3-2 (referable to Genus 7, as Theme A). The Scherzo's initial Theme C and figurations in the dovetailed second section (from bar 16) definitely frequent the lower tetrachord, with set 5-24 (of Genera 7/11) and 3-2 (most likely of Genus 7, as for the Romance).

Other illustrations of a distinct partitioning of material within a theme include Theme D, whose first motive presents material A, set 3-7 (Genus 7, as Theme A), followed by the second motive with material B, set 5-23 (Genera 7/11, as the Prélude counterthemes). Theme E operates in converse fashion, presenting material B (set 5-24: Genera 7/11) across its first phrase, followed in the second phrase by material A (sets 4-2, 5-2 of Genus 6, or, in recognition of the chromatic voice-leading ascent, (C–C♯–D), i.e. subset 3-1, Genus 5). The Coda also demonstrates complementary processes, balancing set 4-2 and subset 3-3 (of Genus 6) on either side of its modal divider, as a reinvocation of the Fugue.

In generic summary, the predominant source of reference is the 'chromatic-diatonic' Genus 7 (sometimes supported by the 'diatonic' Genus 11, one of whose progenitors is the 3-9/9-9 'blues' scale); Genus 7 co-exists with more overt manifestations of the blues that subscribe, through set 3-3, to Genera 6 and 8 (together with further localized chromaticism denoted by Genus 5). One can scrutinize these generic findings by means of the Squo equation, although, since the abstracted schema of Ex. 4.21 represents an assemblage of discrete, localized motivic/thematic constructs, rather than an interpretation of a through-composed musical excerpt, the results are somewhat misleading. Obviously the Squo can offer a useful overview, but not one which particularly respects internal groupings, or associations, within the matrix. Nonetheless, the Squo indices generally endorse the status of Genus 11 (.157), and, the most frequently invoked, Genus 7 (.121); the more contentious aspects involve a raising of status for Genus 5 (.125), which merely duplicates part of the role of the more distinctive, yet underplayed, Genus 6 (.101), together with a slight underplaying also of Genus 8 (.089).[121]

The last remarks here on modality concern the pitch outline across the five movements of the *Suite de concert*. It is surely more than coincidence that the modal centres form the pattern (D–d–F♮–F♯–D), since this also represents the most fundamental blues progression. The irony is that no genuine piece of jazz would be so prescriptive, or, in the words of André Hodeir, show 'such faithfulness to the letter'![122]

Finally, concluding the comparative aspect of this study, the main differences between the original ballet and the chamber version are of superficial arrangement, reordering, omission, and compression. Although Op. 81*b* expresses only part of the whole, and loses something of the instrumental effects of Op. 81, it exhibits new qualities: clarity, precision, and a more overt neoclassicism than the original ballet. The *Suite de concert* is effective chamber music, and a valuable contribution to the piano quintet repertory.

---

[121] The Squo calculations here are based around eleven sets: 3-2, 3-3, 3-7, 3-9/9-9, 4-2, 4-4*, 4-11*, 5-2, 5-11, 5-23, and 5-24 (* denoting a singleton set): Squo(G11) = ((5/11)/29) = .157; Squo(G5) = ((4/11)/29) = .125; Squo(G7) = ((6/11)/45) = .121; Squo(G6) = ((5/11)/45) = .101; Squo(G8) = ((4/11)41) = .089. As stated elsewhere, the precise Squo calculations can seem too strongly slewed by the respective sizes of the different genera (as a more theoretical concern which lies beyond the music in question), and consequently sometimes under-represent the actual presence and extent of certain genera in any one musical context.

[122] Hodeir, *Jazz: Its Evolution and Essence*, 252.

CHAPTER FIVE

Neoclassicism: Refined Modality

❦

En réaction contre l'impressionnisme des postdebussystes, les musiciens voulaient un art robuste, plus clair et plus précis, tout en demeurant humain et sensible.[1]

Après tous les brouillards impressionistes, cet art simple, clair, renouant la tradition de Scarlatti et de Mozart ne serait-il pas la prochaine phase de notre musique?[2]

NEOCLASSICISM is the main style (or, rather, aesthetic) to emerge in Milhaud's music of the 1920s, coexisting with, and then superseding the jazz-inspired style. Part of the reason for the coexistence of these complementary traits lies in their common concern in exploring concepts of 'distance' and 'difference'. Parallel with the idea of 'distance as space', signalled in Chapter 4, is the consideration here of 'distance as time' (in conjunction with place and myth), focusing on Milhaud's attitude towards an eighteenth-century (and also a more distant) past, not least as a means of dislocation from the present and most immediate past.

This introductory outline seeks the sources and stylistic nature of neoclassicism in Milhaud's music, and, in a sense, the music examined here represents a stylistic refinement and development of that considered in Chapter 3, because the 'polytonal' experiments in *Les Choéphores* (1915–16), for example, are one of the immediate sources of this neoclassicism. Such 'polytonality' is usually reduced in more overtly neoclassical contexts to a localized bimodality, or a single diatonic modality. This clarification of Milhaud's style may have occurred partly as a result of researching and writing his critical article of 1923, 'Polytonalité et atonalité', although the seeds for change were already sown in works such as the Fifth Chamber Symphony (1922).

Brief discussion of the general characteristics of that notoriously troublesome term 'neoclassicism' seems appropriate (and inevitable), in

---

[1] Milhaud, *Ma vie heureuse*, 81.
[2] Ibid., 82. These opening quotations are translated and discussed above in Chapter 1, pp. 12–13.

order to view Milhaud's approach in context. Arnold Whittall's definition of the 'neoclassical' in music focuses on the revival of 'balanced forms and clearly perceptible thematic processes of earlier styles'[3] as a reaction against the excesses of late Romanticism. Despite the backward-looking nature of neoclassicism, and, in the words of Keller, its 'suppression of expressionism',[4] the aim is not to remove all hint of expressiveness or progressiveness. Indeed, Whittall comments that 'the prefix "neo-" often carries the implication of parody, or distortion, of truly Classical traits.'[5]

Certainly, many neoclassical composers, including Milhaud, do allude to earlier practice, particularly that of the Baroque period, within new contexts that thrive on economy, discipline and wit, and hence the 'Back to Bach' tag attached to much music of the 1920s. Perhaps in Milhaud's case, with his awareness of French eighteenth-century tradition, one would suggest a variant of 'Back to Couperin'. Milhaud's concern to pay homage to (in itself a typically eighteenth-century response), and his need to belong within, a French tradition are arguably amongst the most striking features of his artistic persona. The other striking characteristic has to be his apparent lack of self-criticism (and the resultant unevenness of his output), and even this facet may be related in part to his viewing composition as a re-invocation of eighteenth-century technical craftsmanship—a craftmanship which sometimes exceeds its true inspiration. In terms of a special affinity with François Couperin, one may consider Milhaud's equivalent of Ravel's *Le Tombeau de Couperin*, his orchestral arrangement *Introduction et Allegro*, Op. 220 (1940) of Couperin's Suite *La Sultane*, and, more broadly, his emulation of the fanciful titling so associated with Couperin in a work like *Machines agricoles* (1919)—a trait also echoed by Milhaud's mentor Satie. Such tributes, especially those which quote material directly (e.g. Milhaud's *Suite d'après Corrette*, Op. 16*b* (1937)), raise fascinating questions of musical ownership in a way that sometimes foreshadows postmodernist concerns.

Later in his definition, Whittall invokes Salzman's suggestion that a better, more comprehensive, term than 'neoclassical' would be 'neo-

---

[3] A. Whittall, 'Neoclassical', *The New Grove Dictionary*, xiii, 104.
[4] Keller, as quoted by Whittall, ibid.
[5] Ibid.

tonal'.[6] And although Salzman is right that the pursuit of technical stances often proves more productive than being overly preoccupied by neoclassicism as a stylistic 'bête noire', in the case of Milhaud's music the term 'neotonal' is far too general. Indeed, most of Milhaud's works would fit under a 'neotonal' or at least 'neomodal' umbrella, including the jazz-inspired pieces and early experimental works. Pursuing further the line of Salzman's argument, in his concern with the 'neotonal', Whittall offers a cautionary note, which should be heeded in discussion of Milhaud's neoclassicism:

> the dangers of unproductive over-simplification are probably greater than for any other style or period, and the most valuable approach so far has been that of such analysts as Salzer, whose often very substantial modifications of Schenkerian principles can at least indicate the extent to which certain works may properly be defined as 'tonal' at all.[7]

Finally, Whittall considers that well-documented comment of Pierre Boulez concerning 'dead forms' bringing about 'dead musical ideas',[8] which, in respect of Milhaud's neoclassicism, also seems inappropriate. Milhaud's ideas are, on the contrary, positive, vital and forward-looking: although he may rework 'dead' forms and textures, his work seems to be striving towards a further goal of total contrapuntal independence. And in the 1920s, at least, his neoclassical compositions also assimilate traits from his imaginative early experimentation, and from jazz.

One of the most important pieces of research which tries to grapple with what exactly neoclassicism might mean (and may have meant in the past) is the scholarly historical study by Scott Messing.[9] For this writer, the consequences of musicians having invoked this term so loosely over a considerable period of time have been that 'a collation of usages produced such a variety of meaning that the expression seemed to possess no syntactical weight whatsoever.'[10] Beyond his initial discussion, the chapters of Messing's book with particular pertinence to the present study include those on 'Neoclassicism in France: 1914–1923' and 'Neoclassicism and Stravinsky: 1914–1923'. The former chap-

---

[6] E. Salzman, *Twentieth-Century Music: An Introduction* (rev. edn., Englewood Cliffs, 1974), 44.
[7] Whittall, 'Neoclassical', *The New Grove Dictionary*, vol. 13, 105.
[8] P. Boulez, *Par volonté et par hasard: Entretiens avec Célestin Deliège* (Paris, 1975; Eng. trans., London, 1976), 31, as quoted by Whittall.
[9] Messing, *Neoclassicism*.
[10] Ibid, Preface, xiii.

ter is significant in that this is where Messing refines the neoclassical terminology in relation to historical context, explaining the distinction, operative until about 1923, between the initially pejorative 'néoclassicisme' (suggesting banal imitation, implicitly dominated by German hegemony), and the far more complimentary 'nouveau classicisme' (suggesting a reinvocation of all that was best within French tradition).[11] The second of the two chapters includes a significant quotation from Milhaud's second article of 1923, 'The Evolution of Modern Music in Paris and Vienna',[12] which regards differences between diatonic and chromatic composition as exemplifying respectively Latin and Teutonic temperamental approaches in a way that now seems simplistic and too zealously categorized, and yet his perception of diatonicism and chromaticism as representing opposite expressive 'poles' was highly applicable here in Case Study 3 on the Fifth Chamber Symphony. In ascertaining further contemporary views on neoclassicism, Messing also consults the writings of the 1920s critic, Boris de Schloezer, who perceived

> Pure music, stripped of all psychological meaning; the sentiments, emotions, and desires . . . are here enclosed in a rigorous form which subdues them, purifies them and gives them an exclusively resonant existence.[13]

Messing's overall conclusions are that 'From its birth, neoclassicism was reckoned as an aesthetic idea. . . . Its use as an indicator of style was, by contrast, a relatively late development.'[14] He considers that 'neoclassicism' was a more useful notion in the 1920s than perhaps it is today: 'a convenient code by which French composers could put forward aesthetic ideas based upon a nostalgic evocation of a moribund style';[15] and that 'The gradual disrepute into which the word neoclassicism fell is parallel to the rise in literature on Stravinsky and Schoenberg which has devised increasingly elegant methods for analyzing their music.'[16] Nonetheless, it seems that there is still a place for neoclassicism in musical analysis today (as evidenced perhaps by Joseph

---

[11] Ibid., 82.

[12] Milhaud, 'The Evolution of Modern Music in Paris and Vienna': quoted in Messing, *Neoclassicism*, 124.

[13] B. de Schloezer, 'La saison musicale', *Nouvelle revue française*, 1 (August 1923): quoted in Messing, *Neoclassicism*, 131.

[14] Messing, *Neoclassicism*, 151.

[15] Ibid.

[16] Ibid., 153.

Straus's study discussed below); or, at least, that there is not yet any satisfactory alternative, and although the examples in Messing's work are not directly relevant, his advice and cautions have facilitated a more considered approach to this aspect of Milhaud's music. Finally, endorsing the need for proper consideration of neoclassicism in relation both to musicological and analytical concerns, one should stress that, although the term is bandied about too often and too carelessly, beyond any superficial simplicity, the concept proves to be a highly complex and difficult one emerging as a composite flowering of such diverse late nineteenth-century concerns as the revival of plain-chant and celebration of the cultures of Ancient Greece and Rome (especially dramatic tragedy), in tandem with a direct reaction against the more immediate excesses of late Romanticism (probably reinforced by the First World War).

The final, most recent, contribution to research which lies broadly within the domain of neoclassicism is Joseph Straus's book, *Remaking the Past*.[17] In a brave attempt to mediate between aesthetic and analytical concerns, this work usefully develops the deeply problematic notion of 'Back to Bach' (or Couperin), mentioned earlier. Central to Straus's thesis is that it may be possible to envisage a musical equivalent of Harold Bloom's seminal theory of poetry, *The Anxiety of Influence*, and hence Straus's opening chapter, 'Towards a Theory of Musical Influence'. This involves consideration of the nature of tradition and notions of intertextuality; in accordance with Bloom's poetic theory, musical works are seen not as self-contained but as 'relational events'.[18] Straus explores applications of 'revisionary strategies', deliberate 'misreadings' and 'recompositions' in relation to 'the anxiety of influence' exerted by specific works of musical predecessors, with illustrations taken from the music of Stravinsky and Schoenberg, amongst others.[19] Certainly, where Milhaud is concerned, there is potential in the concept not merely of invoking, but rather of reinterpreting, and

---

[17] See also the continuance of this theme in P. van den Toorn, 'Neoclassicism Revised', in *Music, Politics, and the Academy* (Berkeley and Los Angeles, 1995), 143–78.
[18] Ibid., 12.
[19] It is probably Edward T. Cone's essay in Henry Lang's short book on Stravinsky, back in 1963, which first raises the the idea of a composer subscribing to conventions in order to flout them, and which leads on to the establishment of musical 'models' which may then be deconstructed (Edward T. Cone, 'The Uses of Convention: Stravinsky and his Models', in Paul Henry Lang, ed., *Stravinsky: A new Appraisal of his Work* (New York, 1963), 21–33).

sometimes ironizing, a specifically French musical past. And, whether or not Milhaud struggled consciously with the anxiety of the influence of the immediate past (or, in the terms of Straus and Bloom, a second, more general, 'anxiety of style'), it is undoubtedly the case that he uses a variety of distancing techniques in his treatment of 'classicism'. The most explicit application of Straus's ideas occurs in Case Study 7 on the Clarinet Sonatina which pursues a subtext concerned with rethinking and rewriting sonata form, in some senses an equivalent of Straus's interpretation of Stravinsky's intentions in the opening movement of his Octet.[20]

In defining and exploring neoclassicism in Milhaud's music, one must continue to embrace the composer's own thoughts on the matter, expressed especially in *Ma vie heureuse* (as in the quotations which head this chapter, and which were first discussed in Chapter 1).[21] Milhaud's most obviously neoclassical undertaking before 1930 is the composition of the set of Six Chamber Symphonies (literally 'Little Symphonies': 1917-1923). Some of these have already been discussed here in connection with early experimentation and the development of the jazz style; the series as a whole, however, is underpinned by an increasingly strong neoclassical aesthetic. If one had to cite a neoclassical prototype in Milhaud's œuvre it would tempting to select the First Chamber Symphony (1917), although the style and accompanying techniques are only incipient and still owe something to Impressionism. A less controversial choice would be the Fourth Chamber Symphony, or *Dixtuor à cordes* (1921), with its 'Ouverture', 'Choral' and fugal 'Étude'.

The series of chamber symphonies is best regarded as part of a revival of interest in Baroque structure and proportion, and it is hard to imagine Milhaud's being unaffected by Bach's set of Brandenburg Concerti. Superficially, Milhaud's works (another set of six) also have important dedications, though of a more personal nature, and the subtitle of the First Chamber Symphony, 'Le Printemps', inevitably evokes associations with Vivaldi. Milhaud's set is roughly contemporary with Hindemith's *Kammermusik* series (1922–27); and, interestingly, Milhaud's Fifth Chamber Symphony, Stravinsky's Octet and Hindemith's

---

[20] Straus, *Remaking the Past*, 103–7.
[21] One should acknowledge that Milhaud tends to avoid using the word 'neoclassicism' directly, possibly because of the associations mentioned by Messing. Mention should also be made here of Barbara Kelly's recent doctoral dissertation on 'Milhaud and the French Musical Tradition', which usefully complements the present book, with its historical rather than analytical focus.

Kleine Kammermusik for Wind Quintet, were all composed (or at least begun) in 1922. In *Ma vie heureuse*, Milhaud explains the appeal of this genre:

> Cette qualité sonore si spéciale d'un groupe d'instruments me tenta et je commençai une série de Petites Symphonies pour sept ou dix instruments différents. J'avais hâte d'entendre ces essais d'indépendance tonale: Braga dirigea la Première Symphonie à un de ses concerts. Le public ne sembla pas surpris par les sonorités de ma musique, mais ignorant ou oubliant qu'à l'époque de Monteverdi, le mot 'symphonie' désignait parfois une seule page de musique instrumentale, il s'attendait à entendre une immense œuvre avec un immense orchestre; il fut choqué par la brévité de mon morceau.[22]

He saw the works as 'experiments in tonal independence', containing elements both of concerto and symphony, i.e. concerted music, 'sounding together' in the literal meaning of sinfonia. Where the reference to Monteverdi is concerned, one can only assume that Milhaud is thinking of the 'sinfonia avanti l'opera', or a short instrumental 'intermède' in a similar context.

Despite some reservations about the Fifth Chamber Symphony voiced in Case Study 3, it should be acknowledged that this work was nonetheless the most favourably regarded by both Collaer and Milhaud, and that consequently the work serves as a focus for commentary which can sometimes be applicable more broadly, as with the remark that 'Les accords n'interviennent la plupart du temps qu'aux points d'articulation des sections dont se compose la forme.'[23] This is an appropriate generalization of the role of chordal passages in Milhaud's chamber music, and also serves to highlight common ground with Hindemith's 'pillar chords'.[24]

All the chamber symphonies exhibit formal economy, usually reliant on the principle of exposition of material without traditional develop-

---

[22] Milhaud, *Ma vie heureuse*, 69–70: 'I was attracted by the unusual quality of small groups of instruments, and embarked on a series of 'Little Symphonies' for seven or more different instruments. I was anxious to hear these experiments in tonal independence: Braga directed the First Symphony in one of his concerts. The audience did not seem surprised by the sonorities of my music, but, ignorant or forgetful of the fact that in Monteverdi's day the word 'symphony' was sometimes used to denote a single page of instrumental music, it was expecting to hear a huge work with a huge orchestra; it was shocked by the brevity of my piece.'

[23] Collaer, *Darius Milhaud*, 330: 'Most of the time, chords only occur at the articulation points of the sections which comprise the form.'

[24] Neumeyer, *Paul Hindemith*, 39.

ment. Milhaud employs typically baroque procedures of canon, fugue, inversion, retrograde, augmentation and diminution, together with the concerto grosso concept of 'concertino' and 'ripieno', implicit in the Fifth Chamber Symphony and elsewhere. Significantly, beyond the 1920s, there are no further works of concerted chamber music before the *Aspen Serenade* (1957).

Milhaud's Sixth and Seventh Quartets (1922, 1925) are much more neoclassical in style than the Fourth or Fifth Quartets, although they are not completely free of other traits. The Sixth still involves modal mixture at the third and limited chromaticism; nevertheless, the structures are more compact than in the Fifth Quartet: relative durations are of 8'45", as against 20'40"! As with the ending of the second of the 'Opéras-minute' (Case Study 8), the textures of the finale of the Sixth Quartet, with alternating 3/8 4/8 metre, strongly suggest Stravinskian influence (see Fig. 5.7 below). The finale of the Seventh Quartet, meanwhile, involves a fugal presentation with a witty 'off-beat' conclusion; vestiges of the jazz style, however, persist in the second movement, 'Doux et sans hâte', with melodic presentation of the blues third (in the cello line around bar 52).

Connected to the writing of absolute music for quartet is the continuing interest in the sonata, or sonatina. The Flute Sonatina (1922) still suggests a stylistic mixture, but it is much developed from the earlier, late Romantic Violin Sonatas. The first truly neoclassical product is the Clarinet Sonatina (1927), which also has an added 'dramatic' dimension, acquired through the increased interest in opera, discussed below. The year 1927 also marks a transcription/arrangement of an early nineteenth-century work: *Trois caprices de Paganini* (1927), with three of the extraordinary 24 *Caprices*, Op. 1, for solo violin by Niccolò Paganini (1782-1840) arranged for violin and piano. Milhaud's desire to undertake this exercise again suggests that he finds inspiration for new compositional projects in the past.

This trend is taken to a further extreme in vocal works based on the texts and history of Classical Rome and Greece, such as *Quatre poèmes de Catulle* (1923, Case Study 6), presented in French translation, for voice and violin. This is one of Milhaud's most effectively simple works, which utilizes distancing techniques and provides a superb example of natural modality, although even here there are hints of the blues scale. Registering the significance of the Greek perspective, one may cite the initial example of *Les Malheurs d'Orphée* (1924), together with the three 'Opéras-minute' (1927). In *Ma vie heureuse*, Milhaud considered that '*Les Malheurs d'Orphée* est le premier d'une série de petits opéras de chambre que j'écrivais par la suite; les éléments sonores y sont réduits au minimum'.[25] The composition of the trilogy of 'Opérasminute' in that fruitful year of 1927 represents the epitome of Milhaud's classically inspired dramas of the 1920s. Their combined performance time is only twenty-seven minutes, the idea being to produce 'little showpieces, rather than intense emotional dramas. They are exquisite chamber music, with charming melodic lines, delicate sonorities, and a touch of irony.'[26] Whatever reservations one has about Collaer's wording here, his acknowledgement of irony in treatment of the myths, both by Milhaud and his librettist Henri Hoppenot, is certainly significant, and is pursued below in Case Study 8. The success of these operatic miniatures lies in their clarity of modal language and linear elegance, with the increasingly important dramatic perspective paving the way for the 'grand opéra' projects of *Christophe Colomb* (1928) and *Maximilien* (1930). *Christophe Colomb*, in particular, might be viewed as the culmination of Milhaud's achievement at the close of this present period of study.

Before examining Milhaud's neoclassical traits from a more technical stance (and as a means of developing the context for Case Studies 6 and 8), two implicit aesthetic concerns, which run across several works, should briefly be addressed. The first, already signalled in terms of distancing techniques, involves processes of objectification and detachment, often resulting in the creation of a deliberately artificial, or synthetic, musical artefact. Such objectification in Milhaud has its parallels in contemporary Stravinsky (*Mavra*, the Octet and *Oedipus Rex*), as observed by Stephen Walsh and Glenn Watkins, amongst others.[27] Although this is primarily a facet of Milhaud's neoclassicism, one may draw together the threads across a range of repertory which also embraces some of the exploratory and jazz-inspired works. In the Fifth Chamber Symphony (Case Study 3), the concept of detached and

---

[25] Milhaud, *Ma vie heureuse*, 141: '*Les Malheurs d'Orphée* is the first of a series of chamber operas which I then wrote; the elements of sound are reduced here to the absolute minimum'. Note again the expression: 'éléments sonores'.

[26] Collaer/Galante, *Darius Milhaud*, 103.

[27] S. Walsh, 'Synthesis: *Mavra* and the New Classicism', *The Music of Stravinsky* (Oxford, 1988), 111–33: e.g. '*Mavra* is an essentially artificial product, almost a statement about art' (115). Milhaud was amongst the few who rated *Mavra* highly at its première in 1922 (see *Ma vie heureuse,* 110).

autonomous mechanisms is used as a means of achieving such objectification, thus creating an innate conflict between fixed and free elements. Then, in *La Création du monde* (Case Study 5), distance and deliberate alienation of the audience from the remote, mysterious subject-matter of African legend is achieved dramatically by means of Léger's huge masks which conceal their human inhabitants and so emphasize the untouchable and larger-than-life quality of the spectacle.

The theme is continued in the first song of *Quatre poèmes de Catulle* (Case Study 6), whose text maintains distance through its emphasis on the third, rather than first or second, person (i.e. the subject-matter is 'objectified'), and its choice of tone as matter-of-fact réportage. We are not privy to the raw emotions of the distrustful lover: we only sense his distress indirectly, even then masked by misogyny, as he remarks on the supposed inconstancy, not just of one woman, but of all womankind (a further distancing and depersonalization through universalization). The speaker of the poem is merely a commentator on the action, his sense of alienation built into the structure of the text, and balanced by our own sense of separation from this poetry of another, ancient, world. The furthest extreme of this trend is perhaps represented by *L'Abandon d'Ariane* (Case Study 8), whose objectification, detachment and ironization is achieved by both musical and dramatic means. The musical language is deliberately over-simplified: pure diatonicism that at times borders on the trite in its parodies of common-practice formulae, juxtaposed by extreme chromaticism for moments of emotional instability. Hyperbole and melodrama are employed as the chorus (a clichéd 'Chorus of Gypsy Revellers') commentates, in the distanced third person, on the plight of Ariadne, 'O femme infortunée!': anguish at one remove.

The second aesthetic issue which is essentially part of Milhaud's neoclassicism, even though it appears in a broader range of contexts during his formative years up to 1922, is that of compression. Milhaud is deeply attracted by condensed, compact structures which represent the ultimate in concision, although they are not necessarily 'miniature', as will be demonstrated in discussion of the Clarinet Sonatina (Case Study 7). The trait has already been signalled in discussion of the Fifth Chamber Symphony (Case Study 3), where comparisons were drawn with the economy and wit of the contemporary cartoonist, whilst other examples include the earlier *Catalogue de fleurs* (1920) and the very notion of a trilogy of 'Opéras-minute'. Such a concept is also acknowledged by Straus as one of several techniques important within 'revisionary strategies': '*Compression*. Elements that occur diachronically in the earlier work [or style] (such as two triads in a functional relationship to each other) are compressed into something synchronous in the new one.'[28]

The purpose of this second part of the contextual outline is to survey neoclassical techniques and analytical concepts, and introduce Case Studies 6–8, which exemplify the neoclassical element of Milhaud's music before 1930, with the selection of a song, a sonatina, and a (chamber) opera underlining the variety of genre. There is common ground with Chapters 3 and 4, although Milhaud's techniques are now more sophisticated. Works which illustrate the neoclassical element are listed in Fig. 5.1, with square brackets indicating those already mentioned in Chapters 3 or 4. Principles of form and modality are followed by consideration of the 'triad motive' in the Chamber Symphonies, localized bimodal conflict, third relations, ostinato, pedalpoints, 'pillar chords' and further types of polarity.

Ternary Form is still the most common outline, of which the 'Souple et animé' of the Sixth Quartet (1922) is typical: A (1–14), B (18–34), A' (37–50), Coda (51–5). The short linking passages between contrasting sections (bars 15–17; 35–6) and their incorporation within the coda are characteristic of increased refinements made to the basic ternary structure in Milhaud's mature neoclassical pieces. The finale of the Sixth Quartet illustrates an extended tripartite form: AB/AB/A, with subtlety and variety of treatment in the repeated Section A lying in the rhythmic parameter. The same AB/AB/A format is employed in the third movement of the Seventh Quartet (1925), as a type of sonata form: Exposition of A (1–18), B (19–24), Link (25–26), Development of A (27–33), B (40–46), Link (46–9), Recapitulation of A (50–58). In addition to two balancing subjects (across Sections A and B), two ostinati play an important, independent role; Milhaud also introduces a new idea into the development, and recapitulates this in the final section.

Fugue, with its special Bachian associations, holds a particular fascination for Milhaud and is most significant in neoclassical (more accurately neobaroque) contexts. He greatly admired the fugal masterpieces of J.S. Bach and sought to recreate the spirit of their technical crafts-

---

[28] Straus, *Remaking the Past*, 17.

Figure 5.1   Neoclassical Works

1917	[*Première petite symphonie*, Op. 43]*
1918	[*Quatrième quatuor*, Op. 46 (I, III)]
	Deuxième petite symphonie, Op. 49
1921	*Troisième petite symphonie*, Op. 71
	Quatrième petite symphonie (*Dixtuor à cordes*), Op. 74
1922	*Sixième quatuor*, Op. 77
1923	*Quatre poèmes de Catulle*, Op. 80 (voice & violin)
1924	*Les Malheurs d'Orphée*, Op. 85 (chamber opera)
1925	*Seizième quatuor*, Op. 87
1927	*L'Enlèvement d'Europe*, Op. 94 ('Opéra-minute')
	Trois caprices de Paganini, Op. 97 (violin & piano)
	L'Abandon d'Ariane, Op. 98 ('Opéra-minute')
	La Délivrance de Thésée, Op. 99 ('Opéra-minute')
	Sonatine pour clarinette et piano, Op. 100

* Square brackets indicate works also relevant in a different connection in Chapters 3 or 4.

manship,[29] with the best examples being found in the finales of the Fourth Chamber Symphony ('Étude'), and the Seventh Quartet ('Vif et gai'). This latter movement maintains well the traditional balance of the formal sections: Exposition (1–16), Middle Section (23–37), Final Section (55–67) and Coda (67–70), looking forward, in its formal and modal clarity, to the neoclassical sonatas and concertos beyond 1930. Subject and countersubject operate within a strong Lydian modality on B♭, with ostinato parts on viola and cello which then constitute a second countersubject and 'free part'. These ingredients are first combined in bars 9–12, with the Subject on viola, Countersubject 1 on second violin, Countersubject 2 (ostinato) on first violin, and the 'free part' (ostinato) on cello.

As in those works which are largely exploratory, or jazz-inspired, modality is still the underlying structural concept, now more sophisticated in its usage. The high profile of modality in neoclassical contexts of the 1920s is demonstrated by a particular melodic hall-mark, the 'triad motive'. This simple lyrical gesture, comprising an ascending major or minor sixth, followed by a descending major or minor third interval (or third progression), is hardly remarkable in itself (see Fig. 5.2), but what is striking is the frequency and variety of usage as an

---

[29] For confirmation of J.S. Bach as a major influence, see Chapter 1, p. 2, n. 2; p. 5, n. 14; and Chapter 4, p. 121 above.

instinctive part of Milhaud's vocabulary. Its prominence serves to underline the relative diatonic emphasis of the neoclassical works, and though it may appear most bland, 'The triad', as acknowledged by Straus, 'becomes the locus of the struggle between present and past.'[30] Despite its triadic simplicity, the motive has a clear identity: the pattern commonly occurs as the ascending-descending curve, rather than in inversion, with the stressed pitch usually the third scalic degree. Examples abound in the Six Chamber Symphonies (Figs. 5.3–5.6).

Figure 5.2   Triad Motive

Sometimes the triad motive is part of a main theme, as in the first movement of the First Symphony ('Le Printemps'), presented on piccolo and oboe (bars 20–2), followed by strings (bars 23–4), and then resumed by piccolo and oboe (bars 26–8). A more embellished version occurs in the finale of the Second Symphony ('Pastorale'), within a four-bar flute ostinato which is heard eight times. There are various prefixes and suffixes (and optional decorations), with an example of the former in the 'Calme' central movement of the Third Symphony ('Sérénade'), played by violin doubling bassoon (bars 3, 5, 7), clarinet doubling bassoon (bar 15), and by solo violin (bars 21–2). The motive also forms the start of a phrase in the finale, presented by the flute in a Lydian mode on D (bars 16–18; 25–7). Melodic extension of the motive is demonstrated again in the opening movement of the Fourth Symphony, firstly by the cello emphasizing the third degree of an overall modality on C (bars 10–14: Fig. 5.3*a*), and secondly by the violin on A (bars 26–9). More rarely the motive functions as a suffix to a phrase, such as in the opening 'Rude' of the Fifth Symphony where this idea is heard on clarinet (bars 6–8), or in the fugal finale of the Fourth Symphony where the triad motive both generates and concludes a new countersubject on A, first heard on viola (bars 13–14: Fig. 5.3*b*).

---

[30] Straus, *Remaking the Past*, 20.

Figure 5.3*a* Fourth Chamber Symphony: I, bars 10–14

   b Fourth Chamber Symphony: III, bars 13–14

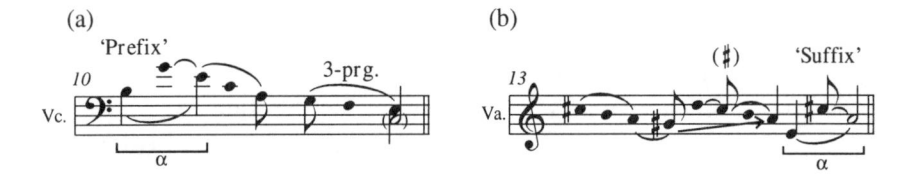

The triad motive may permeate many or all of the polyphonic strata, as in the first movement of the Third Symphony,[31] where the motive appears on bassoon across bars 1–2, 4, 9, 12, through, with some exceptions, to bar 34. In the missing bars it is found transferred to the viola (bars 5–6, 13–15), double bass (bars 9–10, 12–16), violin doubling bassoon (bars 17–18), and to flute and clarinet (bars 20–3). The flute line is particularly effective, with the end of one motivic figure becoming the start of a second within a single instrumental voice: (E,C,A; G,E,C) (Fig. 5.4).

Figure 5.4 Third Chamber Symphony: I, bars 20–3

The next stage of development is the interlinking of statements as a stretto. Occasionally the second statement is an inversion of the first, as with the flute material at bars 14–15 in the first movement of the First Symphony. More commonly the 6th–3rd intervallic pattern is reversed and the shape (ascent-descent) inverted, as in bars 7–8 of the second movement of the Third Symphony: (D,B,G) ascent-descent; (D,B,G) descent-ascent. Similarly, in the second movement of the Fifth Symphony (bass clarinet, bars 22–3), the statements are also interlinked: (E♭,C,A♭) ascent-descent; (C,A♭,F) descent-ascent. In the opening movement of the Sixth Symphony (oboe, bars 22–3), the first statement in bar 22 appears in partial retrograde as (F♯,D,A), as opposed to the usual pitch order which follows in bar 23, (A,F♯,D)

---

[31] The resultant modality of the opening of this movement is discussed below (including Fig. 5.8).

Neoclassicism: Refined Modality

ascent–descent.[32] The first statement ends on the fifth degree, decorated by upper and lower neighbour-notes, prior to forming the start of the next statement. Returning to the opening of the Third Symphony, the motivic figure can occur in original form followed by retrograde inversion, as in the flute line of bars 22–3 where (G,E,C) ascent–descent is balanced by (C,E,G) descent–ascent (see again Fig. 5.4). A final illustration of stretto in use of the motive is provided by the ending of the second movement, where the clarinet supplies the ascending sixth interval: (C♯,D♯–B,G♯), with its latter pitch coinciding with the first pitch of the bassoon: (A-F), and thus signalling the next topic of modal mixture (at the third).

Modal mixture (and upper neighbour-note decoration) in the triad motive is illustrated by the 'Lent' of the Fifth Symphony, with the oboe line of bars 11–15 (Fig. 5.5) and clarinet line of bars 27–9 and 31. Such jazz allusions are continued in the remarkable Sixth Symphony, for soprano, alto, tenor and bass, with oboe and cello.

Figure 5.5 Fifth Chamber Symphony: II, bars 11–15: Modal mixture

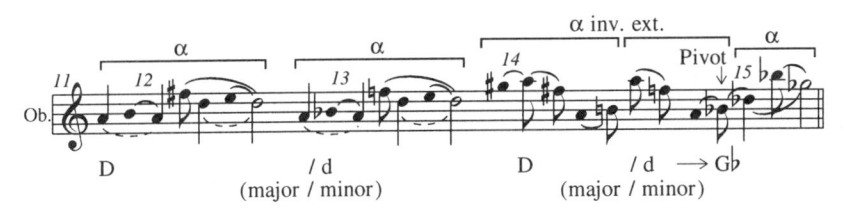

Sometimes the initial sixth interval may be expanded to a minor seventh or octave, as in the final sustained bar of the 'Souple et vif' of the same work. Alternatively, the sixth may be partially filled in by inclusion of a decorative pitch, either a tone above the first pitch, or a tone below the second, as in other instances in the Sixth Symphony (Fig. 5.6*a* and *b*):

The triad motive can be traced back to the first movement of the Third Quartet of 1916 (bar 15) and the opening of the Fourth Quartet. The fifth and seventh songs of *Catalogue de fleurs* (1920) refer to it, as does the opening movement of the Sixth Quartet. In the third of *Quatre poèmes de Catulle* (1923), the motive assumes an important role, concerned with pitches (F♯,D♯,B) in the central section (bars 11–16). In-

---

[32] If this shape and emphasis on the middle, highest pitch were not important to the triad motive, any 'broken triad' could be regarded as a variant.

Figure 5.6a Sixth Chamber Symphony: II, bars 5–6
       b Sixth Chamber Symphony: I, bars 2–3

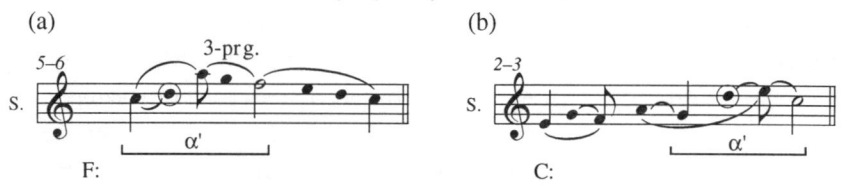

deed, most compositions of the 1920s, other than the jazz-influenced repertory, share the trait, so that general principles of motivic process in Milhaud's neoclassicism are demonstrated by the specific exploration of the triad motive in the Six Chamber Symphonies.

Neoclassical modality also includes further occurrences of the Altered Mixolydian, as in the last song of *Quatre poèmes*, the finale of the Sixth Quartet, and second movement of the Seventh Quartet. Curiously this mode is always encountered with its final on G, in both exploratory and neoclassical contexts. The main chordal sound associated with the mode is (G,B,D,E♭), i.e. set 4-19, more commonly expressed as an augmented seventh chord with E♭ in the bass: (E♭,G,B,D). The finale (III) of the Sixth Quartet, particularly, demonstrates the chordal properties of Altered Mixolydian modality, with the statement of a 'tonic' sonority (G,E♭,G,A,D) 'warmed' immediately afterwards by the necessary B♮ (Fig. 5.7). This chord again embodies polarity between centres a third apart, so that one might view this construct, in Straus's terms, as a tonal axis of competing yet balanced triads: (E♭,G,B); (G,B,D).

In addition to the Altered Mixolydian, more traditional modes are found in authentic and sometimes plagal forms. The Lydian (on F and C) is particularly favoured in Milhaud's neoclassicism, as shown in the finale of the Clarinet Sonatina (Case Study 7). Localized use of Dorian and Phrygian is quite common, with occasional octatonic and pentatonic collections—the latter used for instance in a process of modal complementation in Scene V of *L'Abandon d'Ariane* (Case Study 8). There is also limited use of a hexatonic scale on G: (G,A,B,C,D,E), omitting reference to a leading-note (Case Study 6). Usually, the single large-scale modality operating at background level tends to be of Ionian or Lydian patterning.

Third relations are most prominent in the neoclassical domain, with their importance as a generative melodic force already demonstrated by the triad motive. Milhaud's melodies usually involve a simple triadic

Figure 5.7 Sixth Quartet: III, bars 1–12

framework with integral third relations, and these melodies may also operate in contrapuntal combination, as in the 'Lent' of the Sixth Quartet, where at foreground level, in bar 14, third intervals are exchanged between violin I and cello: (E,C), (D♯,B). At background level, this movement based on B features strong 'bass' emphasis on the third scalic degree: D♯(E♭). A similar enharmonic pivot operates at this same scalic degree in the third of *Quatre poèmes*, also centred on B, with the prominent D♯ (bars 11 and 14) converted to E♭ (bars 19, 21–2) and back to D♯ (bar 23), signalled at a localized level from the outset by melodic third progressions (B,C♯,D♯). The fourth song, 'Ma chérie, en présence de son mari', commences with a derived, minor third Phrygian figure (B,C,D), whose transformation from (B,C♯,D♯) would, in the parlance of Jeremy Drake, embody 'inflectional polyvalency'.[33] The last two vocal bars reinforce this notion with a modification, emphasized by rhythmic augmentation, back to a major third span, now (B♭,C,D).

Third relations can be incorporated into the harmonic perspective simultaneously, in the form of localized bimodality, as in the opening of the Sixth Quartet which involves ambiguity between centres on g (predominant) and E♭ (subsidiary). In bars 1–7, violin II and cello assert a hexatonic mode on G: (G,A,B,C,D,E), whilst the viola subscribes to the harmonic minor and Aeolian on g: (G,A,B♭,C,D,E♭,F♮/F♯,G) so that there is innate modal conflict even before the first violin's introduction (at the end of bar 6) of a five-note major mode segment on E♭: (E♭,F,G,A♭,B♭). Third relations may also exist successively between sections of a movement, often related to ternary form, and between movements of a work. A large-scale third progression across a movement is seen in the 'Lent' (III) of the Seventh Quartet, moving from g to E♭, and involving two ostinato patterns based simultaneously on g and E♭, with a further third connection implicit in that the first subject of the 'development' (bar 27) is heard a major third higher than in the exposition. Third relations across a work are demonstrable through several neoclassical pieces, the overall progression of the Sixth Quartet being I: G, II: b, III: G, whilst that of the Seventh Quartet is I: B♭, II: G (/E♭), III: g–E♭, IV: B♭. The Clarinet Sonatina also involves third relations at various levels, including those between movements: I: b, II: A♭/g♯, III: C.

So the third scalic degree undoubtedly has a high profile; this, however, can make moments where the pitch is omitted even more striking: emphasis through suppression, as at the end of *Quatre poèmes de Catulle*. The main mode is the Altered Mixolydian on G, with its third degree as B♮, and some mixture at the sixth: E♭/E♮. In the coda (bars 22–6), B♮ is replaced by B♭ in a stylized blues inflectional procedure which accompanies the text: 'c'est-à-dire brûlante, embrasée'. After

---

[33] Drake, *The Operas of Darius Milhaud*, 206.

Neoclassicism: Refined Modality 195

this decisive modification, the final two bars are delightfully ambiguous: in bar 25, B♮ returns in reference to the violin's opening accompaniment idea, but in the final bar the third is omitted altogether, concluding with a chord of three open-strings: (G,D,A,G).

In the neoclassical domain, there is some superficial persistence of what Milhaud would term 'polytonality' (preferably polymodality); however, he is now more concerned to elaborate fewer tonalities convincingly than to continue his earlier attempts at sustaining six simultaneous tonalities (e.g. in *Les Choéphores* and *Les Euménides*), which sacrificed the overall sense of directed motion. The first movement of the Third Chamber Symphony (1921) is a useful example because one may begin with Milhaud's own interpretation in 'Polytonalité et atonalité', where he regards an early passage as operating in five keys simultaneously.[34] Such polytonality, though apparent to the eye, would be unlikely to be so perceived by the listener, so that, theoretically, the principles of fundamental bass would tend to produce a single modality on B♭, shown in Fig. 5.8.[35] This small-scale interpretation of B♭ across bars 9–12 is third-related to the movement as a whole, based on D, with the prominent D in the bass acting as a pivot between the 'tonic' of D 'major' and third of B♭ 'major'.

Three movements from the Sixth and Seventh Quartets have already been mentioned as concerned with bimodal balance (and polarity) at the third scalic degree, and thus, bimodality and third relations can be closely related. A final type of bimodal polarity can result from modal complementation, as in Scene V of *L'Abandon d'Ariane* (Case Study 8), where pitches are semitonally opposed between bass and upper voices in a similar, though more sophisticated, manner to that used in the exploratory works up to 1922.

Works of the later 1920s (especially 1927) typically give a higher profile to strong dissonance as part of the increased dramatic effect acquired through the composition of opera. In addition to its appearance in discrete parts of *L'Abandon d'Ariane*, such heightened dissonance is effectively the norm in the Clarinet Sonatina (Case Study 7) where further reference can be made to the 4-7 set, discussed in Chapter 3, as a defiant, semitonal gesture at surface level. By contrast, some neoclassical pieces are largely diatonic (i.e. utilizing pitch groupings of

---

[34] See Chapter 2, p. 22 above.
[35] Hence the stipulation of 'localized [or surface-level] bimodality' in Chapter 2, pp. 54–6.

Figure 5.8 Third Chamber Symphony: I, bars 9–12.

'white-note' modes) and enjoy only mild dissonance, e.g. the Seventh Quartet and *Quatre poèmes de Catulle*, and in such contexts one can successfully implement Hindemith's 'tension theory' to elucidate the treatment and role of dissonance (as in Case Study 6).

There are several means of extending modal structures, including literal and embellished repetition, melodic and harmonic sequence (illustrated in Case Study 7). Ostinato can be a means of pitch prolongation, as a neoclassical equivalent of 'Alberti bass'. Examples abound, as in the 'Lent' of the Sixth Quartet, where a one-bar basso ostinato in B 'major' undergoes various modifications across a substantial time-span. The basic form (bars 1–3) is followed by enharmonic change, D♯–E♭ (within c), and intervallic expansion of a perfect fifth to major sixth (bars 4–6). After the return of the original form (bars 7–11), D♯ is raised to E for a one-bar rendition in C. The ostinato returns on D♭ (bars 16–19), with further intervallic expansion to a minor seventh (bars 17 and 19). By means of a balancing enharmonic change from E♭ to D♯, the original ostinato finally returns in the coda (bar 31). Two such basso ostinato patterns operate in the 'Lent' of the Seventh Quartet: the first consisting of a chromatic encirclement of G: (A♭,G,F♯,G), the second asserting the third relation, E♭, as the bass-note of a second inversion of A♭ (Lydian tendency). E♭ is prolonged, with a whole-tone fragment (A♭,B♭,C,D) above. Another instance occurs in the finale, where an ostinato consisting of habitually displaced octaves functions as a small-scale ground-bass, with cello supported by viola. The material is, in typical fashion, repeated every four bars, before the viola assumes the main subject at bar 9 and the cello at bar 12; meanwhile the ostinato continues in the upper voices as the fugal 'free part'.

The concept of 'pillar chords' articulating the sections, and thereby supporting the overall architecture, has some application for Milhaud's neoclassical repertory. A lucid, small-scale example is the opening of the finale of the Sixth Quartet, mentioned above in relation to the Altered Mixolydian mode. Bars 1–12 employ four, identical quaver-length chords: (G,E♭,G,A,D), which punctuate the texture every four bars and produce a tonic pedal (see again Fig. 5.7).

Some neoclassical pieces show development of earlier metric/rhythmic techniques. The 'Lent' of the Seventh Quartet interpolates 7/8 bars within its 6/8 metre in a similar though more sophisticated fashion to that used in the Third Quartet (1916). Moreover, the finale of the Sixth Quartet has a nine-bar metrical unit, consisting of a mixture of 3/8 and 4/8, with occasional interpolation of 2/8: bars 4–12, 13–21, with a partial unit: bars 22–5 (see again Fig. 5.7). At bar 26, this particular pattern is broken, after which a second unit, of eleven bars' duration, is stated twice, employing some 5/8 metre but no 2/8. There are up to three bars in one metre before a change is made. The effect is to parody a dance, with extra steps incorporated whilst others are absent; the movement has a Stravinskian flavour, brought about by metrical treatment and textural clarity, together with simple melodic shapes, octave doublings, and choice of rhythmic pattern (e.g. quaver–two semiquavers–quaver in 3/8 metre). Sometimes rhythms are set up in metrical opposition, as another kind of polarity. (This movement foreshadows the third movement, 'Léger et cinglant', of the Seventeenth Quartet of 1950.) Another interesting example of neoclassical metric/rhythmic treatment, similar to that used by Stravinsky, is found in the final scene of *L'Abandon d'Ariane* (Case Study 8).

✧

CASE STUDY 6
Modality and Tension Theory in 'La femme que j'aime',
from *Quatre poèmes de Catulle*, Op. 80 (1923)

Preliminaries

Milhaud completed *Quatre poèmes de Catulle* for voice and violin on 4 August 1923, in Aix-en-Provence, with the first performance given in Paris in October, by the singer Vera Janacopoulos and violinist, Yves Astruc. The poems were written by the celebrated lyric poet of ancient Rome, Gaius Valerius Catullus (84–54 BC), and were adapted and translated into French by a linguist whose identity is unknown. These settings are true miniatures with a total duration of just over three minutes. The opening song, 'La femme que j'aime', is extraordinary for its modal simplicity and brevity; it is a mere eleven bars in duration and represents perhaps the purest neoclassicism that Milhaud achieved in the 1920s. The analytical means employed below involve modal partitioning, adapted from van den Toorn, post-Schenkerian voice-leading, and the Hindemith/Neumeyer concept of 'tension theory'.

Analysis

Since the inspiration for the songs stems from the text, it is appropriate to begin by discussing the setting of the poem, which is metrically free, though clearly divisible into two halves:

> La femme que j'aime dit
> qu'elle ne voudrait pas s'unir à un autre que moi.
> Elle le dit;
> mais ce qu'une femme dit à un amant bien épris,
> il faut l'écrire sur le vent et sur l'onde rapide.[36]

The layout of this French version of the Catullus text has been surmised from its punctuation and appearance in Milhaud's score, and has also been informed by an English translation of the original Latin

---

[36] 'The woman that I love says | she would not want to unite with anyone but me. | She says this; | but what a woman says to a truly smitten lover, | one must write on the wind and on the speeding wave.'

text.[37] In his setting of the text, Milhaud adopts a nonchalantly pastoral 6/8 metre with anacrusis (a deliberately ironic choice in view of the subject-matter of love turned sour), whilst the rhythmic treatment is simple and uncluttered, allowing clear enunciation of the words. The most unusual rhythmic subdivision is into four equal dotted semiquavers (bars 8–9), with stressing sometimes purposefully artificial and 'pointed', for example, the placing of the word 'dit' on strong beats: bar 2, beat 1; bar 6, beat 2; bar 8, beat 1. This helps to emphasize the cynicism of meaning, implying that although she 'says' this she does not really mean it. This layering of meaning is reflected in the structural division of the poem into balancing halves (between the poet's perception of semblance and actuality), and is carefully preserved in Milhaud's setting, by means of an imperfect-type cadence, and punctuating rests (bar 5), which act as a caesura. Additionally, Milhaud's setting creates three 'peaks', in terms of the vocal melodic contour and the 'weak-strong' metric placement across the bar-line: 's'u-nir' (bars 3–4), 'é-pris' (bars 8–9) and 'ra-pide' (final two bars). The simple form of the song, shown in Fig. 5.9, reflects that of the poem.

The three analytical examples in the Appendix (Exx. 5.1–5.3), should be regarded compositely; they progress from an introductory perspective on modal partitioning, through a more rigorous post-tonal voice-leading analysis, to an experimental exercise with 'tension theory'. Ex. 5.1 examines the nature of the modality and partitioning, and shows Milhaud at his most diatonic within an Ionian-type mode on G.[38] Set theory is used simply as a supplementary means of identifying the motivic units, so that there is no suggestion that the music is other than modally conceived; and the association between motivic units and 'significant [structural] sets' provides an endorsement of Neumeyer's approach, as considered in Chapter 2.[39]

---

[37] Lesbia says she'd rather marry me | than anyone, | though Jupiter himself came asking | or so she says, | but what a woman tells her lover in desire | should be written out on air and running water.' (Poem 70, from *The Poems of Catullus*, trans. P. Whigham (London, 1966), 182.

[38] The diatonicism, underlined by the almost exclusive use of Forte's 'diatonic-tonal' Genus 12, is striking, since *Quatre poèmes* was written in early August 1923, contemporaneously with *La Création du monde* (first produced in late October). Admittedly, the other songs (especially IV) make more use of the blues scale.

[39] Neumeyer, *The Music of Paul Hindemith*, 125.

Figure 5.9   'La femme que j'aime': Formal Outline

INCIPIENT TERNARY FORM: ABA'

SECTION A
Bars
1   Introduction on violin, with 'tonic' pedal on G
1–5   First sentence of poem
5   Interlude on violin, marking imperfect cadence

SECTION B
6   'Elle le dit;' Opening clause of second sentence, 'dit' balancing occurrence in bar 2
7–9   Continuation of second sentence

SECTION A'
9–11   Return of opening violin figure, with decorated vocal line from bar 2 (and opening modality)
         Conclusion of second sentence
         Cadential ambiguity

The shapes of vocal and accompanying lines tend to be formed of step-wise modal ascents and descents, gradually revealing the nature of the mode on G (a process which is later reversed). The violin pitches of bar 1 suggest the Pentatonic Collection 1 (G,A,B,D,E), set 5-35, with a distinction between lower and upper segments, sounded on the first and second beats respectively. In bar 2, the violin has a second pentatonic grouping: (G,A,C,D,F) with introduction of C♮, though maintaining the lower and upper segments, whilst the voice above (bars 2–3) embraces a hexatonic mode on G: (E,D,C,B,A,G), set 6-32. Thus the terms of reference are increased from pentatonic to hexatonic (with the introduction of F♮ suggesting a resultant modality of Mixolydian on G, indicated below the stave in Appendix Ex. 5.1). The raised seventh only emerges in the vocal line of bar 3, thus focusing the modal identity of Ionian on G (set 7-35), whilst the violin maintains its pentatonicism (with the complementary set 5-35). Significantly, the first instance of contrary motion occurs in the second half of this bar as an expression of modal development. In bar 4, modal identity is clarified further by the introduction of F♯ in vocal and violin lines; thus both parts now use the Ionian on G, although the violin part still maintains its earlier distinction between lower and upper segments, with the tetrachord (C,B,A,G), set 4-11, followed by the trichord (F♯,E,D). This lower tetrachord 4-11, a singleton set referable only to Genus 7, is the only set which does not subscribe to Genus 12;[40] compositely though, set 7-35 (embracing lower and upper segments) maintains the focus on Genus 12.

In traditional tonal terms, bars 4-5 form an imperfect cadence, emphasized by the inclusion of a rest in the vocal line, whilst the violin follows through with a lower pentachord on D (A,G,F♯,E,D), set 5-23 (with bass-line subset 4-11), simply a large-scale chord V in the Ionian on G. In bar 6, the voice re-enters on the G pitch (heard as a dissonance), using the upper tetrachord (G,F♯,E,D), set 4-11, and balanced by the violin pitches across bars 6-7 ((D),C,B,A,G), set 5-23. The recurrence of set 4-11 (of Genus 7) imitates the earlier pitch occurrences, as subsets within the vocal line of bar 4 and the violin line of bar 5; the apparent generic 'dissonance', in conjunction with harmonic dissonance, serves to highlight the phrase 'Elle le dit', as discussed earlier. Bar 7 contains the second instance of contrary motion, as the voice ascends scalically within the Ionian on G (compass E-D), using a pattern repeated sequentially in bars 8-9 (compass F♯-E); below, the violin maintains the Ionian modality with a 'tonic' double pedal across bars 7-8. The violin pitches of bar 8 again feature a division into lower and upper segments, whilst the second beat may also be viewed as an imitation of the vocal line, with the scalic ascent (D-C) suggesting a localized Mixolydian on D. Thus there is further motivic/modal correspondence between the parts.

Bars 1-3 were the result of a process which worked from modal ambiguity to clarity: from pentatonic, through hexatonic and Mixolydian, to Ionian. The opposite process operates across bars 8-11, as the modal identity 'fades', thus complementing the earlier procedure. Bar 8 is the last to feature F♯ (in both parts), after which F♮ returns in the vocal part of bar 9, with the pentatonic collection 1 in the violin part across bars 9-10. The resultant collection for bar 9 is the Mixolydian on G (as in bar 2), with the terms of pitch reference further reduced to hexatonic/pentatonic collections across bars 10-11, where the voice employs (G,A,B,C,D,E) (as bars 1-3), against the violin's pitches (B,A,G; E,D) (as bar 1). Milhaud's fondness of the sixth scalic degree (often in association with pentatonicism) was considered in Chapter 4;

---

[40] Forte's pc set genera in this context rather overplays what is merely a terminological difference, since the actual materials involved are wholly consistent (i.e. all referential to the Ionian mode on G).

on this occasion, the upper segment (E,D) is stressed by means of positioning (on the first beat of bar 10), repetition, and registral transfer.

Motivically, the violin line has the stronger identity, opening with an appoggiatura figure which occurs in embellished (B–G–A) and simple (E–D) forms, extended by sequence in bar 2: (A–F–G), (D–C), with a similar procedure operating across bars 3–4. These figures constitute a stylized 'sigh motive': the appoggiatura is merely a trapping of one of various formulae of common practice music, and thus, although we have the appearance of a 'sigh', this is a hollow gesture devoid of emotion—an attempt to 'cry' without tears. There is some, more limited, vocal representation of this gesture, including the (G–F♯: '4–3') dissonance of bar 6, clinched in bar 9 by the upper registral motion (F–E), which perhaps suggests that there is, after all, a vestige of emotional content. (Additionally, the voice makes frequent use of minor third motives, in both descent and ascent, especially on pitches: (D–B), (G–E), and (F–D).) In pursuit of a small-scaled balance, the original pitches pertaining to the 'sigh motive' as presented on violin, return in the final three bars, with a repetition of the (E–D) motion, and a final synthesized presentation between the two parts (bar 11), as the voice initially supports the sixth degree, but then leaves the violin to finish its fragile harmonics alone, on the fifth scalic degree. Thus the first song ends with an appropriate expectancy. Overall pitch ranges are a perfect 11th (d^1–g^2) for the voice; and two octaves and a tone (g–a^2) for the violin (excluding harmonics).

Ex. 5.2 views the song from perhaps the most important single perspective, that of voice-leading (although no graph should be seen in isolation from another), examining further the functioning of the modality. Standard notation is employed for chords, neighbour-notes, third and fifth progressions, and registral transfer. A 'fundamental line' (from the fifth degree) has tentatively been suggested, and, whilst it does not conform to any Schenkerian model, strong step-wise descents to the tonic (or modal 'final') are noticeable, both in this song and the three that follow.[41]

The choice of a scalic descent from $\hat{5}$ (i.e. D) seems preferable to that from $\hat{3}$, and is reached in fact by arpeggiation from the third degree (B, bar 1). This pitch d^2 is frequently reinforced by its upper

---

[41] The fourth song is also centred on G (featuring chord I with added sixth), and thus offers an element of unity to *Quatre poèmes*.

neighbour-note e^2,[42] and also proves of central importance at the close of the song, with the supporting 'tonic' harmony indisputable. The most feasible point for any descent to start is across bars 4–5, the latter bar providing a convincing dominant harmony (on d^1) to support the second scalic degree a^1.[43] In traditional terms, however, this is very early for such a descent, which might simply be seen as a small-scale replication of some later, more definitive gesture (but one that never quite materializes). In fact the interpretation of a descent at bars 4–5 has its own small-scale replication, or anticipation, in bars 2–3. Although there is an effective 'mirrored' descent in bar 10, this does not carry the necessary tonal weight to constitute the main descent, reduced by this point to Mixolydian and then only hexatonic terms of reference (i.e. no F♯). A second unorthodox feature is that the vocal descent and supporting harmony across bars 4–7 are staggered, though this might be explained as a type of unfolding. A third problem is the short length of any tonic (g^1) in the upper voice, either in bar 7, or in the mirrored descent of bar 10. The ending too is unconventional from a voice-leading perspective, the modality of G rather undermined by the emphasis on D and the avoidance of the tonic, or final. Having said this, chord I is partially implied by the vocal pitch of G (g^1) in bar 10, since the violin sounds the (e4–d4) progression in harmonics, two octaves above its notated register.

'La femme que j'aime' is the most homophonically constructed and simplest of *Quatre poèmes de Catulle*, and thus the experimental inclusion of Hindemith's 'tension theory' proves productive in Ex. 5.3. I have maintained Hindemith's symbols of shaded crescendo and diminuendo marks, as used in the theoretical part of *The Craft of Musical Composition*, to indicate corresponding increases and reductions in harmonic tension. The point at which the diminuendo tails off to nothing indicates a state of pure consonance. Thus, using bar 1 as an example, this approach highlights the gradual increase in tension to the midpoint of the bar. The progression leads from a consonant major 10th (G–B), through a perfect octave (G–G), to a dissonant major 9th (G–A); the second half of bar 1 balances this, at pitches a fifth higher, with

---

[42] In fact, the weighting given to the sixth scalic degree is more significant than the upper neighbour-note interpretation tends to suggest; thus there are limitations in applying traditional voice-leading.

[43] This interpretation supports the literary structure of the hiatus between balancing segments, discussed earlier.

a second major 9th (D–E), resolving back to a perfect octave on the fifth scalic degree (D–D). Interpretation is consistent with the definition of consonance given earlier, and refers strictly to intervals of a third, fifth, sixth, or octave, together with root, or first inversion, triads.

Before examining the full resultant patterns across 'La femme que j'aime', it is worth signalling one of the associated functions of Ex. 5.3, which is to investigate the incidence of types of dissonance (Fig. 5.10), with the major 9th/2nd (0,2) proving most common, followed by the perfect 4th/11th (0,5).[44] The (0,2) major 2nd dissonances: (E,D) provide a symmetry and unity of syntax by opening and closing the song, whilst the harsher minor 2nd has no place, partly because chromaticism is atypically unimportant.[45] Next in incidence is the minor 7th (0,10), followed by the 'compound' (i.e. trichordal) dissonance of major 9th, plus minor 7th (0,2,10). At the other end of the spectrum, it is worth noting how rarely the tritone occurs. Essentially, such dissonance as does occur is far less strident than in earlier compositions and the norm is a consonant one.

Figure 5.10 'La femme que j'aime': dissonant types in order of incidence

Simple dissonances		Compound dissonances	
Major 9th/ Major 2nd	× 12 × 3	Major 9th/Minor 7th	× 3
Perfect 4th/ Perfect 11th	× 7 × 2	Major 9th/Major 7th	× 1
Minor 7th	× 5	Minor 7th/Major 2nd	× 1
Major 7th	× 2	Augmented 4th/Major 2nd	× 1
Diminished 5th	× 1		

In respect of the main concern of Ex. 5.3 with resultant patterning of dissonance and consonance, several 'strategically placed' consonances assist structural articulation, often marking the openings and closes of phrases, such as that which begins bar 1 (repeated at bar 3). Conversely, the first strategically placed dissonance occurs at the end of

---

[44] In contrapuntal terms, the perfect fourth is always regarded as a dissonant, or unstable, interval, which seeks resolution to a major, or minor, third.

[45] The only chromaticism (as a hint of blues 7th) is the lowered 7th, F♮ (occurring three times), in relation to the raised 7th, F♯ (occurring eight times).

bar 2, serving to increase the momentum into the start of bar 3, where the first phrase is subdivided after the word 'dit'. Ensuing consonances on the second beats of bars 5 and 6, both preceded by dissonances on the first beats, create a sequential effect, the end of bar 5 marking the half-way point of the verse.

Further strategically placed consonances occur in the second half, with the consonance on the first beat of bar 9 (the penultimate 'peak') leading to three successive dissonances on the second beat. The midpoint of the bar marks the subdivision of the phrase, balanced in bar 11 by the final 'consonance', a lone pitch on D, following the last appoggiatura (E–D). On the smaller scale, the pattern (consonance–dissonance : dissonance–consonance) occurs five times: in bars 1, 3, 3–4, 4–5 and 11; this is a truly neoclassical treatment of prepared dissonance, which is then resolved. Another common pattern is simply 'dissonance/consonance' stated without preparation, as employed in bars 2, 6, 7, 8 and 9–10, whilst the other frequent pattern is a passing dissonance, denoted by a 'diamond', as used in the moving vocal line in bars 7, 9 and 10.

Conclusion

Thus it is clear that voice-leading alone cannot offer a convincing interpretation, even of Milhaud's most purely modal piece of the 1920s. The most interesting aspect of the piece is its logical increase and then reduction in the terms of modal reference, across such a short timespan. There is justification in incorporating set theory, mainly in attempting to classify motivic units. Furthermore, in such a simple two/three-voiced structure, the Hindemith/Neumeyer approach does produce clear patterning and thus added insight into the song. In bars 1–4, for instance, tension is clearly conceived in terms of the harmonic rhythm of dotted crotchets; in more complex post-tonal contexts, however, 'tension theory' would inevitably become ill-defined and would only serve as a very general guideline.

✧

206   DARIUS MILHAUD

CASE STUDY 7
Sonatine pour clarinette et piano, Op. 100 (1927):
Rethinking Modality and Sonata Principles

Preliminaries

The *Sonatine pour clarinette et piano* is considered as the final chamber work of the 1920s, which, like *L'Abandon d'Ariane* (to be discussed as Case Study 8), was composed during the Summer of 1927 at the family home, 'L'Enclos', close to Aix-en-Provence. It was first performed by the dedicatee, clarinettist Louis Cahuzac, with the pianist M.F. Gaillard, at a concert of the Société Musicale Internationale in Paris, in 1929. A diminutive sonata, the whole work lasts only about 9 minutes.

Although the Sonatina is primarily a product of neoclassicism, and involves a rethinking of some issues of sonata form, as 'an icon of a previous style',[46] the language is highly chromatic, based on notions of allusion and contradiction. This is in stark contrast to the subjects of Case Studies 6 and 8, yet reminiscent of earlier works, such as the opening of the Fifth Chamber Symphony (1922),[47] or the 'Funèbre' of the Fourth Quartet (1918). The structure across the three movements consists of a semitonal progression b–C, also present, and thus prepared, on the smaller scale within the opening movement.[48] The relatively unusual procedure (though anticipated in *L'Abandon*, Op. 98) of thematic connection between first and final movements (both marked 'Très Rude') creates the effect of a single extended movement, with a slow, central episode. Formally, the movements may be viewed in turn as a modified, or reinterpreted, sonata/ternary form, followed by a standard ternary structure, and concluded by another modified sonata form. Although the formal proportions of the first movement and finale

---

[46] Straus, *Remaking the Past*, 18.

[47] The opening movements of the Fifth Chamber Symphony (*Dixtuor d'instruments à vent*) and Clarinet Sonatina share the designation 'Rude'. Indeed, for several reasons discussed below, these two works at least could usefully be regarded, in the terms of Bloom, as 'relational events' (see Straus, *Remaking the Past*, 12).

[48] The Fifth Chamber Symphony also anticipates the overall b–C progression, and exhibits a similar, though less developed, concern with revisiting sonata principles and processes (as do the Fourth Quartet and Prélude of *La Création du monde*). It is also worth pointing out an element of comparison here with Straus's view of the first movement of Stravinsky's Octet, as a reworking of sonata form in which semitonal relations (to some extent superseding tonic-dominant relations) also play a critical role in delineating parts of the formal structure at two distinct levels (Straus, 'Sonata Forms', in *Remaking the Past*, 103–5).

are more obviously akin to ternary form, the inherent principles and processes, centring on 'the polarity of contrasting areas as the essential form-generating element',[49] and notions of initial 'opposition, intensification and [partial] resolution',[50] do bear comparison with those of sonata form. Formal summaries are given at the start of each movement.

Analysis

I. Très rude

The opening movement operates within an all-chromatic scale on b, but its driving force is generated by the tension existing between semitonally conflicting assertions of V–I (as a vestige of more traditional dominant-tonic relations), in terms both of b and the subsidiary, C: hence the prominence of F♯ in the bass, contradicted by G above. Formally, two main sections which delineate distinct and polarized harmonic areas, bars 1–34 (centred on b) and bars 35–56 (exhibiting opposition between C♯/G♯ and C♮), are recapitulated and combined in a final section (bar 57 onwards, centred on b) with a brief coda across bars 87–95, as shown in Fig. 5.11.

The Sonatina is primarily motivic in construction, and one of the most important figures of this type, operating at surface level, constitutes a prefix to the first subject (and is labelled α in Ex. 5.4). This vertical set 4-7 (F♯,G,A♯,B), which includes the Kh-related subset 3-4, is identical to that in the opening of the Fifth Chamber Symphony, and thus indicates another aspect of common ground between the two works;[51] the main horizontal motive is a fifth progression (D,C♯,B,A,G) labelled 'a', subjected to much varied repetition before it is transformed and incorporated into the finale. The first subject group concludes with motive 'b', as an elaboration of the prominent triad motive (also significant in concluding the main theme of the slow movement). In respect of the subtext of this Case Study concerned with 'remaking the past', the Sonatina immediately subscribes to the first of several techniques identified by Straus for this purpose: '*Motivicization.* The motivic content of the earlier work [style] is radically intensified.'[52] The

---

[49] Straus, *Remaking the Past*, 96.
[50] See C. Rosen, *Sonata Forms*, rev. edn. (New York, 1988), 18.
[51] The formation (F♯,G,A♯,B) is also acknowledged as a notable chordal type by Drake (*The Operas of Darius Milhaud*, 210-11). See also Chapter 3, p. 70, n. 31 above.
[52] Straus, *Remaking the Past*, 17.

Figure 5.11 Clarinet Sonatina: I ('Très rude'): Formal Outline

MODIFIED SONATA/TERNARY FORM

	Bars	Total Bars
SECTION A	1–34	34
First subject group: centred on Aeolian/harmonic minor on b	1–29	
Linking material (into 'second subject')	30–4	
SECTION B	35–56	22
Second subject group, focused on C♯/G♯ (and C♮)	35–52	
Ostinato (preparing for return of first subject	53–6	
SECTION A/B	57–86	30
Modified recapitulation:		
First subject group (varied)	57–72	
Ostinato (E♭/e♭ and C) and part of second subject	72–6	
'Mouvt.': Second subject group (subsequent thematic combination)	77–86	
CODA	87–95	9
First subject group		

opening is based in the Aeolian/harmonic minor on b, with mixture at the fifth: F♮/F♯—hence set 4-18 (B,D,F♮,F♯); there is also, however, a sense of Lydian on G (i.e. third relations: upper voice, bars 1 and 3), as the dominant of a largely implicit C. From the opening bars, repetition and textural thickening (through octave, seventh and ninth doublings) are critical to the style which is expansive and dramatic—aspects which were to become notable hall-marks of Milhaud's middle period (1930–early 1950s).

Generically speaking, the opening tends to oscillate between two of the genera of the blues Supragenus III: Genus 9 (indicated by the presence of 4-18, in conjunction with one progenitor, 3-11, and the pentad, 5-32), Genus 8 (signalled by the 'singleton' set 4-7, and one progenitor, 3-4), together with reference to the progenitors of Genus 10. A matrix showing these data, and including the Status quotient (Squo) calculations, is given in Fig. 5.12 below. Essentially, the Squo measurement endorses the interpretation of Genus 9 as an important source of reference, although it also raises the profile of the diatonic-tonal Genus 12 (appropriate enough in terms of a centric, modal 'backdrop'), and arguably falls short in assigning sufficient significance to the 'singleton' set 4-7 of Genus 8.

Figure 5.12 Clarinet Sonatina: I, bars 1-4
Matrix to show Sets in relation to Genera

Potential Genera:	G1	G2	G3	G7	G8	G9	G10	G11	G12
Sets
3-4					o		o		
3-7				o				o	o
3-8		o							
3-11						o	o		o
4-7*					o				
4-18	o		o		o				
5-32	o	o				o			o
Counts:	2	2	1	1	2	3	2	1	3
	G1	G2	G3	G7	G8	G9	G10	G11	G12
					[SGIII	][SGIV	]

Counts	Squo Indices in descending order with Genera
3	.105: G9 (atonal-tonal)
3	.095: G12 (diatonic-tonal)
2	.070: G8 (atonal)
2	.070: G10 (atonal-tonal)
2	.045: G2 (wholetone)

* denotes a 'singleton' set

Bar 5 marks the occurrence in the clarinet part of a countersubject (shown in Ex. 5.5), emerging out of the initial ideas in terms of the prominence of B, F♯ and G, together with the fifth interval, which also forms something of a basis for the later second subject material. Thus Milhaud's rethinking of sonata principles involves much development in this expository section which serves to blur the distinction between the main thematic areas, as well as the relationship between 'theme' and harmonic area. Thus one may say of Milhaud, as Straus has commented of Stravinsky: 'His so-called neoclassicism had generally been regarded as a kind of extended homage to classical music. There is, however, as much defiance as reverence in these works.'[53] In respect of the piano part across bars 5–8 (Ex. 5.5), the opening motive 'a' in the

---

[53] Straus, 'Sonata Forms', *Remaking the Past*, 107.

treble is repeated, now with a localized 'Locrian' inflection (F,E,D,C,B) within a possible dominant seventh in C (G7, in upper parts). This conflicts with second-inversion chords of b♭ minor in the bass, which can be seen enharmonically as a substitute dominant of b♮. Much melodic use is made of the fifth progression, both perfect and diminished. Amongst the invariant intervallic shapes are again 3-4 and 3-7. (It is worth mentioning that bars 5–8 of the published score have the dubious distinction of containing as many as five misprints, which have been corrected here in Ex. 5.5.) Bars 9–10 pursue the dominant G of C, which is stated unequivocally in the bass, although in fact the full triad is initially an augmented set 3-12 (G,B,E♭), with (E♭–D) as a decorative appoggiatura, whilst the horizontal span of the upper line of the left hand produces the diminished set 3-10 (E♭,C,A).[54]

In summarizing the opening ten bars, Ex. 5.6*a* regards the most important localized reference as the 3-4/4-7 construct (of Genus 8), whilst Ex. 5.6*b* suggests the most striking, longer-term, phenomenon to be the tension caused by the conflicting V–I progressions, existing in the semitonally polarized modalities on b and C and at different structural levels: F♯–b in the first movement, yet G–C across the Sonatina as a whole. The 3-4 set (F♯,G,B) is common to both, and thus dissonance receives a high profile at foreground and, implicitly, background levels.

At bar 11, the horizontal fifth-motive is partially inverted, whilst the vertical motive is 'expanded' from set 4-7 to 4-8 (C♯,D,F♯,G); the essential identity is maintained by the dissonant minor ninths and the important subset 3-4 (F♯,G,B), encapsulating the b/G ambiguity. Vertical presentation in bar 11 is balanced by the horizontal in the clarinet countersubject at bar 12 (previously heard at bar 5), together with sets 4-20 and 4-5 in the piano; additionally, the bass triads outline 3-4 across bars 12–15. Ex. 5.7 attempts a voice-leading summary of bars 1–16 which, despite the chromatic complexities, shows that there are recurrent pitches of structural importance, especially the third scalic degree in the upper voice, d3. This graph of the opening is in keeping with a larger-scale view which would favour an upper-line descent from a structural $\hat{3}$, d3, embracing the surface-level fifth motive: (D,C♯, B,[A,G]). In support of this, the bass of the whole section up to bar 34, offers a clearly established chord I (on B_I) from bar 2 onwards, even though the most prominent bass-line pitch is F♯ (i.e. displaying

---

[54] A similar mixture of augmented and diminished triads, mostly at surface level, was observed in the 'Funèbre' of the Fourth Quartet (Case Study 1).

Milhaud's typical partiality for second-inversion chordal presentation). The summary is also useful in illustrating the incipient, longer-term tension between b and C (and their respective 'dominants'), as well as the typical 'black-note' pentatonicism (on F♯) in the bass from bar 12 onwards.

The 'Mouvt.' section from bar 16 marks a new phase in the treatment of the first subject group, with further occurrences of set 4-7 and its subset 3-4 across bars 16–20; the dominant F♯ in the bass continues to be prolonged by its upper neighbour-note G♯. In the clarinet (and piano) part of bars 16–19, the b-based third motive, derived from the opening and so labelled as 'a'', is subjected to varied repetition, phrased across the bar and shown in paradigmatic layout in Ex. 5.8a. A similar process operates across bars 20–4 (Ex. 5.8b), embodying phrase extension by sequence with rhythmic development (the third progression of bars 16–20 is now inverted and based on A/f♯). Thus again there is extensive development within what is ostensibly an expository section: in fact Milhaud's rethinking of sonata principles involves a conflation of expository statement and development which continues in the treatment of the second subject area (there is after all no separate development section as such). Continuing this developmental process across bars 24–5, repeated in bars 26–7, the piano restates the gestural flourish labelled α, formed initially by set 4-7, then mutated as set 4-3 (bar 27), and followed by the continuing third motive on b, labelled 'a'' (Ex. 5.9).

Bars 28–34 consist of linking material in the piano as a 'bridge' between the two subject groups of the modified sonata structure. The chromatic ascent of bars 28–9 (Ex. 5.9) places the main tetrachordal emphasis on 4-17, 4-18 (first heard in bar 2), 4-19 and 4-20. This leads to a further occurrence of the gestural flourish at bar 30 formed by set 4-3 (A♯,B,C♯,D: as at bars 27 and 34)—i.e. a combination of parts of 4-7 (F♯,G,A♯,B) and 4-8 (C♯,D,F♯,G).[55] Further repetition and sequential extension fuels intensification and reinforcement of the F♯/G conflict across bars 34–5 (Ex. 5.10): F♯ in the bass (with B above) suggests I$^6_4$ in b 'minor', though with the articulatory function of a dominant, whilst pitches G and B in the treble suggest an implied V of C (which then attempts resolution, largely unsuccessfully, in the next section). This dramatic gesture, at once pregnant and yet curiously final, rather sug-

---

[55] These overlapping 4-7/4-3 constructs were used on the same pitches in the first movement of the Fifth Chamber Symphony.

gests a move to a more far-reaching development section. What ensues is a conflation (or simultaneity) of 'second subject' and development section, with intensification of harmonic opposition. Again, one acknowledges the extent to which Milhaud misreads (in Straus's sense) and rewrites archetypal eighteenth-century models.

The second subject group (bars 35–52) is examined in part in Ex. 5.10 (bars 35–40), the mode now founded on C♯ with emphasis on the fifth, G♯,[56] preparing the ground for the second movement on A♭. Once more, the music operates at different levels. The correspondence of this material with C♯ (bars 35ff.) could enable it to be construed as representing the structural 2̂ of a large-scale voice-leading descent, although of course the unorthodox features would be the non-alignment of the 2̂ and chord V, and, more particularly, the long period across which the 2̂ would need to be prolonged, in conflict with C. The strong semitonal opposition of C♯ and C♮ (as the future tonic of the finale) suggests rather that the two coexist as 'substitute' dominants, in the sense that each represents an overt polarity to reinforce b as the overall pitch centre. In this respect, certain parallels can be observed with Stravinsky's remaking of sonata form in the Octet where first and second subjects are also articulated by semitonal relations.[57]

The most frequent 'triads' in this section are sets 3-9 and 3-3; set 3-9 (C♯,D♯,G♯), (A♯,B♯,E♯) features both harmonically (bar 36) and melodically (bars 42, 50) against a C-based or at least 'white-note' bass.[58] Generically, the presence in the piano's 'descant' countermelody (bars 36 ff.) of set 3-9, as a progenitor, in conjunction with 5-35 (and the singleton subset 4-23: (F♯,G♯,C♯,D♯), produces a localized allusion to Genus II. The second subject on the clarinet (first statement: bars 35–41; second statement: bars 44–8) balances a phrase in the Mixolydian on C♯, with prominent G♯ and sequential fourth-patterns (also evident

---

[56] The stressing of the fifth is further evidence of the lingering legacy of jazz, epitomized in *La Création du monde* (Romance), Case Study 5.

[57] Straus, 'Sonata Forms', *Remaking the Past*, 103. Stravinsky's pitch centres create a descending figure, E♭–D (balanced in the recapitulation by E♮–E♭, with thematic reversal), as opposed to Milhaud's concern with b–C♮/C♯. However, Milhaud does use the descending formula (B♮–B♭) to articulate distinct sections in the related context of the Fifth Chamber Symphony (opening movement).

[58] The concept of 'white-note' modality polarized against 'black-note' in Milhaud's music was first proposed by Drake (*The Operas of Darius Milhaud*, 206). Such black/white modal conflict, existing in horizontal strands, is by now a typical feature, also to be found in Scenes III and V of *L'Abandon d'Ariane*.

harmonically), against a phrase based in the pentatonic on F♯, with prominent C♯, thus leading back to the localized 'tonic' of C♯.

In allusion to classical practice, further sequential patterns extend the piano part of bars 48–52: a chromatic bass descent G♯–D♭(C♯) is balanced by ascent E♭–A♯(B♭), with small-scale reference sets still 3-4 and 3-7, whilst the clarinet continues with its more overt focus on C♯–G♯. Repetition continues to have a high profile in bars 53–6, with an ostinato which anticipates and prepares for the return of the opening subject; typically, the pitch and rhythmic components are of differing lengths, the bass pitch pattern four crotchets long, against a rhythmic pattern of five crotchets. Further use of melodic sequence (bars 53–6) involves the unification of a bimodal passage: triads of d and E (set 6-Z29), by means of third progressions.[59] Additionally, a sense of the continuing influence of jazz is maintained by appearances of the blues tetrachord 4-17 (E,G♮,G♯,B), a repeated minor third figure, syncopated rhythms on clarinet, and expansion to 5/4 metre.[60]

Bar 57 marks the return of the opening section (as a type of recapitulation), where there is more subtlety in reworking of material than in earlier works: the Locrian modality of the clarinet line is striking, centred on b and then on f♯, created by sequential treatment (at a perfect fourth) of a phrase with a diminished fifth span. In terms of a possible voice-leading interpretation, this passage could be construed as returning to the structural $\hat{3}$ of the opening, and thus creating an interrupted structure: $\hat{3},\hat{2} // \hat{3},\hat{2},\hat{1}$. Such a stance would, however, be compromised by the fact that the supporting structural I is not clearly restated. What is indisputable is that with the 'recapitulation' returns the gestural flourish of set 4-7 (F♯,G,A♯,B), together with the innate tension of the opening; the addition of C in the clarinet produces set 5-6 (used in a similar context in the opening of the Fifth Chamber Symphony). The presentation of 4-7 is developed across bars 59–71 in a fragmented dialogue,[61]

---

[59] The superimposition of modal centres a major second apart, i.e. set 6-Z29, also featured in a similar context in 'Ipanema' (Case Study 4). This practice also occurs in the 'Opéras-minute', especially in *La Délivrance de Thésée*. The d/E combination is used strictly, as demonstrated in Milhaud's article of 1923.

[60] This short 5/4 passage seems to anticipate Copland's style in *El Salón México* (1936): perhaps it is simply the composers' similar responses to Latin American inspiration.

[61] The idea of repeating and extending the semiquaver fragment (bars 70–1) anticipates a similar device in the short piece for viola and piano, 'Le Wisconsonien' from *Quatre visages* (1944).

whilst between bars 59 and 67, and at bar 71, the 4-7 construct is contained within 5-21 (F♯,G,A♯,B,D)—a set also used in Scenes II and V of *L'Abandon d'Ariane*. An overview of bars 59–71 would emphasize the pentatonic pitches in the bass patterning (A♭/G♯, C♯, F♯) used to affirm the G♯(A♭) centre (the future pitch focus of the second movement), set against conflicting patterns above. This also forms something of an allusion to the second subject area. From the enharmonic perspective, the A♭s (bars 59 and 62) set amidst the sharps, prepare for the conversion of D♯ to E♭ (bar 72: Ex. 5.11).

Bars 72–6 involve the clarinet's premature presentation of a shortened, varied version of the second subject, now in C; meanwhile the piano part utilizes conflicting (white/black) bimodality at the minor third (Ex. 5.11), as a varied recapitulation of the triadic ostinato previously heard across bars 53–6. The treble part supports C 'major', whilst the upper part of the bass affirms E♭ 'major-minor', further confused by a D♭ progression unfocused in the depths beneath. A sense of blues third results when treble and upper bass parts are regarded together as C 'major-minor' in first inversion (the E♭/D♯ bass pedal is itself part of a third relation with the tonic, b). Vertically, the first beat of bar 72 presents the blues tetrachord 4-17 (including 3-11), as part of a compound set 5-16, followed in bar 73 by 4-18 (on the same pitches as in bar 2), and still embraced within 5-16; horizontally, the salient figure is the blues trichord, 3-3. Appropriately enough, these bars subscribe clearly to the atonal-tonal Genus 9, with its blues connections, first invoked in bar 2. Thus, on the larger scale, bars 72–6 reinforce the opposition of C and b.

In the following bars 77–82 ('Mouvt.'), the countermelody (as at bar 36) is restated in the treble of the piano, now largely naturalized in its modal inflection; the reiteration of an F♯ bass pedal below suggests dominant function, although the chord is in fact a second inversion of B 'major'. (In terms of black-note/white-note modal opposition, these bars employ the opposite procedure to bars 42–3.) This is followed by the presentation of another augmented triad (C,E,G♯), with the C pitch supported above at bar 82 by a scalic fragment of Aeolian on c. Bars 83–6 (shown in Ex. 5.12) combine the two subject groups (a technique used from the Fourth Quartet onwards), with the clarinet's second subject now set in the main recapitulatory modality on b, in association with the first subject material of bar 12, including the recurrent set 3-4 (F♯,B,G). The full pentatonicism of the bass-line

(F♯,G♯,A♯,C♯,D♯), which maintains allusion to the second subject area, also includes the pitches of the dominant triad (F♯,A♯,C♯), significant in terms of b.

The Coda (bars 87–95) serves to reaffirm previous details as merely a slightly varied version of bars 1–9,[62] offering a final statement of the first subject, with its localized reference set 4-7, and subset 3-4; F♯ in the bass of bars 87-8 and 90-91 reinforces the sense of the dominant seeking resolution, combined again with the Lydian on G and Aeolian/Locrian mode on b. Whilst the presence of dominant constructs reinforces the somewhat fragile centre on b, the continuing importance of third relations on either side of b (b–G; b–D) represents a significant source of innate tension and disruption in this movement (yet a source of stability and unity in the ensuing slow movement). The final bar simply states the B pitch in octaves, unlike the complex concluding chords of the early 1920s (e.g. Fifth Chamber Symphony); nevertheless, the 'argument' which occasioned the first movement remains unresolved.

II. Lent

The more romanticized 'Lent' employs a simplified ternary form. In its use both of third relations (encompassing enharmonic change) to delineate Sections A and B, and of the minor inflection of the tonic (major), it is perhaps characteristic of an early- to mid-nineteenth-century sonata movement.[63] The main centre on A♭ (prepared as G♯ in the first movement), leads to a central episode on E, and, following a return to A♭ major, finally concludes on the tonic minor (see Fig. 5.13). There is a Lydian tendency to the modality (shown in Ex. 5.13) with emphasis maintained on the fifth degree, both melodically and harmonically, by an E♭ bass-pedal. As in the first movement, ideas operate at more than one level: the fifth progression (E♭,D♭,C,B♭,A♭) is relevant both in terms of the first part of the initial melodic phrase,

---

[62] Interestingly the pianist's reference to the triad motive on b at bar 4 is balanced by a reference to the motive on C at the equivalent bar 91.

[63] It may be mere coincidence that the slow movement of Beethoven's Sonata in C minor, Op. 13, the 'Pathétique', based in A♭ major (with occasional inflection as tonic minor, bars 37ff.), also enjoys a modulation through to E major within its central episode (bars 37–50), its point of arrival (bar 44) similarly articulated by a marking of reinforcement.

labelled 'a', and the overall melodic structure of the movement.[64] Section A (bars 1–13) is dominated by the E♭ pedal as the bass of chord I⁶₄ (thus to some extent comparable with the F♯ pedal used in parts of the first movement): the device creates appropriate instability or expectancy and also prepares the leading note (D♯) for the central section on E (and thus semitonal relations have a role here too). E♭ is prolonged through bars 1–6, reinforced by the upper neighbour-note F, and returns at bar 13. Its temporary removal across bars 7–13 leads to greater harmonic movement, where blues-type chords, e.g. 4-17, abound; the bass at bar 7 effects a modulation to the sixth scalic degree, as a kind of interrupted cadence (E♭–F: V–VI). Sequence with localized variation extends the upper piano textures through this opening section, together with literal repetition of the bass progression across bars 7–8. Bars 6 and 13 feature further instances of the ubiquitous triad motive (Ex. 5.14: ascending sixth, descending third, labelled 'β'), as an extension of the second part of the initial phrase, labelled 'b' (Ex. 5.13: bars 3–4), and as a general hall-mark of Milhaud's neoclassicism in the 1920s.

Bars 14–16 (shown in Ex. 5.15*a*) lead into the central Section B ('Un peu moins Lent': bars 16–36), with the left hand of the piano at bar 14 featuring exchange of pitches (B♭/A♭ and A♭/G♭), and across bars 14–15 third progressions (A♭,B♭,C). In bar 15, the fourth interval is reintroduced (as at the opening) to promote expectancy. The E♭ (i.e. D♯, 'leading-note') and F of bar 15 provide a chromatic encirclement of the impending new 'tonic' of E♮. Such use of enharmonic change across bars 15–16 creates a cyclical aspect when connected with the prominent G♯ of the first movement's 'second subject'. At the end of the central section (Ex. 5.15*b*: bars 35–40), the modulatory procedure is simply reversed ('Retrogression'), so creating a balanced formula which moves from an area of four flats to one of four sharps, and back again. This large-scale symmetry, or mirror-imaging (co-ordinated by third relations, and summarized in Ex. 5.15*c*), is typical of the early 1920s,[65] and of the final period beyond 1950.

---

[64] There are also similarities in the step-wise fifth descent with melodic material from the opening of the first movement: (D,C♯,B,A,G), and subsequently with material from the finale: see the final summary in Ex. 5.26.

[65] The 'Fugue' in the Fourth Chamber Symphony (1921) uses this palindromic technique.

Figure 5.13   Clarinet Sonatina: II ('Lent'): Formal Outline

TERNARY FORM

	Bars	Total Bars
SECTION A	1–16	16
Main subject material on A♭		
(Lydian tendency)	1–13	13
Link into second section		
A♭–G♯ (mediant of E)	14–16	3
SECTION B	16–40	25
Contrasting 'second subject'		
material on E: statement–response	16–36	21
Dovetailed link into return of first		
section: G♯–A♭	35–40	6
SECTION A'	41–53	13
Return of first section and main subject		
material; back in modality on A♭		
CODA	54–8	5
Modality of a♭ minor		
Piano reference to Section B		
Conclusion on dominant		

The melodic material of the contrasting (or 'second') subject appears from bar 16 onwards, involving mainly the clarinet and treble of the piano (Ex. 5.16). The material consists of a 'statement' in the Lydian mode on E, labelled 'a', followed by a 'response' in the Locrian mode on b, labelled 'b' (embracing the tritone (F–B) also used across bars 5–9 and 92–5 of the first movement). Possible vestiges of jazz influence include the repeated minor third figure (B,A♯,G♯), which may be linked with a broadly similar, though re-inflected, one (B,A,G♯) in bars 53–6 of the opening movement.[66] Again emphasis is on the fifth, B, possibly significant in preparing the C♭, mediant of a♭ minor, for the start of the Coda. Balancing vestiges of jazz against more forward-looking features (from Milhaud's point of view), the marking 'dramatique', as at bar 16, was never used in Milhaud's chamber music before the mid 1920s, and seems much bound up with his contempo-

---

[66] This could be seen as an illustration of Milhaud's inflectional 'polyvalency' within modal treatment. The 'diatonic skeleton' is preserved, despite alteration of some accidentals: cf. Drake, *The Operas of Darius Milhaud*, 206.

rary interest in opera (a preoccupation which also leads on into the 1930s).

Subsequent presentation of material across bars 19–21 involves the now typical combining of statement and response, with parallel thirds and another occurrence of a blues chord (on E, with G♮/G♯). Bars 22–30 still subscribe to a background structured on E, though obscured by much chromaticism, whilst the forceful V–I (F♯–b) progression of bars 32–3 (as the localized 'dominant'), together with textural intensification in 'fortissimo' triple octaves of the tritonal gesture (B–F♮: bars 33–4), creates further allusion to the first movement.

The opening, A♭-based, material returns at bar 41, following enharmonic conversion from G♯, as the third degree of E. Such third relations (E–G♯/A♭) are the catalysts of background unity in the 'Lent', whereas in the opening 'Très rude' third relations either side of b were the cause of tension and disruption. After the reprise which is almost identical to bars 1–13 (but for occasional embellishment in the piano part), there follows a brief coda (bars 54–8: Ex. 5.17), with the change to 'minor' modality on a♭ reserved for this moment, supported now by a tonic pedal. The restricted harmonic progression consists of: I–(♭VI)–I–(♭VI)–V, with the upper line of the left-hand of the piano part featuring the fifth scalic degree, E♭, prolonged by reference to its chromaticized upper neighbour-note F♭, as a modified inflection of the opening bass line. Above references to part of statement 'a' from the contrasting 'second subject' (piano part: RH), the clarinet traces a diminished seventh chord, 4-28 (E,D♭,B♭,G), contained within the harmonic minor scale on a♭, as second, fourth, sixth and seventh degrees. The reduction in the rhythmic identity of the clarinet line, now merely enunciating the dotted crotchet pulse, has become a familiar closing technique, as used in the Prélude and Fugue of *La Création du monde*. Pitches B♭ and G (clarinet: bar 56) act as pivots between the diminished chord and the dominant, upon which the 'Lent' finishes. Whether or not this inconclusive non-ending represents another vestige of jazz,[67] it certainly creates apt expectancy for the finale.

---

[67] There are again parallels with the central Romance movement of *La Création du monde*.

III. Très rude

As with the opening 'Très rude', the finale is also a modified sonata/ternary form (shown in Fig. 5.14), making use of a similarly chromatic language, now founded on C (Ex. 5.18), and stressing B as the leading-note.

Figure 5.14 Clarinet Sonatina: III ('Très rude'): Formal Outline

MODIFIED SONATA/TERNARY FORM

	Bars	Total Bars
SECTION A	1–27	27
First subject (a and b):		
Lydian-tendency mode on C (importance of F♯/G)		
Chromaticism and high level of dissonance		
Reiteration of A♯/B♭	*14ff.*	
SECTION B	28–60	33
Contrasting 'second subject':		
Phrygian mode on f (reduced level of dissonance)		
Most distant episode (invoking F♭)	*36–44*	
Return to f 'minor'	*47ff.*	
Use of sequence	*51–4*	
Last four bars of section, as bars 51–4, decorated	*57–60*	
SECTION A'	61–82	22
Recapitulation (integral coda):		
Lydian-tendency mode on C, with repeated cadential formula		

Thus the centres of the three movements of the Sonatina (b,G♯/A♭,C) are connected by third relation; additionally, the first, and main, subject material of the finale resembles that of the preceding movements, as a descending statement of two consecutive third progressions (B,A,G; F,E,D) labelled 'a', followed by a response: (C–E,D–F,G–E) labelled 'b', as annotated on the score extract in Ex. 5.18, and summarized in the final Ex. 5.26. The tritone is of continuing relevance, both melodically on (B–F♭) again, and as part of the textural 'thickening' of the bass (C–F♯). These observations further support the large-scale view of the Sonatina as a single, essentially monothematic, movement, with a slow central episode.

Figure 5.15 Clarinet Sonatina: III, bars 1–5
Table to identify Invariant Subsets

Cardinality/Set	Invariant pitch-classes aligned
3-5	(0, 1, 6)
3-8	(0, 2, 6)
3-10	(0, 3, 6)
4-13	(0, 1, 3, 6)
4-27	(0, 2, 6, 9)
4-Z29	(0 4, 6, 7)
5-9	(0, 1, 2, 4, 6)
5-10	(0, 1, 3, 4, 6)
5-Z12	(0, 1, 3, 5, 6)
5-32	(0, 1, 4, 6, 9)
5-Z36	(0, 3, 5, 6, 7)
6-18	(0, 1, 2, 6, 7, 9)
Dyad set 2-6	* *

Bars 1–5 are illustrated with a set-theoretic bias in Ex. 5.18, the opening sonority, set 4-Z29 (C,F♯,D,B), recurring in bar 4 as (B,F♮,G,E), and encapsulated within 6-18, which occurs three times, and may provide a possible 'reference' set. The opening pitch structure stresses two sets of transposed 'triads' with tritonal input, 3-8 and 3-5 (as respective trichordal progenitors of the wholetone Genus 2 and atonal Genus 1) within a musical surface that features strong contrary motion between treble and bass, texturally intensified at the tritone, ninth, seventh, or more rarely the octave. In support of the set-theoretic perspective, Fig. 5.15 identifies the invariant subsets, focusing on the tritonal dyad 2-6.

The unusually high profile of the tritone here is appropriately supported by the suggestion of a predominant, synthesized Supragenus I (Atonal Hybrid), founded on the joint progenitors of Genera 1 and 2 (3-5 and 3-8). These progenitor sets are effectively fused to create variously sized referential constructs, starting with the critical subset 4-Z29 as the essential product of the combined progenitors, sounded on the first and third beats of the 4/4 metre, in both original and transposed forms. This subset construct is expanded through set 6-18, to a possible referential superset 7-29. Fig. 5.16 below lists the sets of the opening in relation to feasible genera, and lists the relevant Squo indices.

Arguably, the Squo measurement is in this case misleading, since, although it endorses Supragenus I overall, the emphasis is on Genus 3, simply because this genus is two-thirds the size of Genera 1 or 2 (and therefore has a greater proportional representation). A designation of

Figure 5.16 Clarinet Sonatina: III, bars 1–5
Matrix to show Sets in relation to Genera

Potential Genera: G1 G2 G3 G4 G9 G10 G12

Sets

	G1	G2	G3	G4	G9	G10	G12
3-5	o						
3-8		o					
3-10			o				
3-11					o	o	o
3-12				o			
4-13	o		o				
4-27		o	o				o
4-Z29	o	o					
5-9	o	o					
5-10	o	o	o				
5-Z12	o	o					
5/7-14	o	o					
5/7-29	o	o	o			o	o
5-32	o	o			o		o
5-Z36	o		o				o
6-18	o	o	o			o	o

Counts: 11   9   8   1   3   3   6
                  G1 G2 G3 G4 G9 G10 G12
                 [SGI   ]   [SGIII] [SGIV]

Counts   Squo Indices in descending order with Genera
8   .116: G3 (diminished)
11   .109: G1 (atonal)
9   .088: G2 (wholetone)

Genus 3 would seriously distort the character of this passage; it contributes very little to its profile (and, significantly, nothing to its recapitulation: see Coda, Ex. 5.25). The progenitor, 3-10, occurs only once, and even then merely as a 'passing' harmony, so that one could probably discount it anyway by means of Forte's rule 5, 'The Rule of Reduction', which omits 'passive genera'.[68] Although it may be unorthodox to suggest a composite Genera 2/1, founded on 4-Z29 (significantly absent from Genus 3), the decision is supported both by the fact that these two genera yield the lowest possible Difference quotient (Difquo: .01666), together with the connected fact that, as

---

68 Forte, 'Pitch-Class Set Genera', 234.

Forte himself notes, the genera of Supragenus I are unusual for their high level of common ground with respect to their hexachordal (and indeed pentachordal) components.[69]

Mediated by the concern with genera, the set-theoretic emphasis of Ex. 5.18 is balanced in Ex. 5.19 by the search for a more exact modal identity. The prominence of F♯/G (as in the first movement) favours both the Lydian (Ex. 5.19*a*) and the octatonic Model A on C (0,1,3,4,6,7,9,10), the latter embracing both the C–F♯ polarity and blues third (E♭/E♮) (Ex. 5.19*b*). This octatonic interpretation cannot, however, explain satisfactorily the prominence of the 'leading-note' B, often heard with F♯/G as subset 3-4, and thus another cyclical aspect from the opening movement; and although the other octatonic collection on B (B,C,D,E♭,F♮,F♯,G♯,A) would explain (B/C) and the prominence of F♯, it could not do justice to the semitonal pair (F♯/G), or the blues third.

Consequently, there is a need to combine and develop the most useful set-theoretic and modal interpretations. Ex. 5.19*c* considers set 6-18 set, its subset 4-Z29, and extended set 7-29, in terms of a scalic collection on C which, appropriately, does exhibit much common ground with the modal collections given in Ex. 5.19*a* and *b*. It is especially fitting that the significant set sonority 4-Z29 (bar 1: B,C,D,F♯) is also that which is created by the pitches of the intersection of the Lydian and octatonic Model A modes (i.e. C,E,F♯, (G)). All of the sets indicated in Ex. 5.19*c* fall within the terms of reference of Supragenus I (as a fusion of Genera 1 and 2). Additionally, set 6-18 is particularly well connected in its Kh subcomplexes since all of the following Kh-related sets are present in bars 1–5: cardinality 3   -5, -8, -10, -11; cardinality 4   -13, -27, -Z29; and cardinality 5/7   -14, -29. Furthermore, set 6-18 is strategically placed on prominent metric beats: the first and third beats of bar 3, and first beat of bar 5.

Nonetheless, even this modally enlightened set-theoretic stance needs further qualification. It should be stressed that embracing Forte's loosely styled 'Atonal Hybrid' Supragenus I is, emphatically, not to suggest that this music is other than modally conceived, and ultimately centric. Moreover, although the progenitors and resultant constructs of Genera 1 and 2 are inextricably intertwined, it is still arguably the 'wholetone' Genus 2 (rather than Genus 1) persona of this music that is foregrounded; and although, in Kh terms, set 6-18 is the

---

[69] Ibid., 225.

strongest candidate for nexus set status, even it cannot explain certain incompatible sets: 3-12 and cardinality 5-9, -10, -Z12, -32, -Z36. In the longer term, Ex. 5.19c could also be criticized for overlooking pitch G as the traditional dominant of C (and as part of the intersection of the Lydian and octatonic Model A collections), which is still of some significance. The most satisfactory compromise is to envisage a flexible Lydian mode on C, with chromatic encirclement around tonic and dominant: (B–C♮–C♯; F♯–G–A♭, as shown in Ex. 5.19d). Such a mode would still preserve the set constructions of Ex. 5.19c, recognizing the motivically important progenitor sets 3-8 (C,D,F♯) (F♯,G♯,C) (D,E,G♯) (F,A,B), and 3-5 (B,C,F♯) (F♮,F♯,C) (E,F,B) (C,F♯,G).

Bars 5–9 maintain the basis on C (Ex. 5.20), and the motivic preoccupation with elements 'a' and 'b' of the main subject, now joined by an elaborated descent of a fourth, labelled 'c'. Vertically, vestiges of blues syntax are suggested by set 3-3: (F,G♯/A) (D,F♮/F♯) (C,D♯/E), whilst, horizontally, discrete pentatonic patterns of set 3-7: (G♯,F♯,D♯; F♯,D♯,C♯), occur in the bass of bars 7, and 9–10. The interpolated semiquaver flourishes of bars 6, 8, and 12, articulate tonic and dominant constructs alternately, reminiscent of the dissonant flourishes of the first movement in their use of minor ninths. Bars 10–13 provide further affirmation of C as the main centre of the finale, endorsed by an incongruously clear-cut V^7–I progression across bars 11–12. However, the now typical white-note/black-note conflict reasserts itself across bars 14–20, with (C,E,G) presented in the treble of the piano against pitches (A♯[B♭],C♯) of a possible tritonally opposed F♯ triad beneath, whilst the clarinet line, in a sense, combines the two within a localized octatonic-type framework, 4-28 (B♭,E,G,C♯). Across these same bars occurs another of Milhaud's typical hall-marks: contradiction between repeated rhythmic patterns and metre, essentially creating 3/4 within 4/4. The continuing preoccupation with third motives here offers further connection with the preceding movements, especially the first.

Bars 21-7 (Ex. 5.21), constructed as one of Milhaud's favoured mirror-images, equate to a 'bridge' between first and second subjects, and, simultaneously (in terms of overall formal proportions) between expository and developmental sections, although, as in the first movement, development is continuous. There is a significant paradox in respect of a transitional bridge-passage which has undergone, in Strausian terms, '*Symmetricization*', so that 'Traditionally goal-orientated harmonic progressions and musical forms (sonata form, for example) are made inversionally or retrograde-symmetrical, and are thus immobilized.'[70] The piano part of bars 21–3 emphasizes the tritone (B♭–E), as opposed to (C–F♯), sometimes combined with G, in a 3-10 diminished triad. There follows a four-bar interjection for piano alone, consisting of a two-bar repeated unit (bars 24–5 and 26–7). The patterning in bars 21–3 and 24–7 is quite distinct: sets 7-22, 7-29, 7-14, followed by the reverse (then repeated).[71] Generically, the first two constructions: (3-10, 4-18) 7-22; and (3-10, 4-27) 7-29, subscribe clearly to the diminished Genus 3, whilst the third construction around 7-14 is far more equivocal. Nonetheless, use of the Squo indicator offers a general endorsement of Genus 3, with the highest quotient across bars 21–3.[72] In terms of significant pitches, these bars suggest an overall prolongation of B♭, as a means of mediating between C and f. This dramatic, rhetorical gesture is not typical of Milhaud's earlier neoclassicism, but is again connected with his increased interest and success in opera.

The first part of Section B (bars 28–35) is similar in its relative consonance to the second subject group of the first movement, utilizing a Phrygian mode on f: (F,G♭,A♭,B♭,C,D♭,E♭,F) with occasional naturalizing of the sixth scalic degree. The simple, contrasting 'second subject', played by clarinet, consists of yet another fifth interval (C–F), followed by an elaborated third progression (B♭–A♭–B♭, C–A♭). Structure and balance are again generated by judicious repetition, with bars 28–9 (as one, repeated, bar) providing the material for bars 31–2, 34–5, 38–9, and 42–3. A 'dominant' half-close formula used to conclude the initial three-bar phrases, at bars 30 and 33, is balanced by a 'tonic' full-close in bars 31–2 and 34–5. Harmonically, the most remote region is across bars 36–44, where a repeated three-bar formula concludes on a chord of F♭ (incidentally, chord VI of the coda in the second movement), in chromatic opposition to f. These bars serve to remind one of the developmental aspect of this section. Highly dissonant interjections (essentially with 'dominant' function) serve to disrupt the relative tranquility in bars 41–2 and 45–6 (Ex. 5.22). Modified inversion of the initial melodic figure of the first subject is coupled with more minor ninth/major seventh thickening; the right-hand parts of bars 41–2

---

[70] Straus, *Remaking the Past*, 17.

[71] In respect of the first and last sets of 7-22, it is worth drawing attention to the occurrences of subset 4-18, which connect back to the first movement, and to the continuing tendency to oppose pitches semitonally: E♭/D; G♭/F; A/B♭/B♮.

[72] Squo calculation based on a total of seven sets across bars 21–3 (3-10, 3-11, 4-18, 4-27, 5/7-14, 5/7-22 and 5/7-29): Squo(G3) = ((5/7)/43) = .166.

(labelled as 'a' and 'b' for basic identification) are exchanged in bars 45–6, with emphasis on the construct (C,E♭/E♮), as both the local 'dominant' and overall tonic of the finale.

Bar 47 marks the return to f 'minor' for the second part of Section B (bars 47–60), dominated initially by piano textures. On a larger scale, the dissonant semiquaver gestures of bars 47 and 48 compare both with bar 6 and the start of the first 'Très rude'. At bars 49–50, the centre on f temporarily gives way to a conflict between the Dorian on g with blues third: (G,A,B♭/B♮,C,D,E,F,G) and an F♯/G♯ oscillation below, reminiscent of bars 77–9 of the first movement. Again, in a wider sense, this perpetuates the tritonal opposition between F♯ ('black-note') and C ('white-note'), with part of the tension caused by the F♯ also due to its previous role in the first movement as the dominant of b. Bars 51–4 are predominantly scalic and sequential, the mode f-based once more in bars 51–2 (Ex. 5.23), though now Dorian in inflection (with blues third). Within its sequential descents, the clarinet interpolates an extended variant of motive 'c' from the first subject.

Tension is gradually heightened in advance of the recapitulation, with f 'minor' pitches still discernible above a bass which is increasingly chromatically excited (bars 53–4). Bars 55–6 represent an elaboration of bars 49–50, with the lowest bass pitches (D♯/E) perhaps again suggestive of blues third in the overall context of C. The final four bars before the recapitulation (bars 57–60: Ex. 5.24) are loosely as bars 51–4, with neobaroque invertible counterpoint, and a 'double-dotted' presentation of set 3-9 on clarinet involving subsequent rhythmic diminution. Baroque/classical trappings are also evident in the placing of the two-bar trill, with its inbuilt sense of expectation, so endorsing the 'modulation' from f/F to (chord V of) the 'tonic' C.

The recapitulation (bars 61–82) commences with the clarinet's reworking of the first subject, accompanied by varied quasi-cadential statements of bars 1–2 on piano which serve to reaffirm the tonic. Constant oscillation between 4/4 and 3/4 adds to the sense of forward momentum. The opening sonority of 4-Z29 occurs on every first beat of the 4/4 metre, with a process of increasing elaboration operating through the reiterations of the cadential gesture (embracing sextuplet groupings and further octave doublings). There is a sense of the piano part being locked into its own self-contained formula, and so dislocated from the rest of the discourse (similar to the procedure at the end of *L'Abandon d'Ariane*). Across bars 73–6, the f 'minor' melody on clarinet (stressing the subdominant relation in the recapitulation, as if in allusion to some late Classical model), is typically combined with the cadential formula. In respect of Milhaud's rethinking of sonata form, the constant cadential reiteration of this section hints at a conflation of recapitulation and coda (balancing the earlier conflation of 'second subject' area and development section).

The integral two-bar coda ('Sans ralentir': Ex. 5.25), with its final cadential statement on the piano, is similar in its condensed brevity to that of the first movement of the Fifth Chamber Symphony (1922), although executed here with more power and drama, and an overt '$\hat{3}$–$\hat{2}$–$\hat{1}$' voice-leading descent in the clarinet line. The (C–F♯) conflict, with Lydian and octatonic associations, is maintained right up to the close of this descent. Generically, bar 81 subscribes, as did the opening of this movement, to a composite Genera 2/1, endorsed by balanced Squo measurements.[73] The eventual arrival on the structural $\hat{1}$ cues a closing diatonic bar of Ionian modality on C (with its accompanying generic resolution to the 'diatonic-tonal' Genus 12, also endorsed by the Squo indices): only then is the progression (b–C) complete. Even so, there is a sense that, although the theoretical resolution may finally have been attained, its extremely brief articulation has been almost too fleeting to register: a case of too little, too late!

Conclusion

The Clarinet Sonatina represents the furthest point reached specifically by Milhaud's chamber music of the 1920s, in terms of its uncompromising modality, and far-reaching modifications of sonata forms. It is a mature if somewhat idiosyncratic Sonatina, operating within a sophisticated modality, rich in its varied allusiveness. As Joseph Straus comments, in general fashion, but with apposite application here, 'Sonorities like the triad, forms like the sonata, and structural motions like the descending perfect fifth are too profoundly emblematic of traditional tonal practices to meld quietly into a new musical context.'[74]

---

[73] The relevant sets for bar 81 are 3-4, 3-5, 3-8, 4-Z29, 5-19, 5-24, 5-28, 5-30 and 5-32, with Genera 2 and 1 each represented seven times; since Genus 1 is fractionally smaller overall than Genus 2, its Squo is very slightly higher: Squo(G1) = ((7/9)/63) = .123, as against Squo(G2) = ((7/9)/64) = .122.

[74] Straus, 'Toward a Theory of Musical Influence', *Remaking the Past*, 1.

Yet simultaneously 'the [sonata] forms lose their original significance in order to take on their new responsibility of evoking the past.'[75]

Certainly, the nature of Milhaud's modality has affected profoundly the extent of his rethinking—or wilful misreading?— of sonata forms. Milhaud enjoys exploring the polarities and dualities, primarily of modal identity (though hand-in-hand with thematic identity), which are, in tonally equivalent terms, at the heart of the eighteenth-century sonata principle.[76] Paradoxically, however, he explores so many polarities more or less simultaneously (e.g. tonic-dominant relations, third relations, semitonal and tritonal oppositions) within a complex concept of modality, that some of the definition is inevitably lost, and the destruction of the very idea itself is threatened. Furthermore, operating in the realms of a flexible modality, as opposed to the tonality which underlies the sonata principle, there is inevitably less scope for 'modulation' as such, which in turn reduces opportunities for formal expansion, again questioning the very foundation of the form. This is no doubt one practical reason for Milhaud's conflation of the second subject area and development section in first and final movements, which might be deemed to reduce the form to no more than a glorified ternary structure—after all, one of Milhaud's most commonly used forms. (On balance, though, the sonata form principles of this work remain well founded in terms of Milhaud's awareness of the duality and innate opposition of the first and second subject areas.) More positively, such concision and compression have already been signalled as intrinsic to Milhaud's neoclassical aesthetic, and are highly appropriate within the self-imposed confines of a Sonatina.

Beyond the problematics of modality and polarity in relation to form, one should add that Milhaud's mature use of modality promotes a linguistic consistency and unity across the work, achieved especially through thematic connections (see Ex. 5.26), fifth and third progressions, and voice-leading descents. These unifying elements are sufficiently strong and numerous to afford real credibility to the large-scale view of the work as a single, extended movement.

---

[75] C. Rosen, *The Classical Style: Haydn, Mozart, Beethoven*, rev. edn. (London, 1976; repr. 1987), 460.

[76] The emphasis on tonal or harmonic contrast as an eighteenth-century phenomenon within the sonata concept is supported by Straus ('Sonata Forms', *Remaking the Past*, 96–7), as a consensus of most standard accounts of sonata form.

Case Study 8
L'Abandon d'Ariane, Op. 98 (1927) as the Culmination of Milhaud's Neoclassicism in the 1920s

Preliminaries

L'Abandon d'Ariane is the second of a trilogy of 'Opéras-minute', so-called not only because of their short durations, but also because of their relatively small instrumental and vocal forces, and methods of construction. In the words of Collaer/Galante (all be they somewhat simplistic): 'the quantity of material is replaced by the quality of inventiveness'.[77] The function of the choruses is to comment on the action, in the manner of classical Greek tragedy. Staging involves difficult issues since it is not appropriate for scenery and acting to mimic the conventions of grand opera; there must be the same economy and concentration of effect as in the composition itself. Thus, we look towards some refined, neoclassical ideal, through a re-invocation of classical Greek mythology and drama. As in Case Study 6, the notion of distance as time (and place) is critical here; Milhaud's music balances the choice of subject-matter with its own exploration of distancing techniques, involving, for instance, objectification and detachment of musical material by means of ostinati and other discrete formulae. Connected with this is Milhaud's engagement in processes of ironization, both within the confines of the work and beyond, in terms of his attitude towards the past.

The compositional approach of the 'Opéras-minute' first emerged in *Les Malheurs d'Orphée* (1925) and is similar to Hindemith's in *Hin und zurück*. Indeed, it was Hindemith who invited Milhaud to take part in the festival at Baden-Baden where *Hin und zurück* and *L'Enlèvement d'Europe* were first performed in the same programme. Milhaud explains the background to these operas in *Ma vie heureuse*:[78] he had originally composed *L'Enlèvement* (nine minutes' duration) to be produced in conjunction with Toch's *Die Prinzessin auf der Erbst* (sixty minutes), Weill's *Mahagonny* (thiry minutes) and Hindemith's *Hin und zurück* (fourteen minutes). However, the managing director of Universal Edition did not consider publication of such a work a viable commercial proposition and suggested the trilogy. Thus Milhaud came to

---

[77] Collaer/Galante, *Darius Milhaud*, 103.
[78] Milhaud, *Ma vie heureuse*, 167–76.

compose *L'Abandon d'Ariane*, 'Opéra-minute en cinq scènes', in Aix-en-Provence in early August 1927, having requested a further two libretti from Henri Hoppenot. The work, of merely ten minutes' duration, was first performed as part of the triptych, in April 1928, at the theatre in Wiesbaden, conducted by J. Rosenstock.

One wonders if, in selecting the myth of Ariadne on Naxos, Milhaud was inspired by Richard Strauss's one-act opera, composed for performance after Molière's comedy *Le Bourgeois gentilhomme*. Indeed, Milhaud remarks in his autobiography on having seen Strauss's *Ariadne* in the production staged at the Opéra in 1922, and on his particular interest in Hofmannsthal's libretto.[79] Might he also have been aware of Stravinsky's shorter dramatic works, such as *Renard* (1916), or Satie's *Socrate* (1918)?

The Greek legendary subject matter of the 'Opéras-minute' is certainly an appropriate choice for the neoclassicist. Ariadne, daughter of King Minos of Crete, has been shipwrecked on the island of Naxos with her twin sister Phaedra and her hateful husband Theseus (who treats her contemptibly despite her having helped him to solve the mystery of the Labyrinth on Crete). Ariadne's loathing for Theseus is matched only by her sister's longing, and unrequited love, for the same man. The machinations of Dionysus, at first disguised as an old man, enable each sister to resolve their respective predicaments. With the aid of Dionysus's wine, the inebriated Theseus later returns to Athens with a veiled Phaedra (whom he believes to be Ariadne), so abandoning Ariadne, who is thus released from the source of her torment and eventually finds happiness in marrying Dionysus. Ariadne's tomb is reputedly to be found on Naxos, where two festivals of commemoration are still held: the first mournful, bewailing Ariadne's death; the second joyous, celebrating her marriage to Dionysus. Although neither event occurs literally in Milhaud's opera, *L'Abandon* maintains the conventional, emotional antithesis. The musical language is largely diatonic, with chromaticism reserved for heightening passages of increased emotion.

L'Abandon d'Ariane is the final work selected for analysis here, since it illustrates well Milhaud's increased interest in neoclassical style and practice in the late 1920s, showing how certain features of the early chromatic and jazz phases have been preserved and incorporated. Another reason behind the selection is that comparison may be made

---

[79] Milhaud, *Ma vie heureuse*, 117.

with Jeremy Drake's essay on the neoclassical operas.[80] Although the work is undoubtedly modal, pitch-class set notation is used as a supplementary analytical tool, in order to draw attention to features that might be overlooked in the voice-leading and functional harmonic analyses (and to facilitate the large-scale interpretation of pc-set genera in Milhaud's music). It should be noted that although the musical examples refer principally to the published vocal score,[81] the orchestral score (available only on hire) has also been consulted.

The opera requires four vocal soloists: Ariane (soprano), Phaedra (soprano), Theseus (tenor) and Dionysus (baritone), together with two small choruses: the male chorus of three shipwrecked sailors consists of soli tenor, baritone and bass, and is balanced by a female chorus of three revelling gypsies: soli soprano, mezzo-soprano and contralto. Instrumentally, the requirements are for 2 flutes (1 doubling piccolo), oboe, 2 clarinets in B♭, bassoon; horn in F, 2 trumpets in C; percussion; 2 violins, viola, cello, and double bass. The percussion section includes timpani (tuned mainly to C and E, but on occasion to B♭, D♭ and F), snare-, tenor and bass drums, cymbals and tam-tam.

General principles of orchestration include much doubling of melodic lines: flute and violin I; oboe and violin II; cello, bassoon and double bass (often pizzicato). More dramatically, Milhaud uses doublings, at four octaves' distance, between piccolo and bassoon, as at bar 8 onwards, and in the final 'Vif'. (Such doubling was discussed as a typical feature of earlier pieces such as 'La Lieuse' from *Machines agricoles*, Case Study 2.) Sometimes instrumental sections are used antiphonally, especially woodwind and brass contrasting with strings; equally, similar effects can be obtained within sections, as in bars 1–7 where melodic material undergoes discrete division within the wind section. Particular timbral effects include the muting of horn and trumpets, and use of pizzicato, harmonics and trills on strings. Such effects, in addition to strategic placing of tutti and soli passages, may contribute to conveying the pitch-structure: timbral distinctions may clarify a passage of bimodality, whilst percussive punctuation on timpani may emphasize a significant pitch.

---

[80] Drake, *The Operas of Darius Milhaud*, Chapter 9, 'The neo-classical operas II: Essay in stylistic analysis'.

[81] Vocal score (Vienna: Universal Edition, 1928; 2nd edn. (German version), 1953; 3rd edn. (English version), 1963). All references are to the 1963 edition unless otherwise indicated; translations, however, are my own.

Overall, the vocal score constitutes a faithful reflection of the full score, although inevitably some doublings are unmarked. Pitches in the treble are sometimes notated an octave lower than in the full score, whilst, more rarely, those in the bass are notated an octave higher, though not compromising the functioning of the bass-line. Occasionally, pitches considered insignificant (e.g. the fifth of a chord, or other types of textural thickening) have been omitted in the published vocal score: such pitches have been selectively restored in the annotated vocal score used in the analytical examples.

Analysis

Before discussing each scene in turn, it is appropriate to give a formal outline of the work. The attention paid to the recapitulation of material produces, at background level, an arch structure, illustrated in Fig. 5.17. This structure has a broadly triadic outline of pitch centres: (C,E♭,G,E♭,C), with the Mixolydian mode on G restricted to the centre-piece of the 'Tango' (Scene III). Symmetry, at least in outline, is thus preserved. Such symmetry is also evident in patterns of harmonic stability and instability: the opening and conclusion of the piece are both essentially 'white-note' diatonic and fairly consonant, whilst the areas of greatest instability, chromaticism and dissonance are located in Scene III (bars 121–9; bars 178–87, 188–96), as far away from the outer 'pillars' as possible (and balanced by other instances in Scenes II and IV). It should be stressed that 'diatonicism' here is not synonymous with functional triadic harmony; the harmonic character is such that there is a point beyond which dominant discords, for instance, dissolve into 'sets'—vertical events which cannot usefully be described as alterations of triads and seventh chords.

The basic scene for the chamber opera is a 'desolate and deserted' landscape on the island of Naxos. In the background is a 'mound of rocks whose tops are outlined against the sunset. During the piece, twilight descends and by the end it is almost night.'[82]

SCENE I. 'Modérément animé'

This first scene has a pastoral atmosphere, employing a lilting 6/8 metre. Ex. 5.27 quotes and annotates the introductory bars 1–7, whose language is entirely diatonic (within the Ionian mode on C), reminis-

---

[82] Preface to 1953 edition.

Figure 5.17 *L'Abandon d'Ariane*: Formal Outline

ARCH STRUCTURE

	Modality	Bars	Total Bars
SCENE I			
SECTION A	Ionian on C	1–30	30
SCENE II			
SECTION B	Dorian on c/Lydian on E♭	31–103	73
	Heightened chromaticism	*43ff., 67ff.*	
	Aeolian on c/Lydian on A♭	*76*	
SECTION A'	Ionian on C (similar to Scene I, bars 8–23)	104–19	
	Linking material on E♭	120	17
SCENE III			
SECTION C	Aeolian on c (Ionian on A♭)	121–200	80
	Chromaticism (descent)	*121–9*	
(SECTION B')	Similar to opening of Scene II	*140ff.*	
	Forceful chromatic climax	*178–87*	
	Chromaticism (ascent)	*188–95*	
	Linking material	*196–200*	
	'Tango': Mixolydian on G	201–17	17
SCENE IV			
Section B'	Dorian on c/Lydian on E♭	218–34	17
	Chromaticism (similar to Scene II, bars 43ff., 67ff.)	227–34	
SCENE V			
Section D	Modal complementation: 'black-note/white-note'	235–54	20
Section C	Mixolydian on F (blues 3rd) (Hint of 'Tango')	255–82	28
Section A'	Ionian on C (similar to Scene I)	283–308	26

cent in this respect of the opening of *Quatre poèmes*. Although the 'language' is diatonic, in that the pitches are 'white notes', the 'grammar' is of course less traditional. However, since these bars are based entirely in one key, C, the stridency of dissonance is limited since the only available semitonal dissonances are (E/F) and (B/C): thus there is only 'internal dissonance' within the mode, rather than 'external dissonance' between foreign pitches or conflicting modes. Jeremy Drake comments on this use of diatonic modality in his essay on stylistic analysis: 'In Milhaud's neo-classical works, purity of mode is a characteristic feature'.[83]

The opening instrumental introduction sustains the dominant of C, sounded in second inversion with a low pitch D (D_1) on double bass; this first chord, 'V^{11}', is the pentatonic set 5-35 (D,G,F,C,A). The double bass is grouped with cello and bassoon to form various tri-chords, mostly of set 3-7 (as one progenitor of Genus 12), which ascend by step, in two-bar phrases. Above, another two-bar pattern, consisting of triads in second inversion (i.e. 3-11, as the other progenitor of Genus 12), works in descent. This descent of the melodic material provides an overly literal word-painting in anticipation of bars 8–9, 'Le soir tombe'; the phrasing and sense of balance are emphasized by discrete instrumental groupings in the wind section, whilst strings provide a constant 'background'. The style is almost naively simple, bordering on the trite, with frequent vertical thirds, sixths and melodic step-wise progressions, the deliberate blandness of which immediately creates a distancing effect: a sense of detachment, or alienation. Bar 7 features a clichéd pause chord on V^{11} (set 5-29), after the 'V^{13}' (set 6-32), of bar 5, creating a strong sense of expectancy for the resolution to the tonic at bar 8.

Before leaving these opening bars, it is worth elaborating briefly on their generic perspective. This introduction is indisputably diatonic, and seemingly uncontroversial: in terms of 'raw' count, all sets are referable to a single genus, the diatonic-tonal Genus 12 (whose two progenitors are present: 3-7, and 3-11, as the ubiquitous triads in the treble stave). If, however, one were to insist on implementing the Squo indicator, the value of Genus 12 would be only .222, as against .241 of Genus 11.[84] Thus the Squo measure would compromise the view of this passage, simply by virtue of the smaller size of Genus 11 (and its consequently greater proportional representation), irrespective of the profiles of the two genera within the passage.

---

[83] Drake, *The Operas of Darius Milhaud*, 205.

[84] All 10 sets are referable to Genus 12: 3-7, 3-11, 4-22, 4-27, 5-23, 5-25, 5-29, 5-35, 6-Z26, 6-32; 7 of these are also referable to Genus 11. Therefore, the resulting Squo calculations are as follows: Squo(G12) = ((10/10)/45), where 45 is the total number of sets in Genus 12, as against Squo(G11) = ((7/10/29), where 29 is the total number of sets in Genus 11. The full set content of each genus is given in the appendix at the end of Forte, 'Pitch-class Set Genera', 264–6.

Bars 8–11 are examined in Ex. 5.28, as representative of the whole scene. At 'Mouvement', the chorus of shipwrecked sailors offers its passive, descriptive commentary, the three lines being doubled by violins and viola. Most striking is the ironized use of simple modal sequence in the Ionian on C, as a banal musical equivalent of rhyming couplets, and one which corresponds well with the four-square text: 'Le soir tombe; les troupeaux rentrent'.[85] Furthermore, this understated melody, consisting merely of two third progressions (C,D,E,C) (D,E,F,D) followed by a descending fifth figure (with bars 15–18 offering a melodic retrograde), seriously over-reaches itself in providing the thematic basis of scenes II, III and V. The sparse instrumental accompaniment utilizes another two-bar pattern (sounded in octaves on bassoon and piccolo): an arpeggiated chord of C with D and B neighbour notes, which, in combination with the vocal progression (C,D,E) and inverted bass-pattern (E,D,C), allude to a passing $^6_4$ construct (i.e. I^6–V^6_4–I, as a voice-exchange). This loosely cadential 'trapping' of common practice music, equates nicely with the sense of stability and closure offered by 'nightfall' itself, as a time of comparative peace for Ariadne beyond her tormentor. (Thus she seeks final refuge in the night sky at the end of the opera). The centre on C is reinforced by timpani rhythms on this pitch across bars 8–23.

The sadness of Ariadne's plight is initially evident only at one remove, in the commentary of the chorus of shipwrecked sailors: 'par l'amour de Thésée, Ariane meurtrie',[86] confounded by music which is as yet still pastoral and lacking in harmonic tension. Across bars 20–4 (Ex. 5.29), however, metrical tension is increased by the change to simple metre for the choir and strings (2/4, 3/4, 2/4), whilst the arpeggiated line of bassoon and piccolo continues in compound metre (6/8, 9/8, 6/8), the conflict of 2 versus 3 quavers suggesting an instance of what Drake would describe as Milhaud's 'polymetricality'.[87] Despite

---

[85] 'Night is falling, the flocks return . . .' It is worthing pointing up the parallel between the homecoming of the flocks before nightfall and the goal-directed nature of the modality on C.

[86] 'Ariadne scarred by her love for Theseus' (bars 14–16). The static quality of a chorus commenting on the action shares something of the 'statuesque' with Stravinsky's *Oedipus Rex*, 'in which the classical idea of verbal elucidation without overt action would be carried to an extreme' (Walsh, *The Music of Stravinsky*, 137). Like *Oedipus Rex*, the chorus in *L'Abandon* also performs a 'pivotal structural role' (ibid., 139).

[87] Drake, *The Operas of Darius Milhaud*, 197.

this, metrical/rhythmic treatment is still far simpler than in early works such as *L'Homme et son désir*.

Bars 24–30 balance bars 1–7, also functioning as a postlude or interlude between the first and second scenes: bars 24–9 sustain 'tonic' harmony within two-bar phrases, whilst bar 30 focuses on IV^{13} (F^{13}). The overall shape of Scene I is a typical ABA' structure, with A as the 'prelude' and A' as the 'postlude'. The restriction of the 'pianissimo' timpani part to the central B section helps to clarify these formal divisions. Finally, as noted in *Machines agricoles* and *Quatre poèmes de Catulle*, one should stress that the wordsetting here is deliberately artificial and stylized in its nature, thus again achieving distance, especially in respect of the chorus which is already distanced from the action.

SCENE II. 'Modéré'

Ariadne and Phaedra appear on stage, identical in height and costume (thus preparing the way for one of two instances of conventional dramatic irony). The second scene commences with Ariadne singing a miniature aria, bars 31–40, appealing to her father, King Minos: 'Ô Père! Ô Juste Minos! Ta fille, objet de ta tendresse, naufragée aux bords de Naxos subit l'époux grossier à qui tu l'as donnée!'[88] The main mode (C,D,E♭,F,G,A,B♭,C) is Dorian on c, or possibly Lydian on E♭ (i.e. a typical ambiguity of centres a third apart), with an apparent move to B♭ at bar 40. The B and E pitches of Scene I have been flattened in accordance with the increasingly melancholic sentiments. From bar 31 the melodic line is derived from the opening of Scene I, within more anguished, repeated phrases, accompanied by alternating pairs of clarinets and flutes, plus viola (a trio texture being maintained across bars 31–7). The predominant melodic motive is still a third progression, contracted now between C and E♭; the bass line (provided by viola) also states four third progressions, commencing (E♭–D–C) across bars 31–2. Meanwhile, the lilting 6/8 metre of Scene I continues, though its use tends to be restricted to the solo passages of Scene II.

The harmonic character of Ariadne's solo favours some mild dissonance, although the concept of increased chromaticism for heightened emotion is developed further in the 'Plus allant', bars 43–9:

---

[88] 'O father! O just Minos! Your daughter, object of your tenderness, shipwrecked on the shores of Naxos, suffering the uncouth husband to whom you gave her!'

Ex. 5.30.[89] With some justification, Drake actually describes the passage from bar 41 onwards as a 'polymodal ostinato'.[90] Ironically, the second chorus, 'Chœur des bacchantes tziganes', operating (as the chorus in Scene I) at one remove, succeeds in commenting on Ariadne's distress far more colourfully than does she herself! These bars are further characterized by the metrical change to 5/4, followed by common time, and the 'tutti' instrumentation including timpani on C (bars 43–8), and cymbals (bars 45–6). Drake continues by remarking that 'any incipient tonal associations are quashed by inflectional dissonance',[91] and although this passage certainly thrives on chromatic ambiguity, there are still distinct pitch patterns. A broadly symmetrical structure, using contrary motion, emerges in the independent vocal parts across bars 43–4 (Ex. 5.30), the structure being similar to those in the Fourth Quartet and the Fifth Chamber Symphony.

The blues type triad 3-3 occurs most frequently and is part of the extended set 4-17 (C,E♭,E♮,G), heard on the first beats of bars 43 (within set 5-6) and 44.[92] This vertical conflict of the third degree suggests a return to pastiche blues treatment, whilst the detached ostinato accompaniment (bars 43ff.) derives from the melodic third progressions of Scene I: (C,D,E♭; D,C,D) with parallel motion a third higher. This c 'minor' identity of the upper parts and timpani is contradicted by the bass (C♯,E,F♯,G): in other words there is a process of chromatic complementation (C♯,E,F♯); (C,E♭,F). Octave displacement of successive quavers within the discrete basso ostinato is again reminiscent of the Fourth Quartet, and is viewed by Drake as 'an unmistakeable fingerprint of his [Milhaud's] neo-classical style'.[93] The prominent figuration in the bass spans the tritone as set 4-13: (C♯,E,F♯,G) (E♭,G♭,A♭,A♮), whilst this interval also comes to the fore in linking the treble, on C, and bass, initially on C♯/F♯. A fondness for centres a tritone apart (also exemplified by the Clarinet Sonatina) is another legacy from *L'Homme et son désir* and *Saudades do Brazil*, and thus Milhaud has maintained the most effective techniques of the early chromatic and jazz elements and incorporated them into his developing neoclassicism. Despite the

---

[89] 'Ô Spectacle tragique! Ô Femme infortunée! Dionysos! Dionysos! Abaisse tes regards sur elle!'

[90] Drake, *The Operas of Darius Milhaud*, 216.

[91] Ibid., 217.

[92] Set 4-17 is also heard on these pitches at the end of the Fifth Chamber Symphony.

[93] Drake, *The Operas of Darius Milhaud*, 190.

superficial conflict, a background level interpretation of these bars would still view the music as centric about C, with a sense of $V^{9/11/13}$ on the final two beats of bars 43–5, and throughout bar 47. (Interestingly, in the broadly comparable bars 227–34 of Scene IV similar chromatic conflicts, presented without a pedal on timpani, crystallize out in favour of a Phrygian mode on d.)

From bar 50 onwards, Phaedra's solo in the Aeolian on c[94] balances that of Ariadne, with another trio texture of violins and pizzicato cello (doubled by alternating bassoon and horn). Bars 54, 58, 62 and 66 are distinctive in cadencing onto an open octave or perfect fifth interval, as a reinterpretation of what might be deemed a 'trapping' of medieval modal practice. The balancing of musical treatment across the two sisters' solos supports the emotional antithesis of the two texts: the cause of the unhappiness of one would constitute the joy of the other. This is followed, and balanced, by the second chromatic choral section (bars 67–75, 'tutti'), now reinforced by both choruses bewailing the sisters' sad destinies. The formal outline of Scene II thus far is: A (bars 31–42), B (bars 43–9), A (bars 50–66) and B (bars 67–75).

At the 'Lent' (bars 76ff.), Dionysus enters as the 'deus ex machina' (appropriate enough in terms of one of his several identities as the 'god of drama'), typically incognito as a beggar holding out his hand: thus this 'Opéra-minute' plays along with the conventional requirement to engage in dramatic irony. Dionysus sings a line which, independently, seems based initially in the Aeolian on c (bars 76–9), 'modulating' to the Lydian on A♭ for the second part of the phrase (bars 80–3). As Drake rightly observes, 'The lydian mode is astonishingly common in Milhaud's works of the 1910's–1930's and even beyond.'[95]

Developing further the modal perspective across bars 76–83, it is interesting that Milhaud restricts the vocal range to a perfect fifth (A♭–E♭), according nicely with his respect for authentic and plagal forms. Melodic association with Scene I continues with prominent melodic third motives (C–E♭), whilst Dionysus's concluding descent to A♭ (bars 82–3) uses an equal division of 6/8 into four dotted quavers, reminiscent of Scenes I (bars 13–14) and II (bars 39–40). The basic reference set for the accompaniment is a pentatonic construct: 4-26 (E♭,F,A♭,C), the C pitch sometimes inflected as C♭. Overall, the modality is delightfully ambiguous: the cello's pedal (E♭–A♭) suggests the second inversion of

[94] The modal identity is supported by Drake, *The Operas of Darius Milhaud*, 203.
[95] Ibid.

A♭, whilst the vocal melody initially supports the Aeolian mode on c: a further ambiguity of centres a third apart. However, the pedal on E♭ (punctuated by pizzicato double bass) may be significant on a larger scale, across the opera, as part of a third progression: (E♭–C). Regarding orchestration, bars 76–83 are further characterized by the subtle use of 'pianissimo' tam-tam and bass drum.

Bars 84–92 ('Très lent') consist of balanced phrases from Ariadne and Phaedra, as each offers money to the beggar, thus passing their ritualistic testing by the disguised Dionysus, and so securing their deliverance. Melodic allusion in the vocal parts is again to bar 8 of Scene I: (A♭,B♭,C; B♭,C,D♭), so that, supported by further third intervals on C,A♭ (violin I) with D♯(E♭) in the bass, localized modal associations are towards A♭, within a dissonant context. In respect of the bass, bar 84 marks the enharmonic conversion of E♭ to D♯ (and A♭ to G♯), as the basis of the first of two chords oscillating between D♯ and E, once again suggestive of a large-scale blues third in C. The full ostinato comprises two main set sonorities of 5-21 (D♯,G♯,E,B,C) and 5-22 (E,A,F,D♭,B♭) (including the common trichord, 3-4), which are presented by lower strings, and are significant as a source of material for Scene V. In traditional fundamental bass terminology, the oscillating chords emphasize quartal components, in the manner of the open-string tuning of the double bass. Drake describes the construct as another 'polymodal ostinato',[96] although there is no real, balanced opposition of distinct modal entities: this seems simply a case of localized instability within a large-scale bass progression (E♭–E♮–F), across bars 76–103. Surface tension is increased across bars 84–95 by agitated rhythms on tenor drum, and across bars 99–103 by a trill on viola: D resolving on to C at bar 104.

Bars 104–19 are broadly similar to bars 8–23 of Scene I; the two choruses function antiphonally, balanced by more condensed hyperbolic responses from the sisters in respect of Theseus's imminent return: 'Ah, je fuis!' (Ariadne); 'Ô bonheur!' (Phaedra). The compression and juxtaposition of these exaggerated responses ironizes the dramatic convention of antithesis by its bordering on the ridiculous. Formally, the overall design so far is ternary: Scene I, Scene II, modified return of Scene I material. At bar 120, the C 'major' mode is converted to 'minor', so that pitches (C,D; E♭,F,G), heard in 'fortissimo' octaves across the whole ensemble, act as a type of pivot from C to E♭ (as the

---

[96] Ibid., 216.

dominant of A♭). This prepares for Scene III, based around A♭/Aeolian on c. Perhaps, though, the underlying centre never wavers from C, as suggested by the timpani which asserts the pitch consistently across bars 104–20.

Scene III. 'Moins animé'

The scene commences with Theseus's insistent cries for the traitorous, cruel Ariadne to come to him: 'Ariadne! Ô Volage! Ô Cruelle! Accourez!', with his characterization reduced to two-dimensional caricature as a force of evil. Theseus enquires of Dionysus the whereabouts of the fleeing Ariadne; Dionysus in turn responds that she will surely arrive soon but that Theseus might appreciate a little fine wine while he waits.

The dissonant, chromatic modality is still ambiguous between A♭ and the Aeolian mode on c. D♭ can be viewed as a Neapolitan-inflected second: thus Theseus's anguished and insistent exclamations (Ex. 5.31), outlining a third progression: (C,E♭,D♭,C), constitute yet another derivative of the third progressions of Scene I. However, the chromatic descent of the double bass across bars 122–9: G♯(A♭) to C♯(D♭), is unstable, with repeated trichords of set 3-5 on lower strings, as the progenitor set of the relatively unusual, atonal Genus 1. All nine sets here are referable to Genus 1 (endorsed by a definitive Squo calculation: Fig. 5.18), and although the set segmentation here concentrates on the orchestral accompaniment, inclusion of the vocal pitches does not alter the generic outcome.

Bars 122–9 illustrate a tritonally corrupted quintal harmony, commencing at bar 122 with 5-32 (G♯,D,A,F,C), the last two pitches being double-stopped by violin I. Strict quintal harmony appeared frequently in Milhaud's music before 1917, but less commonly in the 1920s, so that its corrupted presentation here could almost be read as self-parody. Despite the generic view of these bars operating in the atonal Genus 1, the modality of C still remains at background level: bar 123, for instance, uses a dominant-type construct on G, whilst G♯/F♯ (bars 122, 124) are, in context, subordinate to G/F. The drama of these bars is heightened by the first use of the snare drum and interjections on trumpet. Following the conclusion of the chromatic descent (bars 130–2), the centre on C is quietly reaffirmed by the chord (C–G–D), played pizzicato on the cello, the C pitch doubled by bass and timpani.

Figure 5.18 *L'Abandon d'Ariane*: III, bars 121–9
Matrix to show Sets in relation to Genera

Potential Genera:	G1	G2	G3	G7	G8	G9	G10	G11	G12
Sets									
3-5	o								
4-6*	o								
4-9*	o								
4-16	o	o							
5-14	o	o			o			o	
5-20	o	o				o			
5-25	o	o	o	o					o
5-32	o	o				o			o
5-Z38	o	o	o		o	o	o		o
Counts:	9	6	2	1	2	2	2	1	3
	G1	G2	G3	G7	G8	G9	G10	G11	G12
[SGI			]						

Counts	Squo Indices in descending order with Genera
9	.159: G1 (atonal)
6	.104: G2 (wholetone)
3	.074: G12 (diatonic-tonal)

* denotes a 'singleton' set

Bars 140–7 and 154–72 loosely resemble the early part of Scene II, through similar rhythmic treatment in 6/8 metre, and introduction of pitches B♭ and E♭. The textures, however, are more complex, and the modal identity more ambiguous, between Ionian on B♭ and Lydian on E♭. Four central bars (148–51) are more obviously focused on G♭ 'major' (and do highlight some shortcomings in the vocal score, with omission of two bass pitches on G♭ and the counterpoint of violin II, together with a misprint in bar 149: bass D should read D♭). Theseus's vocal line across bars 172–7 (in which he sings the praises of the wine he has just drunk) extends a scalic figure derived from bars 14–16 of Scene I, though with the inflected pitches B♭/E♭. This passage is founded on a sustained double bass pedal on F (bars 172–5: another omission from the vocal score).

A forceful climactic point, amongst the most dissonant of the opera, is reached by the ensuing bars 178–87. Third progressions return in the upper parts on flute, clarinets, trumpet and violin I: (G♭,F,E♭; F,E♭,D♭), whilst the lower lines are harder to define, using further quintal harmonies. Powerful use of timpani offers some clarification though, retuned now to pitches D♭ and B♭. The 'Moins animé' section (bars 187–96) then exhibits similar harmonic instability (and melodic patterning) to the opening of the scene, with a balancing chromatic ascent in the bass: (D♯–G♯), producing another ABA formal outline. The loud interjection in octaves at bar 196 corresponds with that at bar 186, both functioning as transitional bars. The introduction to the stylized 'Tango' (bars 197–200) makes further reference to the double bass pedal on F (again unclear in the vocal score). Melodic third progressions are evident again, in clarinet and viola: (D,C,B♭) (A,G,F) (C,B♭,A), with accompanying thirds above: (B♭–D, A–C, G–B♭). The pitch centre modulates from a localized B♭ through to G 'major' for the 'Tango' (bars 201ff.), with the inherent B♭–B♮ progression reminiscent of the blues third.

Bars 201–17 (Ex. 5.32*a* and *b*) are a delightful 'Mouvement de Tango', with the wit and humour typical of the neoclassicist: one is reminded of Stravinsky's treatment of the 'Tango' in *L'Histoire du soldat* (1918). This vestige of interest from the Brazilian phase of *Saudades do Brazil*,[97] is now used to enhance the neoclassical effect. There is a case here for an interpretation as bimodality (see Ex. 5.32), as opposed to Drake's 'polymodality',[98] although the centres alternate between (C♯: bass, G: treble) and (D: bass, F: treble). Essentially, this is another instance of the now familiar technique of pitting white-note modality in the treble (supported by the clichéd 'chorus of ship-wrecked sailors') against black-note modality in the bass (E♯,C♯,G♯; F♯,D,G♯). The resultant chords of the instrumental accompaniment can be viewed as sets: most frequent is the 4-17 blues tetrachord, followed by 4-18, 4-19, 4-26 and 4-27 as the seventh-type construct. (4-Z29, heard at the start of bar 202, also opens Scene IV.) The genus with predominant role is Genus 9, appropriately enough as a representative of the so-called 'blues' Supragenus III.[99] Nonetheless, eight of the thirteen chords can still be

---

[97] This observation is supported by Drake, *The Operas of Darius Milhaud*, 187.
[98] Ibid., 216.
[99] Forte's Squo indicator endorses the interpretation arrived at by the judicious use of a 'raw' count, with the status of Genus 9 measured at .139 ((4/7)/41), as against that of Genus 12 at .095 ((3/7)/45). Since both Genus 9 and 12 have singleton representatives, 4-17 and 4-26 respectively, it is logical that the primary genus is determined by the first 'Rule of greatest status quotient' (Forte, 'Pitch-Class Set Genera', 234). These bars might also be elucidated by means of Parks's '8-17/18/19-Complex Genus': see Chapter 6 below.

described as triads with a chromatic note attached to root, third or fifth, which simply serves to reinforce a modal interpretation. The important, repeated modal progression C♯–D is part of a larger chromatic ascent (C♯–D–E♭), completed at the start of Scene IV.

So, the predominant mode of bars 201–17 is one on G, despite the apparently conflicting C♯–D progression in the bass. There are two alternative interpretations, the first of which involves the octatonic Model A: (0,1,3,4,6,7,9,10) (G♮,G♯,A♯,B,C♯,D,E,F). This collection affords sufficient status to the C♯–D progression, accounting well for the bass arpeggio (C♯–E♯–G♯), e.g. bars 201–3, and also explains the G–B♭ oscillation in the vocal bass-line of bars 205 and 207. The octatonic mode cannot, however, give sufficient weight to the balancing, triadic sequences on G and F (since pitches A and C are absent), and also suggests greater semitonal activity than is in fact the case. The more plausible interpretation favours the Mixolydian on G, appropriate in a jazz-type setting, with hints of blues seventh (F♮/F♯, bar 203), and flattened third (B♭, bars 205 and 207). The timpani reiterates the flattened seventh, whilst the treble part of the accompaniment (horn, trumpets, upper string harmonics), and the chorus of male voices, feature two-bar sequences of G and F triads. All of this reinforces the Mixolydian mode, which Drake sees as one of three main modes in Milhaud's neoclassical operas, the others being Aeolian and Lydian. Melodically, the vocal lines of bars 201–8 employ further third progressions in this strongly triadic context: (D–B–D),(G–E); (F–A–F); (E–G–E); (D–F). Third progressions are also found in the treble of the accompaniment (bars 201–4 and 209–12) and in the bass (bars 216–17). The only complication with the Mixolydian interpretation is in explaining the C♯–D progression, which may be seen as a chromatic appoggiatura leading to the (chromaticized) dominant chord: (D,F♮/F♯,A), bars 203–4; alternatively, C♯ might simply be viewed as another Lydian inflection, common in Milhaud's music.

Finally, one should acknowledge that the 'Tango' is an appropriately drunken dance: in keeping with its banal rhyming text, sung by the chorus of sailors, 'Ô Vieillard! Ton vin le trouble! Il en a bu! Il voit double!', simple syncopations abound, heightened by the percussive additions of bass drum (bar 205) and snare drum (bar 209). The significance of Theseus's 'seeing double' (nicely matched by the modal duality) is that he leaves for Athens with Phaedra alone, concealed by a veil, believing that he has taken both women as the second instance of dramatic irony. The conventional emotional antithesis is now adopted by Theseus in his response to each woman: 'Passez par là, Ariane adorée! Suivez-la, Phèdre sans saveur!' (bars 209–12).

SCENE IV. 'Très modéré'
This short scene is quite dissonant, exhibiting modal conflict and ambiguity, although essentially it may just be a simple melody in a less simple context. Drake views bars 218–20 as an example of 'genuine polymodality', though the effect is really more atonal, since there are no clear modal identities. The main sonorities on the first beats of bars 218 and 220 are the Z-related pair: 4-Z29 and 4-Z15, but, beyond this, sets are not very productive either. It is, however, indisputable that Milhaud characterizes each contrapuntal line by giving it a distinct instrumental colour, within a quartet texture of horn, bassoon, clarinet and oboe. The nine-bar instrumental introduction (bars 218–25) features a re-iterated bass pedal on E♭ (horn), comparable with bar 76 of Scene II, coupled by loose modal sequences above (oboe). Bar 226 is reduced to a dyad (D,F) on horn and trumpet, in advance of the 'Plus Allant' of bar 227. This passage connects with those similarly marked at bars 43 and 67 of Scene II, in terms of increased chromatic conflict coupled by third progressions in the orchestral accompaniment. The heightened musical tension accords with the drama of Ariadne's release from her fate, as Dionysus declares: 'Avancez sans crainte! Il emmène Phèdre désormais seule Reine, bon gré ou mal gré, de son cœur'.[100] Despite the localized chromatic corruption, bars 227–34 do exhibit greater modal clarity than their earlier counterparts in Scene II: thus Drake rightly regards this passage as operating in an overall Phrygian modality, presumably on d, with blues third and seventh: (D,E♭,F♮/F♯,G,A,B♭,C♮/C♯,D).[101]

SCENE V. 'Très lent'
The start of Scene V, derived from the start of Scene IV, is a slow chorale-like passage, broad and dignified, suggesting another possible association with *L'Histoire du soldat*. Ariadne sings of her newly found happiness in a miniature aria: 'Ô joie inespérée! Ô ravissant bon-

---

[100] 'Come forward without fear! He is taking Phaedra alone henceforth, for better or worse, as the only Queen of his heart.'
[101] Drake, *The Operas of Darius Milhaud*, 204.

heur!';[102] the expressive marking 'avec beaucoup d'émotion' is unusual for Milhaud and is indicative of increased lyricism. Of course the dignity of the chorale is almost overdone, and so matches the hyperbolic exclamations of the text, as one of several ironizations in *L'Abandon* which thrive on an encoded layer of added meaning. Ex. 5.33*a* shows the opening of Ariadne's diatonic melody and contrapuntal accompaniment, heard on alternating 'quartets' of wind (oboe, clarinet, bassoon and trumpet) and strings.

This passage illustrates chromatic, modal complementation, articulated by distinct instrumental colours. Drake believes the harmony to result from clearly articulated modal counterpoint,[103] appropriate for a composer with melodic priority. The mode of the three upper instrumental lines (and voice itself) is ambiguous and could be Dorian on d, Aeolian on a, Mixolydian on G, or a pentatonic segment with prominent fourth patterns: (D–A),(C–G),(D–A). Whatever its specific identity, the mode is clearly 'white-note', and distinct from the bass's conflicting 'black-note' pitches, also featuring fourths: (E♭–A♭),(B♭–E♭). (The (E♭–A♭) sonority is comparable with that in Scene II, bar 76, also associated with Dionysus.) Furthermore, each component is diatonic within its own horizontal stratum, as supported by the Genus 11 designation in Ex. 5.33*b*, which involves a conflation of instrumental and vocal material. All eight sets, including the progenitors 3-7 and 3-9, are referable to Genus 11 which is usefully endorsed here by an unusually high status quotient.[104] Consequently, there is a strong case for a bimodal interpretation, focusing on opposed modalities of Aeolian on a and the pentatonic collection 3 on A♭: (A♭,B♭,[D♭,]E♭,G♭). Drake considers that the 'frequently exclusive use of "black" notes in the bass . . . would presume a pentatonic usage not elsewhere to be found in Milhaud's music',[105] and whilst the pentatonicism of the bass is not in doubt, the usage is indeed found elsewhere in Milhaud's music: the Fourth Quartet is just one of several examples.

Even though Milhaud most likely placed his compositional emphasis here on the contrapuntal workings of the different instrumental voices, there is a fascination in exploring the resultant harmonic aggre-

---

[102] 'Oh unimaginable joy! Oh rapturous happiness!'

[103] Drake, *The Operas of Darius Milhaud*, 208.

[104] Squo(G_{11}) = ((8/8)/29) = .345. Arguably, one aspect which has been rather overlooked here is a localized wholetone figure in the clarinet line (bars 235–6, 239–40).

[105] Drake, *The Operas of Darius Milhaud*, 228.

gates: after all there is a chorale-like perspective to the scoring of these bars, and so one wonders about the nature of 'progression'. Returning to Ex. 5.33*a*, the alternative vertical segmentation, still incorporating the vocal line, produces a rather more equivocal picture, corroborated by the more equivocal nature of the generic perspective. Nonetheless some patterns may still be discerned: the most frequent vertical sets are 4-10 (C,D,E♭,F) and (G,A,B♭,C) on the first beats of bars 235–7 and 239–41, together with 4-19 across bars 237–8 and 241–2.[106] Interestingly, set 4-10 would also form the tetrachords of a modal interpretation of Dorian on d: (D,E,F,G),(A,B,C,D), whilst set 4-19 also had a role in the 'Tango' of Scene III. From the generic viewpoint, although 4-10 maintains some status as the singleton set referable to Genus 7, with the second highest Squo, essentially the Squo indicator endorses Supragenus I (Genus 3, supported by 2 and 1), thus raising the profile of sets 4-12, 4-13 and the Z-related pair 4-Z15/Z29, but rather ignoring the contribution of 4-19.[107]

Adopting a broader overview, a moderate level of chromaticism and dissonance persists across bars 235–42, though the restrictive pentatonic collection with its bias towards A♭ affords a reasonable harmonic stability. The neoclassical effect of this aria is enhanced by the simple two-bar phrasing and balanced structure: A (235–6), B (237–8), A' (239–40) and B' (241–2). Additionally, there is a cyclical aspect to this final scene, with bars 242–6 reminiscent of the chromatic descent at the start of Scene III (bars 122–9), descending now from A♭ to D. Further hints of Scene II (bars 43ff.) occur in bars 245–6, followed by phrase A" across bars 247–50, where complementation between melody and bass persists, reinforcing the sense of centric ambiguity.

Bars 251–4 contain the Bacchantes' exclamations of 'Dionysus', in answer to Ariadne's request that his identity be disclosed: Dionysus and the Bacchantes throw off their rags, revealing gleaming white gar-

---

[106] The segmentation that produces set 4-19 in bar 238 discounts the passing pitch on A in the trumpet; if this were included in preference to the vocal pitch G (as happens in due course in the music of bar 242), the resulting set would be 4-Z15, as in bar 242; if A and G are both included, the resulting set on the first beat of bar 238 is 5-30. In order to observe the repetition of set 4-19 at pitch: (A♭,C,E,G) across bars 237 and 241, the embellishment pitches D and F in clarinet and voice have been omitted; if pitch D is included, the final beat of bar 241 produces a second instance of set 5-30.

[107] Results produced from a total of ten different sets: 3-3, 4-10, 4-12, 4-13, 4-Z15, 4-19, 4-Z29, 5-10, 5-25 and 5-Z37: Squo(G3) = ((4/10)/43) = .093; Squo(G7) = ((4/10)/45) = .089; Squo(G2) = ((5/10)/64) = .078; Squo(G1) = ((4/10)/63) = .063.

ments which suggest a godliness. These bars are again comparable with the vocal lines at bar 45 of Scene II; the original phrase is now inverted and heard in powerful ascent, as a literal musical portayal of the idea of higher deistic forces. Collectively, vocal and instrumental components are suggestive of an overall V^{13} (C^{13}) construct within F. A definitive pedal on C sounds on timpani across bars 249–53, whilst the bass-line makes a step-wise descent to a B♭ pitch, as the emphatic seventh (appropriate in view of the reminiscence of the 'Tango' at bar 255). The resolution of the perfect cadence is melodramatically delayed by a bar's silence before arriving on the tonic of F (bar 255) when Dionysus sings again, now as a handsome young man. In respect of the plot, Dionysus explains that the sisters' kindness to an old man has enabled their desires to be realized; he then asks Ariadne, in true fairy-tale fashion, whether she has any other wish.

Bars 255–82 consist essentially of a linking passage, in allusion to the 'Tango', between the moment of revelation and the final ecstatic 'Vif'. The overall formal framework is A (bars 255–8), A' (bars 259–62), B (bars 263–6, with bass D♯–F♯), A' (bars 267–70), C (bars 271–4), A" (bars 275–9) and A" (bars 280–2). Milhaud's reference to the 'Tango' (bars 255ff.) involves alternating chords on F and G, in the Mixolydian on F. Such 'vamping' in association with Latin American rhythms frequently employs I–II–I, as opposed to I–V–I, as acknowledged by Drake.[108] (On the large scale, the pitches (F–G) may be seen as chords IV–V of the main modality on C.) The main ostinato figure of bars 255–62 (and 267–70) yields set 4-26, as used in the 'Tango', and 5-21 (as used at bars 84ff. of Scene II), or triads of F/d, G/E♭, as further examples of Milhaud's ambiguous centres a third or sixth apart; increasingly, though, the harmony is pitch-centred on C. Such centricity is supported by the timpani which maintain their presence on pitch C (bars 255–62 and 267–70), as the dominant of F (and large-scale tonic). Neoclassical surface detail emerges in the treatment of ornamentation, with single and double grace-notes; equally, vestiges of jazz persist in mixture at the third degree: G♯ (bar 266), moving to A as the third degree of F (bar 267: violin I, doubled by flute).

The chromaticism in Dionysus's line: (C♮,C♯,D♮,D♭,C: bars 267–70), as he repeats his question 'Que pourrais-je faire encore?', reinforces the main pitch on C, whilst the phrase concludes with Milhaud's well-tested triad motive (ascending sixth, descending third): ((C,D) C–A–

---

[108] Drake, *The Operas of Darius Milhaud*, 213.

F). Ariadne's line above is once more reminiscent of Scene II (bars 31–2), ending with its own embellished triad motive: (G–(D,C)–E♭–C). Melodically, the next two phrases of Ariadne and Dionysus (bars 271–4 and 275ff. respectively) are nicely matched, utilizing the ascending-descending scalic curve first heard in Scene I. Bar 274 features another vestige of jazz with vertical blues pastiche on strings: (C,E♮,C,E♭,G),[109] with the centre on C then confirmed across bars 277–8. From this point on the vocal writing, at least, is entirely diatonic, as at the start of the opera. The accompaniment of bars 281–2 supports with a V^{13} chord (presented typically in second inversion), which creates expectancy in advance of the 'Vif' (bars 283ff.) similar to that first used in the introduction (bars 7–8). Such expectancy is appropriate since Dionysus has just agreed to grant Ariadne's wish to wander the firmament from dusk to dawn.

The dramatic culmination of the final 'Vif' (bars 283–308) sees Dionysus climb with Ariadne at dusk to the top of the rocks; a crown of lights surrounds her head and hanging from her hand is her star-constellation. The triumphant, joyous text of bars 287–308 is sung by the combined choruses (treble and bass), the lowest parts of which each enter one quaver later: 'Au sein d'or des nébuleuses, dans le chœur des astres purs, elle émerge, glorieuse, des profondeurs de l'azur!'[110]

The cyclical aspect of *L'Abandon d'Ariane* is maintained here, with bar 287 and beyond recalling the vocal movement in thirds and sixths from Scene I (bar 8). Melodic embellishment in Scene V of statements from Scene I is illustrated in the comparative Ex. 5.34. The main ostinato figure (with added lower fourth) is again as used in Scene II (around bar 84), except that the order of chords is reversed, whilst the chordal alternation with adjacent bass pitches is also reminiscent of the 'Tango'. Beyond these unifying aspects, the construction of the finale largely from one ostinato figure acquires new meaning in the light of the drama. This relentless, and somewhat mechanical, orchestral ostinato constitutes a fine example of detachment and subsequent objectification, which mirrors Ariadne's own detachment—the literal depersonalization of her removal from mere mortal life, and her ulti-

---

[109] The low pitch C (C¹) on double bass is unfortunately omitted from the vocal score.

[110] 'In the golden bosom of hazy clouds, among the choir of untainted stars, she emerges, glorious, from the depths of the firmament!'

mate objectification as a star-constellation in the celestial spheres. Whilst the bass of the ostinato remains immovably earthbound, its mesmeric repetition effectively conveying the state of ecstasy bestowed by Dionysus, the strong scalic ascent of the vocal lines points skyward.

The last section of music (bars 283ff.) operates in a blues-type mode on C: (C,D,E♭/E♮,F,G♭/G♮/G♯,A,B,C), with the E♮/E♭(D♯) blues third important to the end (see Ex. 5.35 for the final appearance of this repeated material). In each bar, the reiterated chromatic gesture (E/D♯) is heard in the depths on double bass, whilst the timpani stress E and C. Additionally, there is something of a Stravinskian texture here, with 25 bars of alternating metre (6/8, 5/8), rare in Milhaud's music though anticipated in the Seventh Quartet (1925). Instrumentally, the rhythmic groupings (3 + 3),(3 + 2) create patterns of quaver–crotchet (× 3), crotchet (× 1), whereas the vocal lines have the opposite 'long–short' pattern. Both the dance-like momentum, and the conflict between bar-lines and the seemingly anacrusic commencement of the enclosed rhythmic groupings (Ex. 5.35*b*), are strikingly similar to those of Stravinsky, and one wonders whether Milhaud was familiar with *Les Noces* (1917–23). Despite this localized association, as Drake rightly points out, 'Milhaud rarely indeed followed Stravinsky down the path of ametricality. Rapid changes of metre are practically non-existent in his music'.[111]

Although the set-theoretic segmentation of this final section (Ex. 5.35*a*) concentrates on the orchestral textures, the main vocal pitches are almost always included too, often as a consequence of the instrumental doubling of vocal pitches. The main ostinato figure, mentioned above, employs repeated trichords of 3-4: (E,A,F),(D♯,G♯,E), forming a combined set 5-6; vertically, the sets are 4-14 and 5-21, punctuating first and second beats respectively.[112] Drake sees these bars as another 'polymodal ostinato',[113] although the centre on C is surely indisputable, supported unequivocally by numerous broken-triadic formations in the treble (set 3-11), and only 'muddied' slightly in the bass by mixture at the third, and some added pitches. Developing this stance generically, the passage subscribes convincingly to the hybrid

---

[111] Drake, *The Operas of Darius Milhaud*, 192.

[112] Small variants of pitch occur in bars 291, 293, 299, 301, and the penultimate bar 307.

[113] Drake, *The Operas of Darius Milhaud*, 216.

'atonal-tonal' Genus 10 of Supragenus III (with a supporting role for Genus 8, and Genus 9 which includes the 'singleton' set 4-17), thus acknowledging the vestigial traces of blues third in a context that is nonetheless clearly centred. The selection of Genus 10 is supported by the highest Squo indicator (see Fig. 5.19 below), together with the fact that both trichordal progenitors and the 'singleton' set 4-14 feature prominently (the only set not referable to this scheme is 5-9).

Figure 5.19 *L'Abandon d'Ariane*: V, bars 303–8
Matrix to show Sets in relation to Genera

Potential Genera:

Sets	G1	G2	G3	G4	G5	G6	G7	G8	G9	G10	G11	G12
3-4								o		o		
3-11									o	o		o
4-14*										o		
4-17*								o				
5-9	o	o		o	o	o						
5-11				o	o			o		o	o	o
5-20	o	o								o		
5-21				o				o	o	o		

Counts:

2	2	0	1	2	2	1	3	3	6	1	2
G1	G2	G3	G4	G5	G6	G7	G8	G9	G10	G11	G12
						[SGIII			]		

Counts	Squo Indices in descending order with Genera
6	.183: G10 (atonal-tonal)
3	.091: G9 (atonal-tonal)
3	.091: G8 (atonal)
2	.086: G5 (chromatic)

* denotes a 'singleton' set

Across bars 303–8 all voices now hail in rhythmic unison: '[sur la grande voûte étoilée,] la fille de Minos et de Pasiphaé!' (see Ex. 5.35*a*). Bar 303 marks an imperfect-type cadence, focusing within the combined choruses on a G major triad (pitch D on top). This is balanced vocally across bars 305–6 by a corresponding resolution on to the C major triad (pitch C on top: possible structural î), representing the main perfect cadence, confirmed instrumentally across bars 307–8. In voice-leading terms, the melodic line of the accompaniment has prolonged the fifth degree throughout the 'Vif', with its descent to î in bar 306 consolidating the vocal resolution. Further support is offered by the modified instrumental ostinato of bar 307 (as bars 291 and 301), with a strong 'tenor' descent on cello and horn: (F,E♮/E♭,D), finally resolving on to C at bar 308. Overall, the harmonies of bars 307 (beat 1: D,G,E♭/E♮,C; beat 2: D♭,G♭,D,B,G), parody a cadential ⁶₄ progression, the second chord having a Neapolitan inflection, before the final resolution at bar 308 on to a brief C major triad.

Conclusion

L'Abandon d'Ariane is regarded as the dramatic culmination of Milhaud's neoclassicism in the 1920s because of its governing aesthetic concerned with, in Straus's words, 'remaking the past'. This aesthetic manifests itself in various ways, including allusion to classical practice and dramatic convention, with subsequent reworking and occasional ironization of both music and text. Examples of the latter practice include the incorporation of musical banalities; 'trappings' of tonality in alien contexts; chromatic exaggeration matched by textual hyperbole and caricature; and a playing along with the conventions of dramatic irony. The concept of recomposition is inextricably bound up with Milhaud's use of modality which foregrounds diatonicism (in the sense of 'white-note' harmony), focusing especially on Dorian, Lydian and Mixolydian patternings, together with various cadential formulae, triadic themes and third relations.

Supporting the interpretation of the work as a neoclassical culmination is its preoccupation with the small scale: the short duration facilitated by compression and control; the scoring for chamber ensemble, and the insistence on select choruses of just three singers. Typical are the brief and balanced melodic phrases of two bars' duration, the detached and objectified ostinati, the closed forms (e.g. ternary form), and the neobaroque chorale-like opening of Scene V. Additionally, as Stephen Walsh commented of Stravinsky's *Oedipus Rex*, *L'Abandon d'Ariane* portrays specific, discrete 'affects', 'in which the ceremonial, the ornate, the pastoral, the pathetic and so on are treated as distinct "characters" or "modes".'[114] (The 'pastoral' for Milhaud is unequivocally diatonic within C, 'the pathetic' involves chromatic 'heightening',

---

114 Walsh, *The Music of Stravinsky*, 139.

whilst 'the ceremonial', certainly at the start of Scene V, involves a more complex black/white bimodality.) As a connected concern, *L'Abandon d'Ariane* also befits a neoclassical interpretation in respect of its Greek mythological subject-matter and the use of choruses as commentators on, rather than participants in, the action. For all this, *L'Abandon d'Ariane* is not 'pure neoclassicism' (if such a phrase is not intrinsically contradictory): Milhaud continues to assimilate the most effective techniques of his chromatic and jazz phases to enhance the neoclassical 'core', including chromatic bass progressions, limited bimodality and the continuing, if less rigorous, use of blues third and seventh.

Finally, it seems appropriate to conclude by reaffirming association with Stravinsky, whose influence is evident especially in metrical and choral treatment (for instance, the stylized accentuation of the text-setting): relevant works here are *L'Histoire du soldat* (1918), with which Milhaud's chamber opera *Le Pauvre matelot* (1926) was coupled, as well as *Les Noces* (1917–23), and *Mavra* (1922) which particularly impressed Milhaud. Rather as in the case of Stravinsky's *Oedipus Rex* of the same year (notwithstanding the differing statures of the works, and that *L'Abandon* is just one part of a trilogy), Milhaud's *L'Abandon d'Ariane*, with its radical and forward-thinking neoclassicism, is indicative of emergent concerns to be pursued further in the somewhat grander operatic and dramatic designs of the 1930s and beyond. From this small-scaled trilogy of the late 1920s (preceded by the *L'Orestie* trilogy), to a large-scaled representation in the three Latin-American operas, *Christophe Colomb*, Op. 102 (1928), *Maximilien*, Op. 110 (1930), and *Bolívar*, Op. 236 (1943).

CHAPTER SIX

Conclusion: Milhaud's 'Total Entity'

❊

> ... from his adolescent years to the end of his life, he conceived his artistic creation as a total entity, the various elements of which could be drawn forth at any moment for whatever purpose.[1]

INDIVIDUAL conclusions have already been offered at the end of each of Case Studies 1–8, so the main purpose here is to pull together the various emergent threads, encompassing both analytical and broader stylistic issues, and, finally, to suggest a number of pointers for further research both into Milhaud's music and that of other early twentieth-century repertories.

Modal and Structural Perspectives

From the case studies presented, it is clear that there are structural concepts and constructs which connect and develop across the complementary stylistic elements of Early Exploration, Brazilian/Jazz-inspired Music and Neoclassicism. The most important common ground concerns modal collections and their typical constructs, at all structural levels: a free and flexible modality predominates far beyond considerations of 'polytonality' or 'atonality'. And, as implicit in the title of this book, the nature and functioning of the modality does have a profound influence on the resulting structures (and forms), so that the two concepts are inextricably linked. This fundamental idea is illustrated in *La Création du monde* (Case Study 5) where, as a founding principle of the work, modal partitioning governs the entire thematic structure, and where, in the specific context of the Fugue, the structure of the fugal device is inseparable from Milhaud's handling of the blues modality. Similarly, in 'La Lieuse' (Case Study 2), and the first movement of the Fifth Chamber Symphony (Case Study 3), it is the modal articulation of semitonal relations which delineates the ternary forms; and, in the first movement of the Clarinet Sonatina (Case

---

[1] Collaer/Galante, *Darius Milhaud*, 208.

Conclusion: Milhaud's 'Total Entity' 253

Study 7), it is again the articulation of modal polarities that generates the hybrid of a modified sonata/ternary form.

Milhaud's modality embraces the 'ecclesiastical' modes, of Greek origin: Ionian, Dorian, Phrygian, Lydian, Mixolydian, Aeolian, and occasionally the so-called Locrian, in authentic and sometimes plagal (or pseudo-plagal) forms;[2] it also encompasses the chromatic scale, pentatonic, wholetone and octatonic collections,[3] Altered Mixolydian and the blues scale (as perhaps the ultimate expression of Drake's 'inflectional polyvalency'). In addition, essentially as a compositional procedure, one mode may be combined with another (or indeed the same mode) at a different pitch, although, inevitably, one tends to perceive such a combination as a single, composite modality, with 'dissonant' infiltration.[4] And thus, although the chromatic scale is identified as an entity in itself, chromaticism (i.e. the limited introduction of foreign pitches in order to embellish any distinct collection) permeates all modes to varying degrees. Comprehensive use of the chromatic scale is rare and tends to be a localized phenomenon, although there are occasionally more extended examples, as across bars 25–36 of the finale of the Fifth Chamber Symphony (Case Study 3).

There are patterns (or distinctions) in the usage of different modal types across the three stylistic areas, with chromatic, pentatonic and octatonic collections and instances of Altered Mixolydian mode being most frequently encountered in exploratory works before 1922, as for instance in the final song of *Machines agricoles*.[5] Although each mode has a distinct identity, Milhaud's music 'modulates' freely in and out of different modes, and utilizes more nebulous inter-modal regions; specifically, there may be interaction, or pivotal linking, between modes—Milhaud's musical language frequently employs the pitch

---

[2] Beyond considerations of authentic versus plagal forms, Milhaud's music commonly respects a scalic division into upper and lower tetrachordal segments, as illustrated by Case Studies 1, 2, 5 and 6. See also 'complementation' below.

[3] This tendency to use octatonic and other 'exotic' scales is ultimately a typical product of the French interest in Russian exoticism, and thus Milhaud's name may again be linked with that of Stravinsky.

[4] Back in 1954, this was already the perception of Humphrey Searle in his own circumscribed exploration of 'Milhaud and Polytonality': 'the ear tends to try and resolve the total effect of what it hears into one main tonality plus a number of incidental notes, however complex the fabric may be' (*Twentieth Century Counterpoint*, 42).

[5] Refer back to Chapter 3, Fig. 3.2.

grouping (0,2,5), set 3-7, and the expanded form (0,3,5,8), set 4-26, as connective building units for melodic and harmonic constructions. Significantly, this unit figures prominently in pentatonic and hexatonic collections (as, for example, in *Quatre poèmes*, Case Study 6), as well as in the Altered Mixolydian mode.[6] The (0,2,5) and (0,3,5,8) units are relevant in a wide range of modal contexts, and such areas of motivic connection are critical to the working of Milhaud's modality.

Use of the blues and wholetone collections is concentrated in the Brazilian/jazz-inspired repertory, which is where the incorporation of blues techniques reaches its developmental peak. Use of blues-type procedures seems, however, a natural part of Milhaud's vocabulary, even before his Brazilian visit (e.g. incipient in the Third Quartet of 1916), and after his formal renouncement of jazz in 1926 (as, for instance, in the Clarinet Sonatina and 'Opéras-minute'). The most notable characteristic manifested by the blues collection is that specific chromaticism: the melodic bending of third, seventh and occasionally sixth degrees. And the main distinction between usage of blues third in Milhaud's jazz repertory, epitomized by the treatment of the Fugue in *La Création du monde*, and usage elsewhere, is that authentic representation favours the melodic (linear) blues third, whereas stylized 'pastiche' favours the harmonic (vertical) third. Blues third is of course just one type of third relation.

The more sophisticated use of 'diatonic' (generally 'white-note') modes, including further instances of the Altered Mixolydian (in, for example, the Sixth and Seventh String Quartets), tends to be reserved for Milhaud's neoclassically conceived works. Nonetheless, chromatic and pentatonic collections still have roles to play in, for instance, the Clarinet Sonatina and 'opéras-minute', even though such collections feature less prevalently than was the case up to, and including, 1922.

A further area of common ground between the three stylistic tendencies lies in third relations at all structural levels, though the feature is most evident in the neoclassical repertory. Apart from the blues third phenomenon, third relations range from large-scale pitch relations across separate movements, as in the Flute and Clarinet Sonatinas,[7] through to discrete ternary structures with Sections A and B a

---

[6] For further detail, refer back to Fig. 2.4: Pentatonic Model, and Fig. 2.8: Altered Mixolydian Mode, in the final section of Chapter 2.

[7] A summary of these relations is given in the introductory outline of Chapter 5, with separate formal plans for the Clarinet Sonatina detailed in Case Study 7.

Conclusion: Milhaud's 'Total Entity' 255

third interval apart. Third relations may be elaborated by means of a seventh construct, viewed somewhat along the lines of Joseph Straus, for example (E♭,G♭,B♭; G♭,B♭,D♭; E♭,G♭,B♭) in 'Ipanema' from *Saudades do Brazil* (Case Study 4). In turn, seventh chordal axes may represent common ground between the blues collection (e.g. chord I^7) and the Altered Mixolydian mode (e.g. I^7; VII^7). The high profile of third relations is also governed by the very nature of the modal collections, particularly in the case of pentatonic and Altered Mixolydian modes: in the pentatonic collection, full triads only occur on chords VI and I, i.e. centres a minor third apart,[8] and in the Altered Mixolydian the most frequently used sonorities are again VI^7 and I^6, e.g. (E♭,G,B♮,D); (G,B♮,D,E♭), in a mode on G. Additionally, as a more theoretical concern, the chords of interaction between blues and octatonic (Model B) collections stress third relations, with full triads occurring only on chords I, III, and VI, as for instance in the interaction of collections on D: (I) D,F♮/F♯,A; (III) F♮/F♯,A,C; and (VI) B,D,F♮/F♯.[9]

At localized levels, third relations include passages of bimodality at the third, (for example, centres on F and A at the start of the Fourth Quartet), often assisted by balanced, uncluttered contrapuntal textures; such phenomena connect to the underlying concept of polarity. From the Third Quartet onwards melodic third progressions occur frequently, especially at foreground level, as, to some extent, a post-tonal 'prolongational' device: such progressions have a high profile in the 'triad motive', especially prominent in neoclassical contexts (for example, those of Chamber Symphonies 1–6) since these tend to be the most strongly triadic.

The most characteristic means of formal extension across the three complementary elements is ostinato, and its jazz equivalent, the riff, operating at foreground and middleground levels. Such devices, which may embody some measure of dissonance, are also associated with a post-tonal equivalent of 'prolongation'. Large-scale ostinati are employed most frequently in works of the early 1920s, as in the finale of the Fifth Chamber Symphony. In the jazz context, there are many examples which range from simple I–II–I chordal vamping (with added

---

[8] Refer back to Fig. 2.4: Pentatonic Model, Collection 1: Chords, in the final section of Chapter 2.

[9] This follows on from Fig. 2.7: Interaction of Blues and Octatonic Scales, in the final section of Chapter 2.

sevenths and ninths) in *Trois rag-caprices*, and *Saudades do Brazil*, through to more extended patterns in the Final of *La Création du monde*.

Finally, concerning form, ternary structures (mentioned above in connection with third relations), predominate across the three main elements as represented by Chapters 3–5. There are many variants of scale, proportion, number of subdivisions, means of dovetailing between sections, and types of embellishment. Apart from these diverse ternary forms which have already been discussed extensively, there is one formal device which should be acknowledged separately: fugue. The use of fugue extends from exploratory fugato exercises in the second movements of the Second Quartet (1914–15) and Fourth Quartet (1918, Case Study 1); through a similar type of canonic 'fugato' in 'La Lieuse' from *Machines agricoles* (1919, Case Study 2), to fully worked-out fugue, such as the finale ('Étude') of the Fourth Chamber Symphony (*Dixtuor à cordes*, 1921). There are also important contemporary examples in the full orchestral repertory, such as the third movement of *Cinq études*, Op. 63, for piano and orchestra (1920), mentioned in Chapter 3. Milhaud's fascination with fugue continues to develop in the jazz domain, as, most famously, in the second movement of *La Création du monde*. The last illustration of the device, specifically in chamber music of the 1920s, is the finale: 'Vif et gai' of the highly neoclassical Seventh Quartet in B♭ (1925); in the operatic domain, however, the culminating example must be that provided by the *cancrizans* six-part canon in *Christophe Colomb*, Op. 102 (1928)

Summary and Critique of Analytical Approach

Several analytical means have proved effective in tackling Milhaud's early chamber music—some much more so than others. It would be tempting to conclude by advocating the consistent use of one approach to Milhaud's music: to do so prematurely, however, would be neither scholarly nor realistic. The most widely applicable analytical means has been a flexible mixture of post-Schenkerian voice-leading (tending towards Salzerian models), supplemented by the basic tools of Forte's set-theoretic analysis (including pc set genera). This has formed the basis of Case Studies 1–8, although particular contexts have caused one method to be favoured almost to the exclusion of the other.

In respect of an extended voice-leading approach to Milhaud's music, a framework of referential pitches often emerges, and one can travel some distance by means of the notion of a post-tonal mimicry of prolongational types and spans,[10] especially in respect of melodic activity which is contained within any individual horizontal stratum. In saying this, one is well aware of the spectrum of writing on 'the [multifarious] problem[s] of prolongation in post-tonal music' which extends from Roy Travis's pioneering consideration of a 'tonic sonority', with the possibility of 'dissonant prolongations', back in the late 1950s, through Straus's suggestion of an 'associational middleground' in the latter 1980s, and beyond.[11] Indeed, some would doubtless argue that the dangers inherent merely in mentioning the notion, however heavily qualified, outweigh any potential benefits.

At the risk of stressing the obvious, although a vestige of hierarchy has to survive if the music is to be regarded as in any sense tonal or modal, the resulting structures are not strictly (or sometimes even loosely) reductional; there will always be at least some 'rogue' pitches whose contributory functions cannot easily be defined. Indeed, there are also contexts where even mere prolongational 'mimicry' proves unnecessary, since some of Milhaud's structures are so compressed that the emphasis is on motivic statement, rather than on extension (as in parts of the Fifth Chamber Symphony). But even if, as Whittall suggests, 'post-tonal theory can easily seem to offer a parody of what it seeks to replace rather than a genuine alternative',[12] in the case of Milhaud's music of the 1920s the idea of embracing parody within our interpretation of that music is not inappropriate. Inevitably, and rightly, the analytical approach connects with the aesthetic concerns of a reinterpretation of classicism (as foregrounded in Chapter 5); as Straus comments of Schoenberg's Op. 19 No. 2, 'This is not a strange, deformed tonal piece. It is a rich, idiomatic post-tonal piece that, with ironic effect, mimics tonal structure.'[13] Although contextually derived strategies may represent the safest way to approach Milhaud's music, there is nonetheless extensive and overt allusion to wider tonal principles. To deny or understate this phenomenon would be to deprive the

[10] Straus, 'The Problem of Prolongation', 15.
[11] R. Travis, 'Toward a New Concept of Tonality?', *Journal of Music Theory*, 3 (1959), 257–84; Straus, 'The Problem of Prolongation'. Apart from the body of writing contained in the *Journal of Music Theory*, the contributions of other theorists such as James Baker, Arnold Whittall and Michael Russ are also highly pertinent here (as discussed in Chapter 2).
[12] A. Whittall, review of texts by Kostka, Lester, Simms, Straus and Watkins, in *Music Theory Spectrum*, 13 (1991), 79–88, on 87.
[13] Straus, 'The Problem of Prolongation', 19.

music of much of its associative meaning in evoking and 'remaking' the past.

Examples of various 'trappings' of tonal music, which may still maintain some prolongational potency, and which certainly embody a good measure of connectiveness, include chordal notes (exemplified by the 'triad motive'), diatonic and chromaticized neighbour-note gestures (in both treble and bass, as in the I–II–I vamping figures of *Saudades*), passing-notes as 'directed motion' within scalic figures (exemplified by the passing $^6_4$ constructions in Scene I of *L'Abandon d'Ariane*, Case Study 8), together with ubiquitous third progressions and frequent fifth progressions (exemplified by the Clarinet Sonatina, Case Study 7). In furthering the harmonic perspective, tonal or modal centres are still, at some level, cadentially affirmed, as in the concluding portions of the music of Case Studies 7 and 8 (with mimcry of the cadential $^6_4$ progression); there is still some notion of tonic-dominant relations, although these are compromised by the rather greater emphasis that is placed on semitonal relations (again evidenced by Case Study 7).

Occasionally, voice-leading descents appear to ape their tonal precedents, as perceived within common practice music (Case Study 6, and to some extent Case Study 2, together with small portions of Case Studies 7 and 8), although once again these beg many questions about actual meaning. Such descents are problematized in terms of curious patterns of pacing; the placing of interruptions (i.e. unorthodox divided descents); staggering of treble and bass events, or absence of supporting harmony; registral disruption; extent of peroration; and the existence of integral chromaticism. Yet, perversely, despite the many qualifications necessary in the perception of large-scale voice-leading structures (which do involve substantial reinterpretation of classical principles and processes on Milhaud's part), extended voice-leading techniques still have much to offer on the small scale, as a means of focusing on the musical surface. Notwithstanding the caveats of Russ regarding the 'present obsessive concern with the surface',[14] this is by far the most engaging aspect of Milhaud's music.

Meanwhile, the application of set theory has produced some useful common sets, which may be regarded up to a point as favoured 'sonorities'. Mention of particular trichords is held in reserve for their significant role as progenitors in discussion of genera below. In respect of tetrachords, one should highlight the 4-7 'signature' set (Case

---

[14] Russ, 'Four Studies in the Analysis of Post-tonal Music', 219.

Conclusion: Milhaud's 'Total Entity'

Studies 3 and 7, and other contemporary works), and the blues constructs 4-4 (Case Studies 3, 5, and 7) and 4-17 (Nos. 1, 3, 7 and 8); additionally one finds incidences of set 4-3 (Nos. 2 and 3), the seventh construct 4-27 (Nos. 3 and 4), and an octatonically associated 4-28 (Nos. 1 and 3). Amongst notable pentads are those early instances of pure chromaticism: 5-1 (Nos. 1 and 3), together with the pentatonic construct 5-35 (Nos. 1 and 6); hexachordal sets, generally less significant as common constructs, have included 6-20 (Nos. 1 and 4), 6-Z29 (Nos. 4 and 7), and 6-30 (Nos. 3 and 4). Set 6-30, in particular, highlights theory in practice as Milhaud's 'Chord VI': triadic combination at the tritone. (Other instances within specific Case Studies included 6-Z19 ('Chord' I/XI: Case Study 3), 6-33 ('Chord' II/X: Case Study 2), 5-32 ('Chord' III/IX: Case Study 1), and 5-21 ('Chord' IV/VIII: Case Study 1).)

Having established that a number of referential set sonorities operate across Milhaud's music, together with distinctive set patterning (e.g. symmetries) at more localized levels, a logical further step for future research would be to focus on the partiality for, and patterning of, original versus inverted set forms, achievable by means of Anthony Pople's *SetBrowser* utility.[15] Initial findings here, which need still to be substantiated, would suggest the division between original and inverted forms to be fairly even-handed, with a slight favouring of original forms; the superficial impression is of no particular patterning in usage of the two set types.

Since the concept of pc set genera has been used as part of an attempt to mediate between traditional set-theoretic stances and modal considerations, it makes sense now to summarize the collective results of that investigation. As might be expected, the early exploratory works of Chapter 3 invoke a broad range of generic references. The most overtly chromatic repertory, in the form of the slow movement of the Fourth String Quartet (Case Study 1), subscribes unsurprisingly to Supragenus II, with particular emphasis on the chromatic Genus 5 (which receives one of the highest Squo ratings across the study: .259). From early in the movement, however, such material is pitted against a hybrid 'chromatic-diatonic' Genus 7, as an analogue to 'modal complementation'. Genus 7 itself acts as something of a mediating force, offering a means of connection to later moments of pure diatonicism: the various pentatonic constructs of Supragenus

---

[15] A. Pople, *SetBrowser 1.2* (Lancaster University: CTI Centre for Music, 1994).

IV: Genus 12 and, most especially, Genus 11. Additionally, limited exploration of the diminished Genus 3 (with its associated octatonic agenda), is balanced by more widespread reference to the augmented progenitor of Genus 4. Furthermore, certain sets act as generic pivots, such as 5-21 which enables a 'progression' at the close of the movement from Genus 4 to Genus 9 of Supragenus III,[16] characterized by the main 'blues' tetrachord, 4-17.

Case Study 2 again demonstrates a partiality for complementing chromatic and diatonic material, with a basso ostinato subscribing to the 'semichromatic' Genus 6 which is set against the predominant Supragenus IV, with the main emphasis again on Genus 11. Case Studies 1 and 2 also reveal isolated, yet important, references to Genus 8, in the form of the significant 'singleton' sets mentioned above: 4-7, and the other 'blues' tetrachord, 4-4/8-4. In the incipient blues constructs of Case Study 3, the status of Genera 8 and 9 (Supragenus III) is confirmed by virtue of the dual reference sets, 4-7 (Genus 8), and 4-17/8-17 (Genus 9) of the opening movement, and the significance of 4-4 (Genus 8) in the second movement, and finale. Such findings are foregrounded, together with more occasional instances of Genus 3, against a continuing, somewhat antagonistic, 'backdrop' of the chromatic Genus 5.

In the more overtly centric (and less chromatic) Brazilian context of Case Study 4, the 'diatonic-tonal' Genus 12 comes to the fore, founded on 3-11, 4-27 and 6-Z50/Z29, with 4-27 acting, theoretically, as a pivot in respect of small-scale references to the wholetone Genus 2 (4-16, 4-21). The central section especially reveals localized instances of Genus 3, with an implicit octatonic dimension. At the close, the 'blues' Genus 9, which had been present throughout in a subsidiary capacity (as a 'silent partner'), though lacking the previously critical 4-27, finally achieves an appropriate superiority, embracing 3-11, 6-Z29, 5/7-31, 6-30 and the final sonority of set 6-20. Genera had less of a role to play in the jazz-influenced Case Study 5, although they were invoked in the summary of the Modal Complementation of Themes, largely for the sake of consistency, and to provide data to facilitate overall comparison. Most thematic figures subscribe either to the chromatic-diatonic Genus 7 (in

---

[16] In its use of the common progenitor set 3-3 (i.e. minor/major third), and inclusion of the 'blues' tetrachords 4-17 and 4-4, there is justification in regarding Supragenus III loosely as the 'blues' Supragenus (whilst accepting fully that these set designations are only equally-tempered approximations of the blues phenomenon).

conjunction with Genus 11: invoked by its singleton representative, set 3-9/9-9, as an expression of the blues scale), or to Genera 6 and 8 (set 4-4 again), as more overt manifestations of the blues, connected by their common progenitor set, 3-3.

In the neoclassical repertory of Chapter 5, Genera 11 and 12 (Supragenus IV) are foregrounded. Case Study 6, as the most extreme example of pure diatonicism, is almost exclusively governed by the diatonic-tonal Genus 12. By contrast, the opening of Case Study 7 resumes the earlier focus on the 'blues' Supragenus III (Genera 9 and 8 again), founded once more, at surface level, on set 4-7; and, as in the ensuing Case Study 8, transitional moments present the most rapid generic changes (for example, I, bars 26–9; III, bars 21–7). The finale of the Sonatina is distinctive in favouring a composite Supragenus I (Atonal Hybrid), with the progenitors of Genera 1 and 2 (3-5 and 3-8) fused to create common referential constructs: 4-Z29, 6-18 and 7-29. Only at the very end of the work does the pure diatonicism of Genus 12 supersede (too late and too briefly to achieve a fully convincing 'resolution'). In Case Study 8, Genus 12 (Scene I and latter portion of Scene II), supported by Genus 11 (opening portion of Scene V), represents once more the referential norm, departed from only at moments of variously heightened chromatic/dramatic tension. An unstable transitional passage at the opening of Scene III confirms the existence of localized atonality, referable to Genus 1, whilst the 'Tango' shows, appropriately enough, the infiltration of the more 'bluesian' Genus 9. By the close of the work, the predominant diatonicism and the vestiges of blues syntax (mixture at the third) have been synthesized within Genus 10.

So, invoking pc genera has been useful in pointing up various patterns of practice and partiality for particular genera, which do exhibit a potent interface with the building units of scalic collections. Thus, for instance, although the chromatic genus and chromatic scale are not synonymous, they are still very closely related. Essentially, it has served to confirm and support more intuitive expectations: that Milhaud's early chromatic explorations offer the highest profile to Supragenus II (chromatic Genera 5 and 6) within the context of wide-ranging generic reference that also embraces octatonic concerns allied to Genus 3; that Supragenus III (especially Genera 8 and 9) is emerging in the early works, but is still highlighted in the broadly jazz-influenced sector; and that diatonicism (Supragenus IV: Genera 11 and 12) is maximized in the most overtly neoclassical works. Other, perhaps less predictable, findings include, appropriately enough, the level of common ground that exists across the complementary domains of 'exploration', 'jazz-influence', and 'neoclassicism', in terms of chromatic (or semichromatic)/diatonic interaction (whether as complementation or actual synthesis), and the isolated occurrence of a composite Genera 2/1 in the Clarinet Sonatina, at the end of the period in question.

Conversely, this study has attempted to provide a broad testing of the generic concept, within the terms and self-imposed limits of this book, that could usefully be transferred to studies of contemporary music by Stravinsky and Ravel, amongst others. Undoubtedly the idea has proved most useful in 'awkward', apparently ill-defined, contexts that are not readily approachable by other means, and despite Forte's efforts to broaden the application of set theory through genera to include 'common-practice' music, it has proved least relevant in the overtly modal/centric context of *La Création du monde* (Case Study 5). Having said this, the concept of genera has, nonetheless, offered a modicum of common currency to facilitate comparison across the tonal/atonal divide.

Beyond these preliminary provisos, one should add that the concept must be used with care, and with an awareness of its various shortcomings, including the obfuscation of units which already have a distinct identity achieved by other means,[17] and possible distortions, e.g. pc set genera could give 'false' or compromised readings on small, non-contiguous sections. Furthermore, the concept is obviously entirely dependent on, and could prejudice, the choice of segmentation; it is of course also entirely dependent upon accurate computation of the sets themselves. Where the Squo indicator is concerned, although this means has sometimes provided useful confirmation of a particular generic interpretation, the apparent desirability of 'resolving' generic ambiguities may disguise the fact that such ambiguity, conflict, or genuine complementation, has a legitimate, even crucial, role to play. (This certainly holds true for a considerable proportion of Milhaud's music of

---

[17] This particular shortcoming is illustrated by a referential construct such as 8-17, in the opening movement of the Fifth Chamber Symphony (Case Study 3), which seems both definitive and strongly structured, not least in terms of its significant subsets: 4-1, 4-3, and 4-7; yet, precisely because of these subsets, invoking a generic perspective (which views them as 'singleton' representatives of various genera) may apparently obfuscate and problematize the corporate identity of such a construct in a way which cannot always be resolved convincingly by the Squo indicator and other 'Rules for the Interpretation of Generic Relations'.

the 1920s.) Perhaps more critically, it should be noted that standard use of the Squo measurement takes no formal account of the prominence and frequency of particular set constructs/sonorities in any given musical excerpt. This leads to the further point that pc set genera may, in poor hands, suffer the same general accusation as that levelled at set theory itself: that of being, at least at times, too abstracted from the audible musical surface, and not sufficiently responsive to intuitive perceptions, or hermeneutic approaches.

Finally, although Forte's theory, based on trichordal progenitors, has proved quite appropriate in the context of Milhaud's music of the 1920s (as a logical extension of Forte's original set-theoretic work, and in application to music with a 'triadic' basis, in the broadest sense), Richard Parks's distinctive brand of pc set genera may yet prove to be more flexible, and more conducive to hermeneutic strategies. In particular, future research might explore the application of Parks's 'Diatonic' and 'Chromatic' genera (as well as the possibilities for his 'Octatonic Genus', all be they more limited), together with his '8-17/18/19-Complex Genus'. This latter idea seems to have considerable potential: 8-17 figured prominently in the first movement of the Fifth Chamber Symphony (and yet was problematized in relation to Forte's system of genera: see n. 17 above), whilst its 'blues' tetrachordal complement, 4-17, has enjoyed widespread prominence. Passages such as the 'Tango' from Scene III of *L'Abandon d'Ariane* involved a varied menu of sets, but with the main emphasis undoubtedly on the collective identity of 4-17/18/19.

Next in frequency of application has been the adoption of scalic/modal models, with their partitioning, derived from van den Toorn's approach to octatonicism. Sometimes it was possible to implement van den Toorn's ideas directly, such as in attempting to distinguish between the octatonic Models A and B in 'La Lieuse' from *Machines agricoles* (Case Study 2); in general, Model A proved the more applicable to Milhaud's music (in Case Studies 1, 2, 7, and 8), supporting van den Toorn's view of Model A as the neoclassical collection. The modal models for pentatonic, Altered Mixolydian and blues collections were helpful in providing a structural framework, although relevant contexts for the first two scalic types tended to be more restricted and localized than those for the blues collection. Nonetheless, distinguishing between five related pentatonic collections demonstrated that Milhaud made use of all the available variants, with a possible preference for Collection 1. The products of interaction between modes, such as between the blues and octatonic, and Altered Mixolydian and octatonic, were an interesting, if more theoretical, consideration.[18] Regarding modal partitioning, Jeremy Drake's historical concern to distinguish between authentic and plagal modal forms proved a useful refinement,[19] demonstrated by analysis of the finale of the Fifth Chamber Symphony (Case Study 3). It may be possible to invoke these models and partitionings more strongly in future analyses, though one should be aware of their limitations: distinction needs to be made between unordered and ordered pitch collections.

Certain ideas were usefully derived from Milhaud's article 'Polytonalité et atonalité' and then applied to his music, in an attempt to relate theory and practice. The 'Factors which might aid the Perception of Localized Bimodality' (Fig. 2.9) and 'Suggested Types of Localized Bimodal Classification' (Fig. 2.10), with combinations identified by dyad sets, were practical ways of establishing norms of practice in Milhaud's music. Up to a point this approach is consistent with the valuable notion of pitch polarity, and may be employed quite attractively as part of 'a musical metaphor for jangling simultaneity' (in the words of Perloff),[20] or as musical embodiments of 'double-exposure' (Case Study 3), and 'difference' (Case Study 4). Such bimodality may be indicative of, and supported by, generic complementation measured by the Difquo; it may also achieve an increased sense of polarization by means of supporting instrumental and textural contrasts. Nonetheless, Fig. 2.10 could prove its worth only on a small scale, as in the first song of *Machines agricoles*,[21] and was of only limited usefulness in considering the nature of Milhaud's language: inevitably more of a compositional than analytical aid. Indeed, although the composer Humphrey Searle offers a measure of support for the perception of 'bitonality',[22] he too arrives at the question: 'does polytonality [or, for that matter, bimodality] really exist at all, or is it merely a "paper-tiger"?'[23]

Other ideas worked well in specific instances, but could not on present standing be said to be of general application to Milhaud's music.

---

[18] Refer back to Figs. 2.7 and 2.8, in the latter portion of Chapter 2.
[19] Drake, *The Operas of Darius Milhaud*, 201.
[20] Perloff, *Art and the Everyday*, 184.
[21] See the introductory outline of Chapter 3.
[22] Searle, *Twentieth Century Counterpoint*, 43.
[23] Ibid., 42.

These include Meyer's concept of 'implication-realization' (and, up to a point, Straus's 'pattern-completion'), which was most apposite for the finale of the Fifth Chamber Symphony (Case Study 3), involving an ostinato of gradually increasing length. And, in this context, the idea of segments of a Chromatic Matrix also proved appropriate, though it was difficult to locate other passages which were treated so methodically.[24] Another example of an analytical concept with limited application is the Hindemith/Neumeyer notion of 'tension theory', which proved illuminating in the small-scaled simplicity of the first of *Quatre poèmes* (Case Study 6), but was less manageable, or meaningful, in more complex settings. On a larger scale, the Keil/Meyer proposition of ascertaining the extent of deviation from typical blues formations and practices worked nicely in parts of Case Study 5, but did not lend itself easily to more general application within these case studies.

Analytical ideas concerned with proving the importance of third relations were well suited to Milhaud's music, and have already received some attention above. The broad domain of third relations included Hindemith's notion of 'indefinite third relation' and Straus's concept of the seventh axis, as a means of articulating two triads a third apart, yet regarding them as a single entity. Straus's concept was especially suitable in the context of Case Study 4, although it also had application for passages associated with the blues collection (parts of the Fourth Quartet, and Sonata, Op. 47) and with the Altered Mixolydian mode (e.g. (E♭,G,B♮; G,B,D) within a mode on G).

Finally, viewing dissonance and polarity as positive structural constructs, instead of overstating a rather weak, traditional unity, was refreshing. This notion stemmed from articles by, and discussions with, Arnold Whittall, and from the doctoral thesis of Michael Russ;[25] it focused on a broad spectrum of 'difference' from generalized contrast through to the more specific and rigorous concept of complementation. Such complementation has been regarded here as a special, inherently paradoxical, concept whose founding principle is that the *whole* comprises two sets of elements which are on the one hand polar opposites, yet are on the other hand intricately related, and matching.

---

[24] The Chromatic Matrix (with the relevant portion, as invoked in the Fifth Chamber Symphony, demarcated) is shown in Figure 2.5 of Chapter 2.

[25] For full references, refer back to the section on 'General Analytical Theory' in Chapter 2.

The processes of embedding complementation may result in (neutral) juxtaposition, confrontation, or, more rarely, actual synthesis.

These theoretical considerations led to the observation of processes of chromatic complementation in the 'Funèbre' of the Fourth Quartet (Case Study 1), and in Scenes II and V of *L'Abandon d'Ariane* (Case Study 8), and localized octatonic complementation in 'La Lieuse' (Case Study 2). And such observations were often supported by an accompanying generic complementation, measured by the Difquo, as discussed above. Conversely, consideration of 'focused dissonance' also led to increased awareness of 'strategically placed consonance', within a mildly dissonant norm. This concept was especially useful in 'Ipanema' (Case Study 4), with its balanced consonances a tritone apart on G♭ and C, as a musical metaphor for 'cultural difference'. The focus on dissonance and chromaticism (involving semitonal and tritonal relations) proved most relevant and productive in the exploratory contexts of Case Studies 1–3. Additionally, the concept of a balanced polarity also gave a certain credibility to localized bimodality (most applicable in Chapter 3), and to 'modal complementation' within a particular collection, as a result of partitioning into lower and upper scalic segments, as observed in the thematic structure of *La Création du monde* (Case Study 5). In association with pitch relations, contrast and complementation acquired an instrumental/textural dimension in respect of the concertino/ripieno 'dialectic' of the Fifth Chamber Symphony (Case Study 3). More generally, the notion of giving due weight to types of polarity (whilst investigating further the nature and role of dissonance) seems to offer considerable scope for future analysis of Milhaud's music, and that of his contemporaries.[26]

Stylistic and Aesthetic Perspectives

In addition to identifying structural techniques and experimenting with analytical approaches, Chapters 3, 4 and 5 sought, collectively, to explore three complementary stylistic/aesthetic aspects: Milhaud the apprentice, drawing on the music of his late-Romantic or Impressionist predecessors, as well as starting to explore and experiment for him-

---

[26] The present author is currently preparing an article for forthcoming publication in *Music Analysis* on 'Exploring Complementation: The Case of Bartók's Third Quartet', which will offer a much more detailed exposition and application of the concept of complementation. Nonetheless, the essence of these ideas emerged directly from this study of Milhaud's music.

self, especially in respect of the machine aesthetic; Milhaud the eclectic, attracted by popular musics both from the far reaches of his foreign travels and from nearer home within his native Provence; and, finally, Milhaud the neoclassical purist, reinvoking 'absolute' music and techniques from the eighteenth century.

There are two appropriate sets of images, or metaphors. The first, which has been used consistently through this book, is of Collaer's and Milhaud's 'elements' (early experimentation, jazz, and neoclassicism) emerging from an exploratory 'melting-pot', as characterized in the introductory outline of Chapter 3 and supported by Milhaud's own writing. In terms of the chemical imagery, these elements may be employed singly, or fused into 'alloys' of two or more elements, with more complex combined, or possibly modified, physical properties. Initially, one might imagine an ill-defined assortment of elements (as in 'Early Exploration'), dominated by the immature, late-Romantic style of, for instance, the Violin Sonatas Nos. 1 and 2, and String Quartets Nos. 1–3. As early as 1917, however, an emergent element of mature style comes to the fore: incipient neoclassicism, manifested in its earliest possible form by the First Chamber Symphony; by 1918, the makings of a second element, Brazilian/jazz-inspired music, appear in *L'Homme et son désir*, *Le Bœuf sur le toit* (1919) and *Saudades do Brazil* (1920); and by 1919, a third element embodies radical experimentation, sometimes bound up with a machine aesthetic, as exemplified by *Machines agricoles* (1919) and the Fifth Chamber Symphony (1922). Beyond 1922, the varied exploratory manifestations recede (Chapter 3), whilst jazz and neoclassicism gain in importance (Chapters 4 and 5). Milhaud's works of the 1920s often embody a mixture, or 'mélange', of any two elements and occasionally of all three.

The second possible set of images is founded on the idea of 'texts', and so relates quite attractively to notions of vocabulary, language, grammar, and syntax, as used earlier in this book, and to concepts of 'reading/misreading', 'reinterpreting', and 'rewriting' (and, up to a point, intertextuality), which have emerged from applying ideas of Straus (and, at one remove, Bloom) and Meltzer. Thus, in developing the original 'elements' idea, and looking beyond the apprentice works and initial 'melting-pot', one might arrive at a three-fold notion of: 'reading machines' (crediting Watkins, embracing Milhaud's experimentation and use of the machine aesthetic, and exhibiting a temporal concern with present and future, modernism and Futurism); 'reading jazz' (fully crediting Meltzer, and representing Milhaud's relationship to a broad spectrum of cultural otherness, concerning implicitly the most distant, primordial past evoked by primitivism), and a culminating, overriding 'reading classicism' (crediting Straus and Walsh, and exemplifying Milhaud's relationship with the past, most particularly a past that was either eighteenth-century, or French, or both). Additionally, these suggested 'readings' enjoy a larger resonance in this period beyond Milhaud's own music, and, beyond this period in Milhaud's late music after 1950.

All three 'readings' clearly involve influence (and associated distancing techniques of abstraction, dislocation and objectification), as foregrounded in Straus's *Remaking the Past*. The apprentice works discussed in the introductory outline of Chapter 3 are nicely defined in terms of 'influence as immaturity', whilst the ideas of 'reading machines', 'reading jazz' and 'reading classicism' across Chapters 3–5 are more complex, embracing a combination of 'influence as generosity', and, more rarely, in the words of Straus (after Bloom), 'influence as anxiety', or more appropriately 'anxiety of style'.[27] Although there are certain notable 'misreadings' (involving over-complication and compression of modality, rhythm and form as 'anxiety of style' in various contexts), including the tritonally-related seventh complexes in 'Ipanema' from *Saudades*, the intense 'polyrhythms' in the Fugue of *La Création*, and the highly condensed, modified sonata forms of the Clarinet Sonatina, such 'anxious' misreadings are generally quite unusual. Rather, Milhaud represents a classic embodiment of 'influence as generosity', and yet his homage (and his need to belong within a French tradition) does not exist simply at face value as mere replication; it, too, may assume new, subtle and complex forms which embrace reinterpretation, development and intensification of the sources of his inspiration, in a way that Straus tends to associate only with his main concern of 'anxiety'. (One might add too that Milhaud ought perhaps to have been more 'anxious' with regard to his own identity, and his relationship with his predecessors, than was in fact the case.) As Madeleine Milhaud has observed of her husband, 'He thought that if one borrowed folk tunes or music from the past, one should do something utterly personal and new with it.'[28]

---

[27] Straus, *Remaking the Past*, 18.
[28] Nichols, *Conversations with Madeleine Milhaud*, 87.

In discussing 'mutual generosity' between artists and their predecessors, largely after T.S. Eliot (in association with Rosen and Meyer), Straus comments in a way which seems appropriate to Milhaud in the 1920s on Eliot's view of 'influences as enriching an artist, in the formative years and in the period of artistic maturity as well'.[29] Such influence is not a weakness, but a means of experiencing and being part of a continuously evolving tradition, as the present embodiment of the past. Contemporary with the period in question, Eliot himself speaks of the writer's 'historical sense', which embraces 'a feeling that the whole of the literature of Europe from Homer and within it the whole of the literature of his own country has a simultaneous existence',[30] in a manner which Milhaud would surely have understood, particularly so since, as mentioned in Chapters 1 and 3, he was as much, or more, influenced by writers than by musicians.

Before considering illustrations of combined elements, or 'multiple texts' within works, which may result in a collage-like juxtaposition, contradiction, or true synthesis (to some extent mirroring the stricter analytical notion of complementation), it is worth reaffirming the justification for the basic approach which governed Chapters 3–5. The stylistic/aesthetic elements, or texts, selected can be differentiated, yet they are also loosely complementary, and collectively representative of the larger-scale 'themes' across Milhaud's diverse output before 1930. Such elements have not been invoked dogmatically, and difficulties in placing certain works which exhibit ambiguity, or exemplify more than one aspect, have been discussed openly: indeed, it was part of the exercise to ascertain the degree of tension set up between the technical apparatus of the study and the music. Thus one may encounter a single work which contains multiple texts, whilst conversely the resonances of a particular text may extend across a number of works which exist as 'relational events'.[31] (Several works were accommodated comfortably within one stylistic/aesthetic domain, e.g. *Saudades do Brazil* in terms of 'Brazilian/jazz-inspired Music', and the 'Opéras-minute' and Seventh Quartet within 'Neoclassicism'.) Clearly, though, one cannot appreciate the subtle nature of the 'mélange' which constitutes Milhaud's 'artistic creation as a total entity' if one has not first considered these compo-

---

[29] Ibid., 10.
[30] T.S. Eliot, 'Tradition and the Individual Talent' (1919), in *Selected Essays* (New York, 1950), 4, as quoted by Straus, *Remaking the Past*, 10.
[31] Straus (after Bloom), *Remaking the Past*, 12.

nent parts. As with the common dictum, however, the whole is indeed greater than the sum of its parts, so that it now remains to revisit and restore a selection of works in terms of the elemental/textual collage, confrontation, or synthesis, which creates that whole. This brief is to be achieved by reference to three works: one from each of Chapters 3, 4 and 5.

Elemental or Textual Collage: Fifth Chamber Symphony

The Fifth Chamber Symphony is a useful example of a work involving juxtaposition of the three main elements identified in Chapters 3–5, and developed above as 'reading machines', 'reading jazz', and 'reading classicism'. It is one of Milhaud's most radically experimental pieces, but is not a totally successful product. Many of the original ideas raised are worthy of further exploration, and might have been the stepping-stone to new areas of contrapuntal balance, equality and highly focused dissonance, within an atonal framework; the problem is, however, that there are too many contrasting ideas and approaches within too short a time-span: a confusion of texts.

This Symphony was discussed in Chapter 3 as an early exploratory work because of the high profile of chromaticism (including localized twelve-note contexts) and dissonant pitch mechanisms. From a freer perspective, however, one might perceive evidence of all three stylistic/aesthetic elements. The machinist 'text', which was pursued in Case Study 3 as part of Milhaud's experimental brief, is particularly prominent in the first and third movements, founded on dissonant mechanisms, with biting semitonal oppositions derived from chromaticism. Such a text views the music through the analogy of small-scaled clockwork mechanisms, in association with film and cartoon techniques: camera 'close-ups', double-exposure, compression, pacing, and so on; conversely, the metaphor extends back within the music in its own ironization of rigid (fully chromatic) systems.

By contrast, the second movement shows signs of incipient blues third within its melodic process, especially in the bass clarinet line, and in this respect at least subscribes to the emergent idea of 'reading jazz'. Moreover, several aspects of the finale, and first movement, owe much to a developing neoclassicism, founded on the instrumental and textural dialectic of concerto grosso, in the context of compact design, and clear-cut sectionalized forms. Indeed, the whole notion of a set of chamber symphonies is in accordance with a neoclassical aesthetic.

Conclusion: Milhaud's 'Total Entity' 271

One could pursue this line of thought further, but it would be unlikely to yield much more: suffice it to say that Milhaud is still searching for his aesthetic and stylistic identity. Although there is a measure of common ground in respect of the machinist idea and the interpretation of the ripieno/concertino groupings as 'fixed' (mechanized: chromatic) versus 'free' (unmechanized: diatonic), generally Milhaud has not yet succeeded in balancing, or integrating, the different references: hence the designation here of 'collage' (or juxtaposition), rather than rigorous confrontation or synthesis.

Synthesis of Elements, or Texts, as a 'Relational Event': Clarinet Sonatina

Although one may compare the Clarinet Sonatina with its counterpart the Flute Sonatina (1922), the strongest associations are with the Fifth Chamber Symphony, which undoubtedly influences the later work in several respects: the overall semitonal progression (b–C); the surface-level, dissonant reference set 4-7 (also found in *L'Enlèvement d'Europe*); and the uncompromising character suggested by the marking 'Très rude'. Clearly something of the early experimental spirit of the Fifth Chamber Symphony persists in the Clarinet Sonatina, and thus the two works have already been mooted as 'relational events', or texts. Consequently, it makes sense here to view one as the continuation of the other, still embracing three elements, or texts: a more general exploratory text (with some vestige of the machinist phenomenon), and those concerned with jazz and 'classicism', which are now embedded fully and blended more subtly.

Vestiges of the early exploratory text include, in the first movement, motivic sets operating both harmonically and melodically (for example, bars 88–95), 'mechanized' ostinati (bars 53–6), localized bimodality at the minor third (bars 72–6), melodic combination (bars 83–6), and substitute dominant formations (bars 92–4). Tritonal relations persist, especially in the finale which suggests complementary segments: (C–F♯: bass) and (F–B: treble), and connects with more overt manifestations of tritonal relations in the Fourth Quartet and Fifth Chamber Symphony. Furthermore, with its conspicuous use of enharmonic modulation in the slow movement, the Sonatina looks back further to the late-Romantic, student compositions dating from the period of the First World War.

Some trace of Milhaud's interest in 'reading jazz' is revealed by melodic and harmonic emphasis on the fifth scalic degree, as in the second subject of the first movement, and in the material which opens and 'closes' the 'Lent'. Limited instances of the blues triad persist harmonically and melodically, as do syncopated minor third patterns (for example, I, bars 53–6). The sixth scalic degree maintains a high profile, particularly in conjunction with chords I and V: specific illustrations in the 'Lent' include the opening bass pedal: VI–V (F–E♭), the modulation to the submediant (bars 7–8), and the ending: I–♭VI–V (A♭–F♭–E♭), which neatly mirrors the 3-4 set (B,G,F♯) of the first movement.

As a neoclassical text, this Sonatina is quite exclusive as one of only two sonata-type works of the 1920s. The rethinking of this archetypal genre, and of its structural and formal processes, has already been the focus of Case Study 7, so that it remains simply to summarize and make a few further points. The music is strongly centric, especially in the A♭-based 'Lent', with less bimodal conflict than in earlier works. Apart from the typical emphasis on third relations, melodic fifth progressions feature prominently in all movements, balanced harmonically by dominant pedal-points (I, bars 77-82; opening of II). There is increased emphasis on repetition, literal and subtly varied, with the conclusion of the work focusing on a much reiterated cadential formula (bars 61–72, 73–80). Melodic and harmonic sequences have a high profile (I, bars 20–4), especially in stylized, invertible counterpoint (III, bars 51–60), whilst triads transposed *en bloc* are a connected syntactic feature. Two instances of modal procedure might seem to allude to Schubertian practice: use of the tonic minor at the conclusion of the 'Lent', and stressing of the subdominant minor relation (here Dorian on f) in the finale in C. The balancing of two distinct harmonic areas, with contrasting subjects, especially in movements I and III does suggest the re-emergence of aspects of classical sonata form, whilst the surface level reveals many double-dotted rhythms and diminutions, characteristic of baroque practice (for example, III, bars 57–8).

In addition to synthesizing elements of neoclassicism, jazz and early exploration, this piece shows the stylistic development and refinement which one would expect of a mature work in the late 1920s: this is the sense in which the work is greater than the sum of its parts. More complex structures are used than hitherto, creating more subtle and developed ternary outlines, in synthesis with principles of sonata form; greater economy is evident in the number of ideas, each of which is thoroughly pursued, as shown by the cyclical aspect of this work (and of *L'Abandon d'Ariane*); skilful dovetailing of sections is exemplified by the lead into the 'second subject' of the first movement (bar 35). Metrically, the work exhibits a judicious flexibility, as with the alternating 4/4, 3/4 pattern in the finale (a similar technique to that used in the final scene of *L'Abandon*); metre is also integrated within phrase expansion and contraction, as in the progression: 4/4, 5/4, 6/4; 5/4, 4/4, across bars 51–9 of the first movement. At surface level, texture receives varied treatment, including full textures with octave doublings in the piano part (III, bars 15–20); attention is paid to dynamic, phrasing and expressive markings, including in the slow movement the significant term 'dramatique'. Grand, rhetorical gestures in the finale are surely influenced by Milhaud's increased interest in opera in the later 1920s: the dissonant, wide-ranging piano figures (bars 24–7); the effective use of silence after the 'pianissimo' clarinet figure (bar 40); and the particular drama of the ending, aided by varied phrase lengths, metrical change and full use of register at *fortissimo* dynamic.

The Clarinet Sonatina is not necessarily indicative of Milhaud's overall compositional direction, though it does pave the way for further refinements which lead to the highly neoclassical and economical sonatas of the early to mid-1940s. The work is particularly interesting when viewed in the immediate context of the increased involvement with musical drama in the late 1920s; there is a heightened, dramatic effect in what proved to be Milhaud's last chamber work for five years. After the summer of 1927, Milhaud was diverted from chamber music by the attractions of 'grand opera', and went on to compose some of his most successful works of that genre, including the universally acclaimed opera-oratorio *Christophe Colomb* (1928).

Ultimate Synthesis of Elements or Texts: La Création du monde

La Création du monde provides probably the finest example of synthesis: 'j'utilisai le style jazz sans réserve, le mêlant à un sentiment classique' (although one might argue, more appropriately, in favour of a baroque 'sentiment');[32] additionally the machinist/technological dimension also has expression here, largely in the visual dimensions of Léger's avant-garde 'mechanical theatre' and Börlin's choreography, but also in Milhaud's employment of unrelenting musical mechanisms, most particu-

---

[32] Milhaud, *Ma vie heureuse*, 125: 'I used the jazz style unreservedly, blending it with a classical feel.'

larly the circular, contrapuntal devices in the Fugue, and the punctuating riff in the Final.

Essentially, though, this is Milhaud's jazz masterpiece and certainly the piece by which he is best known (usually with that association), and yet any practising jazz musician would assert that Milhaud's assimilation of jazz and the blues scale is still a far cry from the real, spontaneous art.[33] And this of course is part of the point. In fact, composing for a classically trained ensemble, with music fully notated, such a task would have been impossible; true jazz exists only in improvised performance (albeit planned, to a greater or lesser degree), and Milhaud would have been the first to recognize this. Indeed, he was not attempting to compose a genuine piece of jazz: such would be a contradiction in terms, and undoubtedly the work would have been far less successful and durable had he done so. Although he had previously composed pieces more in keeping with early jazz, such as *Caramel mou* for small jazz ensemble with voice, such works have not captured the public imagination in the manner of *La Création du monde*. In contributing to *La Création* in its original ballet format which evokes creation visually, in terms of African primitivism, as well as aurally, Milhaud, in conjunction with Léger and Cendrars, must have intended a synthesis of Western and African/American negro styles from the start.

In addition to this cultural opposition and subsequent synthesis, there is that of the inherent, technical vocabularies of the texts of jazz and neoclassicism. Much discussion has already focused on the jazz element as the more remarkable achievement of a classically trained composer, whilst the neoclassical features too have been acknowledged, particularly where they have a higher profile in the *Suite de concert* version of the work. What remains is to stress the incongruity of some stylistic and technical oppositions, as well as the seemingly organic synthesis which is what gives *La Création du monde* its charm. There is, after all, a delightful incongruity in using fully developed fugue, the epitome of baroque rigour and restraint (exemplifying 'high art'), as the structural framework for one of Milhaud's most 'bluesy' themes (symbolic of 'low art'), itself most likely derived from the music of jazz-man W.C. Handy. In the Romance, distorted twelve-bar blues structures engage and battle with a refined, 'classical' ternary form: this is to stress the irreconcilable polarities, but of course *La Création du monde* only works because some elements are genuinely fused. As dis-

---

[33] See Hodeir, *Jazz: Its Evolution and Essence*, 250.

Conclusion: Milhaud's 'Total Entity' 275

cussed in the analytically orientated part of the conclusion, the high profile of third relations in Milhaud's handling of the jazz and neoclassical 'texts' provides some of the necessary common ground.

Stylistically, too, one also observes bizarre contrasts. In the original staged version, ballet dancers trained in Europe's most exclusive schools delight in role-play as creatures from exotic regions, which most could only hope to visit in their imaginations. Caucasian classical musicians, trained at the Conservatoire, also act out a role, giving a semblance of the freedom of the negro jazz musician. In the *Suite de concert* version, the 'double' incongruity of a Parisian piano quintet acting out a jazz role within a yet more tightly controlled neoclassical framework is equally striking. Furthermore, the audience who witnessed these rites, in the spirit of *Le Sacre du printemps* of a decade earlier, also entered into a fantasy world, far away from their twentieth-century Parisian life-styles.

So the attraction and greatness of *La Création* lie in this exploration of various oppositions (cultural, stylistic and technical: including the processes of modal complementation which govern the thematic basis) which are then synthesized as a superb 'mélange' of different worlds; and its main technical strength is due to the fact that Milhaud undertook his study of jazz and blues at first hand, and approached the subject with a greater seriousness of purpose than many of his contemporaries.[34] *La Création du monde* is certainly the jazz prototype in 'high-art' music of the 1920s, with many attempted sequels; it is doubtful, however, whether even successors such as Ernst Křenek (*Der Sprung über den Schatten*, 1924; *Jonny spielt auf*, 1925–27), Kurt Weill (*Die Dreigroschenoper*, 1927–28; *Mahagonny* 1927–29), or Aaron Copland (Concerto for Piano and Orchestra, 1926), with the notable exception of George Gershwin (*Rhapsody in Blue*, 1924), had the same understanding and compositional skill within the elusive world of jazz. Their works fall more readily into categories of pastiche or parody than real, developed assimilation.

This perspective on three works has endeavoured to highlight elemental/textual juxtaposition (in the Fifth Chamber Symphony); the continued development of these texts, and the sense in which a work is something more than the sum of its stylistic/technical parts (Clarinet

---

[34] Refer back to the early contextual portion of Chapter 1, and the introductory outline of Chapter 4.

Sonatina); and the ultimate creative synthesis of *La Création du monde*. And so one now has a sense of the various modal, structural, and aesthetic concerns that co-exist in an eclectic balance within Milhaud's 'artistic creation as a total entity', or, in the words of Wilfrid Mellers, his '"global village" ethnicity'.[35]

Final Remarks on Milhaud

The final view of Milhaud might be as a Mediterranean modal lyricist (characteristically inspired by the cultural milieu and surrounding scenery of Aix-en-Provence), who always maintained that he composed polytonally.[36] Flexibility within his means of modal reference is perhaps the most striking trait, sustained across a large and varied musical output which is also, to some extent, unified structurally by an array of variations on ternary form. Typically, his music is imbued with great vigour in fast movements as something of a reinvocation of the French eighteenth-century 'Vif', yet with great sensitivity and intensity in slow, central movements where, in the words of Matthew-Walker, his 'Jewish consciousness' is perhaps most apparent; such 'dualism' within his identity (partly mediated by the Sephardic inflection of his Jewish heritage) has been most clearly expressed in Milhaud's own words (quoted early in Chapter 4): 'Je suis un Français de Provence, et de religion israélite.'

Milhaud represents a relatively rare example of a composer who utilized a so-called neoclassical idiom throughout most of his compositional life (especially before 1930, and beyond 1950), comparable to a point with Stravinsky and Hindemith. (Milhaud's middle years do see a resurgence of a much more overt romanticism, evident especially in the large orchestral/choral projects of the 1940s, such as the Jewish *Service sacré* of 1947.) The mainstay of his style was, as he himself commented, a concern to create a 'simple and clear art, renewing the tradition of Scarlatti and Mozart' (quoted early in Chapter 5), which resulted in some highly successful and attractive works such as the six chamber symphonies. So in embodying 'influence as generosity' (generosity of spirit seems to have been his guiding principle in music and life), he does look back for inspiration to the eighteenth-century craft of composition, refined and rarely overtly emotional. As Wilfrid Mellers has

---

[35] Mellers, 'Polymorphous Celebrations', 717.
[36] Drake, *The Operas of Darius Milhaud*, 221.

remarked quite aptly, maintaining this emphasis on craft and a—largely uncritical—fluency of technique: 'Milhaud's yea-saying is a key alike to his potency and to his impermanence. A professional musicman, he exuded music "regardless", hardly asking whether it was good, bad, or systematic'.[37] Yet Milhaud was also a pioneer: most obviously in his assimilation and reinterpretation of Harlem jazz and blues within 'high-art' music, but also in respect of his manipulations of classical notions and formulae, and in his early experimental involvement with aleatory music and the 'machine aesthetic'. Although he can be criticized, with some justification, for the sheer quantity of his total output (up to Op. 443!) and its inevitable unevenness of quality, this does not detract from the undeniable merits of many works, including several masterpieces before 1930: *L'Homme et son désir* (1918), *Les Malheurs d'Orphée* (1925) and *Christophe Colomb* (1928), in addition to the most obvious contender, *La Création du monde* (1923; 1926).

In addition to his composition and conducting, Milhaud (like Hindemith) also had a role as a respected teacher, both at the Paris Conservatoire and at Mills College, Oakland, California, and this important dimension, related to questions of influence, needs at least to be acknowledged in an informal summing-up that seeks to offer a perception of Milhaud for today. Beyond the Second World War, particularly, Milhaud taught several students who went on to pursue successful careers in composition, although none has continued his style directly. At the Paris Conservatoire Milhaud's students included Iannis Xenakis (b. 1922), Milko Kelemen (b. 1924), György Kurtág (b. 1926), Gilbert Amy (b. 1936) and Jean-Claude Eloy (b. 1938); and at Mills College, Charles Jones (b. 1910), William O. Smith (b. 1926), Robert Moran (b. 1937), David del Tredici (b. 1937), William Bolcom (b. 1938) and the Japanese composer, Sadao Bekku. He also encouraged Dave Brubeck in his ambitions to be a jazz pianist, as revealed recently by Madeleine Milhaud.[38] Undoubtedly though, the best-known American figure is Milhaud's one-time Mills College student Steve Reich (b. 1936), who, like Robert Moran, was also taught by Berio. And—although it may initially seem incongruous—Reich might be seen as the composer who most nearly continues Milhaud's musical philosophy: the adherence to a type of (partly jazz-inspired) modality, the use of mosaic-like repeated, and subtly varied, ostinato patterns

---

[37] Mellers, 'Polymorphous Celebrations', 717.
[38] Nichols, *Conversations with Madeleine Milhaud*, 61.

which move in and out of phase with their fellows and the bar-lines, as well as the belief that music should be appealing and accessible.

Ultimately, Milhaud was a man of his time, in keeping with the Parisian musical aesthetic of the 1920s. He offers us an increased understanding of those colourful and attractive years, both through his music and through his autobiography, and, whilst his music exhibits the fashionable frivolity of this decade, it also possesses a far more serious and pensive aspect. The 1920s did indeed constitute Milhaud's formative years, yielding without doubt some of the finest music that he was to produce across his long life-span, though balanced, as acknowledged by Drake,[39] by a certain correspondence with this early music in his third period beyond about 1950. A sense, perhaps, of full circle—or ternary form? It is to be hoped that in the decade of his centenary, Milhaud's music may receive the greater attention that it merits.

Scope for Future Research

As a result of this book, several lines of further research are indicated, both within and beyond Milhaud's music. Some of these possibilities have already been raised *en passant*, but it seems helpful at least to provide a summary here. Essentially, this book has sought to provide ideas for future analytical study in the broad domain of modality (including localized bimodality, and blues-scale formations), and the search for a modal resultant from the encounter of contrapuntal lines may well assist in analysing the music of other so-called polytonalists such as Charles Ives. Other specific research might usefully include substantiation and nuancing of the idea of 'full circle' in respect of the correspondence between Milhaud's early and final periods (mediated by the overtly neoclassical sonatas of the early to mid-1940s); further exploration of pc set genera in French music, including that of Milhaud and Ravel, along the lines suggested by Parks; and development of a theory of complementation, with application for example in contemporary Bartók.

Generally, little analysis to date has attempted to ascertain the extent of deviation (and 'misreading') of jazz-inspired works from blues scalic formations and formal frameworks (as developed from Keil), so that one could pursue further the blues-scale model (as a 'background'

---

[39] Drake, *The Operas of Darius Milhaud*, 318ff.

structure), partitioned in the manner of van den Toorn's treatment of the octatonic collection in Stravinsky's music, to elucidate analyses of, for instance, parts of Satie's *Parade* (1917), Stravinsky's 'Ragtime' from *L'Histoire du soldat* (1918), Gershwin's *Rhapsody in Blue* (1924), or Ravel's 'Blues' from the Violin Sonata (1927). This concern obviously connects with the larger aesthetic question of 'influence' (post-Bloom), and, beyond the specific instance of the blues, theories of influence and tradition (with application to Milhaud's music, amongst others) could be further developed in relation to philosophies of history and value, along the more sophisticated, recent lines of thinkers such as Hayden White and Frank Kermode.[40] Finally, there is undoubtedly considerable scope for other detailed explorations of the machinist/technological phenomenon, as an off-shoot of that second wave of Futurism, particularly in the music and aesthetics of Varèse, Stravinsky and Ravel.

---

[40] Hayden White's texts extend from his early volume on *Metahistory: The Historical Imagination in Nineteenth-century Europe* (Baltimore, 1973), through *Tropics of Discourse: Essays in Cultural Criticism* (Baltimore, 1978), to his more recent work, *The Content of the Form: Narrative Discourse and Historical Representation* (Baltimore, 1987). See also F. Kermode, 'Value at a Distance', in *History and Value* (Oxford, 1989), 85–107. Additionally, F. Lentricchia and T. McLaughlin, eds., *Critical Terms for Literary Study* (Chicago, 1990) contains informative and stimulating essays on 'Influence' (by L.A. Renza), 186–202, and 'Value' (by B. Herrstein Smith), 177–85.

APPENDIX
Analytical Examples: Case Studies 1–8

Case Study 1

Chromaticism and Polarity in the 'Funèbre' from the
String Quartet No. 4, Op. 46 (1918)

284   Darius Milhaud

Example 3.1 Fourth Quartet: II, bars 1–3

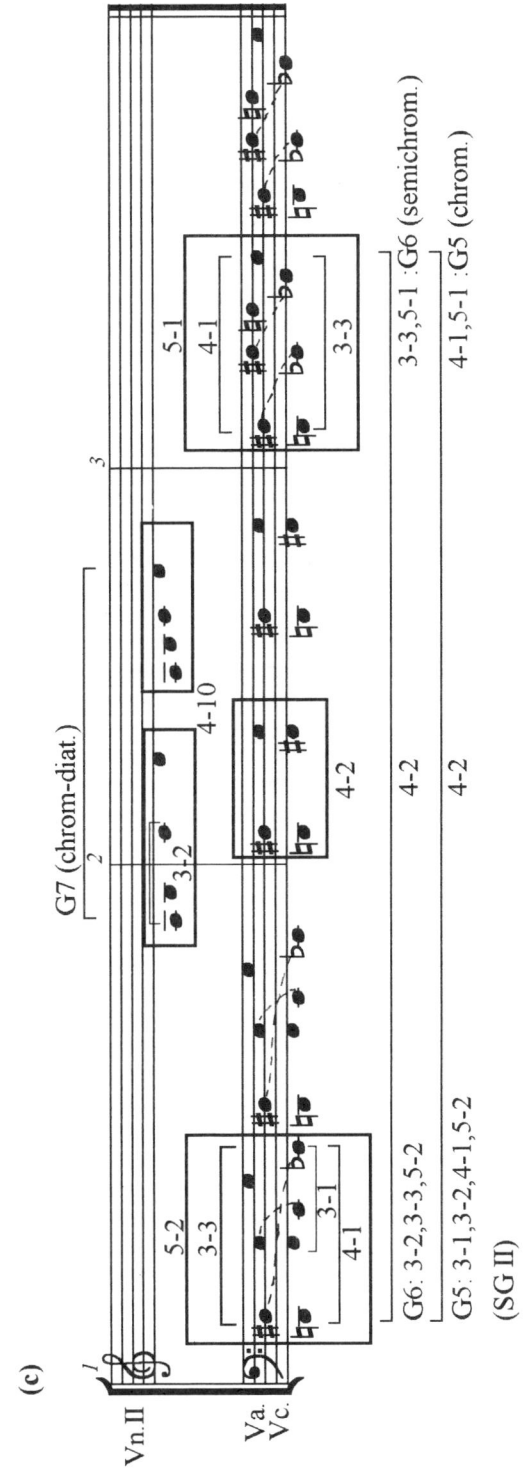

Appendix: Analytical Examples

286 DARIUS MILHAUD

Example 3.1 (continued)

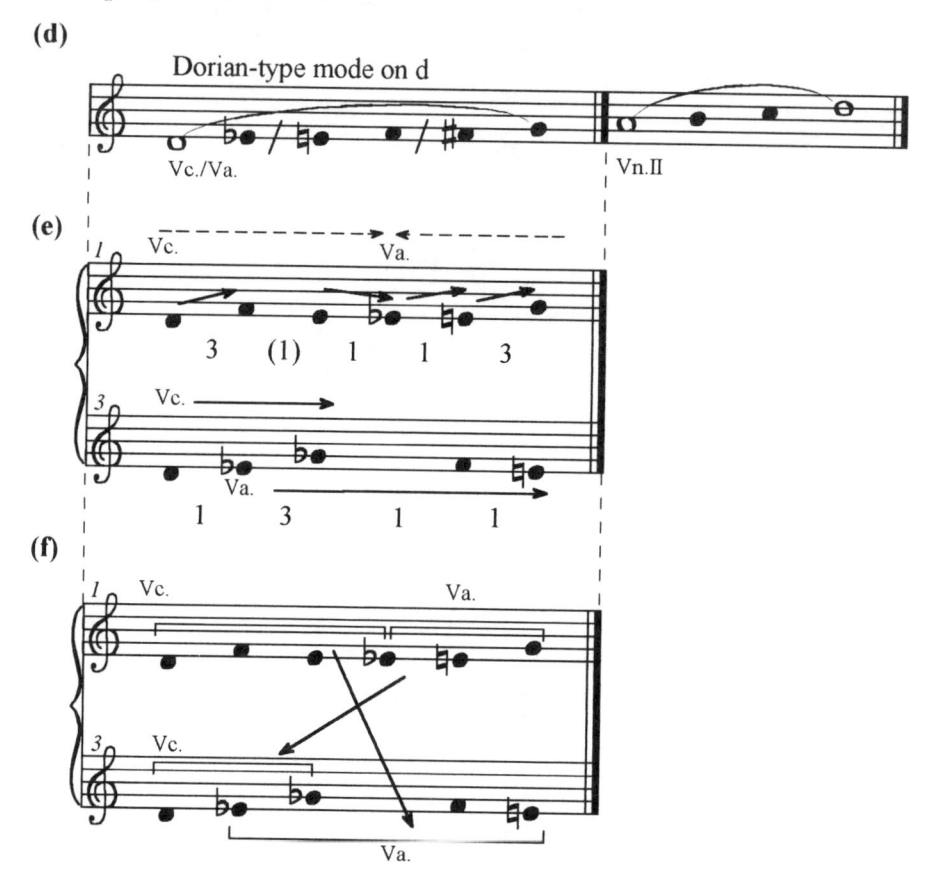

(d)

(e)

(f)

Example 3.2 Fourth Quartet: II, bar 5

288   Darius Milhaud

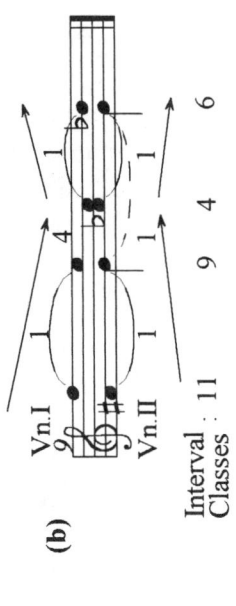

Example 3.3 Fourth Quartet: II, bar 9

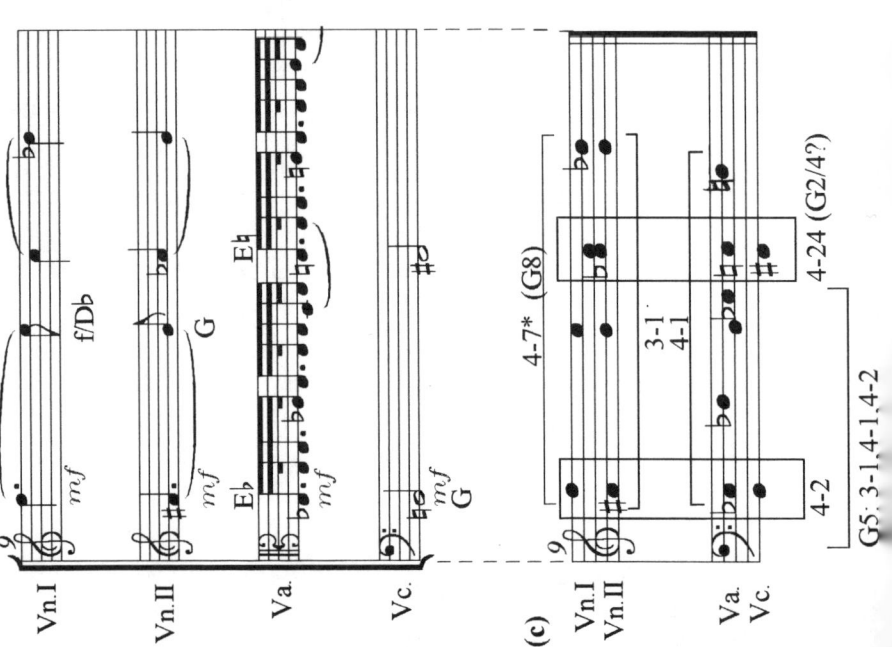

Example 3.4 Fourth Quartet: II, bars 12–16

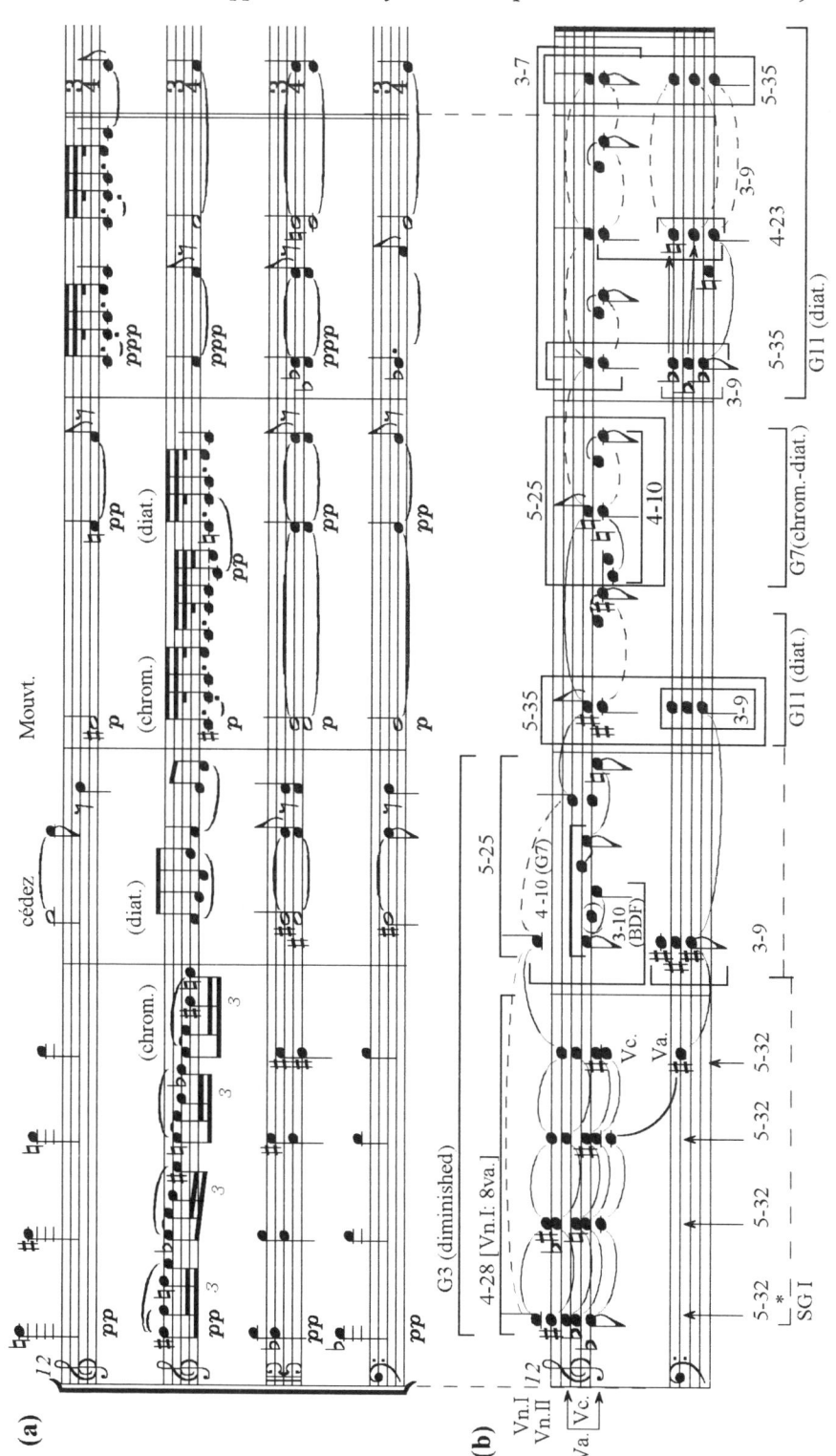

Example 3.5 Fourth Quartet: II, bar 12

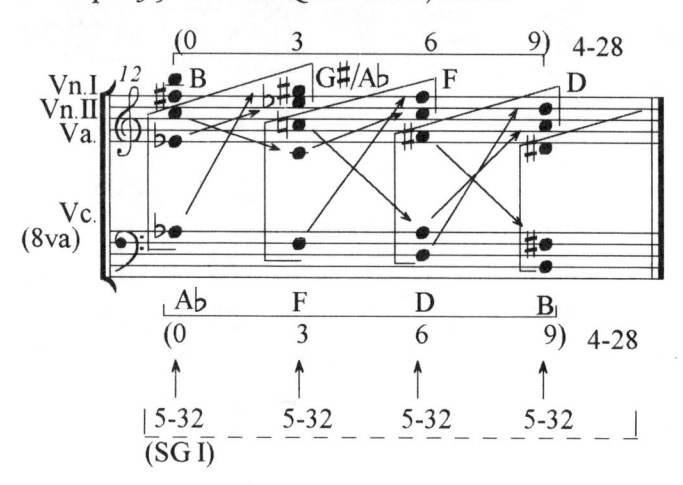

Octatonic Collection: Model A

(0 1 3 4 6 7 9 10)

8-28

Appendix: Analytical Examples 291

Example 3.6 Fourth Quartet: II, bars 17-20

(a) Section A'

Example 3.6 (continued)

(b) Partitioning of Pentatonic Collections

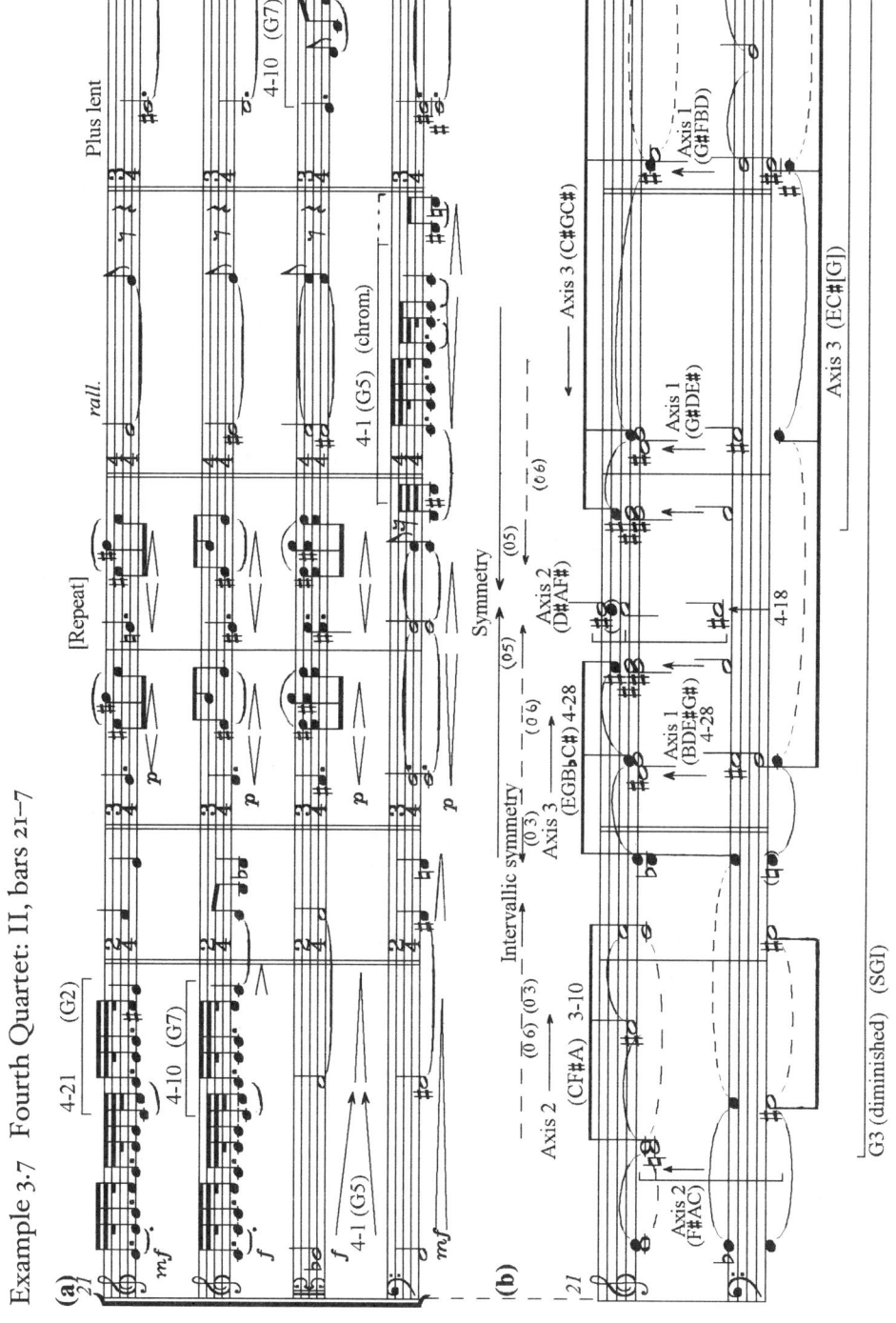

Example 3.7 Fourth Quartet: II, bars 21–7

Example 3.8 Fourth Quartet: II, bars 49–57

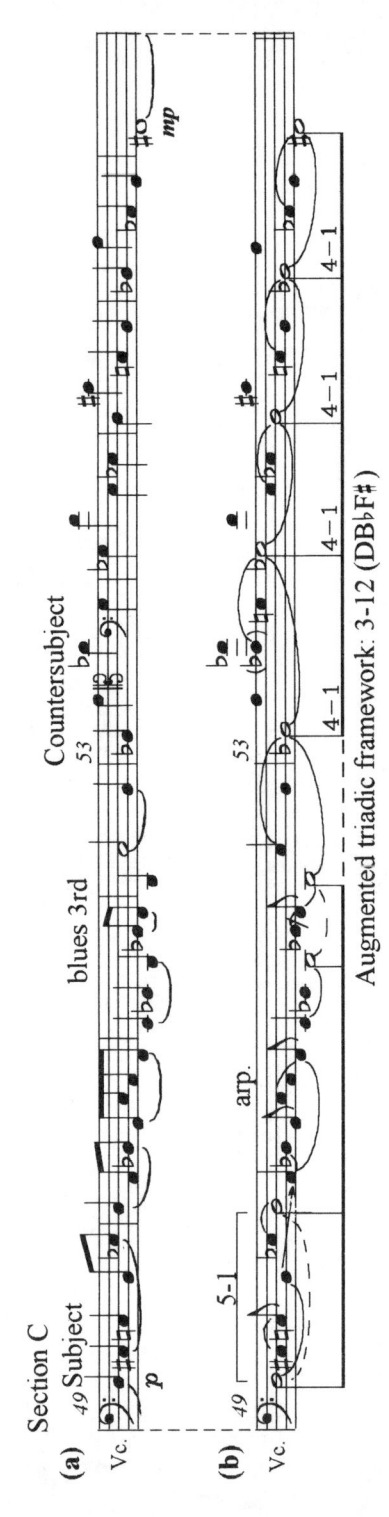

Case Study 2

Chromaticism and Canonic Devices in 'La Lieuse', from
Machines agricoles, Op. 56 (1919)

Example 3.9 *Machines agricoles*: III, bars 1–3

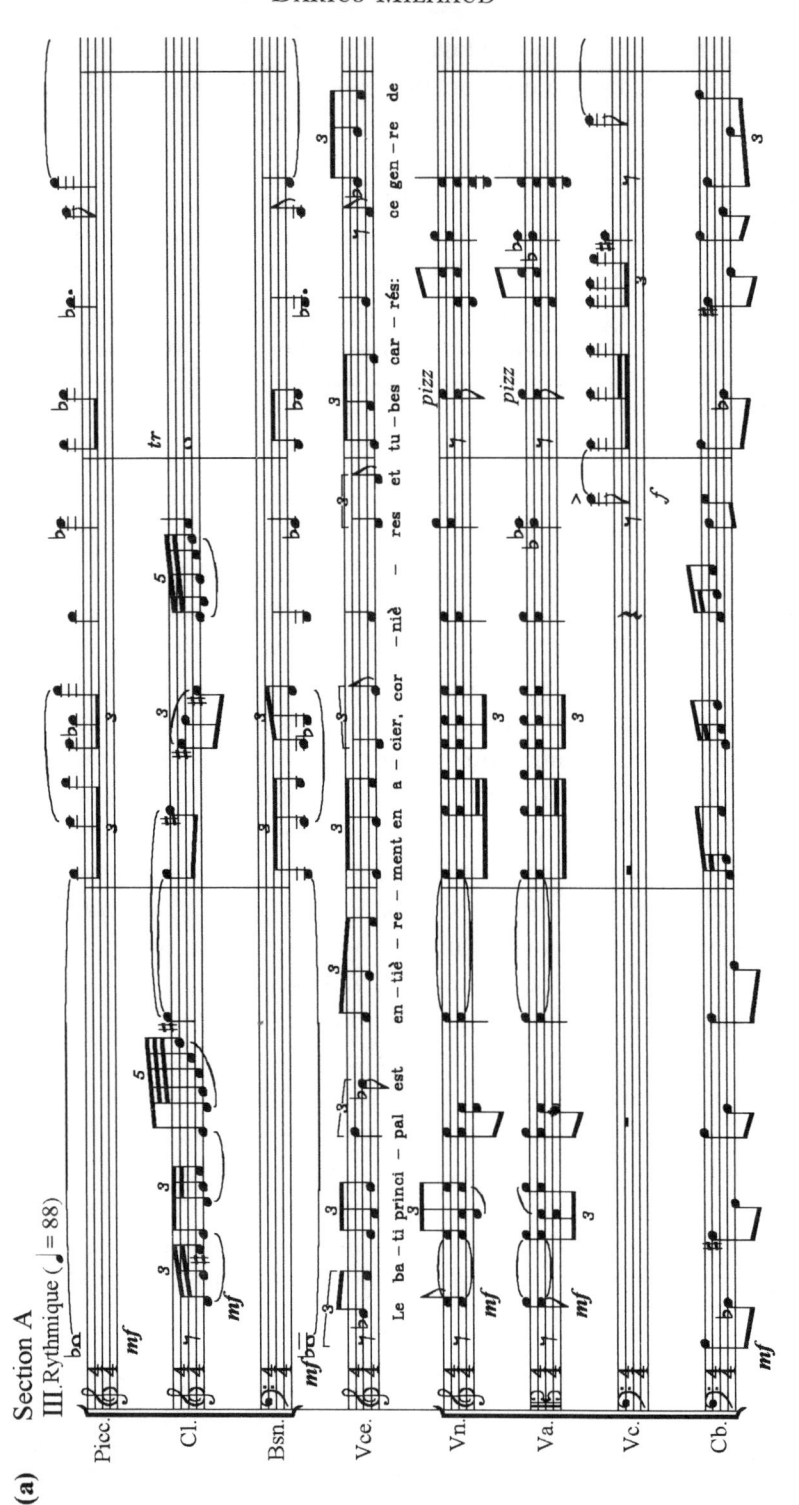

(a) Section A

Appendix: Analytical Examples 297

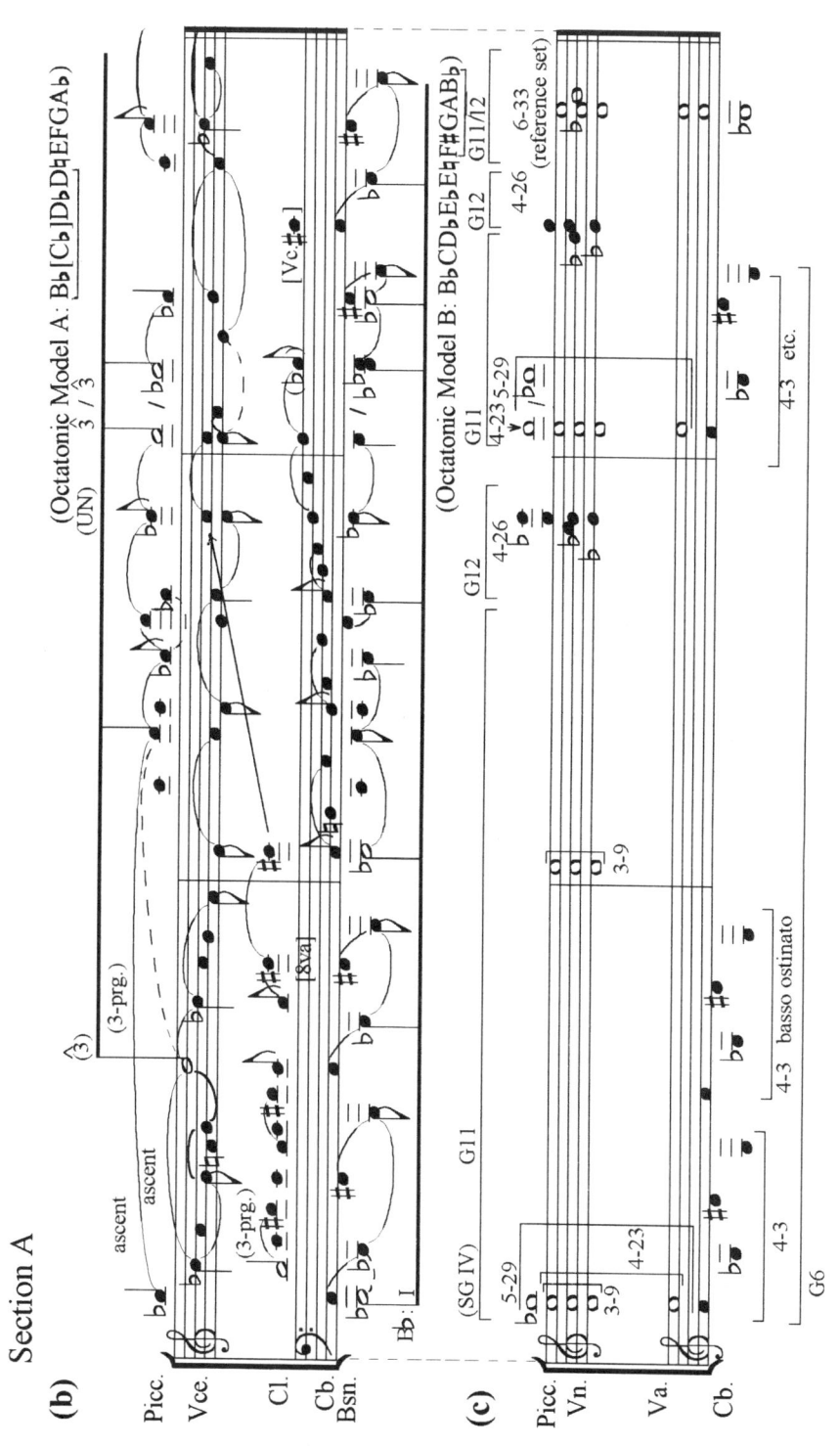

Example 3.10 *Machines agricoles*: III, bars 13–15

Section B

(a)

Appendix: Analytical Examples 299

Example 3.10 (continued)

Section B

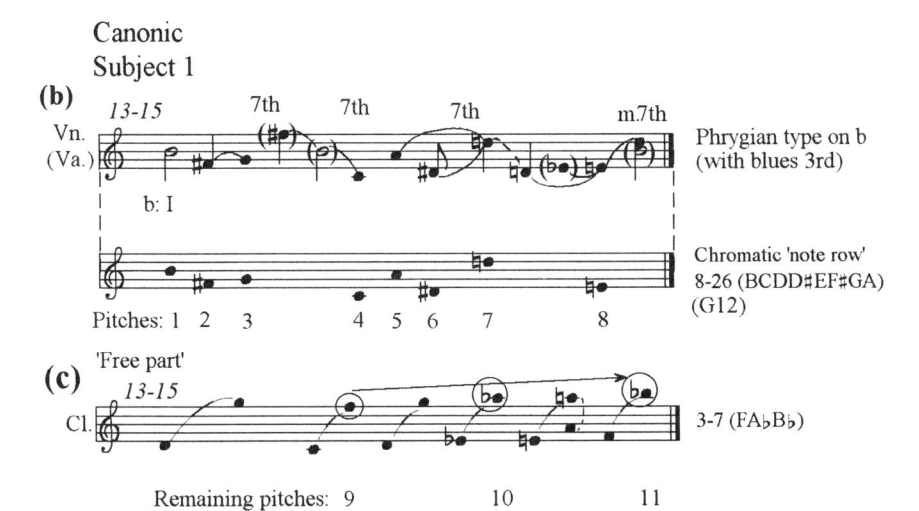

Canonic
Subject 1

(b) *13-15* 7th 7th 7th m.7th
Vn. (Va.)

Phrygian type on b
(with blues 3rd)

b: I

Chromatic 'note row'
8-26 (BCDD♯EF♯GA)
(G12)

Pitches: 1 2 3 4 5 6 7 8

(c) 'Free part'
13-15
Cl.

3-7 (FA♭B♭)

Remaining pitches: 9 10 11

Example 3.11 *Machines agricoles*: III, bars 20–2

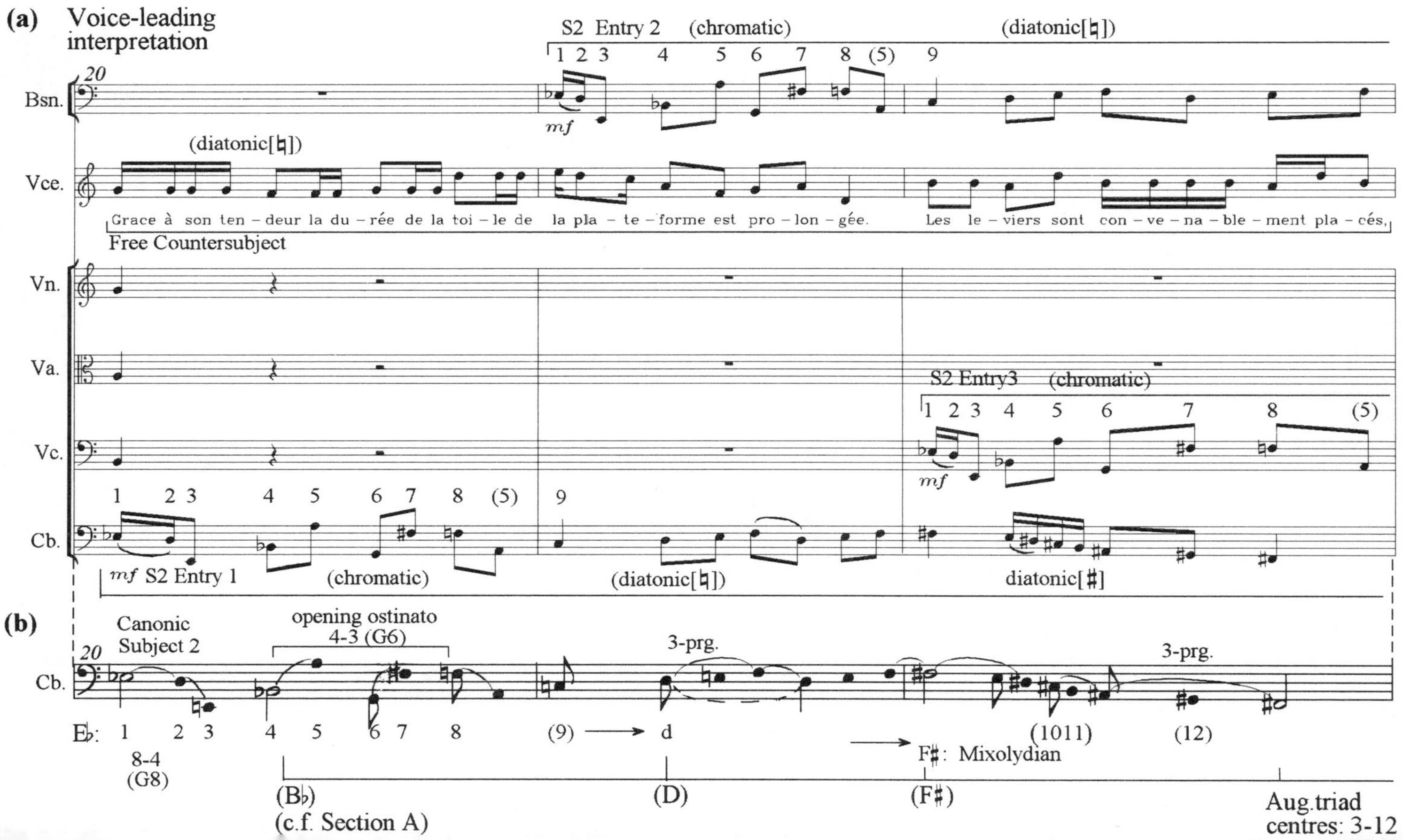

Example 3.12 *Machines agricoles*: III, bars 20ff.

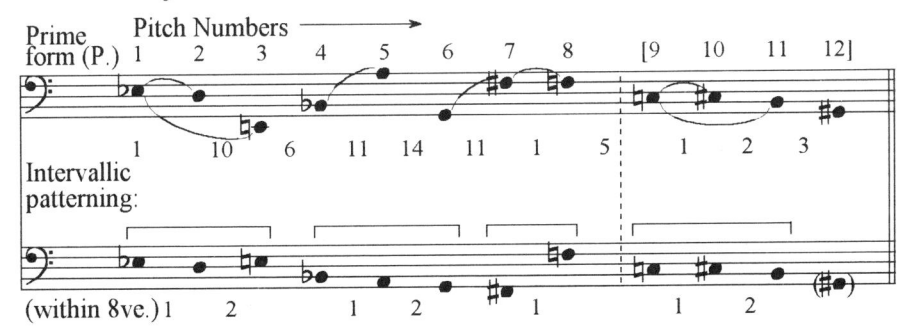

Case Study 3

Dissonant Mechanisms in the
Chamber Symphony No. 5, Op. 75 (1922)

Example 3.13 Fifth Chamber Symphony: I, bars 1–3

Appendix: Analytical Examples 305

Example 3.13 (continued)

(b) Theoretical schema
    Bars 1-3

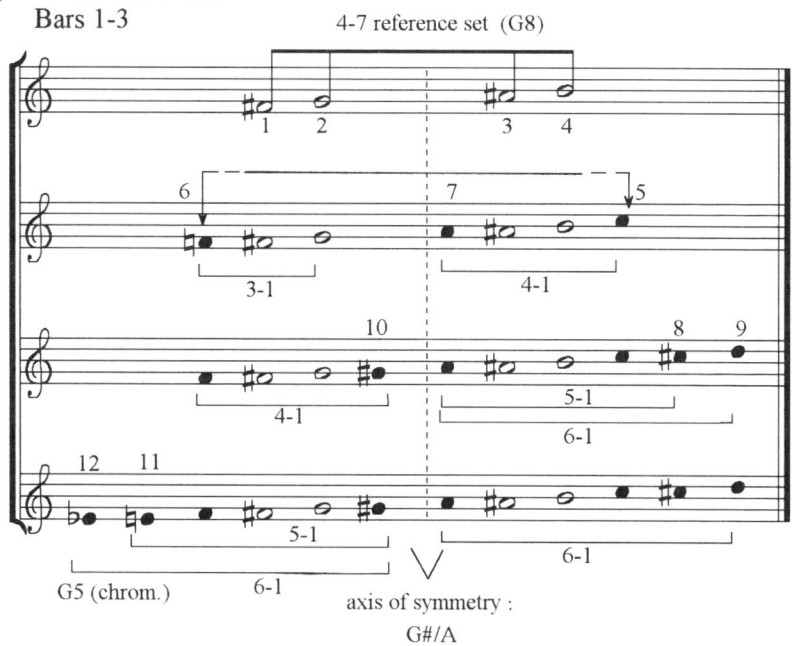

Example 3.14 Fifth Chamber Symphony: I, bars 21–4

Appendix: Analytical Examples 307

Example 3.14 (continued): I, bars 26–9

308 DARIUS MILHAUD

Example 3.15 Fifth Chamber Symphony: I

Theoretical schema: Section A'
Bars 21–29

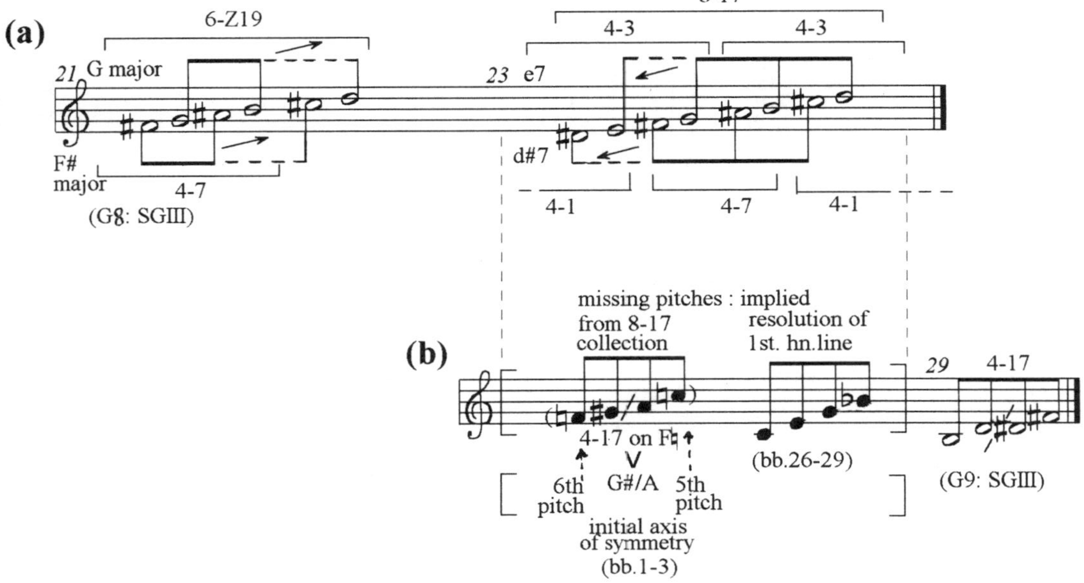

Appendix: Analytical Examples 309

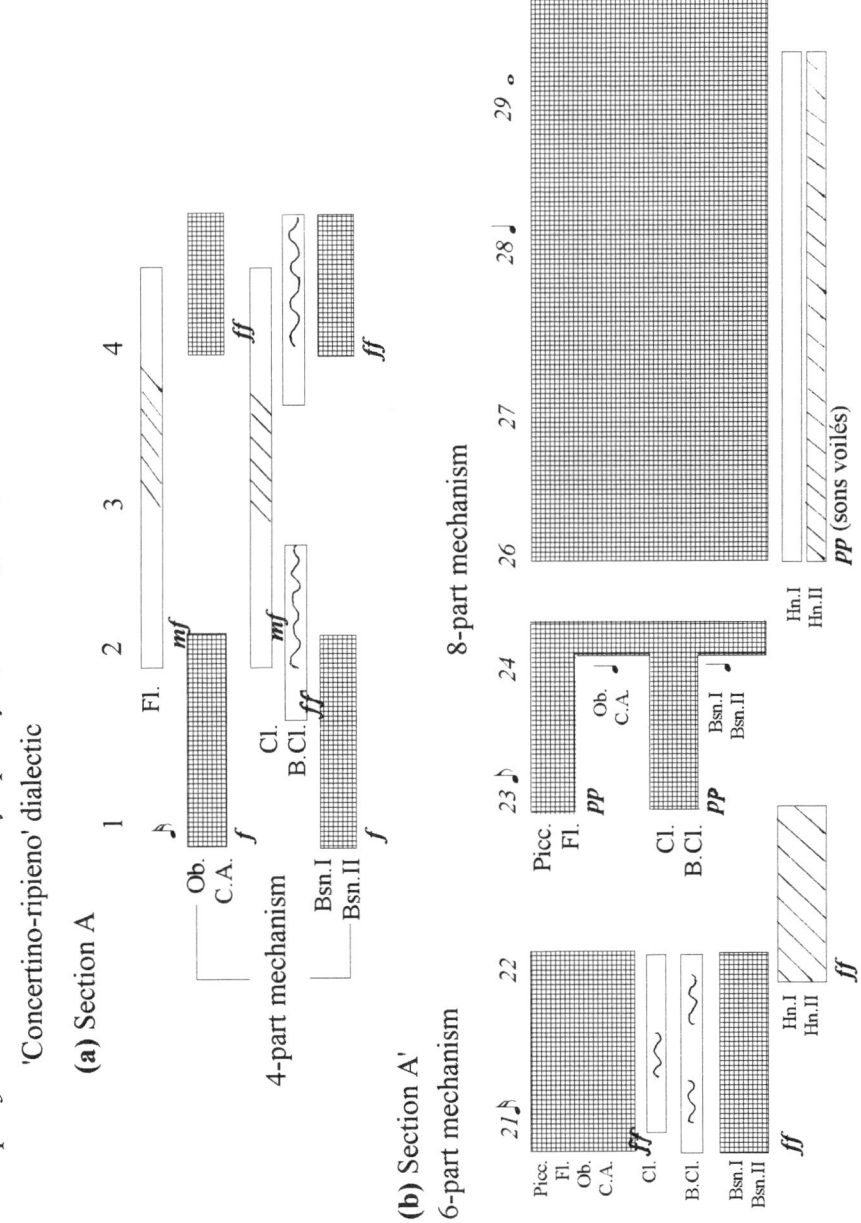

Example 3.16 Fifth Chamber Symphony: I, bars 1–3; 21–9
'Concertino-ripieno' dialectic

(a) Section A

4-part mechanism

(b) Section A'
6-part mechanism

8-part mechanism

310 DARIUS MILHAUD

Example 3.17 Fifth Chamber Symphony: I, bars 15–16

Section B

Appendix: Analytical Examples 311

Example 3.17 (continued)

(b) 4-part mechanism

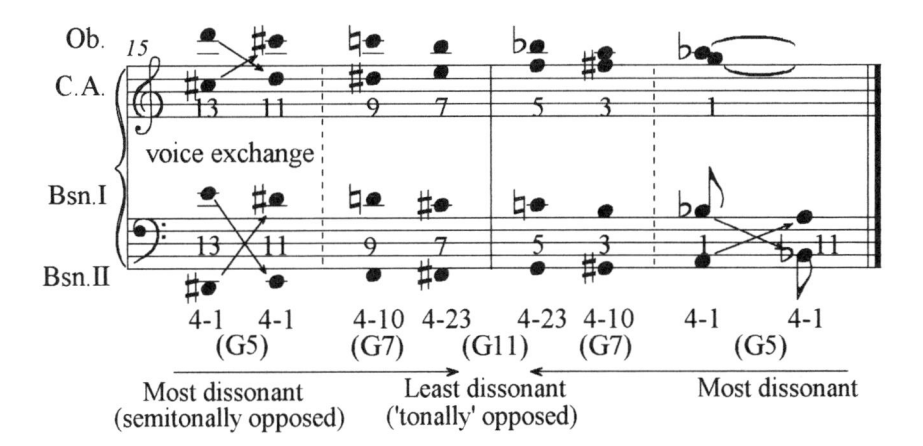

Example 3.18 Fifth Chamber Symphony: I, bars 19–20

Appendix: Analytical Examples 313

Example 3.18 (continued)

(b)   6-part mechanism

Axis of Symmetry: (B♭,C♯,E,G) 4-28

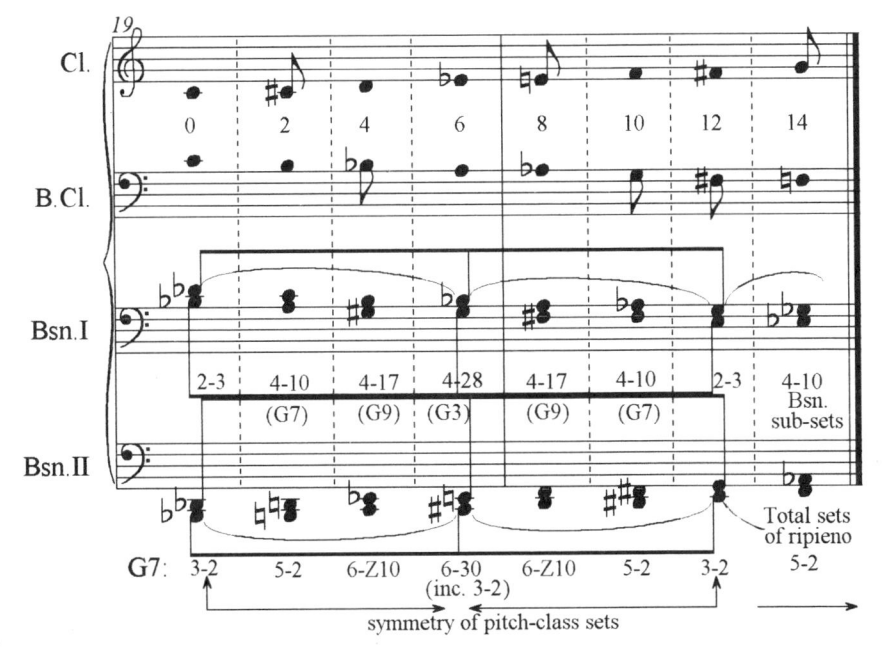

Example 3.19 Fifth Chamber Symphony: I

Theoretical schema
Relations between Sections:

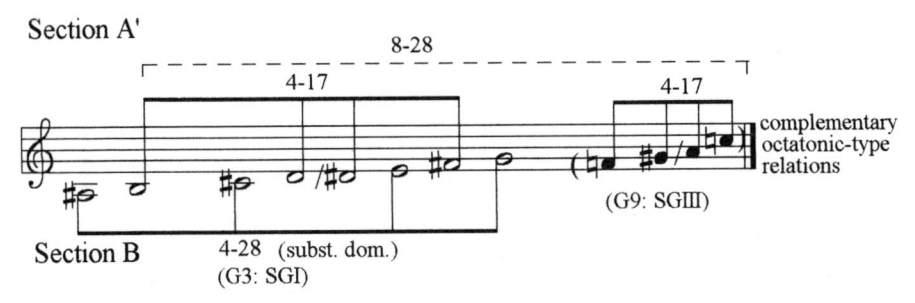

Section A'

8-28

4-17   4-17

complementary
octatonic-type
relations

(G9: SGIII)

Section B   4-28 (subst. dom.)
(G3: SGI)

Appendix: Analytical Examples 315

Example 3.20 Fifth Chamber Symphony: II, bars 1–7

(a) Section A
II. Lent

316　DARIUS MILHAUD

Example 3.20 (continued)

(b) Opening bars

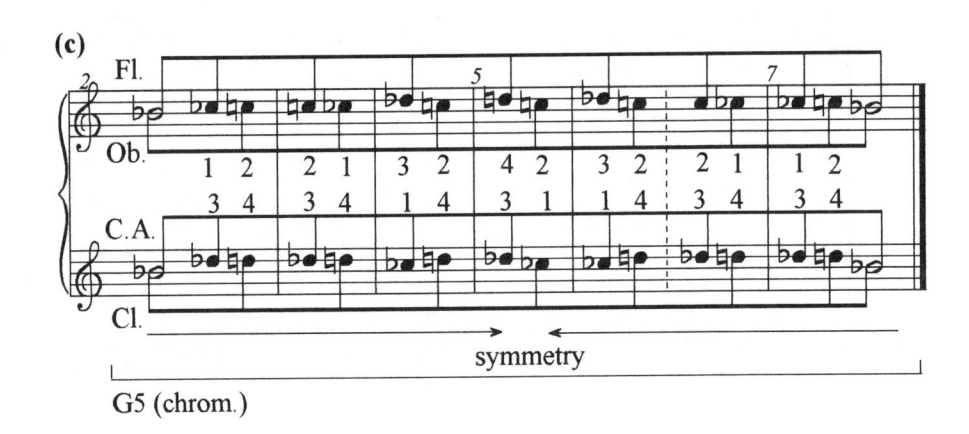

Essential material　　　Fl. II

(B♭)　5-1　　4-1　　　　blues 3rd

(c) Fl.

Ob.

1 2	2 1	3 2	4 2	3 2	2 1	1 2
3 4	3 4	1 4	3 1	1 4	3 4	3 4

C.A.

Cl.

symmetry

G5 (chrom.)

Example 3.21 Fifth Chamber Symphony: II, bars 20–3

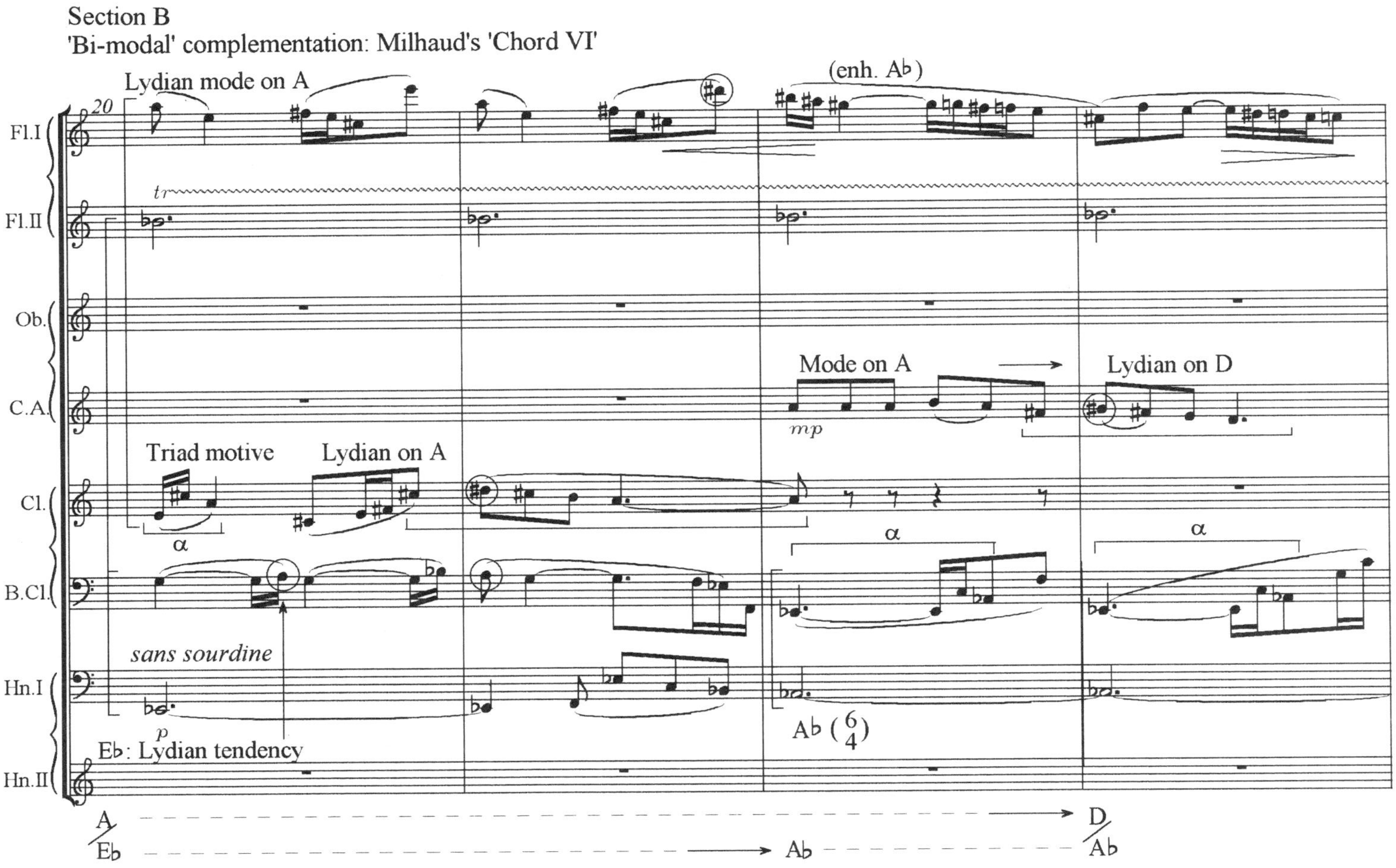

Section B
'Bi-modal' complementation: Milhaud's 'Chord VI'

318　DARIUS MILHAUD

Example 3.22　Fifth Chamber Symphony: III, bars 25–6

Appendix: Analytical Examples 319

Example 3.22 (continued)

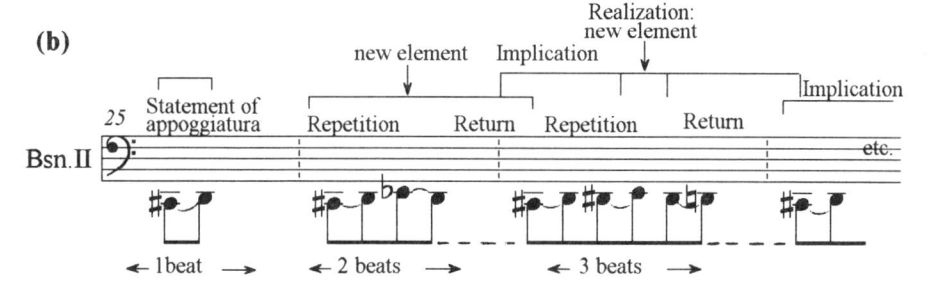

(b)

Example 3. 23 Fifth Chamber Symphony: III, bars 34–6

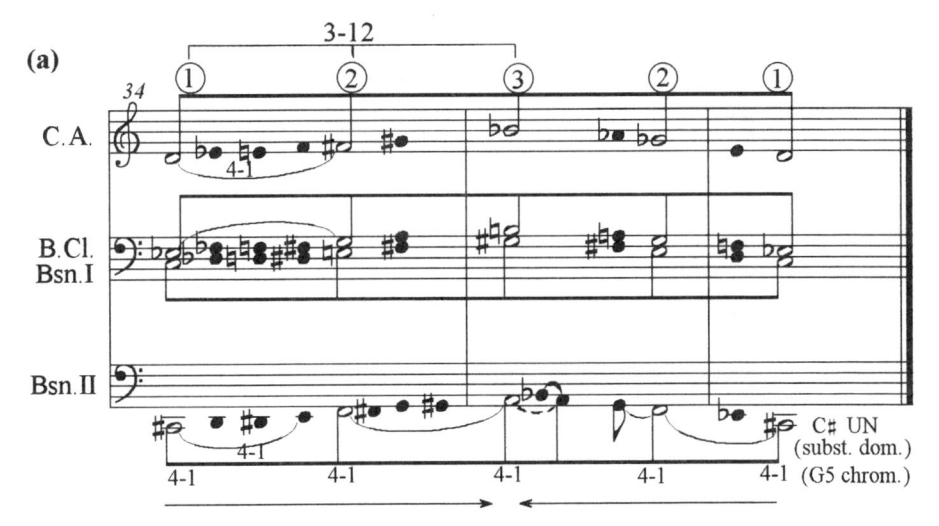

(a)

Example 3.23 (continued): III, bars 34–8

CASE STUDY 4

Seventh Complexes in 'Ipanema', from
Saudades do Brazil, Op. 67 (1920): A Comparative Analysis
with that of Keith W. Daniel

Example 4.1 *Saudades do Brazil*: 'Ipanema', bars 29–34

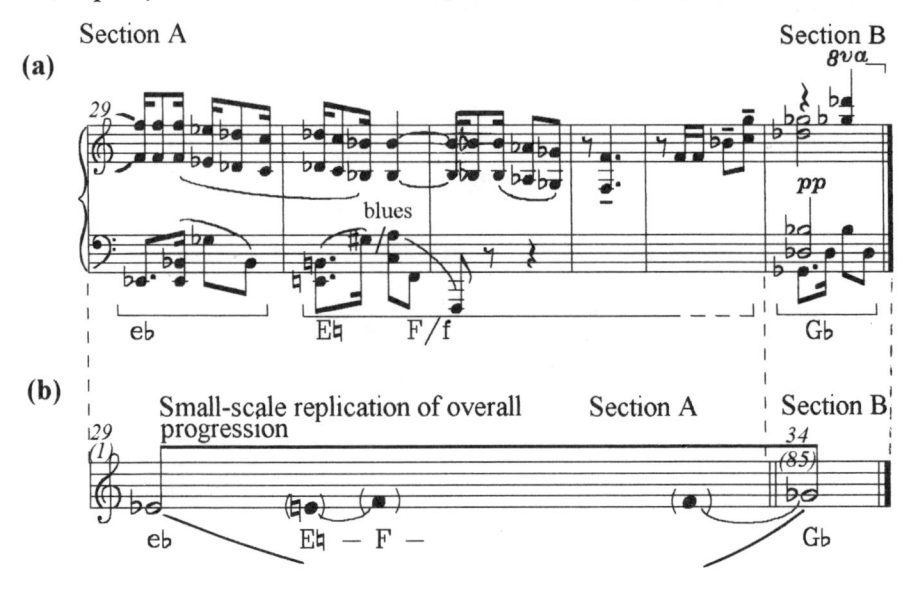

Example 4.2 *Saudades do Brazil*: 'Ipanema', bars 53-7

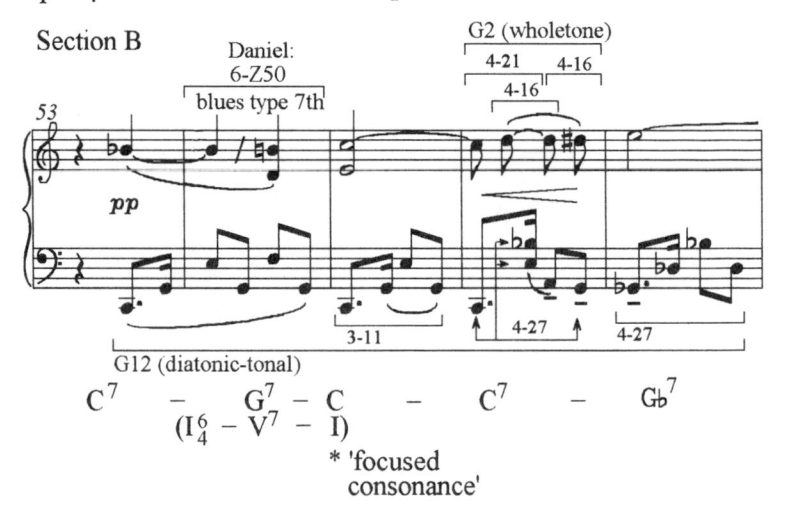

Appendix: Analytical Examples   323

Example 4.3 *Saudades do Brazil*: 'Ipanema'

Theoretical schema: Section B
Tritone-related dominant-seventh constructs

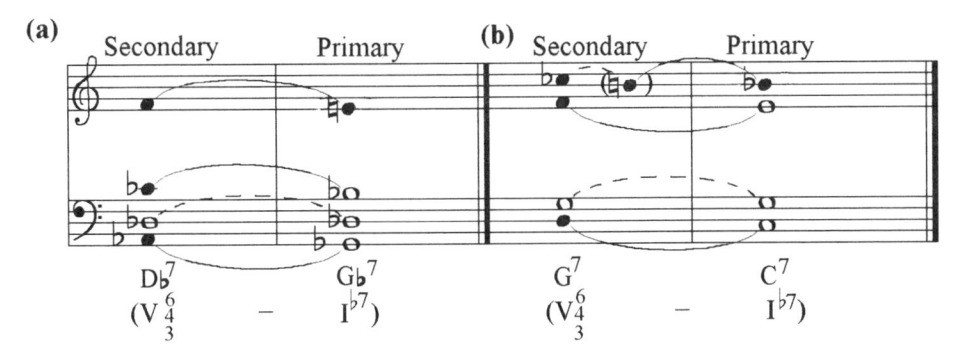

(a) Secondary — Primary

$D\flat^7$ — $G\flat^7$
$(V\begin{smallmatrix}6\\4\\3\end{smallmatrix}$ — $I^{\flat 7})$

(b) Secondary — Primary

G^7 — C^7
$(V\begin{smallmatrix}6\\4\\3\end{smallmatrix}$ — $I^{\flat 7})$

Example 4.4 *Saudades do Brazil*: 'Ipanema', bars 38–40

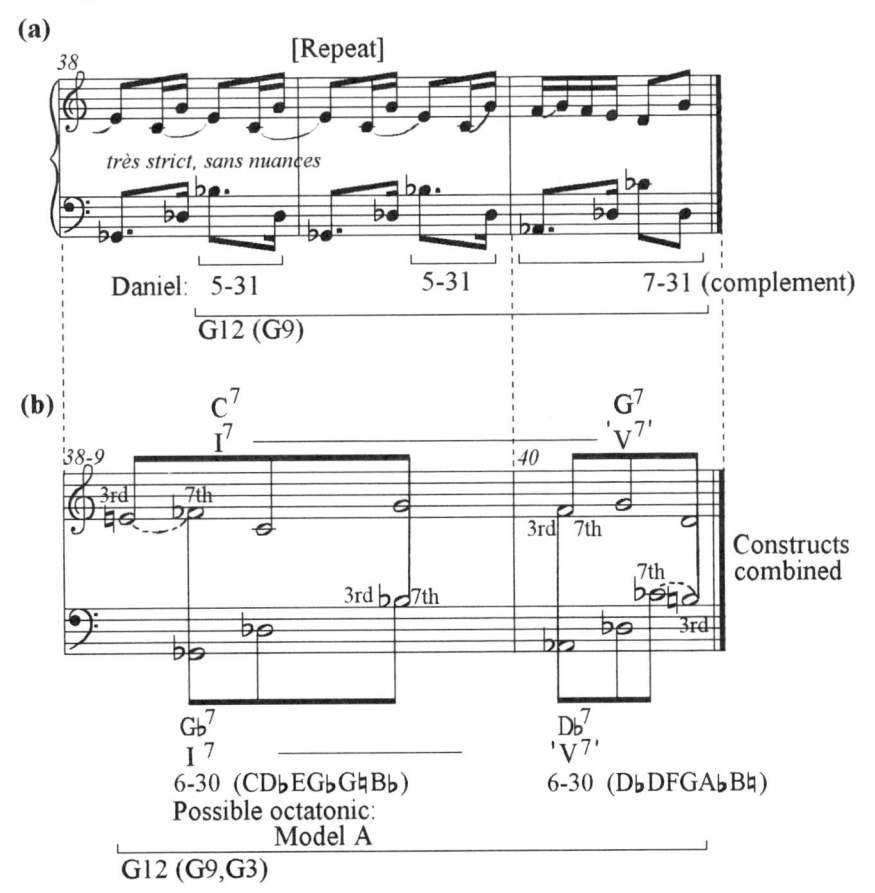

(a)
38 [Repeat]

très strict, sans nuances

Daniel: 5-31   5-31   7-31 (complement)
         G12 (G9)

(b)
        C^7 G^7
        I^7 $'V^7'$
38-9   40
3rd 7th
                                 3rd 7th
                                              Constructs
                  3rd   7th   7th   combined
                                                3rd

        $G\flat^7$ $D\flat^7$
        I^7 $'V^7'$
        6-30 (C D♭ E G♭ G♮ B♭)   6-30 (D♭ D F G A♭ B♮)
        Possible octatonic:
                Model A
        G12 (G9, G3)

Example 4.5 *Saudades do Brazil*: 'Ipanema', bars 1–5

Section A

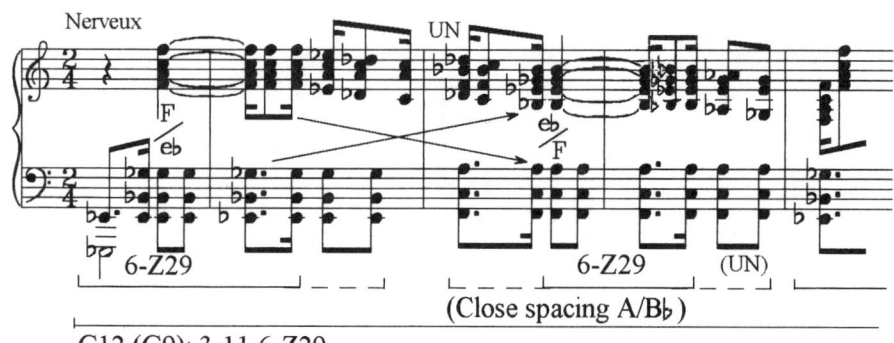

6-Z29   6-Z29   (UN)

(Close spacing A/B♭)

G12 (G9): 3-11, 6-Z29

Appendix: Analytical Examples   325

Example 4.6 *Saudades do Brazil*: 'Ipanema', bars 62–9

Section A'

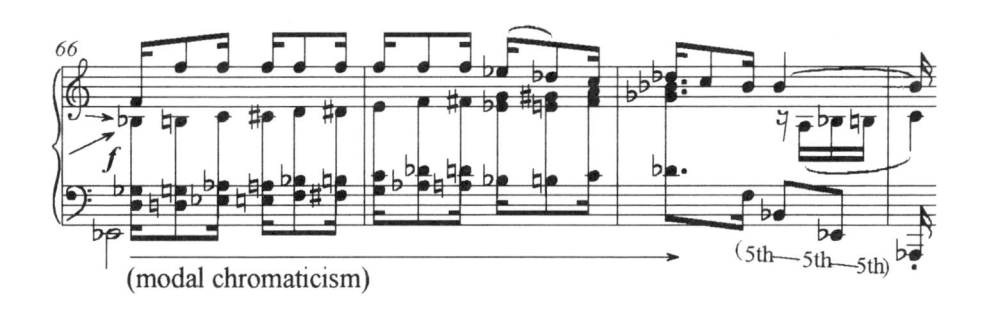

Example 4.7 *Saudades do Brazil*: 'Ipanema', bars 80–5

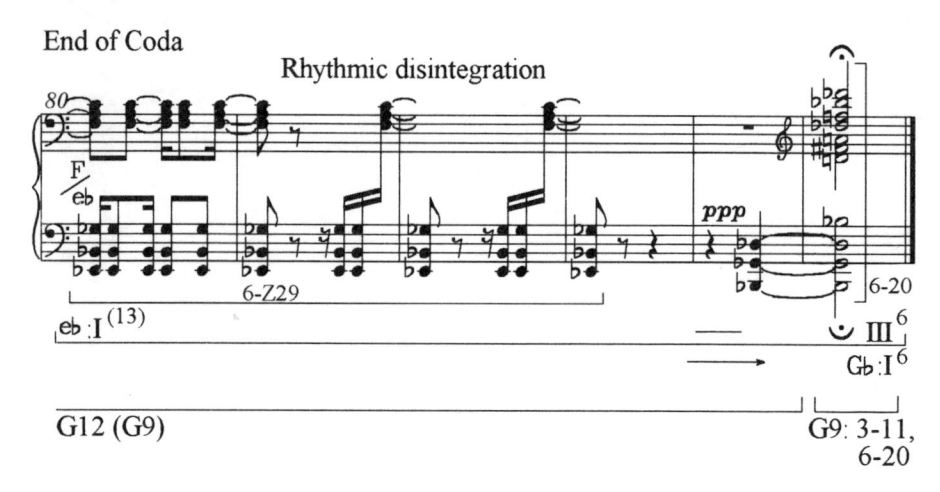

Example 4.8 *Saudades do Brazil*: 'Ipanema'

Theoretical schema

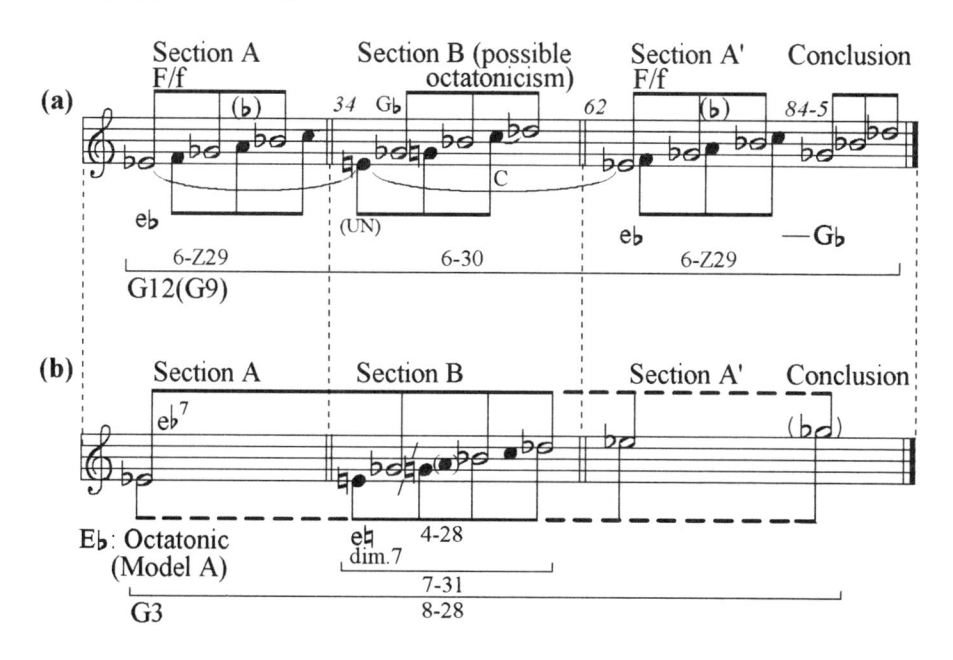

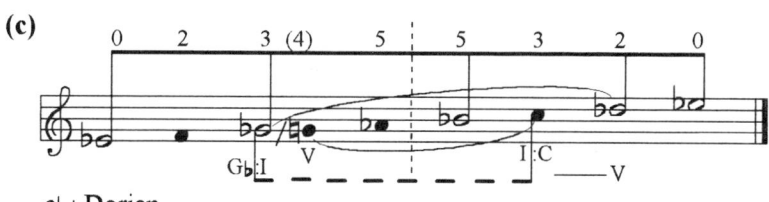

Case Study 5

Blues and Other Modal Formations in
La Création du monde: Suite de concert, Op. 81*b* (1926)

Example 4.9 *La Création du monde: Suite de concert*: I, bars 1–11

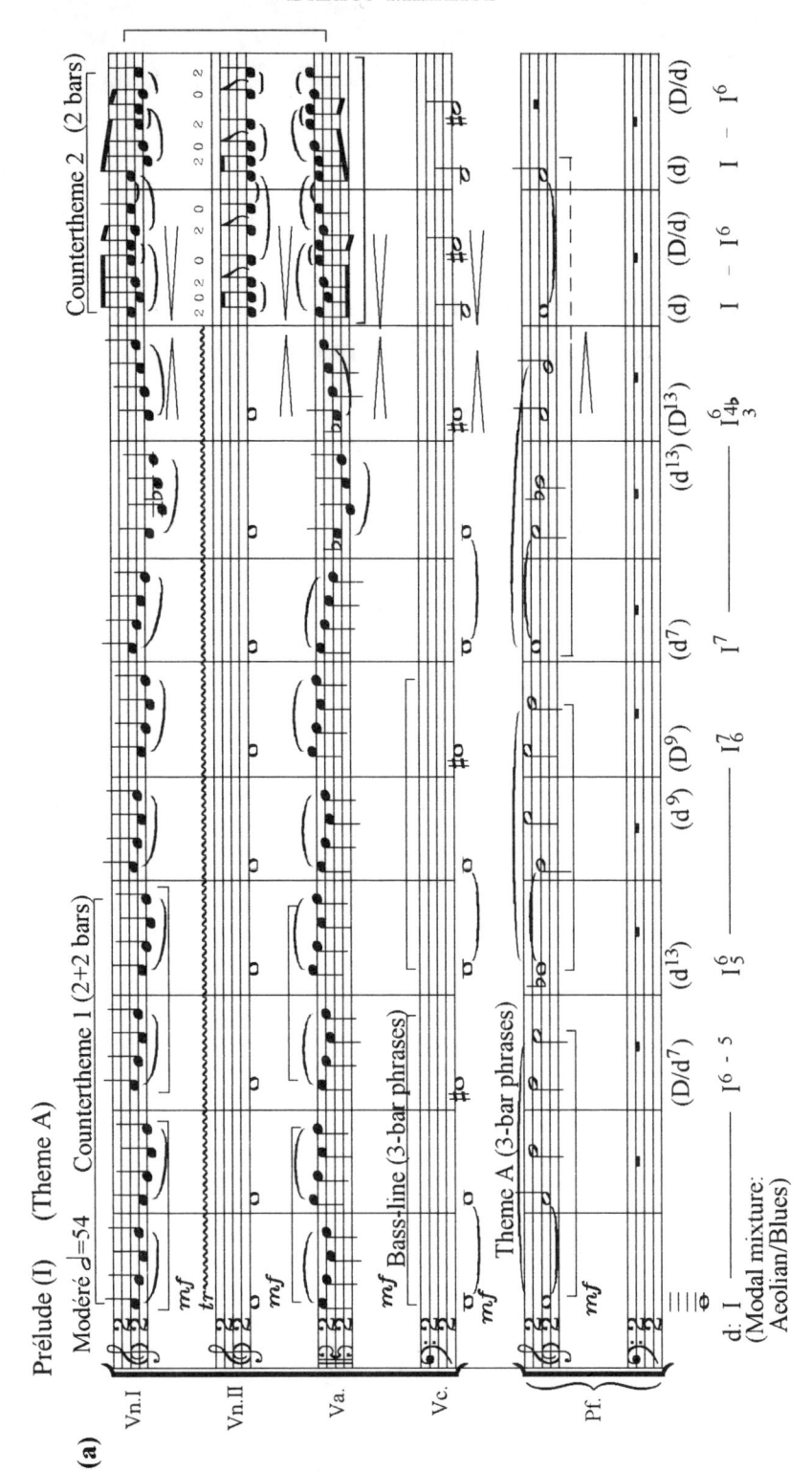

Appendix: Analytical Examples 331

Example 4.9 (continued)

(b) Theme A (first statement)

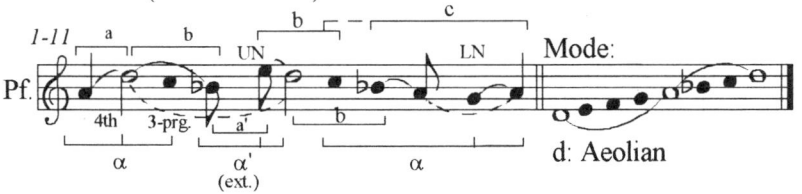

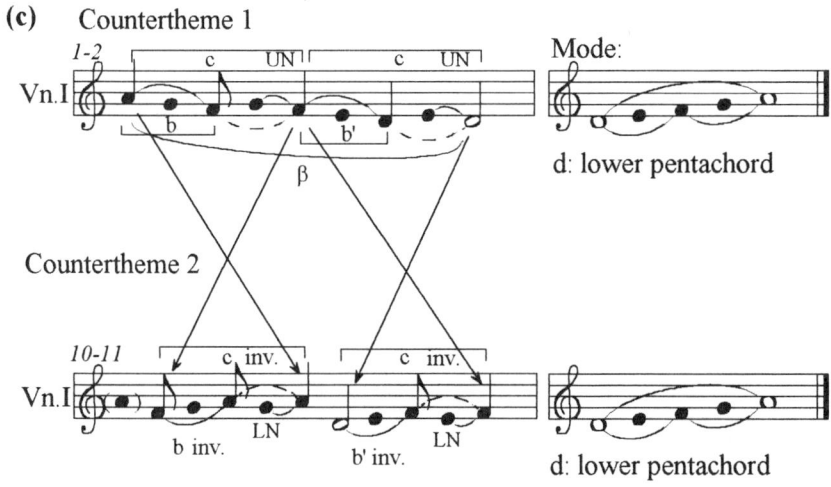

d: Aeolian

(c) Counttertheme 1

d: lower pentachord

Counttertheme 2

d: lower pentachord

(Basis for Fugue: Subject B)

332 DARIUS MILHAUD

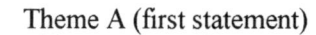

Example 4.10 *La Création du monde: Suite de concert*: I, bars 1–30

Thematic extension and transformation

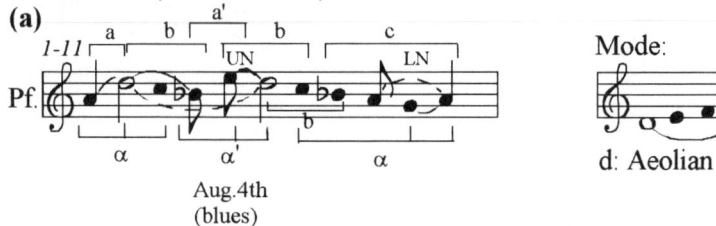

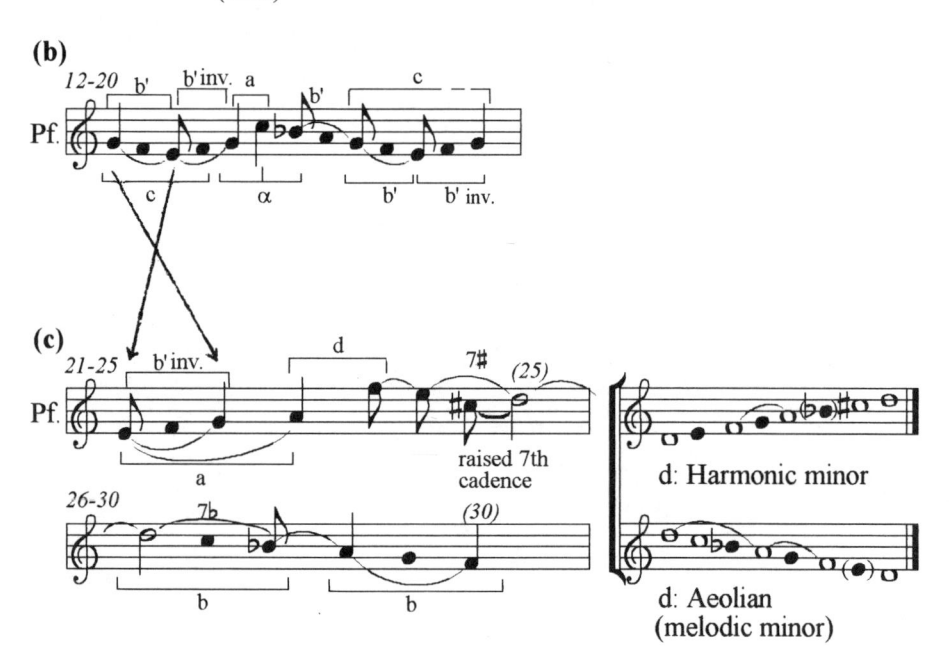

Example 4.11 *La Création du monde: Suite de concert*: I, bars 83–95

Thematic extension and transformation (cont.)

Theme A (fourth statement)

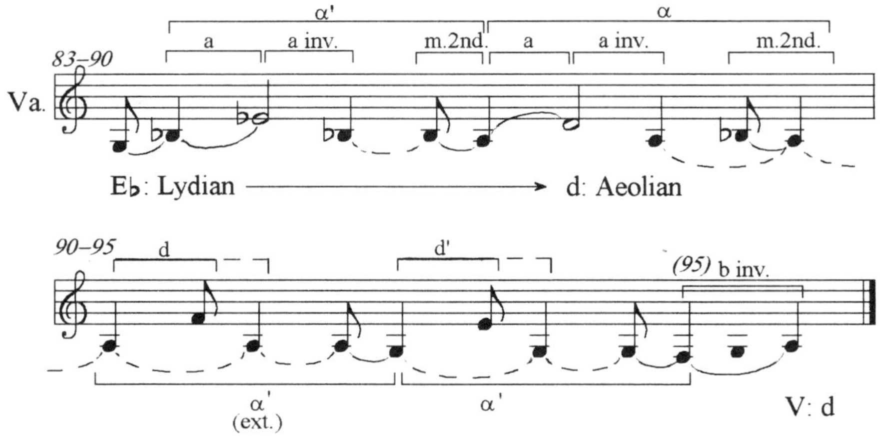

334 Darius Milhaud

Example 4.12 *La Création du monde: Suite de concert*: II, bars 1–6

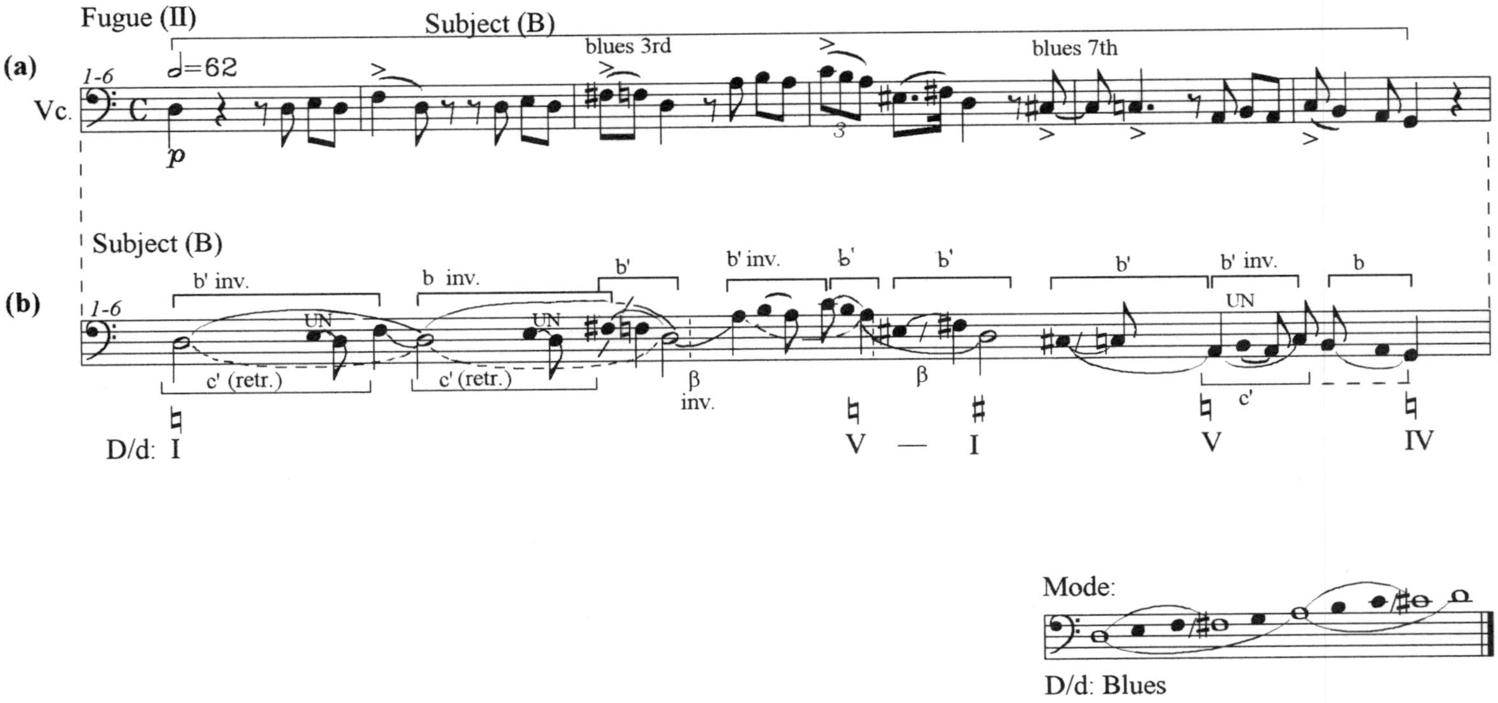

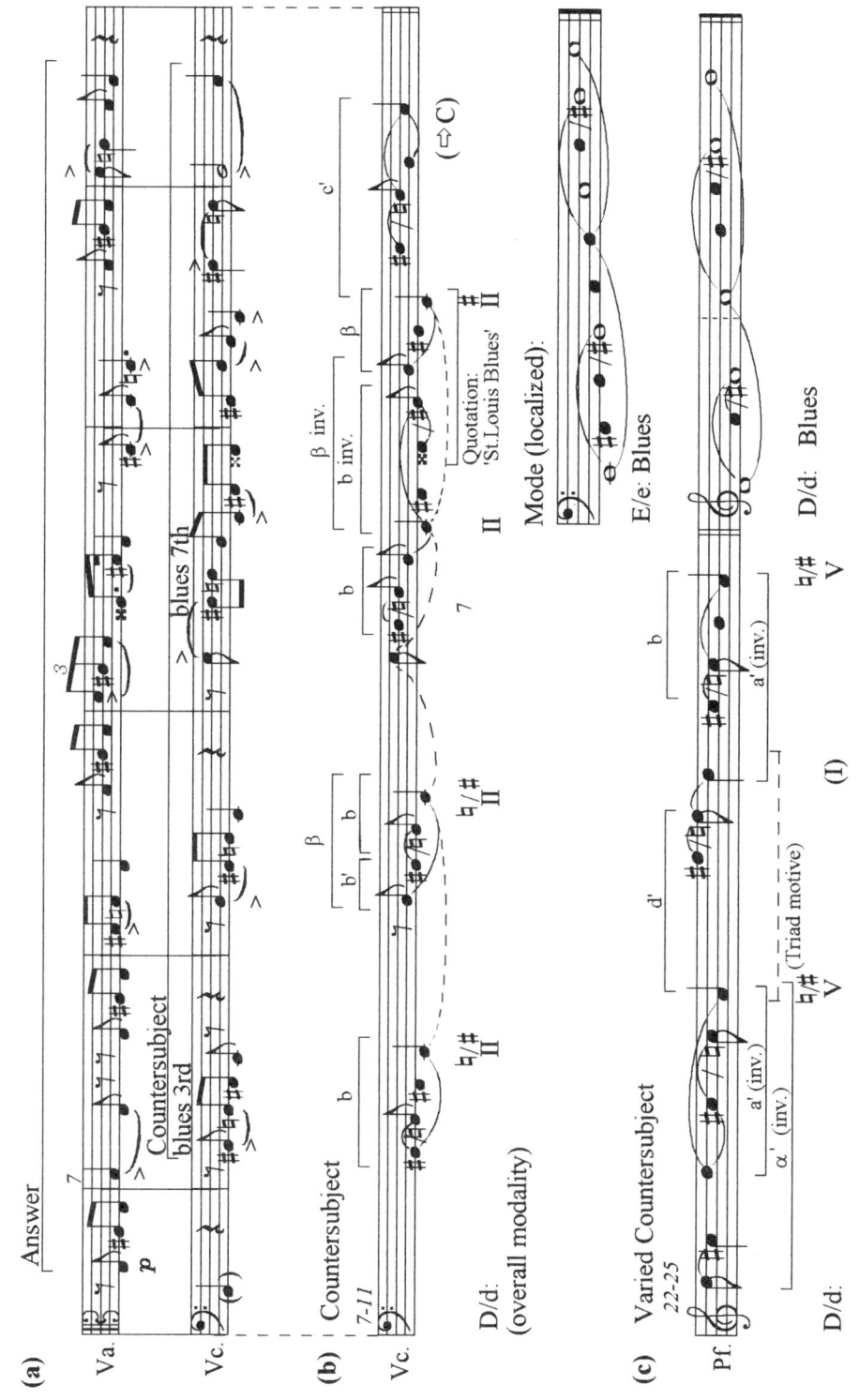

Example 4.12 (continued): II, bars 7–11

336 DARIUS MILHAUD

Example 4.13 *La Création du monde: Suite de concert*: III, bars 1–17

Appendix: Analytical Examples 337

Example 4.13 (continued): III, bars 1–17; 42–6

(b) Theme B (from Fugue)

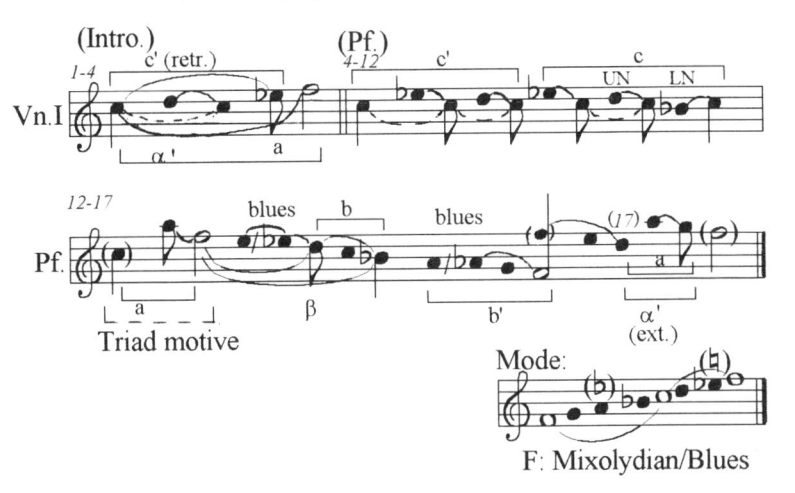

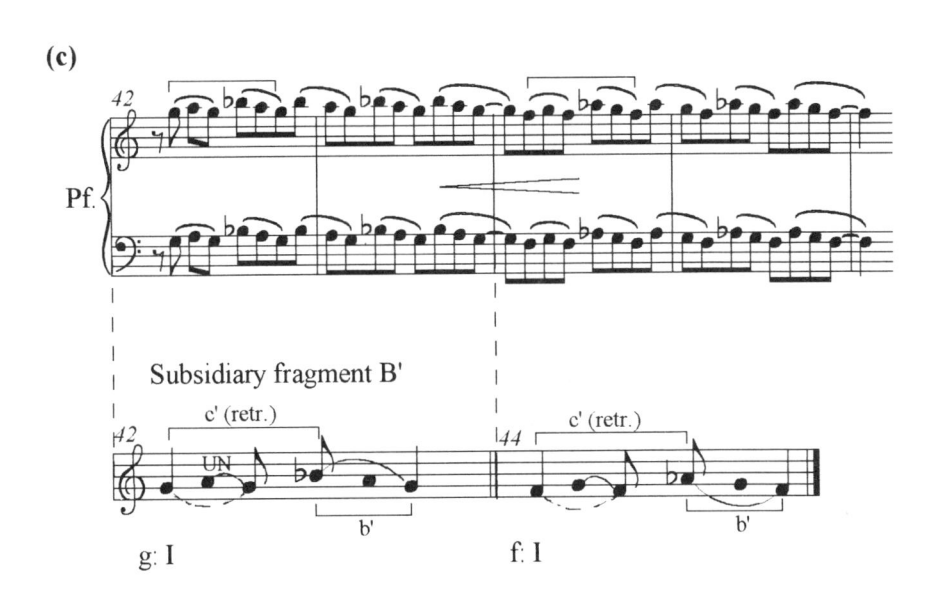

(c)

Example 4.14 *La Création du monde: Suite de concert*: IV, bars 1–8

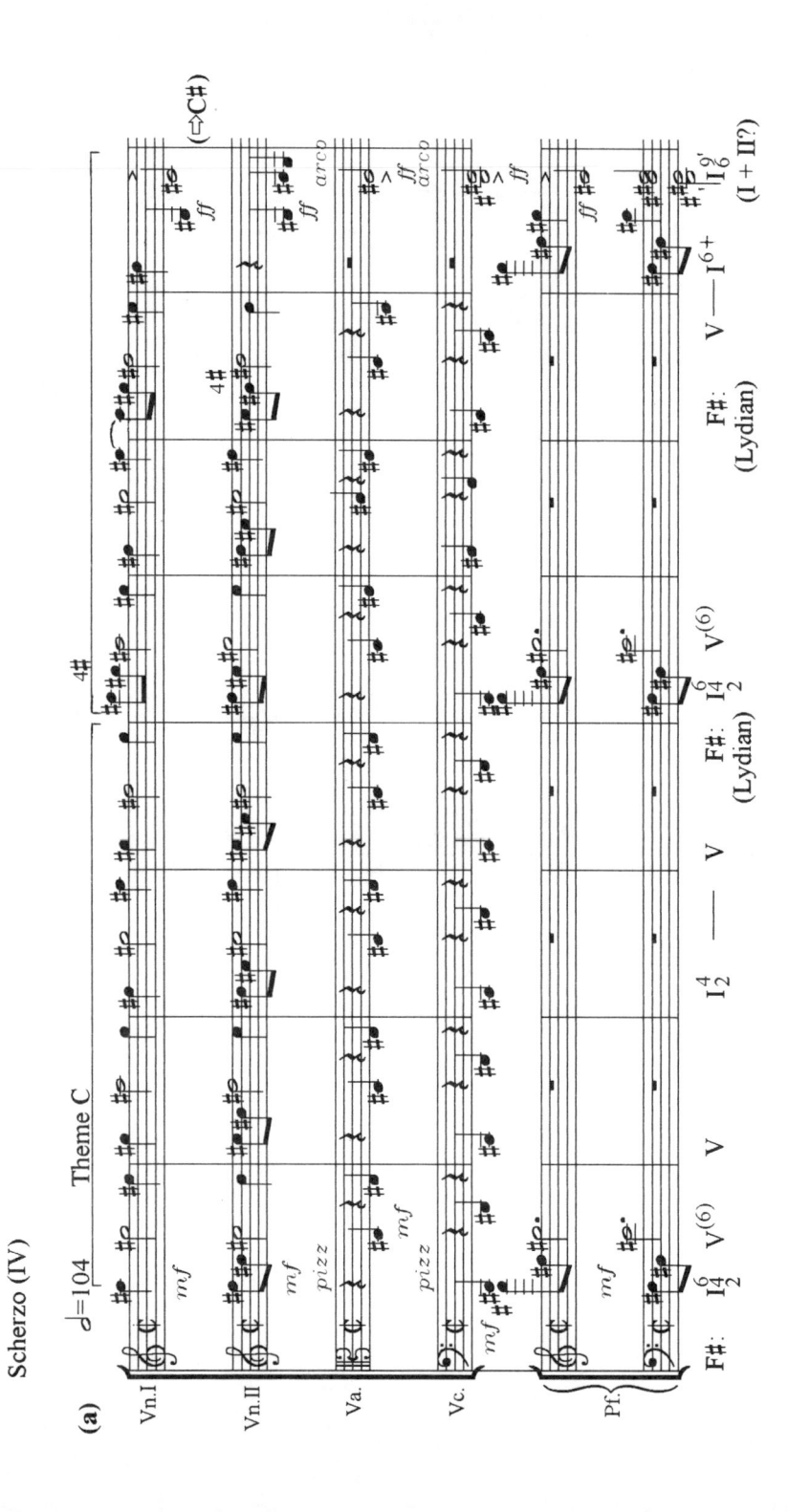

Appendix: Analytical Examples   339

Example 4.14 (continued): IV, bars 1–12; 63–7

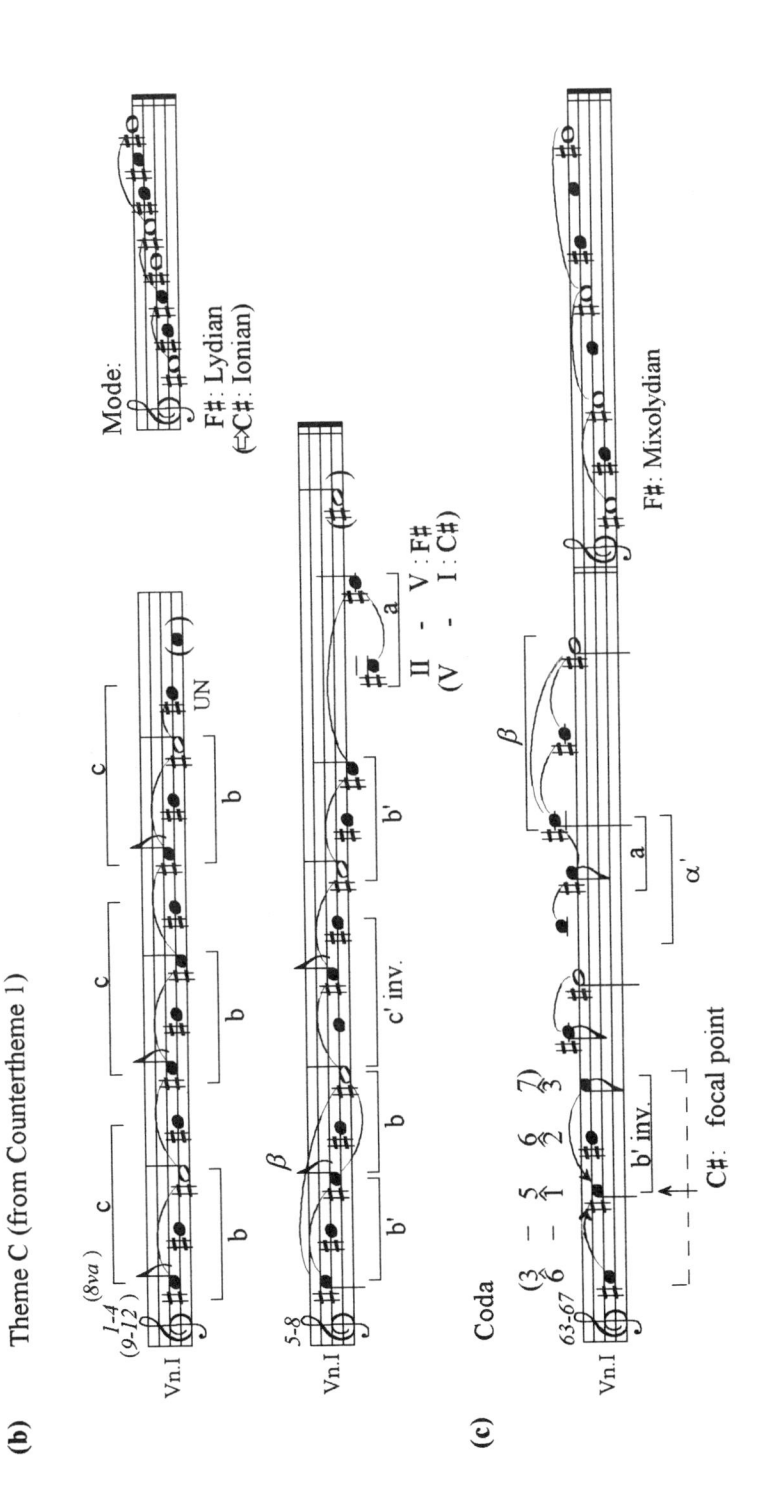

(b) Theme C (from Countertheme 1)

(c) Coda

Example 4.15 *La Création du monde: Suite de concert*: V, bars 1–15

Appendix: Analytical Examples   341

Example 4.16 *La Création du monde: Suite de concert*: V, bars 16–25

Example 4.16 (continued): V, bars 16–30

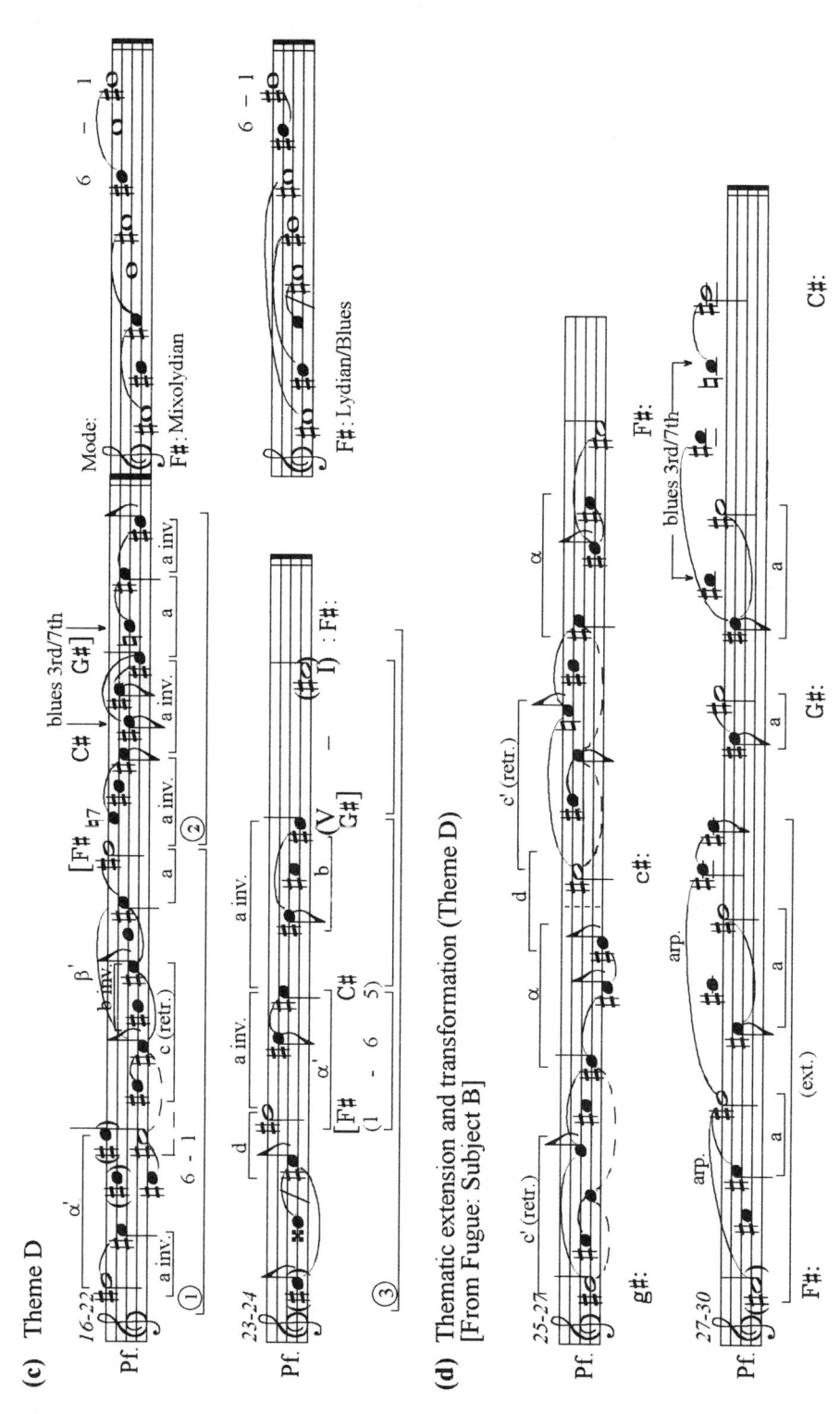

(c) Theme D

(d) Thematic extension and transformation (Theme D) [From Fugue: Subject B]

Example 4.17 *La Création du monde: Suite de concert*: V, bars 60–5

344   Darius Milhaud

Example 4.18 *La Création du monde: Suite de concert*: V, bars 66–71; 72–7

Example 4.19 *La Création du monde: Suite de concert*: V, bars 182–90

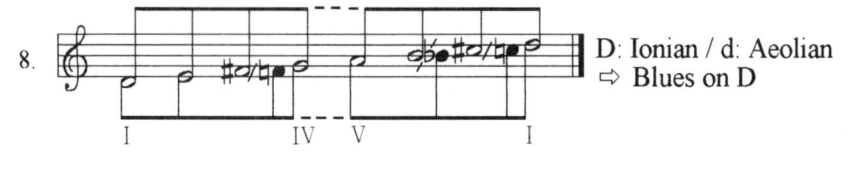

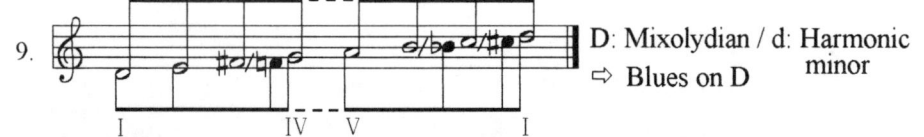

Example 4.20 *La Création du monde: Suite de concert*

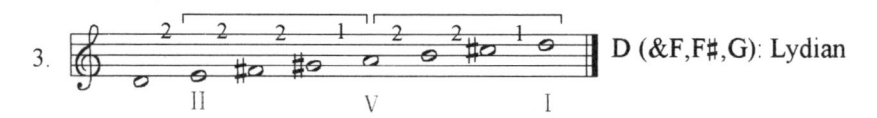

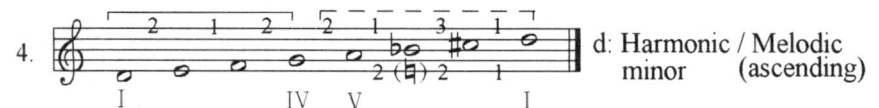

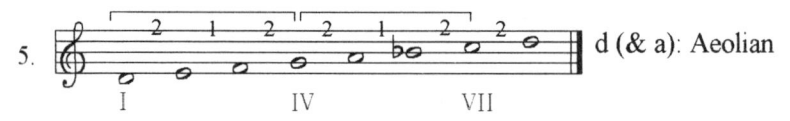

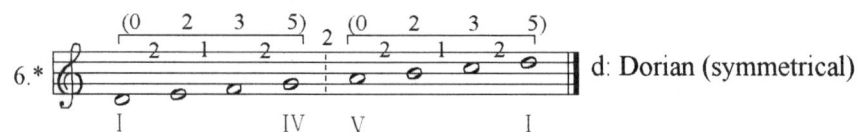

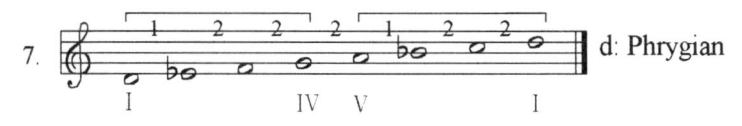

Appendix: Analytical Examples 347

Example 4.21 *La Création du monde: Suite de concert*

Modal complementation of themes

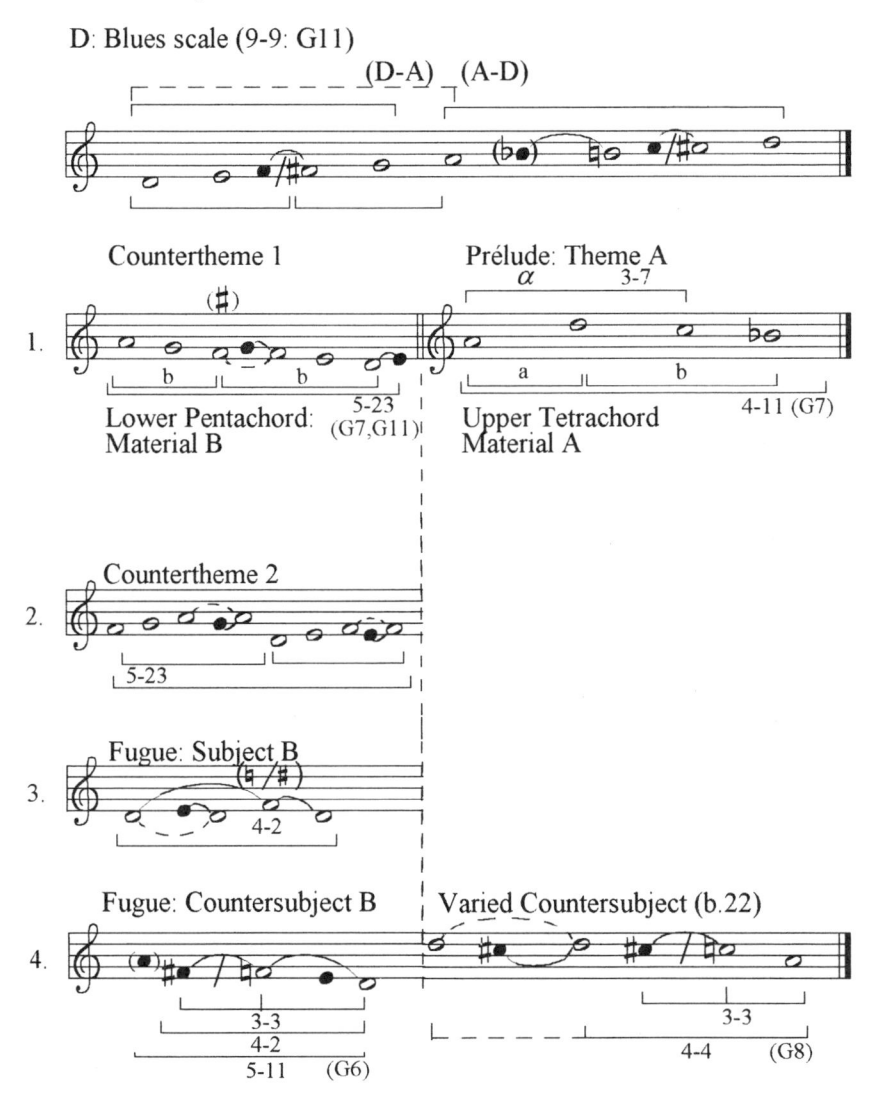

Example 4.21 (continued)

Modal complementation of themes (cont.)

D: Blues scale (9-9: G11)

Case Study 6

Modality and Tension Theory in 'La femme que j'aime',
from *Quatre poèmes de Catulle*, Op. 80 (1923)

350   DARIUS MILHAUD

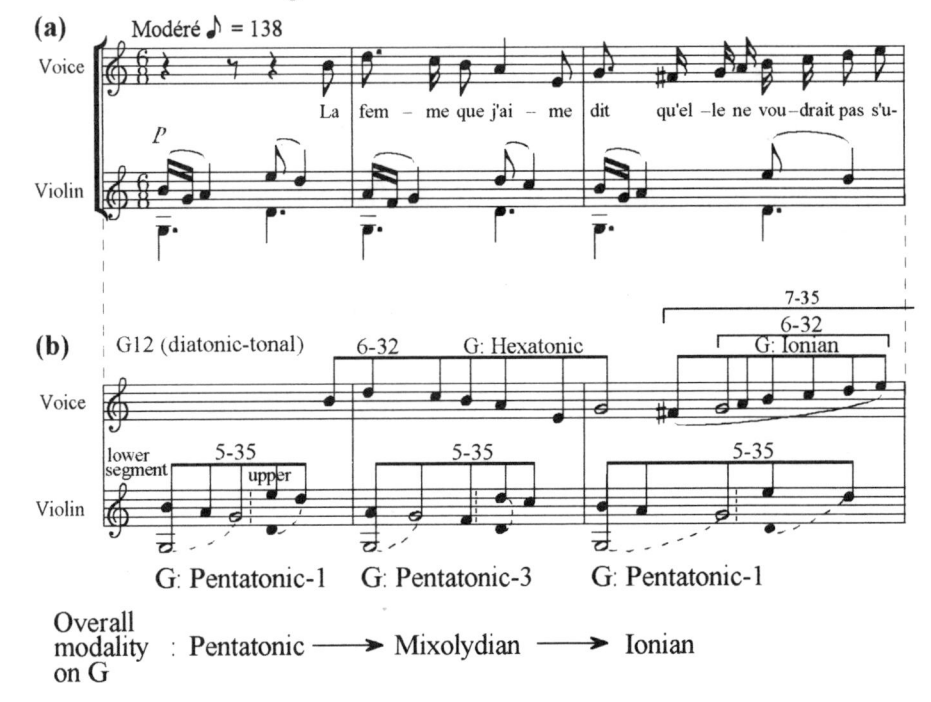

Example 5.1 *Quatre poèmes de Catulle*: I, bars 1–3

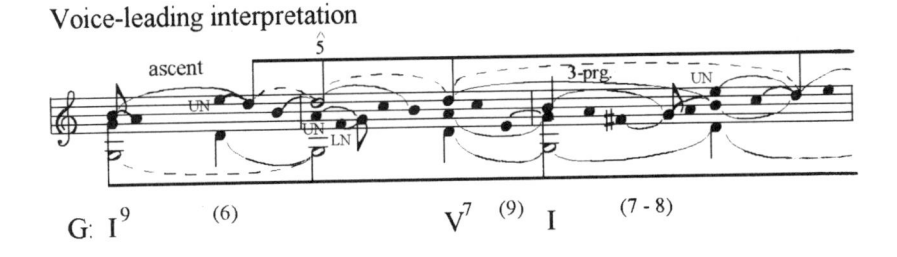

Appendix: Analytical Examples

Example 5.1 (continued): I, bars 4–6

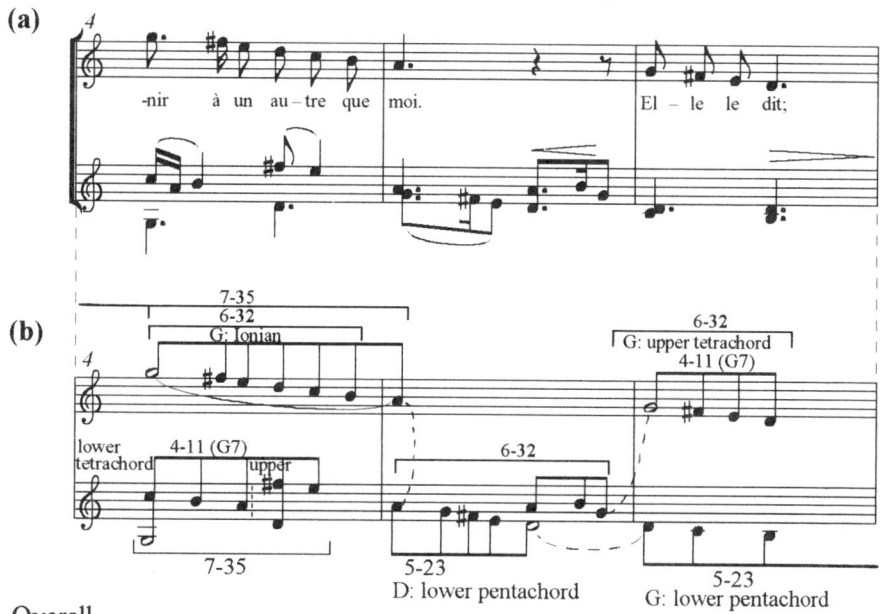

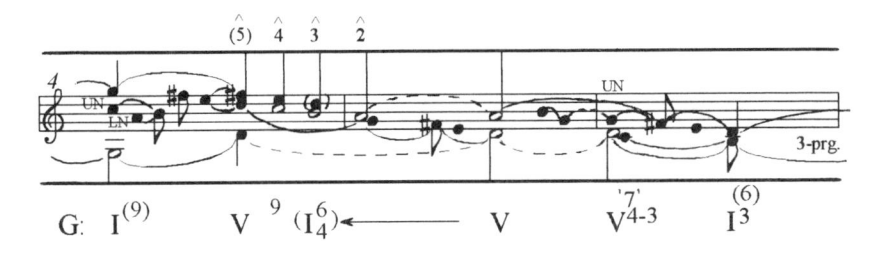

352　　　　　　　　　　　Darius Milhaud

Example 5.1 (continued): I, bars 7–9

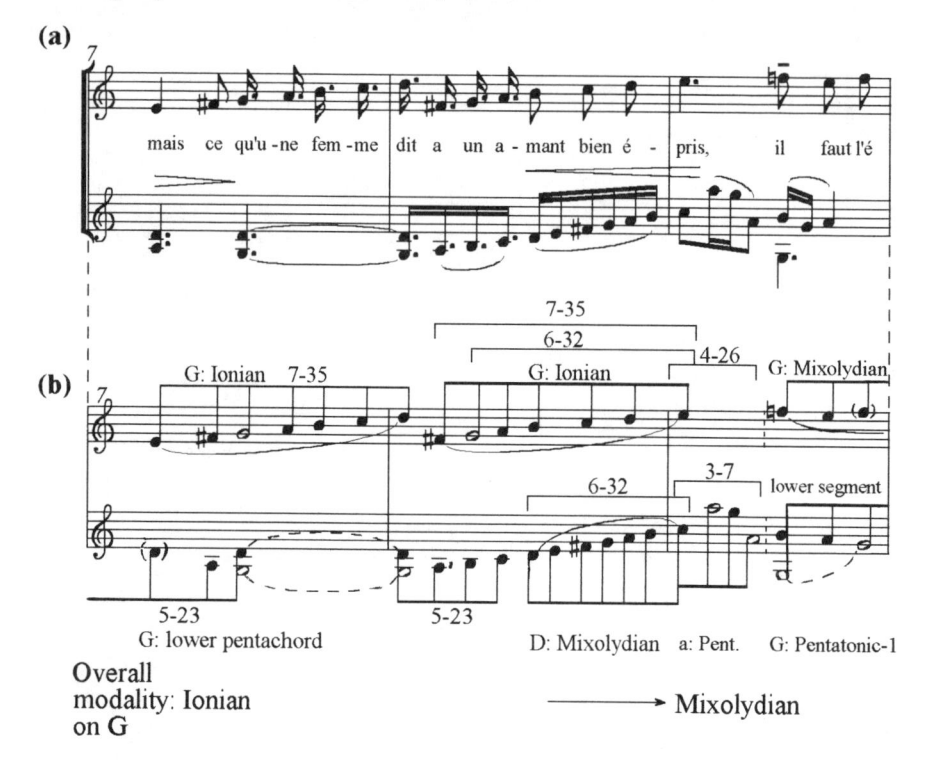

(a) mais ce qu'u-ne fem-me dit a un a-mant bien é-pris, il faut l'é

(b) G: Ionian 7-35 | 7-35 | 6-32 | 4-26 | G: Mixolydian
G: Ionian
6-32 | 3-7 lower segment
5-23 | 5-23
G: lower pentachord | D: Mixolydian | a: Pent. | G: Pentatonic-1

Overall modality: Ionian on G ⟶ Mixolydian

Example 5.2 (continued): I, bars 7–9

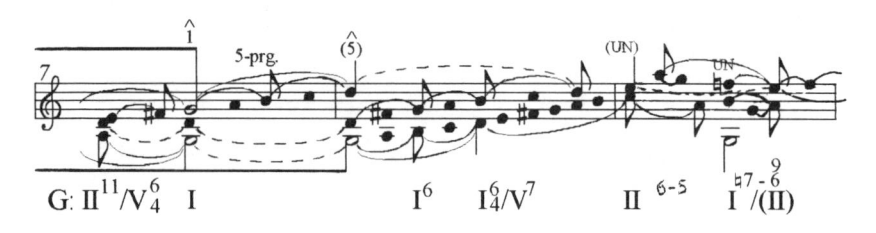

G: II^{11}/V$^6_4$ I   I^6 I$^6_4$/V^7 II $^{6-5}$ I $^{\natural 7 - {6 \atop 9}}$/(II)

Appendix: Analytical Examples 353

Example 5.1 (continued): I, bars 10–11

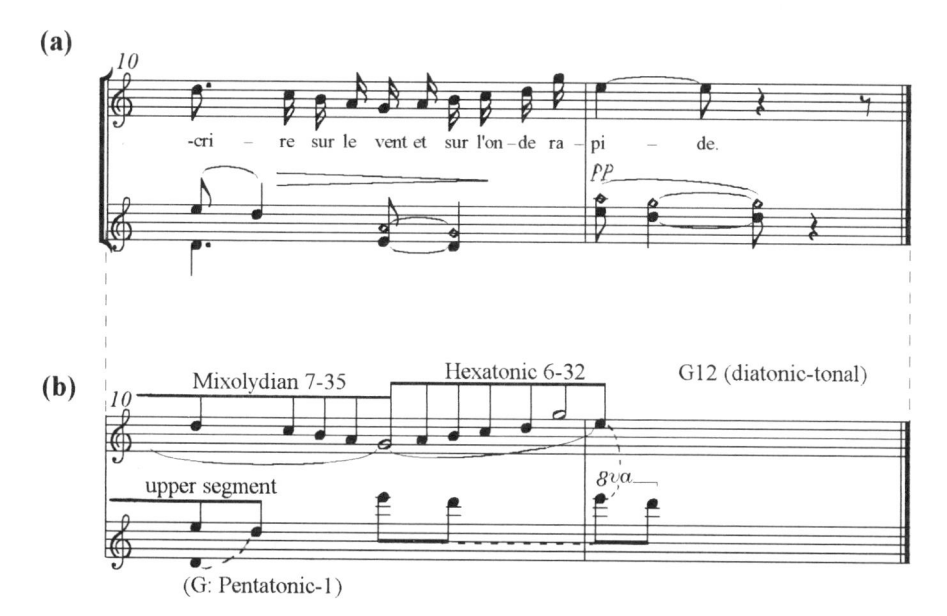

(a)

-cri - re sur le vent et sur l'on - de ra - pi - de.

pp

(b)

Mixolydian 7-35 | Hexatonic 6-32 | G12 (diatonic-tonal)

upper segment

(G: Pentatonic-1)

Overall modality : Mixolydian → Hexatonic on G

Example 5.2 (continued): I, bars 10–11

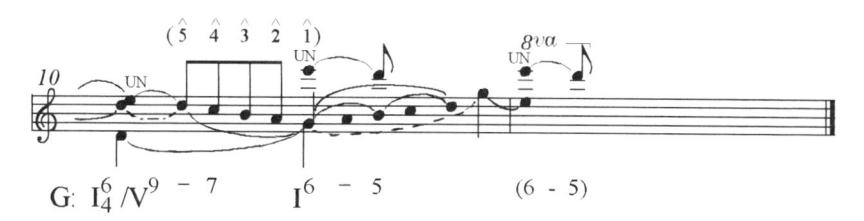

($\hat{5}$ $\hat{4}$ $\hat{3}$ $\hat{2}$ $\hat{1}$)

G: I_4^6 / V^{9-7} I^{6-5} (6 - 5)

Darius Milhaud

Example 5.3 *Quatre poèmes de Catulle*: I, bars 1–6

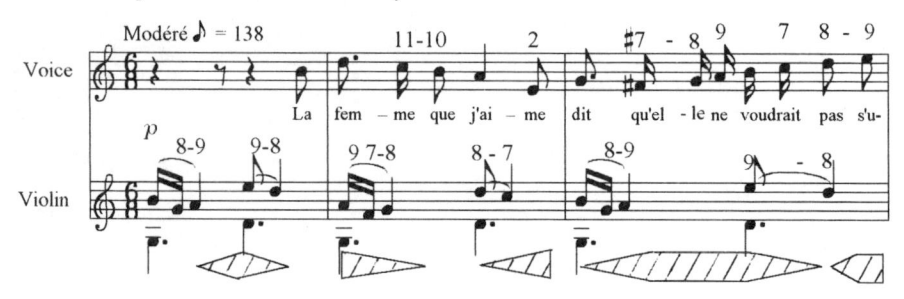

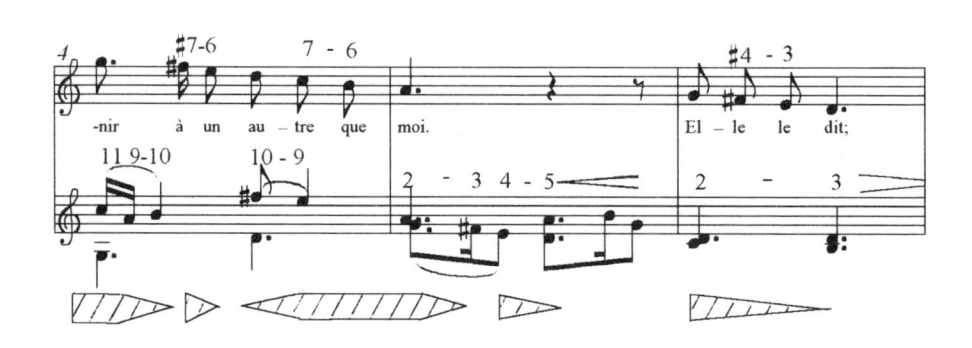

Example 5.3 (continued): I, bars 7–11

Case Study 7

Sonatine pour clarinette et piano, Op. 100 (1927):
Rethinking Modality and Sonata Principles

358 DARIUS MILHAUD

Example 5.4 Clarinet Sonatina: I, bars 1–4

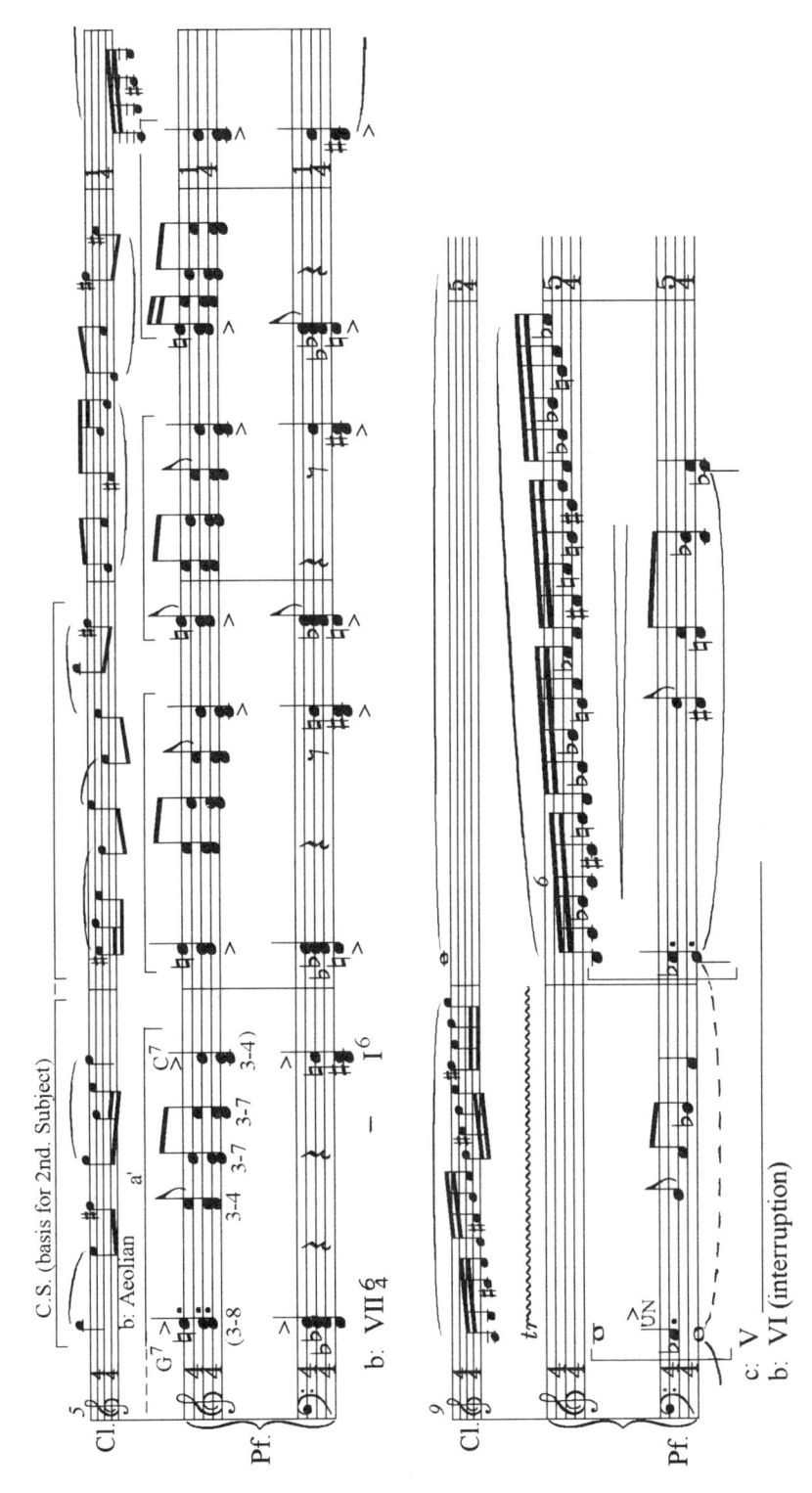

Example 5.5 Clarinet Sonatina: I, bars 5–10

360   Darius Milhaud

Example 5.6   Clarinet Sonatina: I

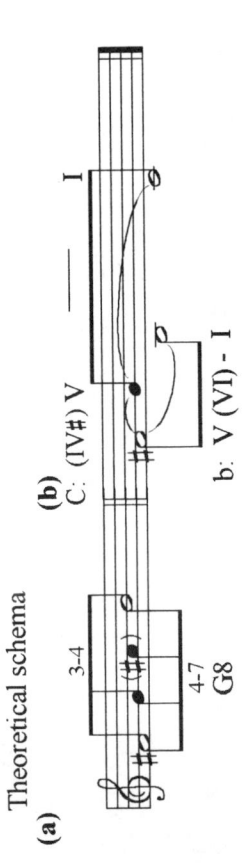

Theoretical schema

(a)   (b)
                          C: (IV♯) V ———— I

                          b: V (VI) - I

Example 5.7   Clarinet Sonatina: I, bars 1–6
Voice-leading interpretation
Foreground level: bars 1-16

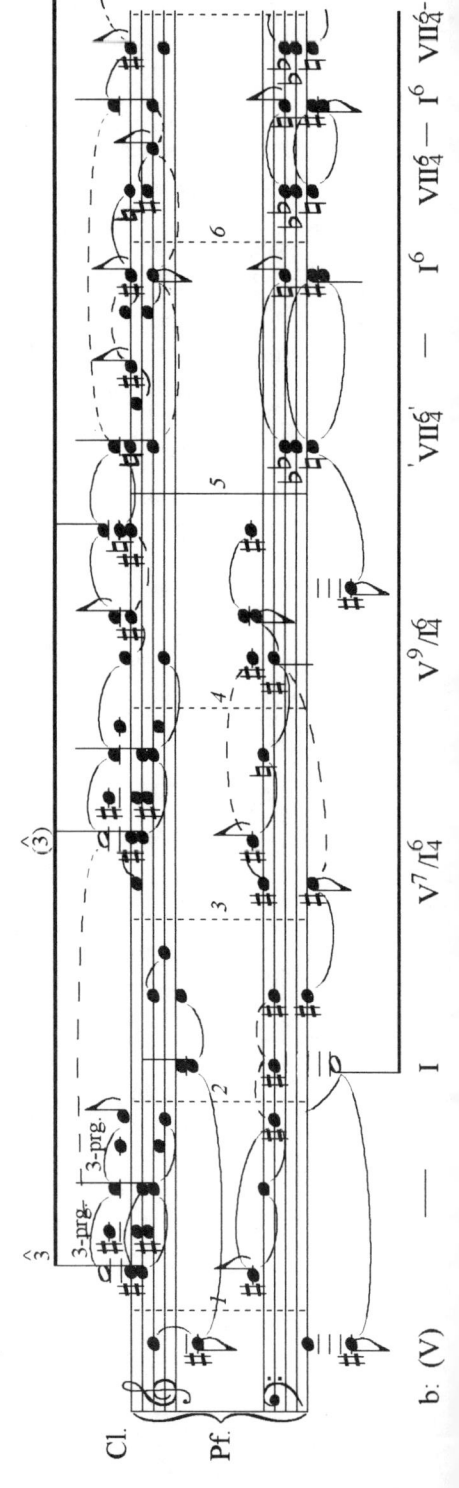

b: (V)   I   V⁷/I⁶₄   V⁹/I⁶₄   'VII⁶₄'   I⁶   VII⁶₄ – I⁶   VII⁶₄–

Appendix: Analytical Examples 361

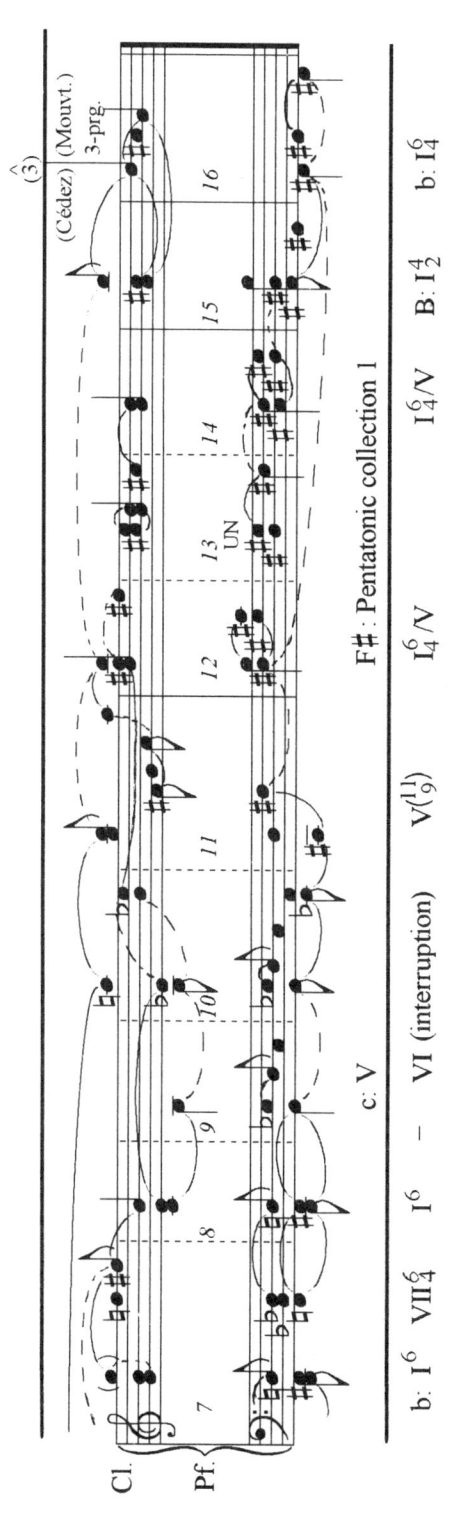

Example 5.7 (continued): I, bars 7–16

362 DARIUS MILHAUD

Example 5.8 Clarinet Sonatina: I, bars 16–19; 20–4

Example 5.9 Clarinet Sonatina: I, bars 26–9

Example 5.10 Clarinet Sonatina: I, bars 34–8

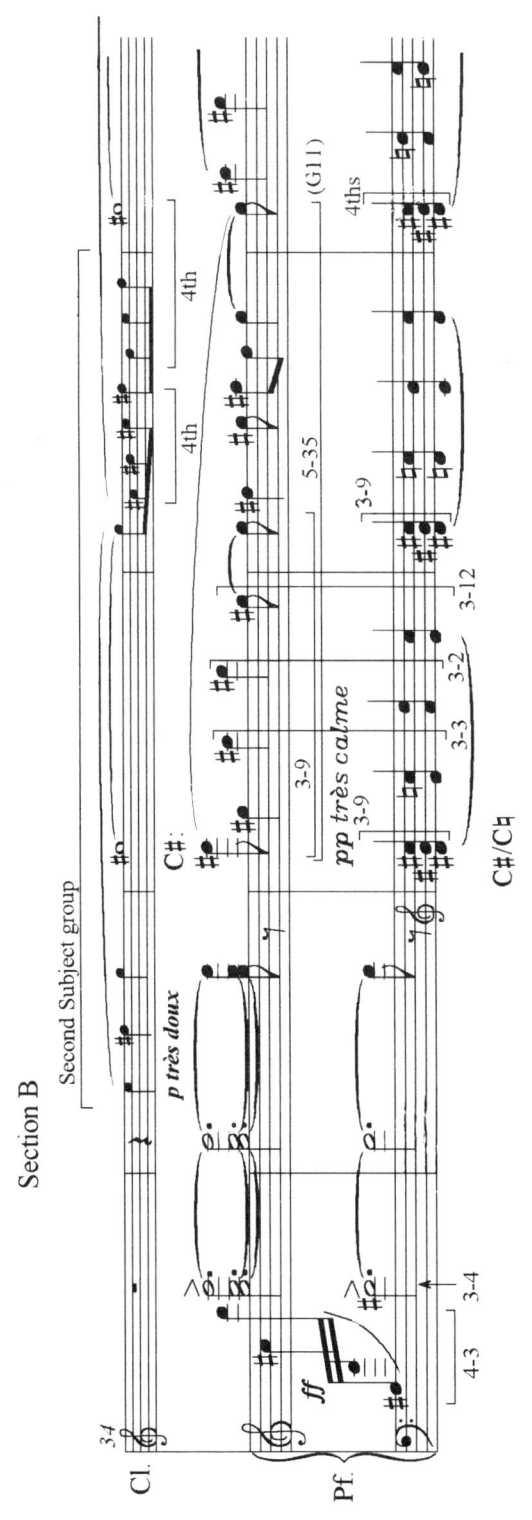

364 DARIUS MILHAUD

Example 5.11 Clarinet Sonatina: I, bars 72–3

[Section A/B]

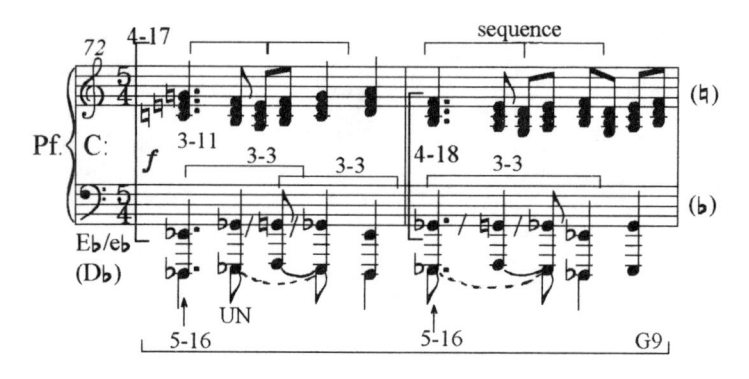

Example 5.12 Clarinet Sonatina: I, bars 83–5

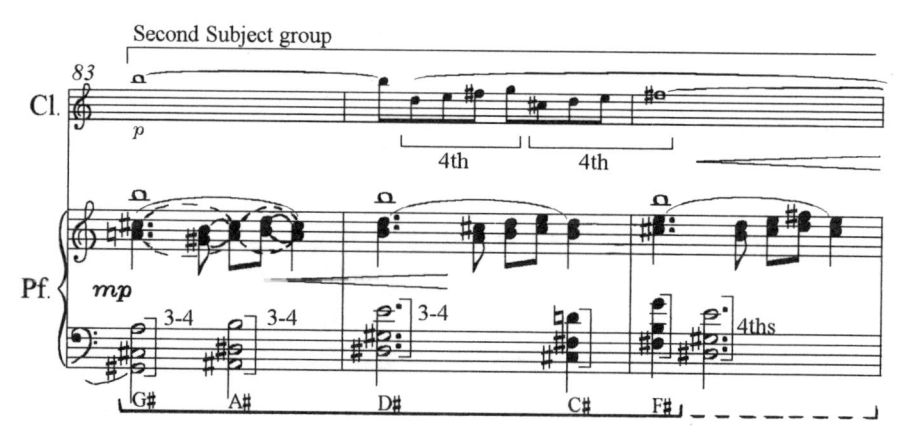

F♯: Pentatonic collection 1 (5-35)

B/b: I$^9_6_4$

Example 5.13 Clarinet Sonatina: II, bars 1–4

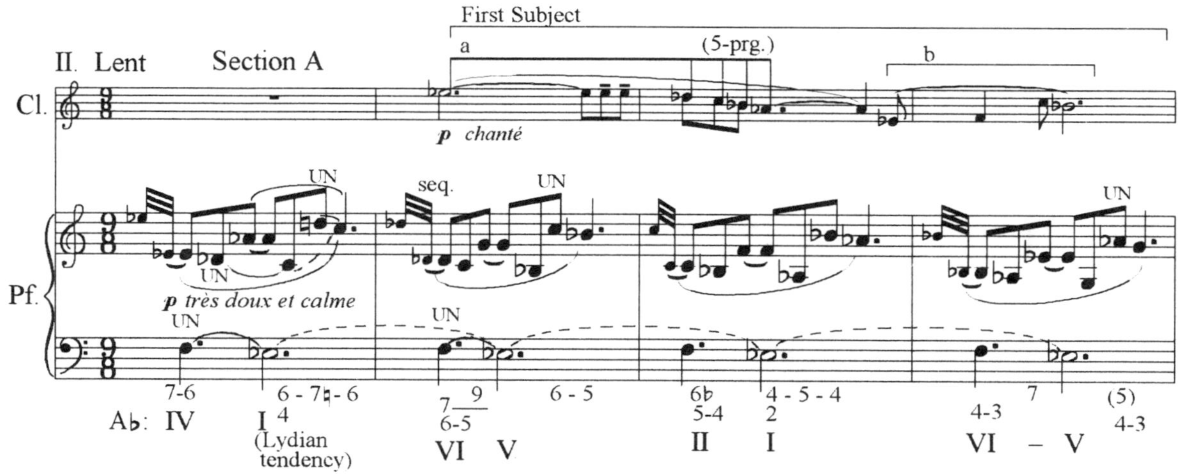

Example 5.14 Clarinet Sonatina: II, bars 6 & 13

366 DARIUS MILHAUD

Example 5.15 Clarinet Sonatina: II, bars 14–16; 35–9

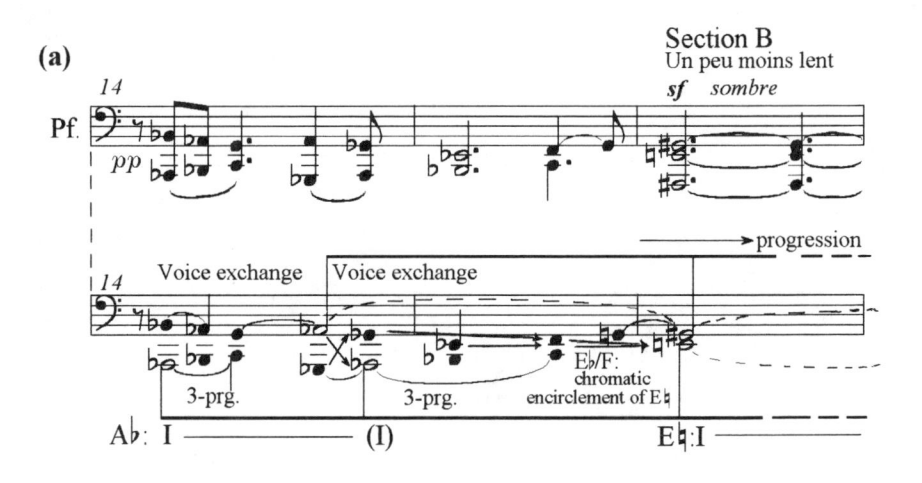

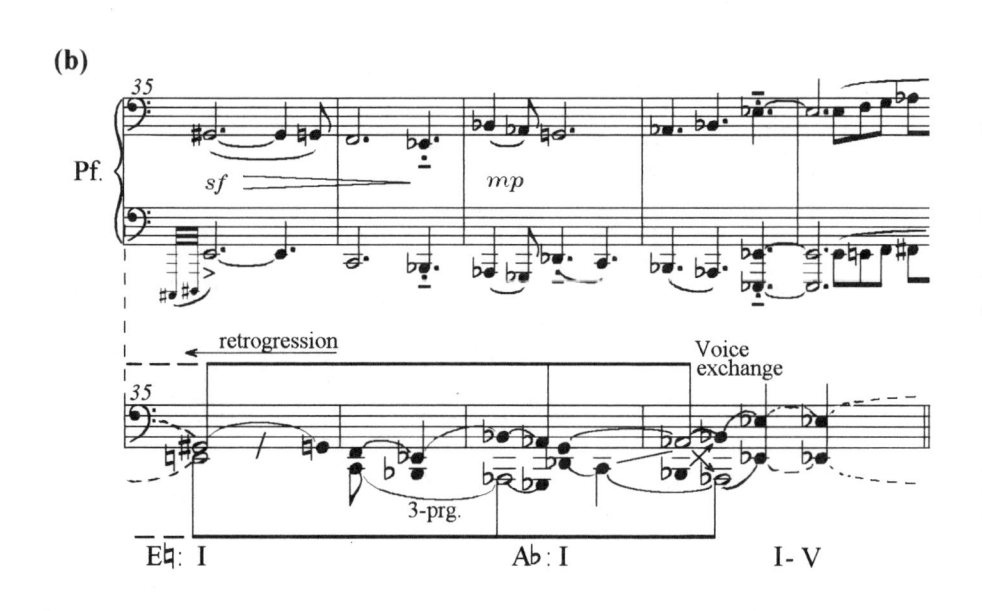

Appendix: Analytical Examples 367

Example 5.15 (continued): II, bars 14–16; 35–37/8

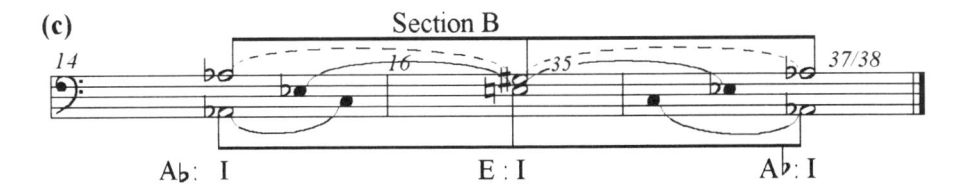

Example 5.16 Clarinet Sonatina: II, bars 16–20(ff.)

Example 5.17 Clarinet Sonatina: II, bars 54–8

Appendix: Analytical Examples 369

Example 5.18 Clarinet Sonatina: III, bars 1–5

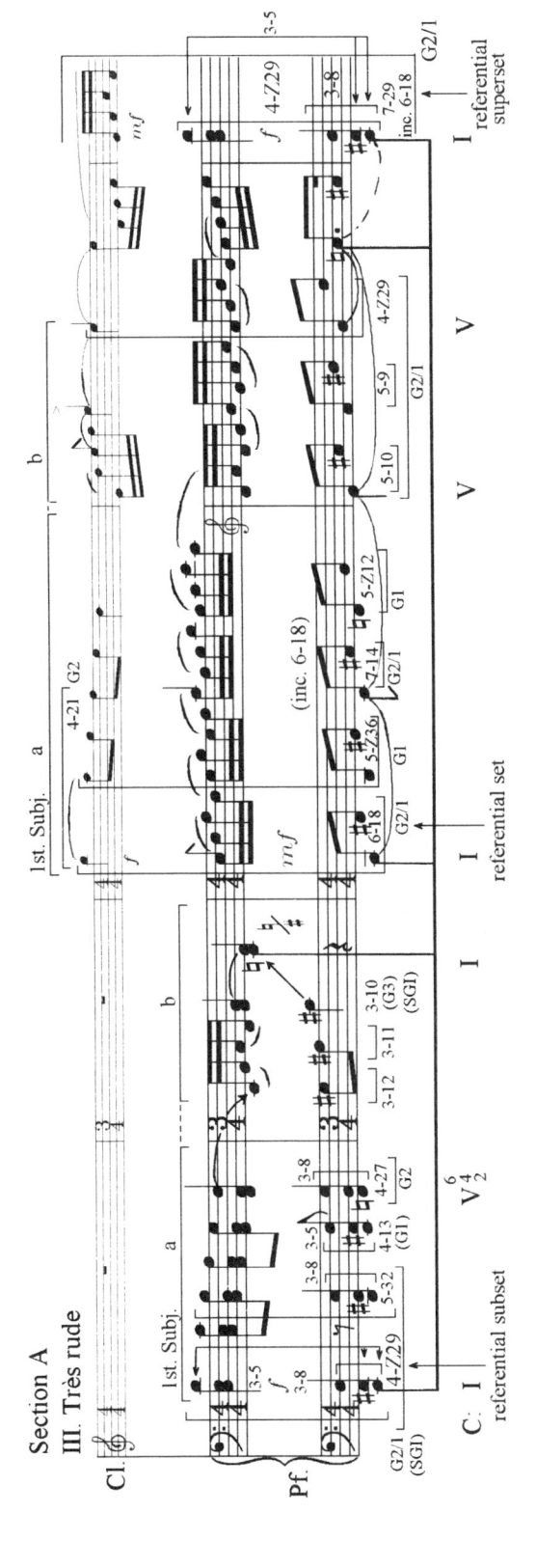

370   Darius Milhaud

Example 5.19   Clarinet Sonatina: III, bars 1–5(ff.)

Modes

(a) C: Lydian

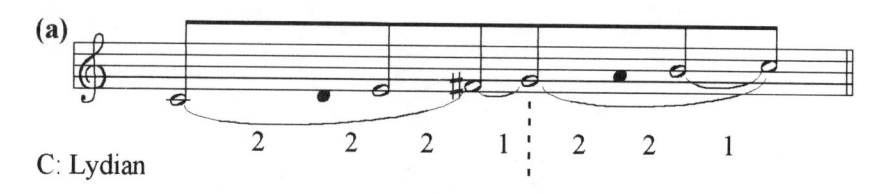

(b) C: Octatonic (Model A)

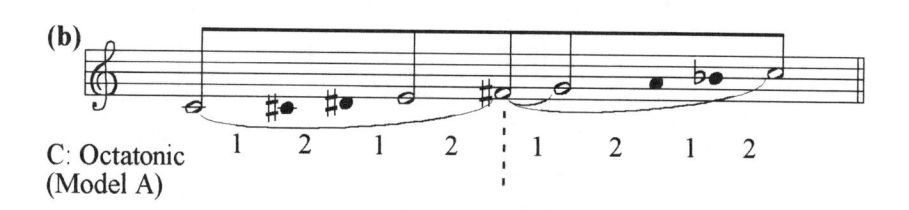

(c) C: Referential Superset

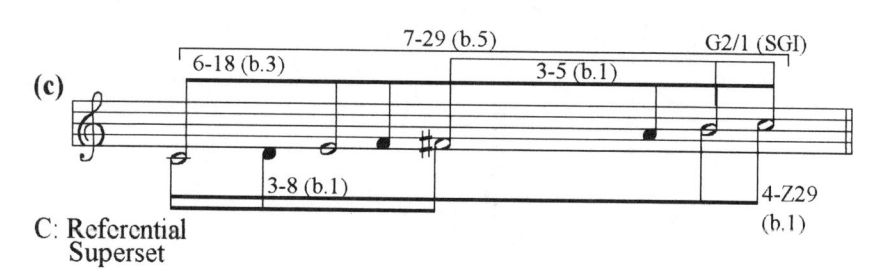

(d) C: Lydian (with chromatic encirclement of I & V)

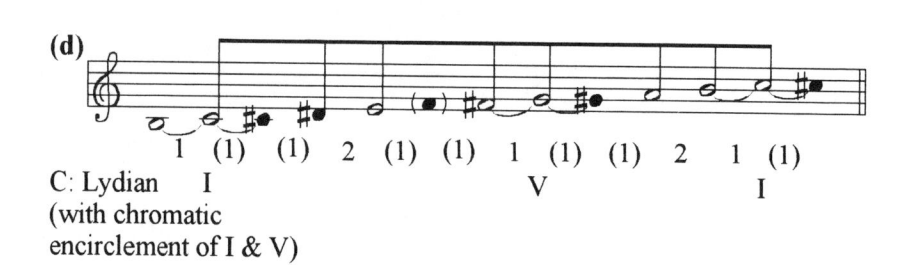

Appendix: Analytical Examples 371

Example 5.20 Clarinet Sonatina: III, bars 5–9

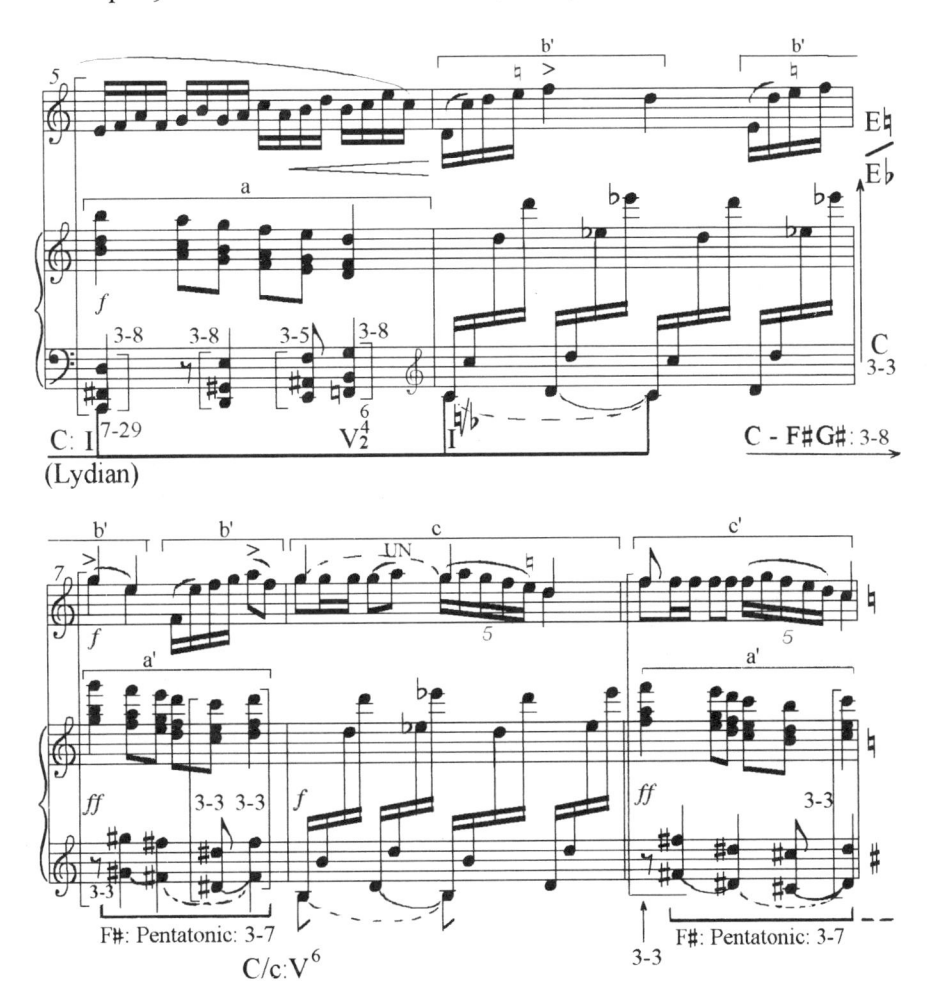

372   Darius Milhaud

Example 5.21   Clarinet Sonatina: III, bars 21–7

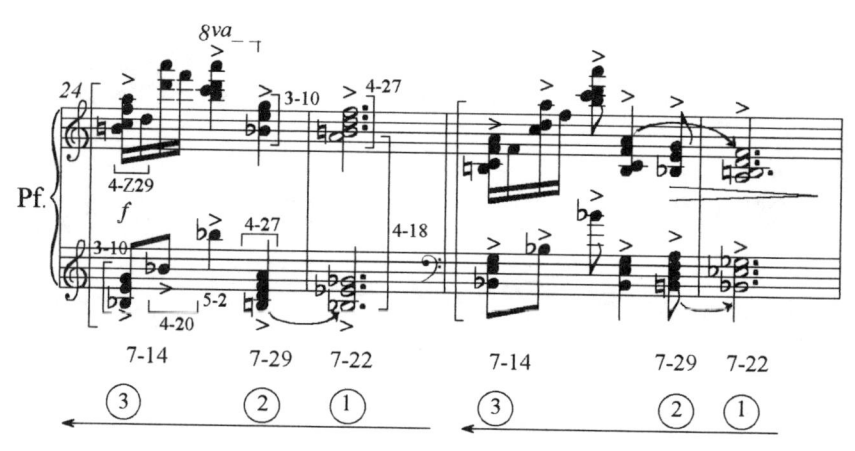

Appendix: Analytical Examples 373

Example 5.22   Clarinet Sonatina: III, bars 41–2; 45–6

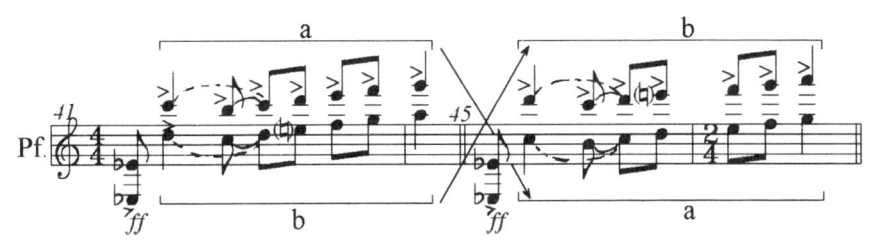

Example 5.23   Clarinet Sonatina: III, bars 51–2

Example 5.24 Clarinet Sonatina: III, bars 57–61

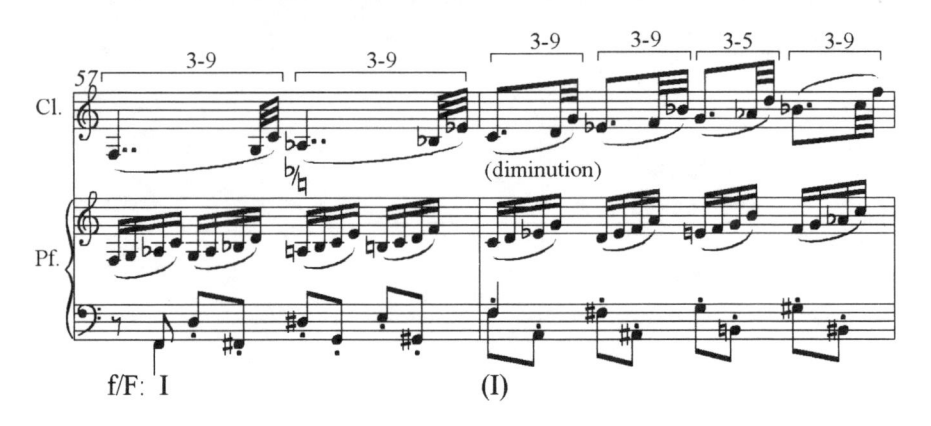

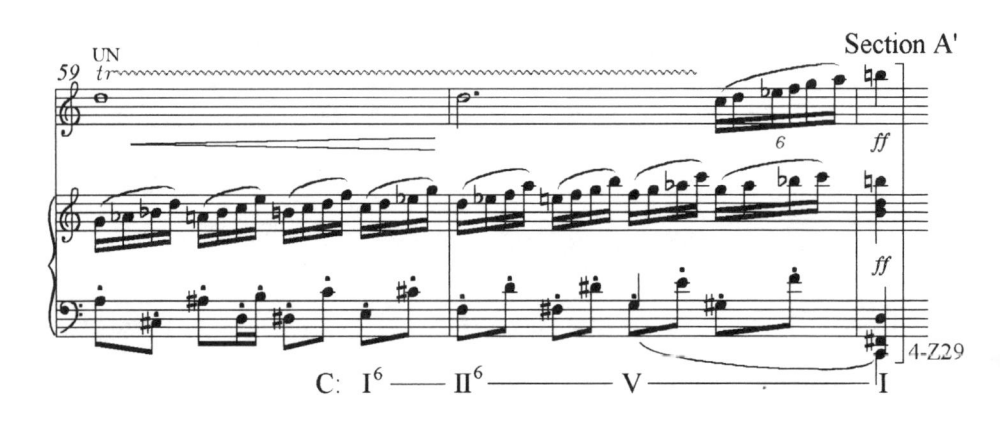

Appendix: Analytical Examples 375

Example 5.25 Clarinet Sonatina: III, bars 81–2

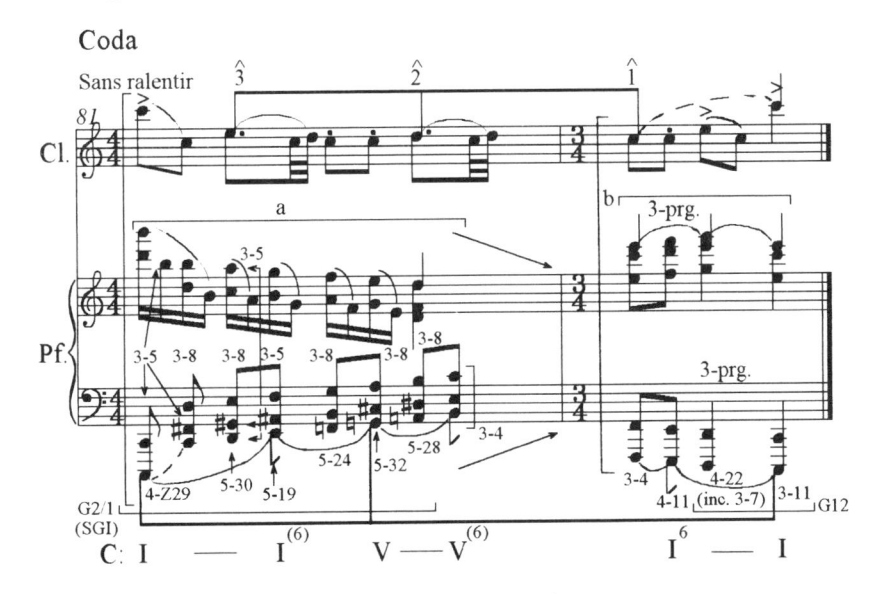

Example 5.26 Clarinet Sonatina: Thematic Connections

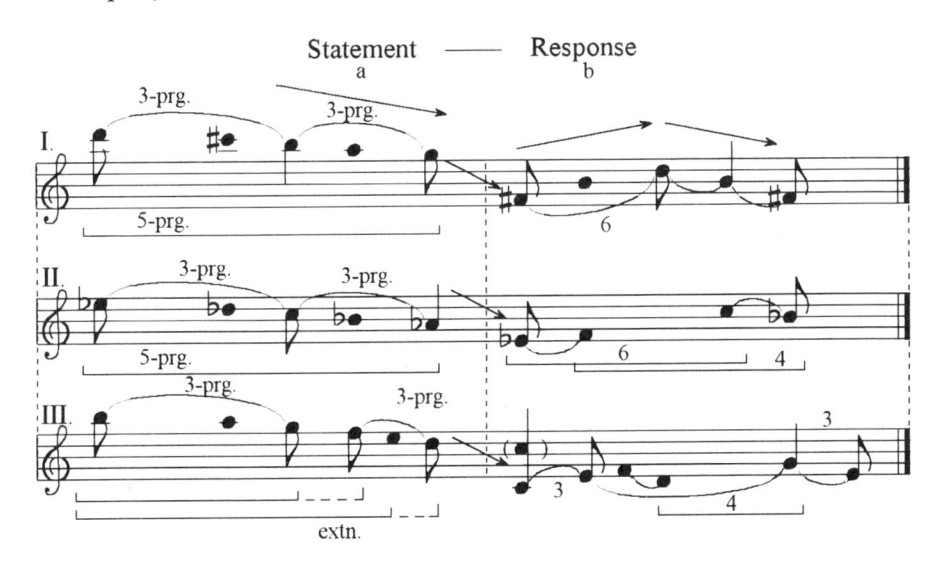

CASE STUDY 8

L'Abandon d'Ariane, Op. 98 (1927) as the Culmination of Milhaud's Neoclassicism in the 1920s

378 DARIUS MILHAUD

Example 5.27 *L'Abandon d'Ariane*: Sc. I, bars 1–7

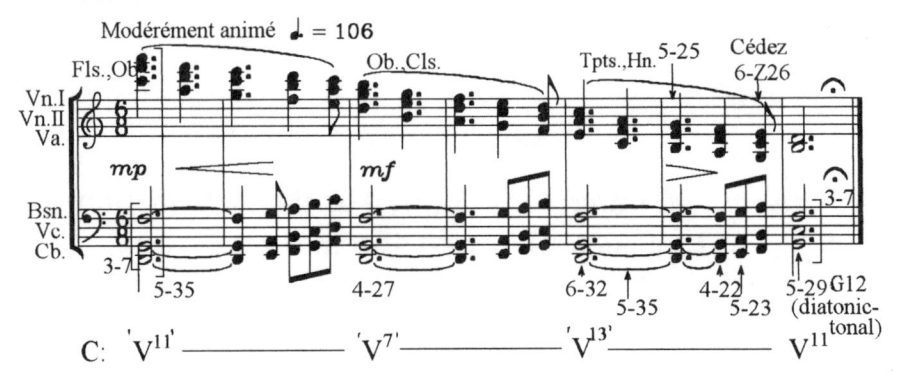

Example 5.28 *L'Abandon d'Ariane*: Sc. I, bars 8–11

Example 5.29 *L'Abandon d'Ariane*: Sc. I, bars 19–23

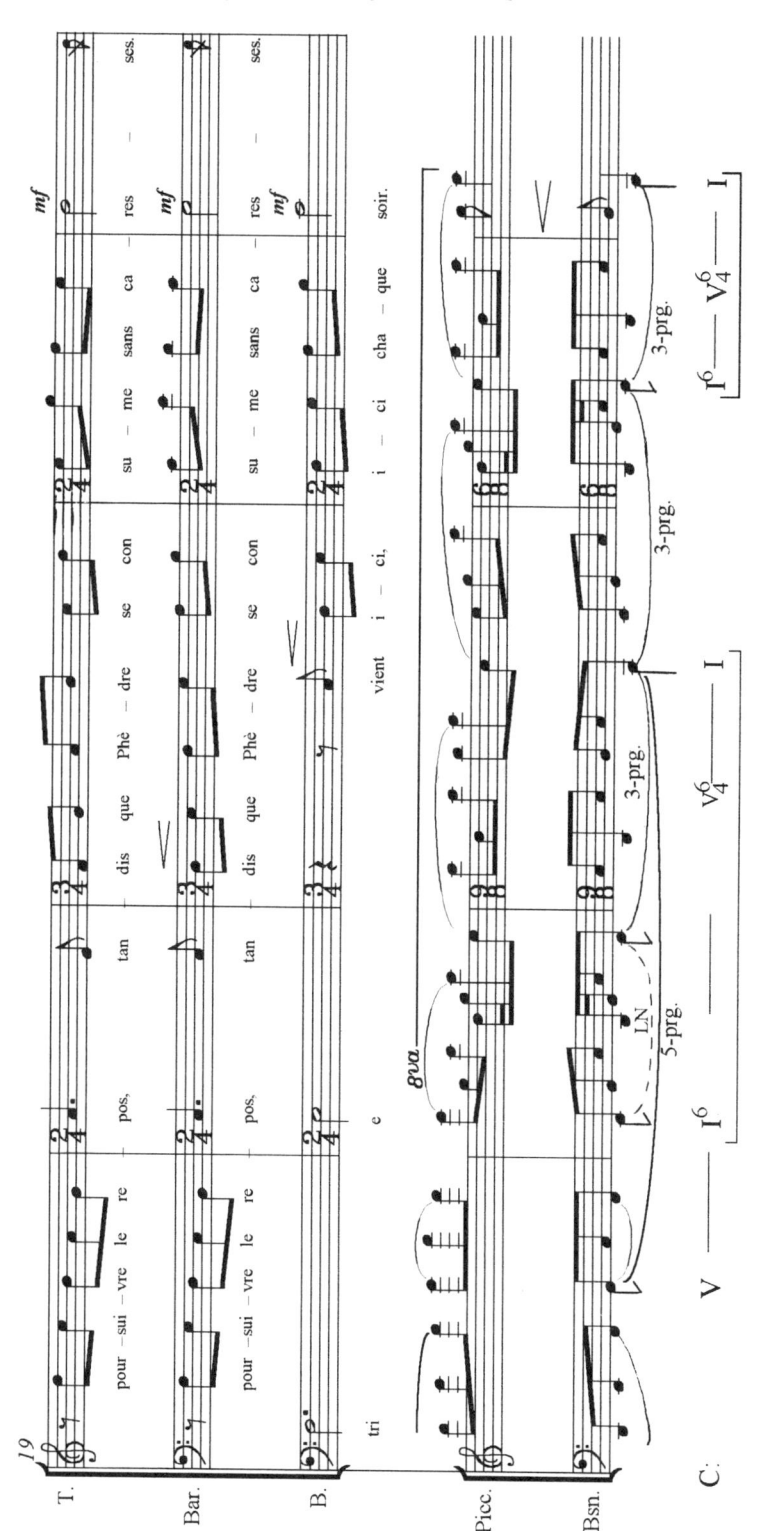

380 Darius Milhaud

Example 5.30 *L'Abandon d'Ariane*: Sc. II, bars 43–4

Appendix: Analytical Examples

Example 5.31   *L'Abandon d'Ariane*: Sc. III, bars 121–9

Example 5.32 *L'Abandon d'Ariane*: Sc. III, bars 201–4 (209–16)

Appendix: Analytical Examples 383

Example 5.33 *L'Abandon d'Ariane*: Sc. V, bars 235–8

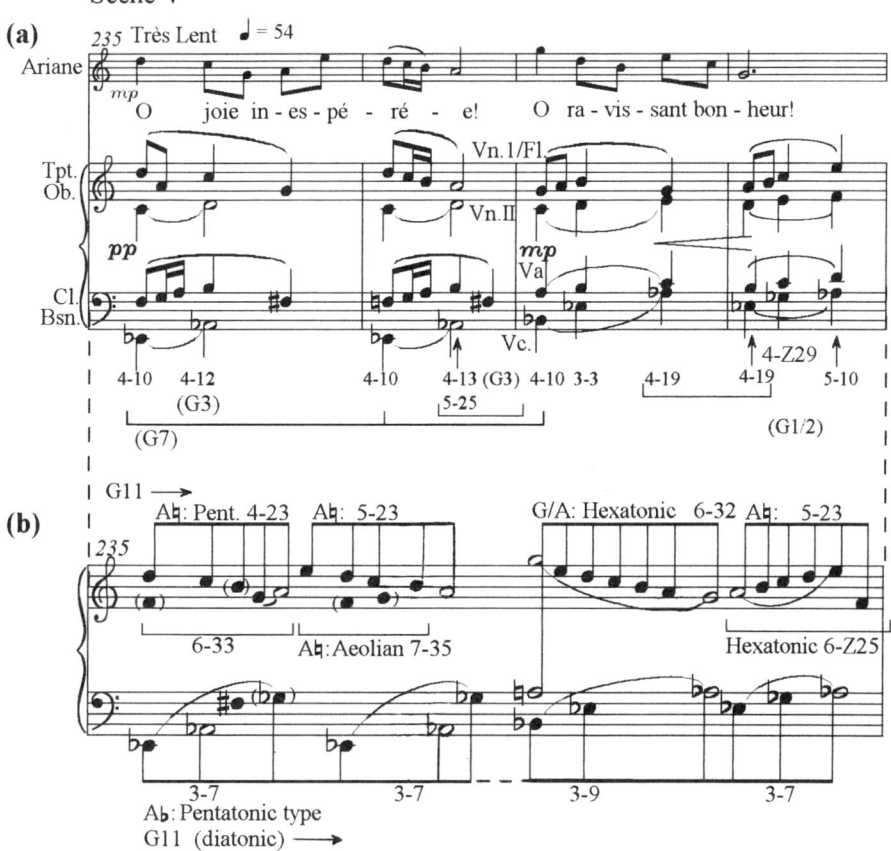

384 DARIUS MILHAUD

Example 5.33 (continued): Sc. V, bars 239–42

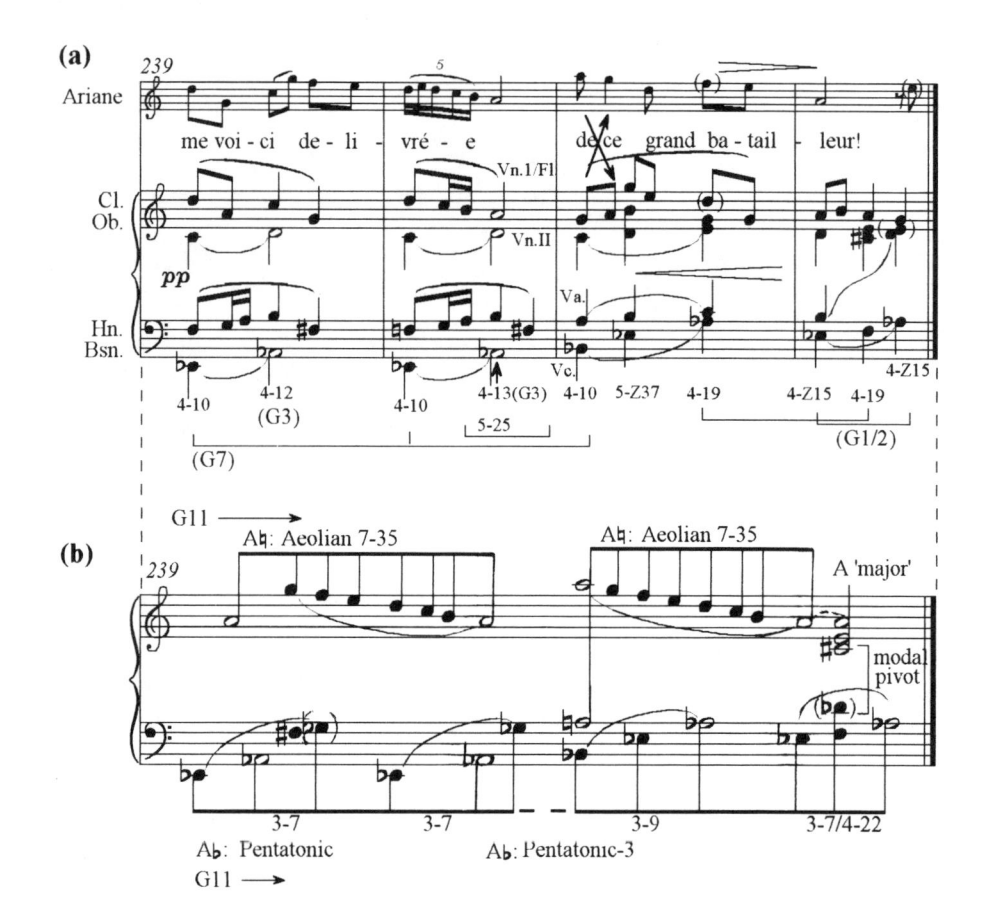

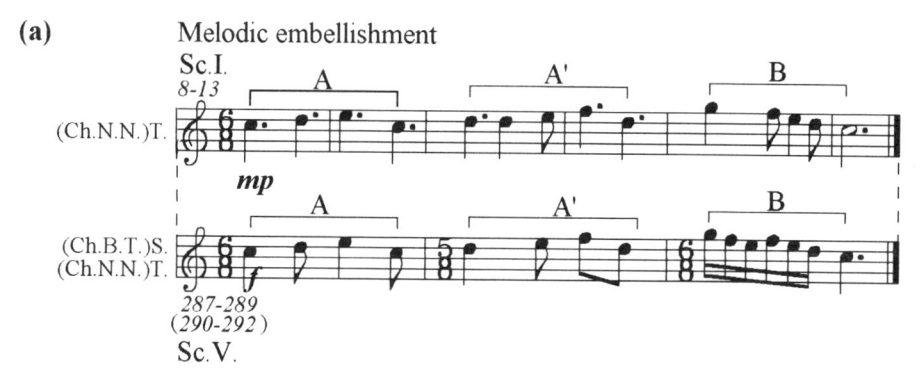

Example 5.34 *L'Abandon d'Ariane*: Sc. I, bars 8–13; 14–16; Sc. V, bars 287–92; 303–8

Example 5.35 *L'Abandon d'Ariane*: Sc. V, bars 303–5

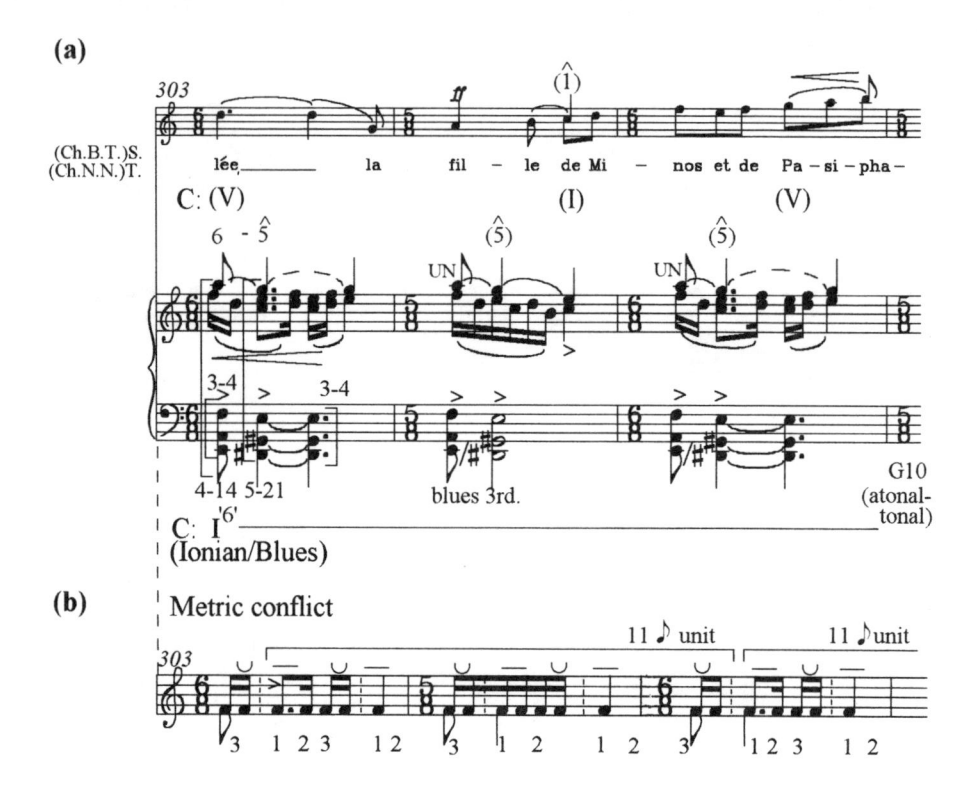

Appendix: Analytical Examples

Example 5.35 (continued): Sc. V, bars 306–8

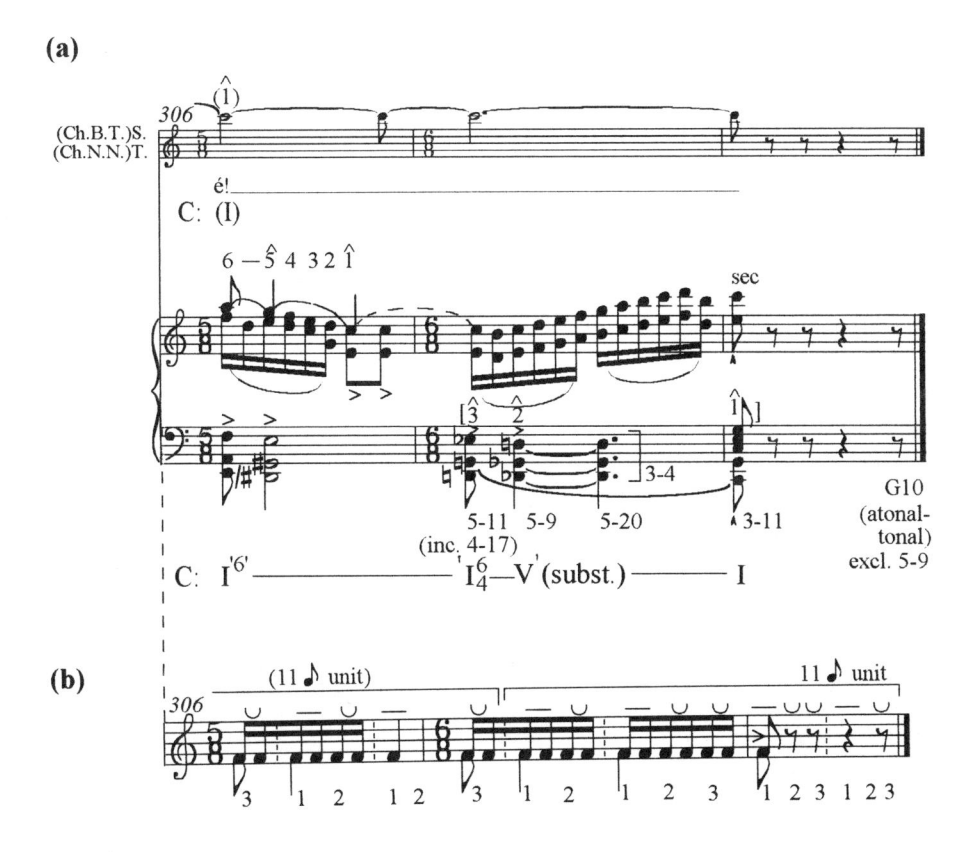

BIBLIOGRAPHY

❧

Auner, Joseph H., review of Watkins, *Pyramids at the Louvre*, in *Journal of the American Musicological Society*, 49 (1996), 161–74.

Baker, James M., 'Schenkerian Analysis and Post-tonal Music', in *Aspects of Schenkerian Theory*, ed. David W. Beach (New Haven and London: Yale University Press, 1983), 156–86.

—— *The Music of Alexander Scriabin*, Composers of the Twentieth Century Series (New Haven and London: Yale University Press, 1986).

—— 'Voice-leading in Post-tonal Music: Suggestions for Extending Schenker's Theory', *Music Analysis*, 9 (1990), 177–200.

—— 'Post-tonal Voice-leading', in Dunsby, ed., *Early Twentieth-Century Music*, 20–41.

Baskerville, David R., 'Jazz Influence on Art Music to Mid-Century' (Ph.D dissertation, University of California at Los Angeles, 1965).

Beck, Georges, *Darius Milhaud: Étude suivie du catalogue complet de son œuvre et discographie* (Paris: Heugel, 1949; supplement 1956).

Bent, Ian, with Drabkin, William, *Analysis*, The New Grove Handbooks in Music (London: Macmillan, 1987).

Berendt, Joachim E., *The Jazz Book, from Ragtime to Fusion and Beyond*, trans. Helmut and Barbara Bredigkeit, with Dan Morgenstern (New York: Granada, 1983).

Berger, Arthur W., 'Problems of Pitch Organization in Stravinsky', *Perspectives of New Music*, 2 (1963), 11–42.

Berry, Wallace, 'Symmetrical Interval Sets and Derivative Pitch Materials in Bartók's String Quartet No. 3', *Perspectives of New Music*, 18 (1979–80), 287–379.

Blom, Eric, 'Darius Milhaud', in *Grove's Dictionary of Music & Musicians*, 5th edn., ed. Eric Blom, 9 vols. plus supplement (London: Macmillan, 1954), v, 758–66.

Bloom, Harold, *The Anxiety of Influence: A Theory of Poetry* (Oxford, Oxford University Press, 1973).

Boatwright, Howard, *Chromaticism: Theory and Practice* (Fayetteville, NY: Walnut Grove Press [Syracuse University Press], 1994).

BOBBITT, Richard B., 'The Harmonic Idiom in the Works of "Les Six"' (Ph.D dissertation, Boston University, 1963).

BOULEZ, Pierre, *Par volonté et par hasard: Entretiens avec Célestin Deliège* (Paris: Éditions du Seuil, 1975); Engl. trans., with foreword by Robert Wangermé, as *Pierre Boulez: Conversations with Célestin Deliège* (London: Eulenberg, 1976).

BRODY, Elaine, *Paris: The Musical Kaleidoscope, 1870–1925* (London: Robson Books, 1988).

BUTLER, Christopher, *Early Modernism: Literature, Music and Painting in Europe, 1900–1916* (Oxford: Clarendon Press, 1994).

CATULLUS, Gaius Valerius, *The Poems of Catullus*, trans. Peter Whigham (London: Penguin, 1966).

CENDRARS, Blaise, *Anthologie nègre* (Paris: Éditions de la Sirène, 1921); also reproduced in id., *Du monde entier au cœur du monde* (Paris: Denoël, 1947).

CHEFDOR, Monique, *Blaise Cendrars* (Boston, Mass.: Twayne, 1980).

CHERRY, Paul W., 'The String Quartets of Darius Milhaud' (Ph.D dissertation, University of Colorado, Boulder, 1980).

CLAUDEL, Paul, *Correspondance Paul Claudel–Darius Milhaud*: see under MILHAUD.

COBBETT, Walter Willson, ed., *Cobbett's Cyclopedic Survey of Chamber Music*, 2nd edn., with supplementary material ed. Colin Mason, 3 vols. (London: Oxford University Press, 1963; repr. 1964).

COCTEAU, Jean, 'Le Coq et l'arlequin' (Paris: Éditions de la Sirène, 1918); also reprinted in *Œuvres complètes de Jean Cocteau*, 11 vols. (Paris: Marguerat, 1946–51), ix (*Le Rappel à l'ordre*), 13–69; Engl. trans. by Rollo H. Myers, as 'The Cock and the Harlequin', in *A Call to Order* (New York: Haskell House, 1974), 3–77.

—— *Correspondance Jean Cocteau–Darius Milhaud*: see under MILHAUD.

COLLAER, Paul, *Darius Milhaud* (Paris and Geneva: Éditions Slatkine, 1982); trans. and ed. Jane Hohfeld Galante (San Francisco: San Francisco Press; London: Macmillan, 1988).

COLLET, Henri, 'Un livre de Rimsky et un livre de Cocteau: Les Cinq russes, les six français, et Erik Satie', *Comœdia*, 16 January 1920, 2.

—— 'Les "Six" français', *Comœdia*, 23 January 1920, 2.

CONE, Edward T., 'The Uses of Convention: Stravinsky and his Models', in *Stravinsky: A New Appraisal of his Work*, ed. Paul Henry Lang (New York: Norton, 1963), 21–33.

COOK, Nicholas, *A Guide to Musical Analysis* (London: Dent, 1987; repr. 1992).

COOPER, Martin, *French Music from the Death of Berlioz to the Death of Fauré* (London: Oxford University Press, 1951).

CRAFT, Robert, *Stravinsky: Chronicle of a Friendship 1948–1971* (New York: Knopf; London, Gollancz, 1972).

—— and STRAVINSKY, Igor, *Expositions and Developments* (New York: Doubleday, 1962).

CRICHTON, Ronald, obituary: Darius Milhaud, *Musical Times*, 114 (1974), 684.

DANIEL, Keith W., 'A Preliminary Investigation of Pitch-Class Set Analysis in the Atonal and Polytonal Works of Milhaud and Poulenc', *In Theory Only*, 6 (1982), 22–48.

—— *Francis Poulenc: His Artistic Development and Musical Style*, Studies in Musicology, 51 (Ann Arbor: UMI Research Press, 1982).

DRAKE, Jeremy, ed., [Darius Milhaud,] *Notes sur la musique: Essais et chroniques* (Paris: Flammarion, 1982).

—— *The Operas of Darius Milhaud* (New York and London: Garland Press, 1989).

DUNSBY, Jonathan, 'Considerations of Texture', *Music & Letters*, 70 (1989), 46–57.

—— ed., *Early Twentieth-Century Music*, Models of Musical Analysis (Oxford: Blackwell, 1993).

—— 'Criteria of Correctness in Music Theory and Analysis', in *Theory, Analysis and Meaning in Music*, ed. Anthony Pople (Cambridge: Cambridge University Press, 1994), 77–85.

—— and WHITTALL, Arnold, *Music Analysis in Theory and Practice* (London: Faber, 1988).

ELIOT, Thomas Stearns, 'Tradition and the Individual Talent' [1919], in *Selected Essays*, 3rd edn. (London: Faber, 1951), 13–22.

EVANS, Edwin, 'Milhaud', in Cobbett, ed., *Cobbett's Cyclopedic Survey of Chamber Music*, ii, 140–5.

FERRARI, Gustave, 'Leroux, Xavier', in Sadie, ed., *The New Grove Dictionary of Music and Musicians*, x, 686.

FORTE, Allen, *The Structure of Atonal Music* (New Haven: Yale University Press, 1973; repr. 1979).

—— 'Ives and Atonality', in *An Ives Celebration*, ed. H. Wiley Hitchcock and Vivian Perlis (Urbana: University of Illinois Press, 1977), 185–6.

—— 'Liszt's Experimental Idiom and Music of the Early Twentieth Century', *Nineteenth-Century Music*, 10 (1987), 209–28.

—— New Approaches to the Linear Analysis of Music', *Journal of the American Musicological Society*, 41 (1988), 315–48.

—— Pitch-Class Set Genera and the Origin of Modern Harmonic Species', *Journal of Music Theory*, 32 (1988), 187–270.

—— and GILBERT, Steven E., *Introduction to Schenkerian Analysis* (New York: Norton, 1982).

GARON, Paul, *Blues and the Poetic Spirit* (London: Edison Press, 1975; repr. New York: Da Capo, 1978).

GILBERT, Steven E.: see under FORTE.

GRIFFITHS, Paul, 'Six, Les', in Sadie, ed., *The New Grove Dictionary of Music and Musicians*, xvii, 358–9.

GUT, Serge and PISTONE, Danièle, *La Musique de chambre en France de 1870 à 1918* (Paris: Champion, 1978).

HÄGER, Bengt, *Ballets Suédois* (London: Thames & Hudson, 1990).

HANDY, William C., *Father of the Blues: An Autobiography* (New York: Macmillan, 1941).

HANEY, Lynn, *Naked at the Feast: A Biography of Josephine Baker* (London: Robson Books, 1981).

HARDING, James, *The Ox on the Roof: Scenes from Musical Life in Paris in the Twenties* (New York: Da Capo Press, 1972).

HARRISON, Charles, *Primitivism, Cubism, Abstraction: The Early Twentieth Century* (New Haven and London: Yale University Press/Open University Press, 1993).

HARRISON, Max, 'Jazz', in Sadie, ed., *The New Grove Dictionary of Music and Musicians*, ix, 561–79.

HASTY, Christopher F., 'Phrase Formation in Post-tonal Music', *Journal of Music Theory*, 28 (1984), 167–90.

HAYES, Malcolm, performance review of Milhaud, *Machines agricoles*, *The Listener*, 115 (6 February 1986), 41.

—— radio review of 'The Harlequin Years', *The Listener*, 115 (3 April 1986), 41.

HELM, Everett, 'Darius Milhaud: A Personal Reminiscence', *Music Review*, 37 (1976), 301.

HERRNSTEIN SMITH, Barbara, 'Value/Evaluation', in Lentricchia and McLaughlin, eds., *Critical Terms for Literary Study*, 177–85.

HINDEMITH, Paul, *The Craft of Musical Composition*, Book 1: 'Theoretical

Part', trans. Arthur Mendel (Mainz and London: Schott, 1942; 4th edn. 1970).

—— [*A Concentrated Course in*] *Traditional Harmony*, Book 2: 'Exercises for Advanced Students' (New York: Associated Music Publishers, 1948).

—— *A Composer's World: Horizons and Limitations* (Cambridge, Mass.: Harvard University Press, 1952).

HINTON, Stephen, review of Neumeyer, *The Music of Paul Hindemith*, in *Music Analysis*, 7 (1988), 356–9.

HODEIR, André, *Jazz: Its Evolution and Essence*, trans. David Noakes (London: Jazz Book Club Edition, Grove Press, 1958).

HORSHAM, Michael, *'20s & '30s Style* (London: Grange Books, 1994).

HURARD-VILTARD, Eveline, 'Le Groupe des Six: ou, Le Matin d'un jour de fête', 2 vols. (Paris: Méridiens Klincksieck, 1988).

JEANNERET, Charles-Édouard [Le Corbusier]: see under OZENFANT.

JONES, Charles, 'Darius Milhaud', in *Dictionary of Twentieth-Century Music*, ed. John Vinton (London: Thames & Hudson, 1974), 487–8.

JONES, LeRoi, *Blues People: Negro Music in White America* (New York: Morrow, 1963).

KAPLAN, Ann, *Fritz Lang: A Guide to References and Resources* (Boston, Mass.: G.K. Hall, 1981).

KAY, Norman, review of Milhaud, *Notes without Music* (1970 repr.), in *Music and Musicians*, 19 (1970), 72.

KEIL, Charles, *Urban Blues* (Chicago: University of Chicago Press, 1969).

KELLY, Barbara L., 'Milhaud and the French Musical Tradition with Reference to his Works 1912–31' (Ph.D dissertation, University of Liverpool, 1994).

—— 'Milhaud's *Alissa* Manuscripts', *Journal of the Royal Musical Association*, 121 (1996), 229–45.

KERMODE, Frank, *History and Value* (Oxford: Clarendon Press), 1989.

KERNFELD, Barry, 'Blues Progression', in Kernfeld, ed., *The New Grove Dictionary of Jazz*, i, 129–30.

KERNFELD, Barry, ed., *The New Grove Dictionary of Jazz*, 2 vols. (London: Macmillan, 1988).

KIELIAN-GILBERT, Marianne, 'Relationships of Symmetrical Pitch-Class Sets and Stravinsky's Metaphor of Polarity', *Perspectives of New Music*, 21 (1982–83), 209–40.

—— 'Stravinsky's *Contrasts*: Contradiction and Discontinuity in his Neoclassic Music', *Journal of Musicology*, 9 (1991), 448–80.

LANG, Paul Henry, ed., *Stravinsky: A New Appraisal of his Work* (New York: Norton, 1963).

LAYTON, Robert, recordings review of Milhaud, String Quartets (various), in *The Gramophone*, 63 (January 1986), 943–4.

LE CORBUSIER [= JEANNERET, Charles-Édouard]: see under OZENFANT.

LEE, Edward, *Jazz: An Introduction* (London: Stanmore Press, 1972).

LÉGER, Fernand, 'The Invented Theater' [1924], in Henning Rischbieter, *Art and the State in the Twentieth Century*, trans. Michael Bullock (Greenwich, Conn.: New York Graphic Society, 1968), 97.

LENTRICCHIA, Frank, and MCLAUGHLIN, Thomas, eds., *Critical Terms for Literary Study* (Chicago and London: University of Chicago Press, 1990).

LESSEM, Alan, 'Schoenberg, Stravinsky, and Neoclassicism: The Issues Re-examined', *Music Quarterly*, 68 (1982), 527–42.

LESTER, Joel, *Analytic Approaches to Twentieth-Century Music* (New York and London: Norton, 1989).

LOCKSPEISER, Edward, 'French Chamber Music', in *Chamber Music*, ed. Alec Robertson (London: Pelican, 1958).

LOUVIER, Alain, 'Gédalge, André', in Sadie, ed., *The New Grove Dictionary of Music and Musicians*, vii, 213–4.

MCCABE, John, *Charlie Chaplin* (London: Robson, 1973).

MCCARTHY, Peter Joseph, 'The Sonatas of Darius Milhaud' (Ph.D dissertation, The Catholic University of America, 1972).

MARK, Christopher, 'Symmetry and Dynamism in Bartók', *Tempo*, 183 (December 1992), 2–5.

MASON, Colin, 'The Chamber Music of Darius Milhaud', *Music Quarterly*, 43 (1957), 326–41.

MATTHEW-WALKER, Robert, 'Milhaud's Jewish Consciousness', *Music and Musicians* [no vol. no.] (November 1984), 14–15.

—— 'Milhaud's *Les Malheurs d'Orphée*', *Music and Musicians* [no vol. no.] (November 1984), 16.

MAWER, Deborah (see also under ROBERTS), 'Darius Milhaud: *La Création du monde*', Analytical Listening Guide [software package] (Lancaster University: TLTP Music Consortium, 1996).

—— review of Boatwright, *Chromaticism: Theory and Practice*, in *Music Analysis*, 16 (1997: in press).

MELLERS, Wilfrid, 'Polymorphous Celebrations' (review of Collaer/ Galante, *Darius Milhaud*), in *Times Literary Supplement*, 4500 (30 June–6 July 1989), 717.

——— *Francis Poulenc* (Oxford: Oxford University Press, 1993).

MELTZER, David, *Reading Jazz* (San Francisco: Mercury House, 1993).

MESSING, Scott, *Neoclassicism in Music from the Genesis of the Concept through the Schoenberg/Stravinsky Polemic*, Studies in Musicology, 101 (Ann Arbor: UMI Research Press, 1988).

MEYER, Leonard B., *Emotion and Meaning in Music* (Chicago: University of Chicago Press, 1956; repr. 1961).

——— *Explaining Music: Essays and Explorations* (Berkeley: University of California Press, 1973; repr. 1978).

MIGOT, Georges, '4e quatuor à cordes', *La Revue musicale*, 2 (February 1921), 167.

MILHAUD, Darius, 'Brésil', *La Revue musicale*, 1 (November 1920), 'Chroniques et Notes', 60–1.

——— 'Polytonalité et atonalité', *La Revue musicale*, 4 (February 1923), 29–44; Engl. trans. as 'Polytonality and Atonality', *Pro Musica Quarterly*, 2 (October 1924).

——— 'The Evolution of Modern Music in Paris and in Vienna', *North American Review*, 217 (April 1923), 544–54; also in *Franco-American Musical Society Bulletin*, 1 (September 1923), 8–16.

——— 'Les Ressources nouvelles de la musique (jazz-band et instruments mécaniques)', *L'Esprit nouveau*, 25 (1924).

——— 'Hommage à André Gédalge', *La Revue musicale*, 7 (March 1926), 256–7.

——— *Études*, La Musique moderne, 3 (Paris: Éditions Claude Aveline, 1927).

——— 'Farewell to Diaghilev', *Modern Music*, 7 (December 1929–January 1930), 12–15.

——— 'Experimenting with Sound Film', *Modern Music*, 7 (February–March 1930), 11–14.

——— *Notes sur Erik Satie* (Paris, 1943; New York: Édition de la maison française de New York, 1946).

——— 'French Music between Two Wars', *Circle*, 7–8 (1946), 106–8.

——— Preface to Stravinsky, *Poetics of Music* (1947 edn.), ix–xi.

——— *Notes sans musique* (Paris: René Julliard, 1949); *Notes without Music*, ed. Rollo H. Myers, Engl. trans. Donald Evans (London: Dobson, 1952); American edn. ed. and trans. Arthur Ogden (New York:

Knopf, 1953; repr. New York: Da Capo, 1970); rev. and enlarged as *Ma vie heureuse* (Paris: Éditions Belfond, 1974; repr. 1987); *My Happy Life*, new Engl. trans. Donald Evans, George Hall, and Christopher Palmer (London: Marion Boyars, 1995).

—— 'Thirty-seven Years', in *Stravinsky in the Theatre*, ed. Minna Lederman (New York: Pellegrini & Cudaby, 1949), 131–2.

—— *Entretiens avec Claude Rostand* (Paris: René Julliard, 1952).

—— 'Hommage à Béla Bartók', *La Revue musicale*, 224 (1955), 16–18.

—— 'Reminiscences of Debussy and Ravel', *The Listener*, 59 (29 May 1958), 896–8.

—— *Correspondance Paul Claudel–Darius Milhaud: 1912–53*, in *Cahiers Paul Claudel*, ed. Jacques Petit, 12 vols. (Paris: Gallimard, 1961), iii.

—— 'Stravinsky: A Composer's Memorial', *Perspectives of New Music*, 9–10 (1971), 9–10.

—— 'In Memoriam I.S.', in 'Canons and Epitaphs (Set 2)', *Tempo*, 98 (1972) [no pagination].

—— *Notes sur la musique: Essais et chroniques*, ed. Jeremy Drake (Paris: Flammarion, 1982).

—— *Correspondance Jean Cocteau–Darius Milhaud*, ed. Pierre Caizergues and Josiane Mas (Montpellier: Université Paul Valéry, Centre d'Études Littéraires, 1992).

MONELLE, Raymond, performance review of Milhaud, *Le Pauvre matelot* and Purcell, *Dido and Aeneas*, *Opera*, 37 (May 1986), 596–7.

MORRILL, George Dexter, 'Contrapuntal Polytonality in the Early Music of Darius Milhaud' (DMA dissertation, Cornell University, 1970).

MUNDY, Simon, '1920s Paris', *Classical Music*, 8 February 1986, 19.

MURET, Maurice, *Le Crépuscule des nations blanches* (Paris, 1925); Engl. trans. as *The Twilight of the White Races*, by Lida (Miller) Touzalin (London: Unwin, [1926]).

NARMOUR, Eugene, *The Analysis and Cognition of Basic Melodic Structures: The Implication-Realization Model* (Chicago: Chicago University Press, 1991).

NATTIEZ, Jean-Jacques, *Music and Discourse: Towards a Semiology of Music*, trans. Carolyn Abbate (Princeton: Princeton University Press, 1990).

NEUMEYER, David, *The Music of Paul Hindemith*, Composers of the Twentieth Century Series (New Haven: Yale University Press, 1986).

NICHOLS, Roger, 'Cock and Harlequin', *The Listener*, 115 (30 January 1986), 30.

—— 'Poulenc, Francis', in Sadie, ed., *The New Grove Dictionary of Music and Musicians*, xv, 163–9.

—— *Conversations with Madeleine Milhaud* (London: Faber, 1996).

OLIVER, Paul, and KERNFELD, Barry, 'Blues', in Kernfeld, ed., *The New Grove Dictionary of Jazz*, i, 121–9.

ORENSTEIN, Arbie, ed., *A Ravel Reader* (New York: Columbia University Press, 1990).

ORLEDGE, Robert, *Charles Koechlin (1867–1950): His Life and Works*, Contemporary Music Studies, 1 (Chur and New York: Harwood Academic Publishers, 1989).

—— *Satie the Composer*, Music in the Twentieth Century (Cambridge: Cambridge University Press, 1990).

—— *Satie Remembered*, with translations by Roger Nichols (London: Faber, 1995).

—— 'Notes from a Happy Life' (review of Milhaud, *My Happy Life* [1995 edn.] and Nichols, *Conversations with Madeleine Milhaud*), *Times Literary Supplement* 4876 (13 September 1996), 10–11.

OSTRANSKY, Leroy, *The Anatomy of Jazz* (Seattle: University of Washington Press, 1960).

OZENFANT, Amédée, and JEANNERET, Charles-Édouard [Le Corbusier], 'Le Purisme' [1921], repr. in *Modern Artists on Art: Ten Abridged Essays*, ed. Robert Louis Herbert (Englewood Cliffs, NJ, 1964), 58–73.

PALMER, Christopher, 'Milhaud at 80', *Musical Times*, 113 (September 1972), 861–3.

—— *Darius Milhaud* (London: Faber, 1976).

—— 'Milhaud, Darius', in Sadie, ed., *The New Grove Dictionary of Music and Musicians*, xii, 305–10.

—— Engl. trans. of Milhaud, *Ma vie heureuse* (with Donald Evans and George Hall): see under MILHAUD.

PARKS, Richard S., *The Music of Claude Debussy*, Composers of the Twentieth Century Series (New Haven and London: Yale University Press, 1989).

PEARSALL, Edward R., 'Harmonic Progressions and Prolongation in Post-tonal Music', *Music Analysis*, 10 (1991), 345–55.

PERLOFF, Nancy, *Art and the Everyday: Popular Entertainment and the Circle of Erik Satie* (Oxford: Clarendon Press, 1991).

PHILIP, Robert, 'Pro Arte Quartet', in Sadie, ed., *The New Grove Dictionary of Music and Musicians*, xv, 277–8.

PICKARD, Roy, *The Hollywood Studios* (London: Frederick Muller, 1978).

POPLE, Anthony, *SetBrowser 1.2* [software utility] (Lancaster University: CTI Centre for Music, 1994).

RAVEL, Maurice, 'Contemporary Music' [1928], repr. in Orenstein, ed., *A Ravel Reader*, 42–3.

—— 'Finding Tunes in Factories' [trans. unattributed], *New Britain*, 9 August 1933, 367; repr. in Orenstein, ed., *A Ravel Reader*, 398–400.

RENZA, Louis A., 'Influence', in Lentricchia and McLaughlin, eds., *Critical Terms for Literary Study*, 186–202.

ROBERTS (now MAWER), Deborah, 'The Early Chamber Music of Darius Milhaud: Style and Structure' (Ph.D dissertation, University of London, 1991).

ROBINSON, J. Bradford, 'Blue note (i)', in Kernfeld, ed., *The New Grove Dictionary of Jazz*, i, 120.

ROSE, Phyllis, *Jazz Cleopatra* (London: Chatto & Windus, 1989).

ROSEN, Charles, *The Classical Style: Haydn, Mozart, Beethoven* (London: Faber, 1971; rev. edn. 1976, repr. 1987).

—— *Sonata Forms* (New York and London: Norton, 1980; rev. edn. 1988).

ROSTAND, Claude, 'The Operas of Darius Milhaud', *Tempo*, 19 (1951), 23–8.

—— *Darius Milhaud: Entretiens avec Claude Rostand* (Paris: René Julliard, 1952).

ROY, Jean, *Darius Milhaud* (Paris: Seghers, 1968).

RUSS, Michael, 'Four Studies in the Analysis of Post-tonal Music' (Ph.D dissertation, University of Ulster, 1985).

SADIE, Stanley, ed., *The New Grove Dictionary of Music and Musicians*, 20 vols. (London: Macmillan, 1980).

SAID, Edward W., *Orientalism* (London: Penguin, repr. 1987).

SALTER, Lionel, 'Milhaud's *Christophe Colomb*', *Musical Times*, 114 (1973), 483–4.

SALZER, Felix, *Structural Hearing: Tonal Coherence in Music*, corr. edn., 2 vols. in 1 (New York: Dover, 1982).

SALZMAN, Eric, *Twentieth-Century Music: An Introduction* (Englewood Cliffs, NJ: Prentice-Hall, 1967; rev. edn. 1974).

SARGEANT, Winthrop, *Jazz: Hot and Hybrid* (New York and London: The Jazz Book Club Edition, 1938; enlarged edn. 1959); rev. and further enlarged as *Jazz: A History* (New York: McGraw–Hill, 1964).

SCHENKER, Heinrich, *Five Graphic Music Analyses* (*Fünf Urlinien Tafeln*), rev. edn., with a new introduction and glossary by Felix Salzer (New York: Dover, 1969).

—— *Free Composition* (*Der freie Satz*), trans. and ed. Ernst Oster (New York and London: Longman, 1979).

SCHLOEZER, Boris de, 'La saison musicale', *Nouvelle revue française*, 1 (August 1923), 238–48.

—— 'Darius Milhaud', *La Revue musicale*, 6 (March 1925), 251–76.

SCHOENBERG, Arnold, *Letters*, ed. Erwin Stein (New York: St Martin's Press, 1965).

SCHULLER, Gunther, *Early Jazz: Its Roots and Musical Development* (New York and London: Oxford University Press, 1968).

—— 'Rags, the Classics, and Jazz', in *Ragtime: Its History, Composers and Music*, ed. John Edward Hasse (London: Macmillan, 1985), 79–89.

SEARLE, Humphrey, *Twentieth Century Counterpoint: A Guide for Students* (London: Williams & Norgate, 1954).

SHATTUCK, Roger, *The Banquet Years: The Origins of the Avant-Garde in France, 1885 to World War I* (London: Cape, 1969).

SHAW, Arnold, *The Jazz Age: Popular Music in the 1920s* (Oxford: Oxford University Press, 1987).

SHEAD, Richard, *Music in the 1920s* (London: Duckworth, 1976).

SILVA, Sagramour Lopes DA, 'L'Aspect brésilien dans l'œuvre de Darius Milhaud' (Maîtrise dissertation, Université de Paris–Sorbonne, 1982).

STEEGMULLER, Francis, *Cocteau: A Biography* (London: Macmillan, 1970).

STODDARD, Lothrop, *The Rising Tide of Color against White-World Supremacy* (New York: Chapman & Hall, 1921).

STRAUS, Joseph N., 'A Principle of Voice-leading in Stravinsky', *Music Theory Spectrum*, 4 (1982), 106–24.

—— 'Stravinsky's Tonal Axis', *Journal of Music Theory*, 26 (1982), 261–90.

—— review of van den Toorn, *The Music of Igor Stravinsky*, in *Journal of Music Theory*, 28 (1984), 129–34.

—— 'The Problem of Prolongation in Post-tonal Music', *Journal of Music Theory*, 31 (1987), 1–21.

—— *Introduction to Post-tonal Theory* (Englewood Cliffs, NJ: Prentice-

Hall, 1990).

—— *Remaking the Past: Musical Modernism and the Influence of the Tonal Tradition* (Cambridge, Mass.: Harvard University Press, 1990).

STRAVINSKY, Igor, *An Autobiography* (New York: Simon & Schuster, 1936; rev. edn. 1975).

—— *Poétique musicale [sous forme de six leçons]* (Cambridge, Mass.: Harvard University Press, 1942); *Poetics of Music, in the Form of Six Lessons*, Engl. trans. Arthur Knodel and Ingolf Dahl (London: Oxford University Press, 1947).

—— and CRAFT, Robert, *Expositions and Developments* (New York: Doubleday, 1962).

STUART, Walter (with Stan Applebaum and 'Bugs Bower'), *Encyclopedia of Improvisation* (New York: Charles Colin, 1972).

SWICKARD, Ralph James, 'The Symphonies of Darius Milhaud: An Historical Perspective and Critical Study of their Musical Content, Style and Form' (Ph.D dissertation, University of California at Los Angeles, 1973).

TARUSKIN, Richard, '*Chez Pétrouchka*: Harmony and Tonality *chez* Stravinsky', *Nineteenth-Century Music*, 10 (1987), 265–86.

TIRRO, Frank, 'Jazz', in *Dictionary of Twentieth-Century Music*, ed. John Vinton (London: Thames & Hudson, 1974), 367–76.

TISDALL, Caroline, and BOZZOLLA, Angelo, *Futurism*, World of Art (London: Thames & Hudson, 1977; repr. 1993).

TRAVIS, Roy, 'Toward a New Concept of Tonality?', *Journal of Music Theory*, 3 (1959), 257–84.

—— 'Directed Motion in Schoenberg and Webern', *Perspectives of New Music*, 4 (1966), 84–9.

TROY, Nancy J., *Modernism and the Decorative Arts in France: Art Nouveau to Le Corbusier* (New Haven: Yale University Press, 1991).

ULANOV, Barry, *A Handbook of Jazz* (London: Hutchinson, 1958).

VAN DEN TOORN, Pieter C., *The Music of Igor Stravinsky*, Composers of the Twentieth Century Series (New Haven: Yale University Press, 1983).

—— 'Neoclassicism Revised', in *Music, Politics, and the Academy* (Berkeley and Los Angeles: University of California Press, 1995), 143–78.

WALDO, Terry, *This is Ragtime* (New York: Da Capo, 1976; rev. edn. 1991).

WALSH, Stephen, *The Music of Stravinsky* (Oxford: Oxford University

Press, 1988).

—— *Stravinsky: Oedipus Rex*, Cambridge Music Handbooks (Cambridge: Cambridge University Press, 1993).

WATKINS, Glenn, *Pyramids at the Louvre: Music, Culture, and Collage from Stravinsky to the Postmodernist* (Cambridge, Mass.: The Belknap Press of Harvard University Press, 1994).

WEBSTER, James, 'Sonata Form', in Sadie, ed., *The New Grove Dictionary of Music and Musicians*, xvii, 497–508.

WHITE, Eric Walter, 'Stravinsky, Igor', in Sadie, ed., *The New Grove Dictionary of Music and Musicians*, xviii, 240–65.

WHITE, Hayden, *Metahistory: The Historical Imagination in Nineteenth-Century Europe* (Baltimore: Johns Hopkins University Press, 1973).

—— *Tropics of Discourse: Essays in Cultural Criticism* (Baltimore: Johns Hopkins University Press, 1978).

—— *The Content of the Form: Narrative Discourse and Historical Representation* (Baltimore: Johns Hopkins University Press, 1987).

WHITTALL, Arnold, *Music since the First World War* (London: Dent, 1977; repr. 1983).

—— 'Neo-classical', in Sadie, ed., *The New Grove Dictionary of Music and Musicians*, xiii, 104–5.

—— 'Music Analysis as Human Science? *Le Sacre du printemps* in Theory and Practice', *Music Analysis*, 1 (1982), 33–53.

—— 'The Theorist's Sense of History: Concepts of Contemporaneity in Composition and Analysis', *Journal of the Royal Musical Association*, 112 (1986–87), 1–20.

—— 'Review Survey: Some Recent Writings on Stravinsky', *Music Analysis*, 8 (1989), 169–70.

—— review of books by Stefan Kostka, Joel Lester, Bryan R. Simms, Joseph N. Straus, and Glenn Watkins, in *Music Theory Spectrum*, 13 (1991), 79–88.

—— 'Tonality and the Emancipated Dissonance: Schoenberg and Stravinsky', in Dunsby, ed., *Early Twentieth-Century Music*, 1–19.

See also under DUNSBY and WHITTALL.

WILSON, Paul, *The Music of Béla Bartók*, Composers of the Twentieth Century Series (New Haven: Yale University Press, 1992).

ZINAR, Ruth, 'Greek Tragedy in Theatre Pieces of Stravinsky and Milhaud' (Ph.D dissertation, New York University, 1968).

INDEX OF NAMES AND WORKS

❧

In this Index, 'names' includes some collective names of groups, societies and ensembles; 'works' includes selected writings of Milhaud, Stravinsky, Hindemith and Cendrars, incorporating some substantive quotations where the author's name is not explicitly cited in the main text. References supported by Figures are denoted by '(& *fig.*)' or '(& *figs.*)', whereas '(*fig.*)' indicates citation in the body of a Figure only. Appendix contents are not indexed separately, since the reader is already directed to specific analytical examples from the main text. In Case Studies 1–8, especially, some discretion has guided the inclusion of references to parenthetical or footnote discussion of a work; entries for some relatively minor cross-references in the text have also been omitted.

Amy, Gilbert 277
Antheil, George 101
   Airplane Sonata 86 n., 101
   Ballet mécanique 101, 146 n.
Apollinaire, Guillaume 146 n.
Armstrong, Louis 124
Arnold ('s American Band), Billy 119, 148
Astruc, Yves 198
Auric, Georges 101, 120

Bach, Johann Sebastian 2 n., 5 n., 19, 121, 178, 181, 187–8
   Brandenburg Concerti 4, 182
Baker, James M. 40, 257 n.
Baker, Josephine 118
Bakst, Léon 117
Ballets Russes 3, 145 n.
Ballets Suédois 3, 145, 147, 148
Bartók, Béla xx, 21, 278
   Fourteen Bagatelles, Op. 6 20
   String Quartet No. 3 97, 266 n.
Baskerville, David 31
Beethoven, Ludwig van 215 n.
   Sonata in c minor, Op. 13 ('Pathétique') 215 n.

Bekku, Sadao 277
Bent, Ian 44 n.
Berg, Alban 6–7
Berger, Arthur 33
Berlioz, Hector 2 n.
Berio, Luciano 277
Berry, Wallace 97
Bertin, Pierre 122
Birtwistle, Harrison 97
   Secret Theatre 97 n.
Bizet, Georges 153 n.
Bloom, Harold x n., 118, 181–2, 267–8, 279
Boatwright, Howard 69 n.
Bobbitt, Richard B. 31
Bolcom, William 277
Börlin, Jean 146–7, 273
   Sculpture nègre 147
Boulez, Pierre 179
Braga, Francesco 183
Brubeck, Dave 277

Cahuzac, Louis 206
Catullus, Gaius Valerius 198–9
Cendrars, Blaise 1, 118, 146–8, 159, 169, 274

Scenario: *La Création du monde* 155, 161, 164, 167, 171, 172
Cézanne, Paul 60
Chaplin, Charlie 102, 110–11
   Modern Times 102
Chefdor, Monique 118 n., 146 n.
Cherry, Paul W. 31
Claudel, Paul xx, 1, 3, 114
   L'Annonce faite à Marie 1 n.
   L'Otage 1 n.
   Le Soulier de satin 1 n.
Cobbett, Walter W. 73
Cocteau, Jean 7, 8, 87, 101, 111, 116, 120
Collaer, Paul xviii, xx, 10, 11, 14, 27, 46, 74, 83, 96, 145, 171, 183, 185, 228, 252
Collet, Henri 1
Cone, Edward T. 42, 181 n.
Cooper, Martin 86
Copland, Aaron 9, 275
   Concerto for piano and orchestra 275
   El Salón México 213 n.
Couperin, François 178
   Suite: *La Sultane* 178
Craft, Robert 4

Daniel, Keith W. xviii, 8, 16, 31, 32–3, 134–41, 144
Davies, Peter Maxwell 41
Debussy, Claude ix, 1, 8, 37, 57, 58, 117
   Children's Corner Suite 118
   Pélleas et Mélisande 58
   Préludes (II):
      'Ondine' 20
      'La Terrace des audiences du clair de lune' 38
Delgrange, Félix 73, 85
   Concerts Delgrange 73
Derain, André 117
Desormière, Roger 145
Diaghilev, Serge xx, 3
Disney, Walt 111
   Plane Crazy 111
   Silly Symphonies 111
   Steamboat Willie 111
Drake, Jeremy xvii n., xviii, 10, 13, 17, 18, 28–31, 35, 46, 132, 230, 232–4, 236–8, 243–4, 246, 248, 253, 264, 278
Dukas, Paul 58
Dunsby, Jonathan 40, 41 n.
Dvořák, Antonín 126
   'American' Quartet 126

Eliot, Thomas Stearns 113 n., 269
Ellington, Duke 158
Eloy, Jean-Claude 277

Fauré, Gabriel 8, 57
   Sonata for violin and piano, Op. 13 66
Forte, Allen xxi–xxii, 35–8, 44, 45–6, 76, 77 n., 81 n., 137, 142, 199 n., 201 n., 221–2, 241 n., 256, 262–3
Franck, César 8
   Sonata in A for violin and piano 66
Freund, Marya 95

Gaillard, M. F. 206
Galante, Jane Hohfeld xx, 46, 228
Gauguin, Paul 117
Gédalge, André xx, 58, 60, 66
Gershwin, George 9, 163 n., 164, 166, 275
   Rhapsody in Blue 9, 156 n., 163, 275, 279
Gide, André 1, 114
Gilbert, Steven xxi n.
Golschmann, Vladimir 134, 145
Goodman, Benny 9
Gounod, Charles François 2 n.
Guerra, Nininha Velloso 134
Guillaume, Paul 117

Hába, Aloïs 25
   String Quartet 25
Handy, William C. 157, 274

Index of Names & Works

St Louis Blues 157
Haney, Lynn 119 n.
Hasty, Christopher F. 38, 44
Hayes, Malcolm 86
Hindemith, Paul xvii, xviii, 2, 4–5, 6, 21, 22, 24–5, 27, 43, 46, 183, 198, 203, 205, 228, 265, 276, 277
  The Craft of Musical Composition 5, 43, 203
  Hin und zurück 4, 228
  Kammermusik series 4, 182
  Kleine Kammermusik 4, 183
  Musik für mecanische Instrumente 101–2
  Suite for Piano 120 n.
Hodeir, André 123, 150, 151, 156–9, 164, 176
Hofmannsthal, Hugo von 229
Homer 269
Honegger, Arthur xx, 7–8, 102
  Horace victorieux 24
  Pacific 231 8, 86
  Le Roi David 8
Hoppenot, Henri 185, 229

Indy, Vincent d' 58
  Sonata in C for violin and piano, Op. 59 67
Ives, Charles 9, 278
  The Unanswered Question 9

Jammes, Francis 1, 114
Janacopoulos, Vera 198
Jones, Charles 6, 277

Keil, Charles 44, 46, 265, 278
Kelemen, Milko 277
Keller, Hans 178
Kelly, Barbara L. x n., 182 n.
Kermode, Frank 279
Koechlin, Charles ix, 9, 27, 59
Kolisch Quartet 145
Křenek, Ernst 275
  Jonny spielt auf 275
  Der Sprung über Schatten 275
Kurtág, György 277

Lang, Fritz 102
  Metropolis 102, 111
Lapommeraye, Pierre de 149
Latil, Léo 1, 11, 58–9, 114
Le Corbusier (Jeanneret, Charles-Édouard) 102
Léger, Fernand 1, 86, 101, 146–8, 273, 274
Leroux, Xavier 57
Levinson, André 148
Liszt, Franz 36
Lunel, Armand 11

McCarthy, Peter J. 31
Mahler, Gustav 152
  Lieder eines fahrenden Gesellen 152
Maré, Rolf de 3, 145 n.
Matthew-Walker, Robert 59, 276
Mellers, Wilfrid ix, 61, 276–7
Meltzer, David x, 14, 118–20, 123–4, 267–8
Mendelssohn, Felix 73
Messing, Scott 179–81
Meyer, Leonard B. xviii, 39, 44, 97, 108–9, 139, 265, 269
Migot, Georges 73
Milhaud, Darius, works of:
  Aspen Serenade, Op. 361 184
  Bolívar, Op. 236 251
  Le Bœuf sur le toit, Op. 58 7, 61, 102, 116, 133, 267
    Cinéma-fantaisie, Op. 58*b* 15, 102, 116, 125, 126, 130
    Tango des Fratellini, Op. 58*c* 116
  La Brébis égarée, Op. 4 58
  'Brésil' 114
  Caramel mou, Op. 68 13, 119–20, 123, 125–30 (*& figs.*), 274
  Catalogue de fleurs, Op. 60 63, 71, 85, 186, 191
  Chamber Symphonies (set of six) 4, 7, 15, 16, 26, 182–3, 187, 189–92 (*& figs.*), 255

No. 1 (*Le Printemps*), Op. 43 xvii, 61, 70, 95, 114, 182–3, 267
No. 2 (*Pastorale*), Op. 49 114, 188
No. 3 (*Sérénade*), Op. 71 22, 70, 71, 188, 195–6 (*& fig.*)
No. 4 (*Dixtuor à cordes*), Op. 74 60, 68, 70–2, 95–6, 182, 188, 216 n., 256
No. 5 (*Dixtuor d'instruments à vent*), Op. 75 (Case Study 3) 3, 4, 9, 47, 49, 63, 70, 95–7, 112, 177, 180, 182, 184, 185–6, 206–7, 211 n., 260, 266, 267, 270–1
   I. 61, 67, 69, 72, 97–105 (*& fig.*), 226, 236, 252, 262 n.
   II. 105–7 (*& fig.*), 128, 130
   III. 65, 66, 107–11 (*& fig.*), 129 (*& fig.*), 253, 255, 264–5
No. 6, Op. 79 95–6, 105, 125, 128–31 (*& fig.*), 133
Christophe Colomb, Op. 102 xix, 8, 15, 26–7, 60, 185, 251, 256, 273
Cinq études for Piano and Orchestra, Op. 63 6, 60, 256
Cocktail, Op. 69 62
Concerto for percussion and orchestra, Op. 109 9
Concerto No. 1 for viola and orchestra, Op. 108 4
La Création du monde, Op. 81 xii, 3, 16, 27, 59, 77 n., 81, 90, 101, 112, 117, 122, 145–50, 174–6, 186, 252, 256, 273–6, 277
   Suite de concert, Op. 81*b* (Case Study 5) xix, 15, 125, 129, 145–6, 149–50, 174–6, 260, 262, 266, 274–5

   I. 150–5 (*& fig.*), 158, 169, 171, 173, 174, 218
   II. 105, 123, 130, 133, 155–61 (*& figs.*), 170, 172, 175, 218, 254, 268
   III. xxii, 126, 131, 161–4 (*& fig.*), 172, 175
   IV. 126, 131, 133, 164–7 (*& fig.*), 175
   V. 132, 167–74 (*& fig.*)
Deux hymnes, Op. 88 114
Deux poèmes tupis, Op. 52 115
Esther de Carpentras, Op. 89 9, 114
Études xxi, 4, 12, 62, 105, 119 n., 123, 145
'The Evolution of Modern Music in Paris and Vienna' xxi, 103, 180
L'Homme et son désir, Op. 48 xix, 3, 15, 32, 72, 114–5, 117, 125, 140, 148, 235, 236, 267
In Memoriam I.S., Op. 435 4
Introduction et Allegro, Op. 220 178
Machines agricoles, Op. 56 8, 16, 27, 32, 54–5, 63, 72, 85–7, 101, 178, 235, 267
   I. 71, 87, 264
   III. (Case Study 2) 61, 65, 70, 78, 85–94 (*& figs.*), 96, 99, 230, 252, 256, 260, 263, 266
   V. 71
   VI. 65–6 (*fig.*), 94, 253
Les Malheurs d'Orphée, Op. 85 3, 59, 184–5, 188, 228, 277
   Sc. IX: 'Duo d'Eurydice et d'Orphée' 129
   Sc. XII: 'Lamentations d'Orphée' 67 n.
   Sc. XIV: 'Chœur des funérailles' 59
Ma vie heureuse x, xx–xxi, 2, 7, 10–13, 28, 57, 60, 85–6, 112,

114, 116, 120–5, 134, 145, 147, 149, 160, 177, 182–3, 185, 228, 273
Maximilien, Op. 110 185, 251
Musique pour Ars Nova, Op. 432 62
Notes sans musique xx–xxi
Notes sur Erik Satie 7
Opéras-minute (trilogy) xix, 3, 17, 72, 185, 186, 254
   L'Abandon d'Ariane (No. 2), Op. 98 (Case Study 8) xi, 3, 13, 29, 186, 188, 206, 228–32 (& fig.), 250–1, 261, 272–3
      Sc. I 231–5
      Sc. II 69 n., 214, 235–9, 243, 266
      Sc. III 132 ('Tango'), 212 n., 239–43, 263
      Sc. IV 243
      Sc. V 192, 195, 198, 212 n., 214, 225, 243–50, 266
   La Délivrance de Thésée (No. 3), Op. 99 188, 213 n.
      Sc. VI 69 n.
   L'Enlèvement d'Europe (No. 1), Op. 94 4, 188, 228, 271
      Sc. V 70 n.
      Sc. VI 70 n.
L'Orestie trilogy 3, 251
   Agamemnon (No. 1), Op. 14 32
   Les Choéphores (No. 2), Op. 24 59–60, 71, 177, 195
   Les Euménides (No. 3), Op. 41 26, 27, 31, 60, 195
Le Pauvre matelot, Op. 92 7, 251
Poèmes de Francis Jammes, Op. 1; Op. 6 58
Poèmes juifs, Op. 34 114
'Polytonalité et atonalité' xvii, xxi, 19–26, 27, 56, 100–1, 104–5, 106, 177, 195–6, 264
La P'tite Lilie, Op. 107 102
Quatre poèmes de Catulle, Op. 80 16, 27, 129, 184, 196, 198, 235
   I. (Case Study 6) 186, 198–205 (& figs.), 232, 254, 261, 265
   III. 191, 194
   IV. 125, 130, 192, 194–5, 199 n., 202 n.
Quatre poèmes de Léo Latil, Op. 20 59
Quatre visages, Op. 238 213 n.
   'Le Wisconsonien' 213 n.
'Les Ressources nouvelles de la musique' 62, 102
Saudades do Brazil, Op. 67 xix, 13, 16, 32, 70, 116, 125, 130, 134, 236, 241, 267
   Group 1:
      'Sorocaba' 116, 125, 128, 132
      'Botafogo' 33
      'Leme' 116
      'Copacabana' 33
      'Ipanema' (Case Study 5) xi, 33, 116, 131, 132, 134–44 (& figs.), 213 n., 255, 260, 266, 268
      'Gavea' 116, 126, 128, 132
   Group 2:
      'Corcovado' 126, 132 (& fig.), 133
      'Tijuca' 126, 128, 133
      'Sumaré' 125, 128, 131
      'Paineras' 132
      'Laranjeiras' 128, 132, 133 (fig.)
      'Paysandú' 116, 132
   Symphonic Suite: large orchestra, Op. 67*b* 134
Scaramouche, Op. 165*b* 148
Service sacré, Op. 279 276
Six chants populaires hébraïques, Op. 86 114
Sonata for flute, oboe, clarinet and piano, Op. 47 63, 66, 72 (& fig.), 128–9 (fig.)

Sonata for piano and two violins, Op. 15 58
Sonata No. 1 for violin and piano, Op. 3 8, 14, 17, 57–8, 61, 63, 64–7, 70, 267
Sonata No. 2 for violin and piano, Op. 40 8, 17, 58, 63, 70, 114, 267
Sonatina for clarinet and piano, Op. 100 (Case Study 7) xvii, xix, 14, 16–17, 32, 41, 72, 97, 112, 182, 184, 186, 192, 194, 195, 206–7, 226–7, 254, 268, 271–3
    I. 207–15 (*& figs.*), 252
    II. 132, 215–18 (*& fig.*)
    III. 219–26 (*& figs.*), 262
Sonatina for flute and piano, Op. 76 17, 64, 69, 128, 132, 184, 254, 271
String Quartets
  No. 1, Op. 5 8, 28, 60, 61, 63, 64, 66, 267
  No. 2, Op. 16 8, 28, 59, 63, 256, 267
  No. 3 (with soprano), Op. 32 6, 8, 13, 59, 63, 65, 67–9 (*& fig.*), 128, 191, 197, 254, 255, 267
  No. 4, Op. 46 8, 54, 63, 64, 72, 73, 114, 271
    I. 56, 71, 84, 127 (*& fig.*), 191, 264
    II. (Case Study 1) 16, 36, 55, 56, 59, 61, 73–84 (*& figs.*), 92 n., 93, 99, 104 n., 210 n., 236, 244, 259, 266, 268, 271–2
    III. 65, 68 (*& fig.*), 84, 128
  No. 5, Op. 64 6, 60, 63, 70, 71, 184
  No. 6, Op. 77 8, 184, 188, 191, 192–4 (*& fig.*), 195, 196–7, 254
  No. 7, Op. 87 129, 184, 187, 188, 192, 194–7, 248, 254, 256
  No. 8, Op. 132 14
  Nos. 14/15, Op. 291 9
  No. 17, Op. 307 98 n., 197
  No. 18, Op. 308 14
String Quintet No. 1, Op. 312 14
String Septet, Op. 408 62
Suite d'après Corrette, Op. 161b 178
Suite de quatrains, Op. 398 62
Le Train bleu, Op. 84 7
Trois caprices de Paganini, Op. 97 184
Trois poèmes de Léo Latil, Op. 2 59
Trois rag-caprices, Op. 78 2, 70, 125–6, 128, 130–3, 256
Wind Quintet, Op. 443 14
Milhaud, Madeleine xx, 1–2, 6, 268
Mille, Agnes de 145
Mitchell, William 36
Monteux, Pierre 4
Monteverdi, Claudio 183
Moran, Robert 277
Morrill, George Dexter 31
Mossolov, Alexandr Vasil'yevich
  The Iron Foundry 102
Mozart, Wolfgang Amadeus 2 n., 12–13, 276
Musorgsky, Modest Petrovich 58
  Boris Godunov 58

Narmour, Eugene 44 n.
Nash Ensemble 86
Nattiez, Jean-Jacques 18
Nazareth, Ernesto 116, 134
Neumeyer, David xviii, 5, 43, 45, 198–9, 205, 265
Nichols, Roger x
Nouveaux Jeunes, Les 1

Orledge, Robert ix, x n., 9 n.

Index of Names & Works

Paganini, Niccolò 184
  24 Caprices, Op. 1 184
Palmer, Christopher x n., 60
Parks, Richard S. ix, 37, 241 n., 263, 278
Perloff, Nancy 61, 119 n., 264
Picasso, Pablo 117
Pinkard, Maceo 145
  Liza 145
Pople, Anthony 259
Poulenc, Francis ix, 7, 8, 87
  Mouvements perpetuels 21
  La Voix humaine 86 n.
Pro Arte String Quartet 73

Quatuor Capelle 73

Ravel, Maurice xii, 1, 8, 58, 102, 117, 262, 278, 279
  Bolero 102
  Sonata for violin and cello 20, 106 n.
  Sonata for violin and piano 118, 279
  String Quartet in F 8, 58 n., 126
  Le Tombeau de Couperin 178
Reich, Steve 115, 277–8
  Clapping Music 115
Réti, Rudolph 155
Rimsky-Korsakov, Nikolay Andreyevich 117
  Shéhérazade 117
Rodin, Auguste 117
Rose, Phyllis 118
Rosen, Charles 113 n., 269
Rosenstock, J. 229
Rostand, Claude 4
Roussel, Albert 106 n.
  Fête de printemps 106 n.
Rubinstein, Arthur 134
Russ, Michael 41–3, 46, 257 n., 258, 265

Salzer, Felix xxi, 179
Salzman, Eric 178–9
Sargeant, Winthrop 150, 157, 167
Satie, Erik ix, xii, xx, 1, 7, 178
  Jack in the Box 7
  Parade 21, 101, 111, 118, 279
  Le Piège de Méduse 122
  Socrate 229
Scarlatti, Domenico 12–13, 276
Schenker, Heinrich xxi
Schloezer, Boris de 26, 27, 55, 180
Schoenberg, Arnold 5–6, 25, 60, 180
  Kammersymphonie (No. 1), Op. 9 4, 6
  Klavierstück, Op. 33a 25 n.
  Pierrot lunaire, Op. 21 6
  Six Little Piano Pieces, Op. 19 257
  String Quartet No. 2 (with soprano), Op. 10 6
  Three Pieces for Piano, Op. 11 24
Searle, Humphrey 26, 27, 54, 60, 68, 70, 253 n., 264
Section d'Or, Concerts 85
Six, Les (Groupe des Six) xii, 1, 7, 59, 120
  Concerts des Six 134
Skryabin, Alexander Nikolayevich 35, 36
Smith, William O. 277
Société instrumentale à vent 95
Société Musicale Indépendante (concerts of) 73
Straus, Joseph N. x, xviii, 2, 14, 39–40, 46, 50, 52, 56, 74, 97, 109, 113, 128, 131, 134, 143, 181–2, 187, 189, 192, 207, 209, 212, 223–4, 226–7, 250, 255, 257, 265, 267–8
Strauss, Richard 229
  Ariadne auf Naxos 229
Stravinsky, Igor Feodorovich xii, xvii, xx, 2–4, 22, 33–6, 39–41, 119, 122, 128, 179–80, 262, 276, 279
  Apollon Musagète 3

Dumbarton Oaks 39
L'Histoire du soldat 3, 33, 118, 241, 243, 251, 279
Mavra 4, 185, 251
Les Noces 33, 248, 251
Octet 3, 34, 182, 185, 206 n., 212
Oedipus Rex 3, 39, 185, 234 n., 250–1
Petrushka 20, 26, 33, 35, 101
Piano-Rag-Music 3, 118
Poetics of Music 4
Ragtime for Eleven Instruments 3, 118
Renard 229
Le Sacre du printemps 3, 40, 117, 147, 148, 275
Study for Pianola 101
Symphonies of Wind Instruments 3, 34
Symphony of Psalms 34, 39, 50, 56
Three Pieces for String Quartet 33
Two Poems of Balmont 41
Stuart, Walter 156
Szymanowski, Karol 25
 Mythes 25

Taruskin, Richard 18, 35
Toch, Ernst 228
 Die Prinzessin auf der Erbst 228
Travis, Roy 39, 42, 257
Tredici, David del 277

van den Toorn, Pieter C. xviii, 24 n., 33–5, 46–7, 50, 74, 79, 97, 198, 263, 279
Varèse, Edgard 279
Verdi, Giuseppe 2 n.
Villa-Lobos, Heitor 115
 Sexteto místico 115
Vivaldi, Antonio 182
Vuillermoz, Émile 148–9

Wagner, Richard 2, 36
Walsh, Stephen x, 14, 185, 234 n., 250–1, 268
Walton, William 85
 Façade 85, 87
Watkins, Glenn x, 14, 61, 117 n., 185, 267
Webern, Anton 38
 Bagatelle, Op. 9 No. 1 38, 42–3
Weill, Kurt 9, 275
 Die Dreigroschenoper 275
 Mahagonny 228, 275
 Symphony No. 2 9, 107
White, Hayden 279
Whittall, Arnold 40–1, 46, 136, 178–9, 257, 265
Widor, Charles-Marie 58

Xenakis, Iannis 277

Zemlinsky, Alexander von 6
Zinar, Ruth 31–3